AMERICAN PUBLIC ADMINISTRATION

AMERICAN PUBLIC

ADMINISTRATION:

Concepts and Cases

Carl E. Lutrin
Allen K. Settle

MAYFIELD PUBLISHING COMPANY

To Kathi Settle and D.R.A. and R.B.K.

Library of Congress Catalog Card Number: 75–44697
International Standard Book Number: 0–87484–314–6

Manufactured in the United States of America
Mayfield Publishing Company
285 Hamilton Avenue, Palo Alto, California 94301

This book was set in Elegante and Vega Light by
Applied Typographic Systems. Cover was printed
by Auto Screen Lehigh and text was printed by
Banta West. Sponsoring editor was Alden Paine,
Carole Norton supervised editing, and Barbara
Pronin was manuscript editor. Michelle Hogan
supervised production, text design by Nancy Sears,
and cover design by William Nagel. Chapter opening
artwork by Jean Michel Folon.

CONTENTS

TABLES AND FIGURES

PREFACE

Although there are no glib answers to the complex questions confronting American public administration today, this book is designed in part to acquaint the reader with some of the noteworthy trends and modern perspectives that aim at seeking solutions to recent problems in the field. In writing the book, which is oriented toward the basic concepts, tools, and issues of public administration, the authors have combined a personal interest in personnel administration, budgeting, decision making, communication, and bureaucratic power on the one hand with an interest in comparative administration, administrative organization, bureaucratic behavior and responsibility, and issues of regulation on the other.

In addition to exploring the most significant background literature in the field and discussing the major instruments of administration, we have devoted considerable attention to difficult questions arising from administrative growth, taxpayer discontent over increased government spending, public employee unrest, the impact on public administration of the Vietnam War and Watergate, and bureaucratic accountability.

To present administrative concepts and related case studies in a single volume was one of the major purposes of this book. The selected case studies attempt to capture the flavor and excitement of various aspects of administration, to provide practical illustrations of some of the administrative fundamentals discussed in the chapters, and to offer the reader who plans to work, or is already working, in the public sector a point of departure for understanding the issues involved in applying administrative concepts to administrative problems. Our grateful thanks to all the authors and publishers of the case studies for their permission to reprint selections from copyrighted material.

Many people have participated in preparing this book for publication. At Mayfield Publishing Company, we wish to thank our fine and capable editor, Barbara Pronin, for her comprehensive reading and comments on the manuscript; also Carole Norton and Alden C. Paine for their additional observations and suggestions. For their reviews and criticism, we owe thanks to John C. Ries, University of California at Los Angeles; Brian Fry, University of South Carolina; Richard Feld, East Texas State University; and Lloyd M. Wells, University of Missouri.

We should also like to thank Aaron Wildavsky, University of California at Berkeley; Francis Rourke, Johns Hopkins University; and Frank Lindenfeld, Cheney State College, for their valuable insights on program budgeting, the bureaucracy, and semi- and nonbureaucratic organizations. Faculty colleagues at California Polytechnic State University in San Luis Obispo who have offered useful observations and encouragement include George Clucas, Irving Babow, and William Alexander. In addition, we wish to acknowledge the intellectual stimulation and training received from David Wood and Stanley Gabis, University of Missouri, and Dean E. Mann and Gordon Baker, University of California at Santa Barbara.

Finally, for typing manuscript drafts, helping to prepare the index, and for numerous related tasks, we are indebted to Lavonne Sanchez, Norma Pieretti, Elizabeth Mace, Merille Looke, Barbara Wilkinson, Linda Hirschkovitz, Bonnie Wall, and Kathi Settle.

INTRODUCTION TO PUBLIC ADMINISTRATION

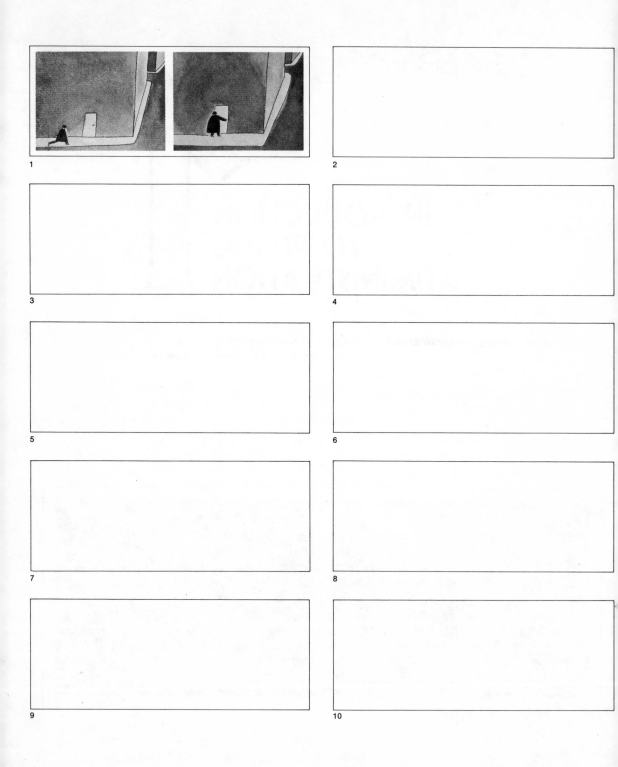

1

2

3

4

5

6

7

8

9

10

. . . The men who create power make an indispensable contribution to the nation's greatness, but the men who question power make a contribution just as indispensable . . . for they determine whether we use power or power uses us.

JOHN F. KENNEDY

1 Power bears watching, wherever it exists. From history books and headlines we have long been aware of power in the political arena and how its use can affect our lives for better or for worse. It is only recently, however, that we have gained some inkling of the awesome implications of power in the bureaucratic sphere, that vast tax-funded domain wherein an army of civil servants and administrators go about their day-to-day business of carrying out public policy. We have been forced to this awareness.

FBI, CIA, IRS. These familiar initials all stand for public agencies once generally respected, if not always admired, for their seemingly dauntless devotion to duty. Now, as a result of recent disclosures of some of their activities, they stand in the minds of many as virtual symbols of trust betrayed. Another such symbol is Watergate. Behind each of these images is a story of administrative power turned against the people who gave it legitimacy.

Why did it happen? How could we have prevented it? What is the likelihood that it will happen again? How well are our public servants really serving the public? We have not merely the right to ask these questions, but the obligation.

This book is all about administrative power and responsibility—what it is, how it came into being and burgeoned to its present proportions, where it exists, and where it is taking us.

3

WHAT IS PUBLIC ADMINISTRATION?

A Preliminary View

No conclusive definition of what public administration is, or ought to be, has been widely agreed on to date. Professor Frederick C. Mosher has observed that "any definition of this field would be either so encompassing as to call forth the wrath or ridicule of others, or so limiting as to stultify its own discipline. Perhaps it is best that it not be defined."[1] Gerald Caiden cautions that knowledge is growing too fast to permit unaltered meanings and permanent boundaries.[2]

According to Pfiffner and Presthus, public administration is essentially concerned with the means of implementing public values, or coordinating individual and group efforts to carry out public policy; as such, it is mainly occupied with the routine work of government.[3] Others believe that it involves the accomplishment of politically determined objectives, and it is true that public administration must be concerned with policy as well as with the technique required for its orderly execution. It must be practical enough to solve problems and to formulate societal goals but innovative enough to seek better methods of understanding what is involved in group efforts.[4] For the purposes of this text, however, public administration will be defined as that part of the public domain that is primarily concerned with the administrative aspects of resolving public issues.[5]

Administrative process is a body of knowledge and techniques employed in different ways by private and public organizations, including the legislatures and courts; its form, determined largely by whom it is intended to serve. In both the public and private sectors, administration is a cooperative group effort concerned with the means of survival in a difficult, sometimes hostile environment. Businessmen often emphasize the risks involved in conducting private enterprise in a competitive market; but commanding armed forces in times of war or sustaining public services against the challenges offered by increasingly militant unions or increasingly less generous taxpayers are not risk-free occupations either. If most businesses are required for their survival to make profits, many public enterprises, such as the postal service or port authority of some large cities, are expected at least to break even (or even to show a loss).

The great difference between private and public enterprises is that the latter are supposed to serve the public interest and are held publicly accountable for their actions. Public agencies face constant scrutiny by taxpayer associations, by the press, by the legislative process at all levels of government, even grand jury review of those departments located in the more than three thousand counties of the United States. In addition, legal mandates determine what public agencies may and may not do. Regulations concerning their operations and conduct are laboriously detailed. Officials are frequently held accountable to legislatures and other public bodies. As James V. Forrestal, the first U.S. Secretary of Defense (1947–49), observed: ". . . The difficulty of government work is that it not only has to be done well, but the public has to be convinced that it is being done well. In other words there is necessity for competence and exposition, and I hold it is extremely difficult to combine the two in the same person."[6]

The private corporation need not necessarily be concerned with the public interest, and many businessmen do not fare well in government precisely because they are not accustomed to having to justify their orders or actions to the public. Frustrated, they complain of red tape, but much of this red tape arises from taxpayers' demands to know how their money is being spent. Prices may rise without comment in the private sector as corporations, in order to ensure a continued profit margin, pass increased operating costs on to the consumer; but a great public outcry invariably accompanies increases in the costs of public services and the increased taxes required to support them. Businessmen may treat one another to expensive dinners and trips at the customer's expense, but high-ranking government officials who may be on important trips for their constituents are criticized for "junketing." Indeed, as Professor Caiden notes, patrons will wait in line with far greater patience in a private bank than in a post office.[7]

In many ways, however, the differences between public and private enterprise are diminishing. There is considerable flow of personnel between the two, especially at the higher management levels; and with increased governmental intervention in the areas of subsidies, taxes, regulations, and contracting, the distinctions between public and private are no longer clear-cut.

Legislatures and courts are of considerable importance in public administration not only as initiators and enforcers of public policy but as objects of administration themselves. Legislatures formulate the policy that public administrators are asked to put into effect; they provide the funds without which there would be no agencies, personnel, or programs, and they also monitor the bureaucracy—that is, they perform the vital function of legislative oversight. If legislatures are to discharge their duties effectively, it is essential that they be well administered themselves, that they have adequate staff and equipment and the optimal number of committees to support their work.

The courts, too, have been centrally important in public administration, particularly with regard to administrative law as it affects regulatory commissions, boards, and bureaus at all levels of government, the enforcement of administrative decisions and procedures, and the liability of public officers. Most problems involving civil liberties and the administrative process arise out of questions of whether a government agency has provided procedural due process in its proceedings against an individual; school desegregation, decreed in the 1954 case of *Brown* v. *Board of Education,* is an example of this. The U.S. Supreme Court can declare executive acts illegal, as evidenced in the case of President Harry S. Truman's seizure of the steel mills in 1952 and of President Richard M. Nixon's withholding of evidence contained in tape recordings in 1974.

Thus, our courts as well as our legislatures must be well administered if they are to function effectively. Most states and scores of cities now have court managers, a position that is beginning to receive wider attention since U.S. Supreme Court Chief Justice Warren Burger and others have indicated their interest in it.

THE GROWTH OF PUBLIC ENTERPRISE

Robert Michels has argued that to speak of organization is by definition to speak of oligarchy, for in any organization ruling power is concentrated in the hands of a small group, or elite, and has usually been based on superiority of wealth, military might, or social position.[8] While Michels's "iron law" generalization invites many exceptions, it nevertheless argues correctly that organizations tend to become increasingly conservative in the course of time and that leaders tend to identify their own interests, which they naturally seek to preserve, with their positions, thereby laying the foundation for a possible conflict of interest between the leaders and the led. The significance of this argument to public administration lies in the context of social equity, a problem that has preoccupied a variety of administrative thinkers since the turn of the century and that remains a major theme of civil service reformers today.

In the United States, especially, the theme of social equity in government has been coupled with a popular concern that government should be more businesslike and efficient. Woodrow Wilson's classic "Study of Administration" (1887) urged greater efficiency at a time when abuses of the spoils system of patronage appointments had favorably disposed the nation toward civil service reform. With the passage of the Pendleton Act in 1883, Congress created the federal civil service system. The efficiency theme, introduced by Wilson and advanced by Frederick W. Taylor and others, and civil service systems were both steps toward greater equity in the organizational structure of government, and both would be supplemented by Leonard White's emphasis in 1926 on personnel administration.[9] Among others, Luther Gulick (director of the Institute of Public Administration in New York in the 1930s) argued that people who are treated equitably will do more efficient work.

The next major emphasis in the development of American public administration was on the administrative organization itself. In 1937 the Brownlow Committee (or The President's Committee on Administrative Management) reported that the executive offices of the president, state governors, and municipal executives must be strengthened if they were to become more professional managers of government. In 1949 the first Hoover Commission on Organization of the Executive Branch of Government concluded further that by strengthening management at the top, improvements would follow down the line.

Several important changes and reorganization plans were adopted as a result of the reports of the Brownlow Committee, the first Hoover Commission, and, to a lesser extent, the second Hoover Commission in 1955 (which was more concerned with the overall functions of government). Their effect was to stimulate a continual reassessment of the efficiency and effectiveness of government and to initiate a continual activity for government reorganization.

The growth of a large American public service primarily reflects our changing attitudes toward the proper role of government in our economy and defense. At the inception of the republic, government played a relatively minor role in both the economy and in society as a whole. In 1800 the U.S. citizenry required fewer than .5 federal bureaucrats per 1,000 inhabitants. By 1900 the ratio had increased to 2.7 per 1,000 inhabitants. On the eve of World War II the figure was 7 per 1,000, and by 1962 it had climbed to 13

Table 1   TOTAL CIVILIAN EMPLOYMENT, 1954–1974

One out of ten
employed by government

1954   Total—60,890,000
Government— 6,751,000

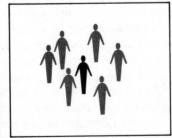

One out of seven
employed by government

1964   Total—69,305,000
Government— 9,596,000

One out of six
employed by government

1974   Total—86,312,000
Government—14,845,950

SOURCE: U.S. Department of Commerce

per 1,000 inhabitants (excluding military personnel).[10] According to Daniel P. Moynihan, the total increase in U.S. employment between 1957 and 1963 can be accounted for by jobs in the public sector.[11]

Personnel increases in state and local government have been even more remarkable. In 1933, 2.6 million people were employed by state and local entities; by 1972 the number had risen to 10.5 million. In 1972 alone, 1.5 million people were added to state and local personnel rosters. By the early 1970s 1 of every 6 gainfully employed Americans was a bureaucrat working for federal, state, or local governments. The reasons for this phenomenal growth are to be found in the public's mounting demand for goods and services which they believe only government can provide—demands that have arisen from the technological revolution, the great transformation of our economy, and America's emergence as a major world power.[12]

Government Growth and the Economy

During the late eighteenth and most of the nineteenth century, Americans asked relatively little of their federal government, which confined itself mostly to matters of defense, foreign affairs, Indian affairs, law enforcement, postal services, taxes, tariffs, land grants, and pensions. These activities were not extensive, and it is therefore not surprising that the entire federal budget was "$4 million in 1790 and only $318 million a century later."[13]

But the founding fathers had known that government would play a major role in shaping the nation's economy. James Madison, the father of the Constitution, wrote: "The most common and durable source of factions has been the various and unequal distribution of property. Those who hold and those who are without property have formed distinct interests in society. . . . The regulation of their various and interfering interests forms the principal task of modern legislation."[14] Indeed, by protecting the right of contract, insuring the rights of creditors, and issuing patents to protect the rights of inventors, the Constitution can be said to have promoted economic interests (a point stressed by Charles A. Beard and others).

The federal government would greatly influence the nation's economic life. The first U.S. Congress provided for tariffs to protect business interests and for subsidies to shippers. More important, it acceded to Alexander Hamilton's Financial Plan for a first U.S. Bank and other governmental measures, although further efforts in this direction, such as Henry Clay's American Plan,* would fall victim to the prevailing American ideology of the day, which stressed laissez faire, states' rights, and rugged individualism.

*Clay's American Plan would have used public works, especially canals, to facilitate interstate commerce.

This ideology did not prevent the states from being active economic participants, however. During the nineteenth century, state activities included giving bounties to agriculture, subsidizing silk culture (nine states), supporting fishing and naval stores' production (Massachusetts), allowing tax exemptions, excusing serving on juries and the militia for individuals in certain industries, fixing prices for goods and services (Pennsylvania), engaging in market inspection, and giving public aid to the poor.[15] In his study of Pennsylvania, Louis Hartz concludes that ". . . virtually every phase of business activity were the constant preoccupations of politicians and entrepreneurs, and they evoked interest struggles of the first magnitudes. Government assumed the job of shaping decisively the contours of economic life."[16]

The extensive economic role of local governments in the nineteenth century is perhaps less well known. By 1861 the local aid movement had been authorized by 2,200 laws in thirty-six states. Local governmental aid was crucial in the development of the railroads. A study of railroads in New York State has emphasized that public (mostly municipal) funds pioneered the way for railroads in that state and bore most of the financial risks. The city of Baltimore invested "$20 million in railroads between 1827 and 1886. Cincinnati with its own railroad outspent Baltimore."[17]

Robert Lively concludes his study of state and local economic activity during the nineteenth century by stating:

> However varied the explanations for public sponsoring of enterprises, the facts supporting these stories can be summarized in one generalization: the movement was virtually unlimited both as to time and place. From Missouri to Maine, from the beginning to the end of the nineteenth century governments were deeply involved in lending, borrowing, building and regulation.[18]

Still, giving land and money to the railroads did not require much personnel, and the American bureaucracy remained small. It was not until the late nineteenth and early twentieth centuries that Americans began to accept the notion that government, especially at the federal level, could serve as a positive economic force in an increasingly urban society.

The post–Civil War period was one of great business expansion and rapid industrialization. Between 1899 and 1929 the value of manufactured goods and services increased six and one-half times. The nation was transformed by the railroads (which linked both coasts in 1869), by petroleum and electricity, by the automobile and telephone, and by mechanized agriculture. We gradually ceased to be an agrarian nation until the 1920 census revealed that the majority of Americans now lived in cities. People became increasingly interdependent as more worked for large corporations as well as for themselves.

These changes were not unmitigated blessings. The essentially unregulated economy produced many unsavory conditions, ranging from the sixty- to seventy-hour work week, the exploitation of child labor, and the sale of contaminated meat and drug-addicting medicines, to the rise of the giant trusts (corporations) at the juncture of the nineteenth and twentieth centuries. The country struggled in the grip of giant business monopolies, but the Supreme Court refused to prosecute the monopolistic practices of U.S. Steel because bigness was no crime. It was the high tide of laissez faire and the Robber Barons; and the Great Depression, which would dominate the American 1930s, was still another result of an unregulated economy.

In the first year of the depression the national income dropped from $81 billion to $40 billion. Businesses and banks failed by the thousands. In 1933, 13 million people (almost one-third of the work force) were unemployed. Reflecting the view that government can be a positive economic force, Franklin D. Roosevelt created scores of governmental agencies to fight the nation's severest economic dislocations. In 1933 the Tennessee Valley Authority was created to improve the standard of living for millions who lived in one of the most economically deprived areas of the nation by providing flood control, navigational improvements, fertilizers, and cheap waterpower, as well as to provide a touchstone by which private companies could be judged. The Civilian Works Administration (1933) employed 4 million people in public works; the Civilian Conservation Corps (1933) employed more than 1.5 million.

Many of Roosevelt's creations would permanently alter the contours of the American economy. The Securities and Exchange Commission (1934) would police the securities industry; the Federal Deposit Insurance Corporation (1933) assured that the government would insure against bank failures; the Public Utilities Holding Corporation Act (1935) limited the activities of public utilities; the Maritime Commission (1936) and the Civil Aeronautics Board (1938) gave the government a voice in shaping maritime and aviation policy.

Workers achieved an important benchmark with the passage of the Wagner Act (1935), which guaranteed their right to organize; the National Labor Relations Board (1935) was created to police labor-management relations. The Soil Conservation and Domestic Allotment Act (1936) and the Commodity Exchange Act (1936) set the pattern for government's pivotal position in agriculture for more than thirty-five years. Many of Roosevelt's social and economic programs would be retained and expanded in post–World War II America. Social security coverage, for example, was greatly expanded and by 1965 included medical care for the aged.

World War II—which marked a major turning point in the nation's policies of defense and foreign relations—and events of the subsequent cold war expanded the growing American bureaucracy in a number of ways. In 1943, under the aegis of the Office of War Mobilization and the National War Labor Board, the United States achieved military production unprecedented in history. Science was brought into the war effort and the bureaucracy with the Office of Scientific Research and Development (1941), which produced the Manhattan Project and the atomic bomb.

By 1945 the United States had become a dominant military and world power, no longer able to rely on a small professional army supported by the militia or to pursue a policy of isolation in foreign affairs. By 1970 the Department of Defense employed 1.25 million civilians as well as more than 3 million persons in uniform; in the same year the Department of State had 39,753 employees.[19] Foreign policy considerations predominated in the creation of the National Aeronautics and Space Administration (1958), which would employ tens of thousands of people and spend more than $30 billion to beat the Soviet Union in the race to the moon. The national hysteria that accompanied the USSR's first successful space launch was responsible for the federal government's first major thrust into education. Thereafter, the 1958 National Defense Education Act would be expanded until, under President Lyndon Johnson, the federal government became a major force at all levels of education.

In 1946 the Council of Economic Advisers was created to encourage and help achieve full employment. In the same year, the Atomic Energy Commission was established to control the development and manufacture of atomic energy. In 1962 the Manpower Development and Training Act was passed to deal with problems of general and technological unemployment; the Area Redevelopment Act of 1962 sought to uplift areas of low income and high unemployment.

m DTA (1962)

The Johnson administration's War on Poverty was an assault on the nation's poverty and malnutrition problems; the Job Corps, Headstart, Community Action programs, and Model Cities were all efforts to this end— all, however, soon yielding to local pressures, extreme racial tensions, and the Vietnam War. By the early 1970s the federal government had also been enlisted in attempts to solve the problems of a deteriorating environment. Smog, oil spills, mercury-contaminated fish, and an energy crisis all led to the commitment of billions of dollars and to the creation of the Environmental Protection Agency (1970). On a percentage basis, however, the fastest growing federal agency is the National Endowment for the Arts, whose budget doubled from 1973 to 1974.[20]

Substantial increases in demands for goods and services have not been confined to the federal government; dramatic increases have also occurred at state and local levels. Municipal income rose from $9.5 billion in 1954 to $26 billion in 1968—almost a tripling in fourteen years.[21] There have been vast increases in demands for improved highways, police services, health, education, and welfare services, and recreational facilities. New programs involving urban development, smoke abatement and pollution control, the building of airports and parking lots, and aid to the arts have also required greater governmental resources.

In short, governmental activity in the American economy has grown enormously. Murray Weidenbaum has estimated that in 1968 the government spent 40 percent of the Gross National Product and that its purchases accounted for another 25 percent.[22] Lloyd Musolf summarizes this interdependence:

> The panorama of public and private economic institutions is vast and there is widespread disagreement on the significance—but not the fact—of the growing public and private sectors. The bankruptcy of Penn Central and the troubles of Lockheed perplex policy-makers. Economists differ on the ultimate significance of the close connections between government and its contractors. For example, Andrew Shonfield, Walter Adams, Murray Weidenbaum, and John Galbraith have regarded these relationships, respectively, as an important step toward rational economic planning, a bestowing of "royal" franchises upon privileged recipients, a fruitful partnership for important and otherwise unattainable purposes, or a stage in the merger of the large corporations into the governmental administrative complex.[23]

The nature and problems of government's enlarged role are especially highlighted at the level of the Pentagon.

Government Growth and the Military

Until 1953 the United States could be characterized as a nation of strongly antimilitaristic sentiment. America's founding fathers, well versed in contemporary political history and the history of militarism in ancient Greece, Rome, and the Italian city-states, believed that democracy and militarism could not coexist comfortably. As Englishmen, they were acutely aware of the excesses of Oliver Cromwell's seventeenth-century New Model Army; as eighteenth-century Americans, their antimilitary attitudes were exacerbated by their interaction with the British occupation forces, composed, according to historian Walter Millis, of ". . . sweepings of jails, ginmills, and poorhouses, oafs from the farm beguiled into taking the King's shilling."[24]

The Declaration of Independence railed against political tyranny, the arrogance of "royal hirelings," and the irresponsible exercise of power by royal standing armies: "A standing army, however necessary it may be, is always dangerous to the liberties of the people." In the *Federalist Papers,* Alexander Hamilton added: "Altho a large standing army in time of Peace hath ever been considered dangerous to the liberties of a Country, yet only a few troops, under certain circumstances, are not only safe, but indispensably necessary. Fortunately for us, our situation requires but few."[25]

Our forebears recognized the need for defense but relied primarily on citizen soldiers known collectively as the militia and personified by George Washington, who stated: "It may be laid down as a primary position, and the basis of our system, that every Citizen who enjoys the protection of a free Government, owes not only a proportion of his property, but even his personal services to the defense of it."[26] Accordingly Washington urged that all men from the ages of eighteen through fifty be provided uniforms and arms and trained as part of the militia, and the militia remained our defensive ideal for generations.

During peacetime a small standing army was permitted. In 1794 Congress authorized an army of ninety privates and proportional officers, not to exceed the rank of captain, to guard the stores at West Point and Fort Pitt. But so great was antimilitary sentiment that Jefferson, during his presidency (1801–09), planned to place the seagoing navy in reserve and to cut the army, while the latter was frequently unable to meet even its small authorized level.

In 1835, with an authorized strength of 7,198 men, the actual number stood only slightly above 4,000. During the Civil War almost 2.5 million men answered the muster, but after Appomattox, as Millis has noted, "The Grand Army of the Republic, the finest military machine in existence made its three-day march down Pennsylvania Avenue . . . and dissolved."[27] From the post–Civil War era to the Spanish-American War, our entire army numbered only some 25,000 men, largely scattered throughout the west enforcing Manifest Destiny. So feeble were our defenses in 1891 that Rudyard Kipling described the nation as " . . . as unprotected as a jellyfish."

Spurred by the naval scholar Alfred T. Mahan and by President Theodore Roosevelt, the American navy underwent a considerable expansion; but by 1908 it was apparent to Roosevelt that it had become impossible to recruit an adequate number of officers and enlisted men. Although 4 million men were mobilized for World War I, the army was gradually reduced by postwar demobilization to 119,000 until, on the eve of World War II, the U.S. Army was about the size of Sweden's. In 1939 the U.S. Navy was composed largely of obsolescent ships and failed to meet even the modest size authorized by the Washington and London naval treaties which had attempted to limit the naval arms race during the interwar period.

During the nineteenth century most European nations were fighting among themselves for the spoils of empire. Because of the remoteness of Europe, the necessity of protecting our two oceans, and also to pursue various domestic needs, the United States eschewed policies that might involve us in entangling foreign commitments. But isolationism and minuscule armed forces became impossible during the twentieth century with the rise of mass communications, the growth of economic interdependence, the challenge of totalitarian ideologies, and the inception of the air, missile, and atomic ages.

In response to the challenge of fascism during World War II, the nation mobilized 11.3 million men and women for military duty. By 1947, however, postwar demobilization had reduced our armed forces to 1.67 million men.[28] During the early postwar period, when Communist activities posed problems for the United States in Greece, Turkey, Berlin, and the Philippines, Secretary of State George C. Marshall observed that we were playing with fire while having nothing with which to put it out. President Truman permitted small increases in the size of the armed forces but felt that the nation could afford to spend only $15 billion for defense.

Our decision to accede to the Rio Treaty, our commitments to NATO, SEATO, and ANZUS,* Soviet intransigence in Eastern Europe, the outbreak of the Korean War, and the specter of nuclear and thermonuclear war—all greatly altered American notions of defense requirements. The idea that the United States should maintain a standing peacetime military force numbering in the millions and consuming between 7 and 12 percent of the Gross National Product dates from 1953. In the aftermath of the Korean War, defense budgets soared. If Truman had attempted to limit defense spending to $15 billion, President Eisenhower sought to keep the figure at $40 billion, while President Nixon, in the mid-1970s, would struggle with a defense budget twice that size. Between 1947 and 1971 Americans spent $1,176 billion on defense, and the U.S. Department of Defense became the largest managerial operation in the world.

Support of national defense required the emergence of a vast bureaucracy, including the Veterans' Administration (1930), the Atomic Energy Commission (1946), the Central Intelligence Agency (1947), and the National Aeronautics and Space Administration (1958). At one time, the disbursements of the Veterans' Administration alone exceeded all those of the government of Belgium. Today the expenditures of the Department of Defense are so great that reducing them poses serious difficulties. A reduction

---

*The Rio Treaty, signed in 1947 by most of the Latin American states, asserted that an attack by one member would be considered an attack on all. The ANZUS Treaty of 1951 involved Australia, New Zealand, and the United States and contained a similar provision.

in defense-related spending contributed to the 1969-70 recession. Again, in 1974 President Nixon proposed closing 40 military bases and reducing 219 others. As the navy was the largest employer in the state of Rhode Island, curtailing naval operations in Newport meant the loss of 21,400 jobs at a time when the state suffered an unemployment rate of 6.4 percent.

Our swollen military has created a great many other problems as well. Defense-related research at major American universities contributed greatly to campus unrest during the 1960s and raised serious questions about the academic integrity of many scholars. The army-CIA coverage of Earth Day activities in 1971—an attempt to emphasize the fragility of, and the importance of protecting, our increasingly polluted planet—opened to public question the amount and scope of military spying in American society. The *Pentagon Papers* (1970) revealed that the military has concealed much information that should have been made available to Congress and the American people. The Nixon administration's decision to raise a large professional army was in total opposition to the advice of America's founding fathers. Finally, the free movement of retired military officers into our corporations, universities, and government has served only to expand the problems of American militarism. As President Eisenhower, a former general, observed in 1961:

> This conjunction of an immense military establishment and a large arms industry is new in American experience. The total influence—economic, political, even spiritual—is felt in every city, every State house, every office in the Federal government. We recognize the imperative need for this development. Yet we must not fail to comprehend its grave implications. Our toil, resources and livelihood are involved, so is the very structure of our society.[29]

PROBLEMS IN PUBLIC ADMINISTRATION

As employer, spender, and decision maker, even as a potential object of corruption and agent of abuse, government has become a pervasive element in American life, raising serious questions about the nature and quality of our public administration and the nature and quality of the services it provides.

As previously noted, government employs one of every six working Americans. Public employees at federal, state, and local levels collectively constitute one of the most powerful special interest lobbies in the nation. They exceed fifteen million in number; their payroll is more than $140 billion annually;[30] and within the next decade they may become the largest, most potent group of organized workers in the United States. Already well organized, they have both the manpower and the money to contribute significantly to political campaigns; they have the special advantage of working in capitals, county seats, and city halls where political decisions are made; and they have not been reluctant to strike when legislatures, supervisors, and school boards have responded sluggishly to their demands.

In the summer of 1974 the San Francisco Bay Area reeled under the impact of strikes by firemen, policemen, nurses, and port workers. Strikes that closed sanitation facilities caused untreated effluent to be dumped into the Bay. Unions have, of course, made enduring contributions to American life, and these public employees undoubtedly had legitimate grievances. But what about public health? What about the public that must pay for, and depend upon, public services? Whether or not we may expect more of those who are employed in the public sector than we expect of those in the private sector, their growing power calls to attention the necessity of recognizing and assessing their potential for its abuse.

Special-interest and public demands for services have placed new pressures and challenges on public administrators and raised new questions as well. Blacks, chicanos, American Indians, women, and other minorities have long been denied access to many of the better jobs and opportunities in public service. In an effort to overcome this, many civil service commissions have encouraged the hiring of minorities under affirmative action programs which aim not only at providing equal employment opportunities but at ensuring equal treatment in hiring, training, promotion, and other aspects of employment.

Equal employment opportunity does not mean preferential treatment of minorities, but some have argued that it has nevertheless brought about reverse discrimination against white majorities. Does affirmative action mean hiring employees who may not be best qualified for the job? And if public administrators do not hire minority applicants who may not meet exact job qualifications, how will they be able to take their rightful place in our society?

In addition to being a major employer, government is also a major spender, consuming approximately one-third of the nation's Gross National Product. Although the federal government's share of public revenue has been declining, the share claimed by state and local governments has increased with growing demands for improved housing, greater employment opportunities, a cleaner environment, more adequate and inexpensive medical care, less crime, and greater national security. At the same time, however, efforts to reduce government spending often create serious difficulties. In the late 1960s, for example, a reduction in the space program brought about severe unemployment in Southern California, and it was partly in response to political pressure that the National Aeronautics and Space Administration ordered a multibillion-dollar space shuttle to alleviate this situation. Can we afford to be for peace if reduction in defense expenditures closes a military base or causes layoffs at the local factory? Both government spending and reduced government spending are problematic; either may affect our employment and economic well-being.

With the stupendous growth of the American bureaucracy in recent years, and especially after the resignations of President Nixon and Vice President Spiro Agnew, administrative accountability has become a major issue for public servants. Examples of corruption, abuse of power, and administrative wrongdoing abound in government and among quasi-judicial agencies as well. Among the latter, the Federal Trade Commission (FTC), the Food and Drug Administration (FDA), and a variety of public utility commissions have been severely criticized for errors in the regulation of industry and of publicly regulated agencies.

For example, scandalized by his sexual views, which were then being taken up by the Beat Generation, the FDA in the 1950s waged a ten-year campaign (at one point spending up to 25 percent of its budget) against psychiatrist Wilhelm Reich, only to be criticized by the press and other government agency officials for destroying credibility in Reich's now highly regarded work on biogenetics and human sexuality.[31] In 1974, for another example, fourteen Food and Drug medical professionals, charging pressure on the FDA by the pharmaceutical industry, testified that they had been hounded out of their jobs because they had been conscientious in testing drugs.[32]

On the local level of administrative wrongdoing, one frequently encounters arbitrary literary censorship—the removal of Richard Wright's *Black Boy* from high school libraries for containing "filthy" material; the 1962 resignation of a Chicago high school teacher whose principal had forbidden him the classroom use of Steinbeck's *Cannery Row;* the banning in 1962 of Steinbeck's *Grapes of Wrath* by the public schools of Amarillo, Texas; the banning of Edgar Rice Burrough's Tarzan novels in Downey, California, because Tarzan and Jane were not married. The mayor of Patterson, New Jersey, once ordered Oscar Lewis's *Children of Sanchez* removed from the city's libraries, while U.S. Customs authorities banned Henry Miller's *Tropic of Cancer* from 1931 to 1959 on the grounds that it violated existing pornography laws.[33]

Corruption of a higher order is not unusual on the state level. To give only two examples: kickbacks and bribes are alleged to be commonplace throughout the New Jersey state government;[34] in August 1974 J. Edward Crabiel became the third New Jersey secretary of state to be indicted for bid rigging. Following Vice President Agnew's conviction it was revealed that there had been widespread bribery of government officials during his tenure as governor of Maryland.

At the federal level one recalls Grant's Whiskey Ring; Harding's Teapot Dome; Truman's problems with the Internal Revenue Service; the bribery conviction of Eisenhower's chief aide, Sherman Adams; the imprisonment of Lyndon Johnson's protégé, Bobby Baker, for abusing his Senate office by influence peddling; but the enormity of the Watergate scandal of 1972–74 has eclipsed these. Previous acts of corruption have principally involved abuses of money, but Watergate was a clear abuse of power. In addition to Nixon's resignation and acceptance of pardon, which President Gerald Ford regarded as an admission of guilt, more than fifty Nixon aides would be indicted or imprisoned for crimes including illegal breaking and entering; use of the CIA and FBI in covering up the Watergate story; an attempted bribe of the Department of Justice by International Telephone and Telegraph (ITT); the Milk Fund scandal, in which campaign contributions resulted in higher federal subsidies to the milk industry; and the creation of a White House "enemies list."

During the final week of July 1974 the House Judiciary Committee voted three articles of impeachment against President Nixon. The first charged conspiracy to obstruct justice by attempting to cover up responsibility for the Watergate break-in of Democratic National Committee headquarters. The second charged Nixon with "uniquely presidential acts," such as Internal Revenue Service harassment of opponents; misuse of the FBI; wiretapping the phones of newsmen; the break-in of the office of the psychiatrist of Dr. Daniel Ellsberg, a former Pentagon and Rand Corporation official; and remaining silent as former Attorney General Richard Kleindienst lied about presidential interference in the ITT bribery case. The third charged Nixon with failure to honor committee subpoenas.

A fourth article accused Nixon of illegally waging and covering up an air war in Cambodia; but this article failed to command the necessary votes, in part because some congressmen believed they had failed to use their own powers to restrain the president. A fifth article involving tax fraud did not win full committee support because it was feared the charges could not be proven.[35] A noted jurist has summarized the scope and challenge of Nixon's actions as follows.

> He believed that he could refuse to carry out programs enacted by Congress, and did so. He claimed broad and final authority to withhold information from the Congress and to avoid accountability for his actions. Members of his staff, seeking to accomplish Presidential purposes, have used the powers of the Presidential office to plan or authorize fantastic acts of lawlessness, violating ancient and fundamental rights of the people.

He has presented us with a challenge to our Constitution—to our basic institutions and our way of life. However well motivated the President may be, however sure he may be of his actions, the net effect of his actions has been an attempted constitutional coup d'etat: a fundamental alteration—a subversion—of our basic constitutional structure.[36]

The republic has survived Watergate and Richard Nixon; indeed, some have regarded the former president's resignation as an affirmation of the vitality of the constitutional system. But numerous events of the recent past—from the Cuban missile crisis of 1963, the Middle East crisis of October 1973, and the long American involvement in South Vietnam, to the Watergate disclosures—clearly demonstrate that decisions made by public administrators can affect not only the United States but the world. For this reason alone the issues of administrative responsibility and bureaucratic power must continue to be explored by students of public administration.

NOTES

1. Frederick C. Mosher, "Research in Public Administration: Some Notes and Suggestions," *Public Administration Review* 16 (summer 1956): 169–78.

2. Gerald E. Caiden, *The Dynamics of Public Administration: Guidelines to Current Transformations in Theory and Practice* (New York: Holt, Rinehart & Winston, 1971), p. 3.

3. John M. Pfiffner and Robert Presthus, *Public Administration*, 5th ed. (New York: Ronald Press Co., 1967), pp. 5–7.

4. M. E. Dimmock and G. O. Dimmock, *Public Administration* (New York: Holt, Rinehart & Winston, 1969), pp. 3, 11.

5. Caiden, *Dynamics of Public Administration*, p. iii.

6. Cited in Felix A. Nigro, and Lloyd G. Nigro, *Modern Public Administration*, 3d. ed. (New York: Harper & Row, 1973), p. 15.

7. Caiden, *Dynamics of Public Administration*, p. 5.

8. Robert Michels, *Political Parties: A Sociological Study of the Oligarchical Tendencies of Modern Democracy* (Glencoe, Ill.: Free Press, 1949).

9. Leonard D. White, *Introduction to the Study of Public Administration*, 4th ed. (New York: Macmillan Co., 1958). White would later become chairman of the U.S. Civil Service Commission.

10. Theodore Lowi, "The Public Philosophy," *American Political Science Review* 61 (March 1967): 5.

11. Daniel P. Moynihan, *Maximum Feasible Misunderstanding* (New York: Free Press, 1969), p. 63.

12. Almost 20 percent of the U.S. employed are on public payrolls (*Los Angeles Times*, 10 February 1973). The U.S. Department of Commerce determined in 1974 that one of every six persons in America is employed by government.

13. Merle Fainsod, Lincoln Gordon, and Joseph C. Palamountain, Jr., *Government and the American Economy*, 3d ed. (New York: W. W. Norton & Co., 1959), p. 3.

14. Alexander Hamilton, John Jay, and James Madison, *The Federalist Papers* (New York: Random House, 1937), p. 56.

15. Robert A. Lively, "The American Business System," *Business History Review* 29 (March 1955): 86.

16. Louis Hartz, *Economic Policy and Democratic Thought: Pennsylvania* (Cambridge, Mass.: Harvard University Press, 1948), p. 289.

17. Lively, "American Business System," p. 87.

18. Ibid., p. 86.

19. *Statistical Abstract of the United States, 1974* (Washington, D.C.: U.S. Department of Commerce, 1974), table 389, p. 298.

20. "Uncle Sam for the Arts," *Newsweek*, 26 March 1973, p. 55.

21. Charles R. Adrian and Charles Press, *Governing Urban America*, 4th ed. (New York: McGraw-Hill, 1972), p. 384.

22. Murray Weidenbaum, *The Modern Public Sector* (New York: Basic Books, 1969), p. 7.

23. Lloyd Musolf, "American Mixed Enterprise and Government Responsibility," *Western Political Quarterly* 24 (December 1971): 780.

24. Walter Millis, *Arms and Men* (New York: Mentor Books, 1958), pp. 14–15.

25. Ibid., p. 37.

26. Ibid., pp. 38–39.

27. Ibid., p. 118.

28. *Statistical Abstract of the United States, 1948* (Washington, D.C.: U.S. Department of Commerce, 1948), n. 246, p. 224.

29. Cited in Robert I. Vexler, ed., *Dwight D. Eisenhower, 1890-1969* (Dobbs Ferry, N.Y.: Oceana Publications, 1970), p. 143.

30. George Skelton and William Endicott, "The Public's Servants: How Big and How Powerful?" *Los Angeles Times*, 10 September 1974.

31. See Nathan G. Hale, Jr., review of *Wilhelm Reich vs. U.S.A.* by Jerome Greenfield, *New York Times Book Review*, 11 August 1974, p. 3.

32. "Protest Hit the FDA," *San Francisco Chronicle & Examiner*, 25 August 1974.

33. See A. K. Pickren, *Pressures from Right and Left* (Palo Alto, Calif.: Palo Alto Library, 1964).

34. "In Jersey: The Names of the Indicted Charge," *New York Times*, 4 August 1974, sec. 4, p. 6.

35. *New York Times*, 4 August 1974, sec. 4, pp. 1, 2; also New York Times Staff, "Articles of Impeachment," *End of a Presidency* (New York: Bantam Books, 1974), pp. 317–23.

36. Abe Fortas, "Mr. Nixon and the Constitution," *New York Times*, 4 August 1974, sec. 4, p. 7.

FORMAL ASPECTS OF ORGANIZATIONS

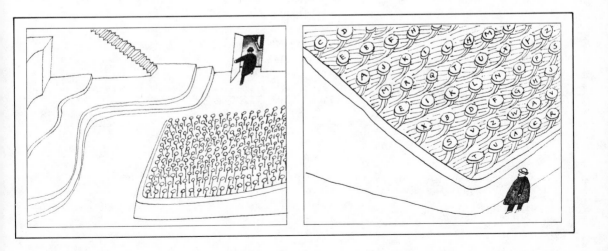

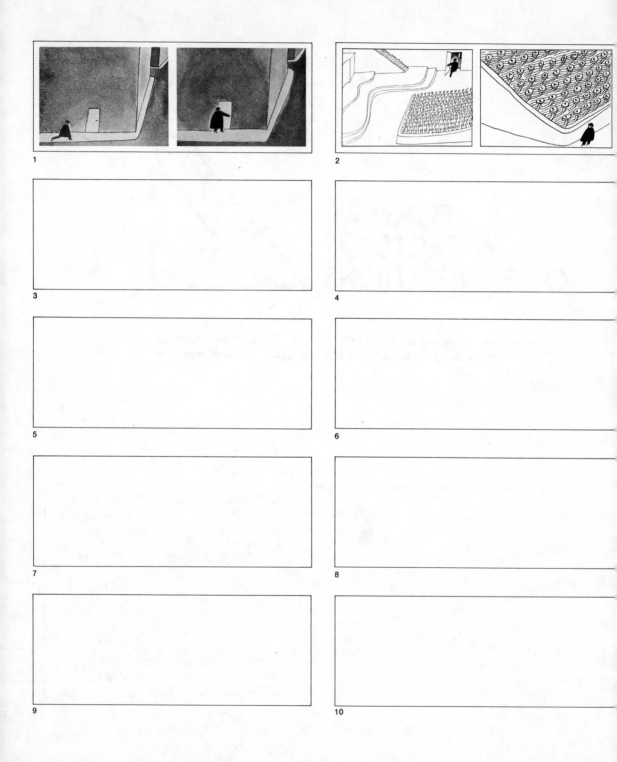

1

2

3

4

5

6

7

8

9

10

New managers always tend to rely more on the rules. They call us up and ask us if we have lists of rules which they can use. They are unsure of themselves and they need something to lean on. After they're on the job somewhat longer they're less worried about the rules.

The Successor's Defenses
ALVIN W. GOULDNER

2 This chapter explores some of the important elements of formal organizational theory, focusing especially on Max Weber's ideal constructs, Frederick W. Taylor's concept of scientific management, Henri Fayol's emphasis on a formal, rationalistic approach to administration, and the ideas of Luther Gulick and Lyndall Urwick on the formal foundations of organization. These men, all concerned with rational, efficient, formal approaches to the study of organization, have been criticized for ignoring such matters as dysfunctionalism, interest in human welfare, goals, and the role of bureaucratic politics both within and outside the organization, but their works have nevertheless profoundly influenced both the study and practice of public administration.

Formalism—a term having particular reference to the legal-rational bases of organizations[1]—dominated the theory and practice of public administration for a half-century. The reorganization and reform movement is still greatly influenced by the legacy of POSDCORB,* and formalistic prescriptions are still the starting point for most studies of organizational behavior. Although much public administration literature and many efforts to improve public management have more recently focused on the informal aspects of organization, formalism is still a vital force in public administra-

*See page 31.

POSDCORB *Planning, Organizing, Staffing, Directing, Coordinating, Reporting, and Budgeting*

23

tion. Indeed, it may be the shortcomings of formal theory that cause public administrators to turn their attention to the more informal aspects of administration. The case study at the end of this chapter, which deals with the issue of bureaucratic succession, demonstrates both the need for, and the limitations of, formal organizational factors.

MAX WEBER (1864–1920)

By the nineteenth century, Prussia was already a highly bureaucratized state. As early as the eighteenth century and well into the nineteenth, a number of noted German intellectuals, including Christian Kraus (a colleague of the philosopher Immanuel Kant), Wilhelm von Humbolt, and Frieher von Stein, had expressed concern about its influence.[2] Max Weber, born in Thuringia, had spent most of his youth in Berlin, the capital of the dynamic Bismarckian Germany. His father had been a trained jurist; his mother, a cultured and liberal-minded woman. Weber had studied law originally, but his Ph.D. in this discipline had eventually led him to examine a field in which economic and legal history overlapped. An original thinker and scholar in the fields of religion, history, economics, political science, and sociology, it is not surprising that he should in the course of time have devoted his genius to the study of bureaucracy as well.

In Weber's view, history moves in a unilinear progress toward technological relationalization.[3] Bureaucracy is a major contributing element in this process, and Weber believed that the ideal bureaucracy was characterized by several precepts.

1. That static and clearly defined jurisdictional areas exist and are determined by law or administrative regulations;

2. That organization and distribution of activities are based on division of labor;

3. That authority to give commands necessary to discharge organizational duties is not arbitrary but stable and prescribed;

4. That bureaucratic management is based on written documents known as "the files," which are preserved in their original forms;

5. That organization of officials is based on hierarchy. Each lower official is under the control and supervision of a higher one, who is in turn responsible to a superior for his own and his subordinates' actions. The superordinate has the right to issue directives, and subordinates have the duty to obey. The nature of directives is fixed by law, but the system affords the opportunity for lower officials to appeal decisions to a higher office;

6. That officials are offered positions on the basis of contracts freely entered into and mutually binding. Personnel are selected for their professional qualifications, and thorough expert training is presupposed for management positions. Ideally, recruitment is based on examination or educational certification congruent with the office.

For Weber, officeholding constituted a career or vocation that consumes an individual's capacity for work over a long period of time. Normally the official is protected from arbitrary dismissal, and the position is held for life. Salaries, pensions, and other emoluments are provided for; compensations and privileges are based on the individual's position within the hierarchy. In short, Weber's system envisions a career personnel structure that provides for advancement within the hierarchy on the basis of either seniority or examination.[4]

Weber believed that bureaucracy, with its greater impersonality, rationality, and efficiency, had a distinct advantage over organizations based on charismatic types. If rational standards of government are to prevail over personal considerations, especially in relations with clients, bureaucracy must function in a detached, impartial fashion. Bureaucratic officials must discharge their duties with neither affection nor enthusiasm;[5] unlike officeholders of the Middle Ages, they must not exploit their offices for personal gain.[6] If the bureaucrat's loyalty is not given to impersonal, functional purposes, he might allow his feelings to blur his evaluations of subordinates or to color his dealings with clients. This aloof neutrality, however irritating it may be to the public, is ultimately to the public's advantage, since detached, impartial evaluation of clients is the only assurance the public has that it will receive fair and equal treatment at the hands of bureaucracy.[7]

Weber felt that bureaucracy was not only technically superior to all other forms of organization but that it also compared favorably with the substitution of machines for nonmechanical production—machines that brought about measurable increases in man's productive capacity.

> Precision, speed, unambiguity, knowledge of the files, continuity, discretion, unity, strict subordination, reduction of friction and of material and personal costs—these are raised to the optimum point in the strictly bureaucratic administration. . . . As compared with all collegiate, honorific and avocational forms of administration, trained bureaucracy is supreme on all these points.[8]

At the same time, however, Weber had reservations about the appropriateness of the legal-rational model for a democracy. He believed that increased bureaucratization and rationalization would have the effect of separating people from the means of production.[9] Because access to university education was tied to economic advantage, he was concerned that the high educational requirement for entry into the upper levels of bureaucracy would create a new elite. He was also apprehensive about the possible domination of bureaucracy in a democracy, fearing that a politician was likely to be less specialized than a bureaucratic expert and therefore unable to control the bureaucratic expert. In Bismarck's Germany, for example, nonelected officials had been permitted to occupy dominant positions in the cities, and the result had been a politically stultified state in which nonbureaucratic elements had been unable to express themselves.[10] Bureaucracy tended to accumulate power, and in 1909 Weber lamented:

> It is horrible to think that the world could one day be filled with nothing but those little cogs, little men clinging to little jobs and striving towards bigger ones—a state of affairs which is to be seen once more, as in the Egyptian records, playing an ever increasing part in the spirit of our administrative system, and especially of its offspring, the students. The passion for bureaucracy is enough to drive one to despair.[11]

Weber has been greatly criticized by a number of social scientists for neglecting the dysfunctional elements engendered by organizational life, for ignoring its informal aspects, for failing to deal with issues of bureaucratic responsibility, and for lack of universal applicability. It has been observed, for example, that bureaucracy's emphasis on prudence and impersonality might cause rules intended as means toward ends to become ends in themselves, might encourage bureaucratic support of the status quo, or encourage conflict with the public it is supposed to serve.[12] Bureaucracy can refuse to implement a policy of social change, as Robert K. Merton has pointed out.[13]

Philip Selznick's classic study of the Tennessee Valley Authority illustrates how organizational purposes can be subordinated to interests of organizational survival, another common occurrence ignored by Weber. Carl Frederick has criticized Weber for ignoring the issue of bureaucratic responsibility, asserting that the Weberian model too closely resembles the Prussian military model of bureaucratic organization to allow even cooperation, let alone consultation.[14]

Weber's analysis treats only the formal aspects of bureaucracy and implies that deviations from this model are idiosyncratic. But informal relations and unofficial liaisons develop without official sanction, and, as Chester Barnard and others have pointed out, these informal relations are essential for both individual and bureaucratic survival.[15] Peter Blau's 1955 study of a federal law enforcement agency found that persistent bending of bureaucratic rules can actually enhance the likelihood of an agency's achieving its goal. Finally, a number of non-Western scholars have asserted that Weber's assumptions about human behavior are not universal.[16] In spite of these criticisms, however, the Weberian model still remains the focal point of most research on organizational behavior. In his day, Weber was alone in his scholarly pursuit of the formal-rational aspects of bureaucracy, and his influence on the study and practice of public administration has been enormous.

FREDERICK W. TAYLOR (1856–1915)

Scientific management—an American movement synonymous with the name of the mechanical engineer Frederick W. Taylor—greatly impressed Weber, who regarded it as a triumph of rational conditioning and training of work performance for greater efficiency.[17] Taylor lived at a time when inefficiency, corruption, political immorality, and the plunder of our natural resources had become national scandals. Said Finley Peter Dunne's Mr. Hennessy: "I knew an Aldherman that was honest as th' sun except whin th' street railroad or th' gas company needed something."

> "Well, there ye are're," said Mr. Dooley. "It seems to me that th' on'y thing to do is to keep pollyticians an' businessmen apart. They seem to have a bad influence on each other. Whinever I see an aldherman an' a banker walkin down th' sthreet together I know th' Recording Angel will have to ordher another bottle iv ink."[18]

The corruption and inefficiency of the Progressive Era gave rise, in Samuel Haber's view, to an efficiency craze:

> . . . a secular Great Awakening, an outpouring of ideas and emotions in which a gospel of efficiency was preached without embarrassment to business, workers, doctors, housewives, and teachers, yes, preached even to preachers. Men as disparate as William Jennings Bryan and Walter Lippmann discussed enthusiastically on efficiency. Efficient and good came closer to meaning the same thing in these years than in any other period of American history.[19]

As Haber has also observed, the Midvale Steel Company was to Taylor what the Big Horn Mountains were to Teddy Roosevelt.[20] Taylor spent six years as a journeyman at Midvale in Philadelphia before becoming its chief engineer in the early 1880s; he later did consulting work, discovered a new method of making steel, became president of the American Society of Mechanical Engineers, and at the age of forty-five retired to lecture and write.

During his industrial career, Taylor became preoccupied with the question of how to get more work out of employees, whom he believed to be naturally lazy.[21] At the time, the dominant managerial method was the piecework system under which workers received higher wages for producing more and lower wages for producing less. The piecework system was inefficient, in Taylor's view, because employers had no way of knowing how much a worker could actually produce and also because it placed initiative for greater production with the worker rather than with management.[22]

Spurred by Theodore Roosevelt's observation that the conservation of America's natural resources was only preliminary to the larger question of national efficiency,[23] Taylor published *The Principles of Scientific Management* in 1911. This book had three goals: to demonstrate the great losses sustained by the United States as a result of the daily inefficiencies practiced by its people; to suggest that the solution to this problem lay in employing people of ability and in the practice of systematic management; and to prove that systematic management was based on definite rules, laws, and principles.[24]

Taylor's method of achieving efficiency was known as scientific management (a term originally coined by Louis Brandeis). Scientific management meant the conscious, deliberate application of rationalism to industrial work; it arose from ". . . the idea that human activity could be measured, analyzed, and controlled by techniques analogous to those proved successful when applied to physical objects."[25] Taylor believed that there was in any trade one best method of work and that the keys to finding this best method lay in job analysis and time and motion studies.

> Now, among the various methods and implements used in each element of each trade there is always one method and one implement which is better and quicker than any of the rest. And this one best method and best implement can only be discovered or developed through a scientific study and analysis of all the methods and implements in use, together with accurate, minute, motion study. This involves the gradual substitution of science for rule of thumb throughout the mechanical arts.[26]

As an example, Taylor cited bricklaying, a trade that had been practiced for hundreds of years with little or no improvement in implements, materials, or methods. In an effort to improve the trade, Frank B. Gilbreth (1868–1925), an efficiency expert and originator of the science of motion study, had studied bricklayers' movements, eliminating all unnecessary movements and substituting fast motions for slow ones. He had noted the exact position that each bricklayer's feet should occupy in relation to the wall, mortarbox, and brick pile so that it would not be necessary for the workman to take a step toward the pile and then back again to the wall each time a brick was laid. As a result of this study, Gilbreth reduced the number of motions involved in laying bricks from eighteen to five. For Taylor, whose concern was to determine which aspects of the operation were essential and to eliminate the rest, Gilbreth's study demonstrated that bricks could be laid under standardized conditions.[27]

Taylor also emphasized that workmen should be carefully selected, trained in the best methods, and given financial inducements to work more efficiently. Prepared to pay for increased productivity, he nevertheless believed that management should train and enforce standards of cooperation. Those who, after being trained in accordance with the new principles, could not, or would not, adhere to these standards should be discharged.[28] In addition, Taylor gave considerable thought to the subject of functional division of labor and planning, noting:

> The shop, and indeed the whole works, should be managed, not by the manager, superintendent, or foreman, but by the planning department. The daily routine of running the entire works should be carried on by the various functional elements of this department, so that, in theory at least, the works could run smoothly even if the managers, superintendents and their assistants outside the planning room were all to be away for a month at a time.[29]

The planning room would deal with routing, preparing instruction cards, time and cost records, and discipline.[30]

The gospel of scientific management was widely spread by the Taylor Society, organized in 1915, and soon exercised great influence in public and private management in the United States, Europe, and postrevolutionary Russia. But Taylor's concepts did not escape criticism by unions or managers or by those who rejected his mechanistic view of the workingman. Under Taylor's scheme of things, wages, hours, and working conditions were to be determined not by collective bargaining or negotiation but by scientific management.[31] At a time when unions were struggling for their existence, labor-management camaraderie was resented, and scientific management was seen as a tool of management.

Many managers resented Taylor's opposition to rule of thumb operations and his view that, without higher education or assistance by highly qualified experts, they were unfit to manage; indeed, their opposition was instrumental in Taylor's having to leave Midvale and Bethlehem Steel in 1893.[32] There can be no question, too, that Taylor's view of workers was cold and calculating or that his scheme left little room for the exercise of individuality. Moreover, it is now axiomatic in management circles that people are not motivated by money alone.

Taylor's time and motion studies also came under attack.[33] Some were criticized by his contemporaries for alleged inaccuracies; one criticism emphasized that managers have been more successful in demonstrating efficient procedures than in getting workers to accept them.[34] Perhaps more serious were the normative questions raised by their usage, as Taylor's "ideal" clearly favored management.

> . . . It was never clear what was being measured. Was it the minimum time in which a job could be done? If so, why the allowances [for differences] and why not select the fastest man for the measurement? Was it the average time—something Taylor would have never admitted? If so, why the attention paid to the elimination of waste motions and the selection of a particular individual to be timed? Was it, perhaps, an ideal time? In a sense it was. But an ideal—however defined—could not conceivably be measured by a stop watch, nor could it be inferred from evidence a stop watch could provide. No measuring instrument could provide an "ought to be."[35]

HENRI FAYOL (1841–1925)

Before becoming a successful manager and highly influential administrative thinker, Henri Fayol, a Frenchman, had, like Taylor, been an eminently successful engineer who had performed important work in reducing fire hazards in the coal mining industry. The formal-rational approach advanced by Fayol, one of the first writers to develop a general theory of administration, would become deeply embedded in the theory and practice of American public administration to the present day. Disturbed by the absence of a general theory and convinced that every citizen should know something about administration, whether practiced in the home or for the state, Fayol urged that the subject be taught at all levels of education and attempted to formulate a body of administrative thought himself.

Fayol's approach emphasized five elements: forecast planning, organization, communication, coordination, and control, with particular attention to "organizational charts" (a graphic display of the organization, depicting lines of authority and responsibility and how they relate to one another). Everyone in every type of organization should know his place in the organizational chart, which Fayol saw as the principal tool of management. Fayol vigorously stressed the concept of unity of command, in which an employee receives orders exclusively from one supervisor; believed that managers, with their power to give orders and exact obedience, must accept responsibility for their actions; and asserted that staff to aid in correspondence, planning, control liaison and improvement was vital.

Although Fayol's views were broader than Taylor's and more concerned with human psychological problems, such as the need for esprit de corps, they were nevertheless not based on scientific observation. Fayol's "principles" were based only on his years of experience as a successful administrator, and he is best remembered today for his emphasis on the formal-rational approach.[36]

POSDCORB AND THE "PROVERBS"

As previously noted, the concept of administrative efficiency gained great impetus during World War I. Luther Gulick (1891-) and Lyndall Urwick (1892-), both of whom had long served on numerous public boards studying various aspects of public administration, were tireless proponents of, and propagandists for, the application of neutral principles aimed at improving administrative efficiency. In particular, they are notable for attempting to derive practical managerial concepts from the writings of Taylor and Fayol to apply them to the study and practice of American public administration. In 1937 Gulick and Urwick edited a volume entitled *Papers on the Science of Public Administration* containing important landmark thought on the formal-rational approach and introducing several original formulations as well.[37]

By means of seven functions summed up in the acronym POSDCORB, Gulick attempted to define the administrative responsibilities of an executive:

1. Planning, that is working out in broad outline the things that need to be done and the methods for doing them to accomplish the purpose set for the enterprise;

2. Organizing, that is the establishment of the formal structure of authority through which work subdivisions are arranged, defined and co-ordinated for the defined objectives;

3. Staffing, that is the whole personnel function of bringing in and training the staff and maintaining favorable conditions of work;

4. Directing, that is the continuous task of making decisions and embodying them in specific and general orders and instructions and serving as the leader of the enterprise;

5. Co-ordinating, that is the all important duty of interrelating the various parts of the work;

6. Reporting, that is keeping those to whom the executive is responsible informed as to what is going on, which includes keeping himself and his subordinates informed through records, research and inspection;

7. Budgeting, with all that goes with budgeting in the form of fiscal planning, accounting, and control.[38]

Three of these principles (planning, organizing, and coordinating) were borrowed from Fayol, to whom Gulick readily acknowledged his indebtedness.[39]

The POSDCORB formulation has many assets and has provided a convenient point of departure for a variety of writers on public administration.[40] At the same time, however, POSDCORB omits many of the realities of organizational life. It ignores personality factors, says little about economic policy or the public interest, and fails to address itself to a number of vital managerial factors, including the importance of internal power struggles and of mechanisms for defining problems, of generating alternatives, and of problems relating to the cultures and subcultures within which administration operates; the problems of dealing with diverse and conflicting social values; and the legacy of previous organizational experiences as guides to current practice.[41]

Gulick and Urwick were also the authors of seven principles, or "proverbs," that are still of considerable influence on the formal aspects of public administration. These principles deal with the need for: (1) fitting people into structures, or organizing; (2) one top executive and unity of command; (3) adequate staff assistance; (4) division of labor; (5) delegation of authority; (6) matching authority and responsibility; and (7) limited span of control.[42]

Organizing, according to Urwick, is determining plans and assigning people to implement them. Individuals should be assigned on an objective basis, without reference to incumbency. Efforts must be made to admit people into the organizational structure and to force them to fit the organization, not to alter the organization to fit them.[43]

Gulick and Urwick both stressed the need for one top executive and for unity of command in the interests of avoiding inefficiency, confusion, and irresponsibility. Urwick criticized the slow, cumbersome character of boards and commissions, noting that well-run government agencies were administered by a single individual. After carefully reviewing the administrative experiences of World War I, Gulick concurred that multiple supervision was inefficient.[44]

Borrowing from Fayol and from the military, Gulick and Urwick asserted that executives needed both special and general staff assistance. The special staff would concentrate on the knowing and planning aspects of administration and would have no administrative authority or responsibility. The general staff would deal with problems of coordination and control, initiating orders, following them up, and smoothing out the kinks in the organizational machinery. In performing these functions, general staff personnel would be acting as agents of their superiors, relieving them of burdensome details so that they could concentrate on broader, more important matters.[45]

With regard to the division and subdivision of labor and of assigning people to the appropriate subdivisions, Gulick stressed the importance of homogeneity. Workers should be assigned according to the purpose served (e.g., controlling crime), the process employed (e.g., engineering or medicine), the persons or things dealt with (e.g., veterans or automobiles), and where the service would be performed (e.g., Boston or Central High School).[46]

On the theory that the fear of delegating authority was a major cause of organizational behavior problems, Urwick stressed that authority must be delegated, that administrators should be concerned only with deviations from set standards, and that responsibility must be matched with authority. People must have the authority to discharge their responsibilities; but responsibility must be clearly defined, and persons in authority must be held personally accountable both for their own actions and for the activities of their subordinates.[47]

Finally, Gulick and Urwick both held that the administrator's span of control must be limited. Urwick believed that because the human span of attention is limited, no supervisor could adequately direct the activities of more than five or six subordinates. Gulick believed that the optimal number of subordinates was difficult to assess with precision but was limited in any case by factors of knowledge and energy.[48]

During the early post–World War II period, the Gulick-Urwick principles were vigorously challenged by a number of scholars, especially Dwight Waldo, Herbert Simon, and Robert Dahl. Waldo objected to the misuse of the word "science," asserting that Gulick and Urwick had not used the scientific method and, in addition, had failed to treat the issue of values—an essential issue in any scientific endeavor.[49]

Thus Urwick in "Organization as a Technical Problem" confesses that personal factors intrude and that "they cannot be ignored." Yet he insists that "individuals are the raw materials of organization." "The idea that organization should be built up around its individual idiosyncrasies, rather than that individuals should be adapted to the requirement of the sound principles of organization, is as foolish as attempting to design an engine to accord with the whimsies of one's maiden aunt rather than with the laws of mechanical science." This is a truly remarkable statement. Do the "laws of mechanical science" have an existence apart from the "idiosyncrasies" of the metals, fuels, and lubricants that constitute an engine?[50]

Robert Dahl also emphasized that public administration cannot be regarded as a science until it rests on a scientific basis. Calling particular attention to the culture boundedness of the Gulick-Urwick principles, he stressed the necessity of testing public administration concepts in cultures other than our own.[51]

Herbert Simon regarded the Gulick-Urwick principles as superficial, simplistic, and frequently contradictory; indeed, in Simon's view, they were not scientific principles at all but more like proverbs.[52] The concepts of unity of command and the need for specialization seemed to him especially incompatible. Gulick and Urwick argued that organization must bring specialization to bureaucracy in order that expert decisions can be made; but expertise is often to be found outside organization. As an example, Simon cites the case of an educational institution in which the accountant is subordinate to the educator. If unity of command is observed, the finance department cannot issue orders regarding the technical aspects of the accountant's work. By the same token, the motor vehicles division of a public works department could not issue orders to the driver of a fire truck on the care of motor equipment.[53]

IMPORTANCE OF FORMALISM

The first fifty years of the discipline of public administration cannot be understood without reference to the formalistic school, whose principles remain the central point of departure for most studies of bureaucracy and administrative reorganization today. As Redford has observed, efficiency was the dominant concern of those engaged in the study and practice of public administration in this country, from Woodrow Wilson to Luther Gulick.[54] In Gulick's words, "In the science of administration, whether public or private, the basic 'good' is efficiency."[55] Frederick Mosher has noted five basic objectives of administrative reorganization, all deriving from the formalistic approach: (1) increased control at the top in the interests of better coordinated operations; (2) decentralization of decision-making and organizational activities; (3) increased productivity and quality; (4) reduced costs and more economical operations; and (5) the application of administrative principles.[56]

Conducted at the University of California at Berkeley under the joint aegis of the Inter-University Case Program and the Institute for Governmental Status, twelve diverse studies in administrative reorganization, concerned with agencies at all levels of government, all concluded that efficiency, rationality, and POSDCORB dicta remain central concerns of administrative reformers today.[57] Another study analyzing thirty years of federal reorganization efforts since 1937 concluded that despite many serious studies and efforts to formulate and test hypotheses, no new principles have been discovered that were not originally to be found in the 1937 report of the Brownlow Committee, which remains the embodiment of formalistic wisdom.[58]

Students of administration continue to debate many of the questions raised by the formalists—among them, the concept of span of control. Urwick maintained that span of control should be small. Herbert Simon, on the other hand, argued that the smaller the span of control, the greater the number of vertical echelons needed, thereby making vertical communication more difficult.[59]

Some interesting scholarship has been done to shed light on this question. In 1950, for example, James Worthy attempted an empirical study of the effect of Sears, Roebuck's "flat" concept of organization—i.e., an organization characterized by a wide span of supervision—in which some forty-four senior vice presidents reported directly to the executive vice president. This system of organization forced much authority to be delegated because the executive vice president could not deal with all his subordinates' problems. Worthy believed this to be a superior method because managers could not constantly be running to their superiors for advice. If, in their freedom, they made mistakes, this only contributed to their growth as managers.[60]

A more recent study has examined the advantages and disadvantages of "flat" and "tall" organization (i.e., an organization with many levels and a narrow span of control) in a laboratory setting. The experiment divided people into four groups of fifteen persons each, two of the groups having the flat and two the tall method of organization. The flat organization consisted of two levels, with fourteen subordinates reporting directly to the president; the tall structure had four levels, with each superior limited to supervising two subordinates; and the groups were given similar tasks to perform. The study concluded that to process decisions through the various layers of the tall organization was more time-consuming, while the flat organization required greater efforts to resolve conflict and coordination problems. The tall organizations were found to be superior in producing higher rates of profits and return on revenue.[61]

The notion of line and staff is another concept that formalism has bequeathed the study of public administration. According to Blau and Scott: "The distinction between staff and line is one that has long informed the study of formal organizations. Line organizations place emphasis on differences in rank, and its members have authority over production processes. Staff organization directs attention to specialization, and its members usually function in a research and advisory capacity. In short, line officials possess formal authority, whereas staff members furnish specialized and technical advice to the appropriate line officials in the organizational hierarchy."[62]

Thus, in a university, individuals engaged in teaching and research might be considered to be performing line functions, while officials engaged in planning, budgeting, and matters of personnel would be considered to be exercising staff duties. The distinctions between line and staff are seldom so clear-cut, however. The professor who is elevated to the position of department chairman is often expected to perform staff functions while continuing to teach—a line function. Much research has been done to investigate conflicts between line and staff organizations, although formalists assumed that no conflict would occur. In his study of managerial officers, Dalton has noted that staff men tend to be younger, better educated, and from different social backgrounds than line personnel. Line managers tended to see staff as individuals who undermined line authority.[63]

James March and Herbert Simon have criticized the formalists on the grounds that: (1) the motivational assumptions underlying the theories are incomplete; (2) there is insufficient appreciation of the role of intraorganizational conflict of interest in defining limits of organizational behavior; (3) the constraints placed on the human being by his limitations as a complex information-process system are given little consideration; (4) little attention is given to the role of cognition in task identification and decision; and (5) the phenomenon of program elaboration is not considered. These and others criticisms of formalism will be examined in subsequent chapters. Here it only remains to be said that although many consider them to be incomplete or outdated, formalistic ideas still persist in the study and practice of public administration.[64] Indeed, Gerald Caiden has stated that the Gulick-Urwick principles, despite criticism, have been strengthened as they have been methodically researched and have also been crucial in telling public administrators how to act.[65]

CASE STUDY 1

The Successor's Defenses
ALVIN W. GOULDNER

The division of employers and employees into different, often intensely hostile camps has been one of the curses of industrial-technological civili-

Reprinted with permission of Macmillan Publishing Co., Inc. from *Patterns of Industrial Bureaucracy* by Alvin W. Gouldner. Copyright 1954 by The Free Press, A Division of Macmillan Publishing Co., Inc.

zation. American history has been marred by a number of ugly events arising from labor-management tensions: the Molly Maguires in western
Pennsylvania in the 1870s; the railroad strike of 1877; the Haymarket Square
bombing in 1886; the Pullman strike of 1894; the IWW strike in Lowell,
Massachusetts, in 1912; the bloody battles in Harlan County, Kentucky, in
the 1930s; and the fierce Detroit riots in 1932. It was partly to bring harmony
to the violent area of industrial relations that the subdiscipline of industrial
sociology evolved. Alvin W. Gouldner's *Patterns of Industrial Bureaucracy*
(1954) is a classic in this field. Although critical of Max Weber's work,
Gouldner acknowledges that it is "a starting point suggestive of critical
problems and fruitful lines of study."

Although the formalists failed to deal with matters of bureaucratic
succession and discipline, it will be seen in this account of the replacement
of a plant manager that these can present very serious problems. The case
study takes place in the late 1940s in a gypsum plant in upstate New York
operated by the General Gypsum Company, which owned several plants
throughout the United States. The Lakeport plant employed 225 people—75
in the mine and 150 in the various surface departments. The central figure
in the case is the new plant manager, Vincent Peele, and the study begins
with a discussion of the problems he encountered as he attempted to assume
leadership. As you read this selection, ask yourself the following questions:

1. *What were Peele's assets and how well did he use them?*

2. *What would you, as Peele, have done differently?*

3. *How would you assess formalistic bureaucratic theory, especially Weber's, in
   light of this case study?*

4. *How important are informal aspects of organizational behavior in explaining
   Peele's dilemmas?*

5. *What does Gouldner's case study suggest for reducing employer-employee tensions?*

These cumulated pressures channeled Peele's anxiety, focusing it into a
suspicion of what was happening down below. One worker assessed the
situation acutely:

> "When Doug was here, it was all like one big happy family . . . Why,
> Doug could *get on the phone,* call up the foreman and have the situa-
> tion well in hand. *Peele has to come around and make sure things are
> all right.* Maybe that's why he's bringing in his own men."

These remarks suggest that "strategic replacement" served to bridge the communication gap between Peele and the rest of the plant and, thereby, to alleviate his own suspicions and anxieties. They also indicate another mechanism used to mend poor upward communications; Peele goes out and "sees for himself," and engages in "close supervision."

Close supervision

Peele's practice of flitting around the plant released a vicious cycle which only intensified his problems; for the men resented his continual presence, feeling it to be an expression of distrust. A sample worker stated this succinctly:

> "Doug *trusted* his men to do a job. Vincent doesn't. Doug didn't come around so much. He *relied* on the men."

Close supervision, which served as a substitute for informal upward communication, violated workers' beliefs that they should be little checked upon, and resulted in even greater exclusion of the successor from the informal system and its communication networks. Mere visitations to the plant, though, did little to dissolve Peele's tensions. He was well aware that the men modified their behavior upon his approach. Peele, therefore, soon took to showing up at what he hoped would be unexpected times and places. In a mechanic's words:

> "Peele is like a mouse in a hole. You don't know when he will pop out."

But Peele could not be truly ubiquitous; try as he might, he could not be everywhere at once personally checking up on everyone. He was compelled, therefore, to resort to methods more congruent with his role. Although as a successor he had no secure position in the system of informal relations and communications, and could not infuse it with his goals, he still had unimpaired use of his official powers as plant manager. He could, therefore, make changes in the formal organization of the plant and move about, or remove, certain of the key personnel.

Strategic replacements

Peele could deal with the problem of the resistant "old lieutenants" in a limited number of ways: (1) He might get rid of the "old lieutenants" and replace them with his own; (2) he could open up new or additional supervisory posts which he could staff, thereby affecting the "balance of power" among the middle managers; or (3) he might decide to "pay off" the inherited obligations to the "old lieutenants." [If he rids himself of "old lieutenants" and replaces them with his own, he will probably face worker resentment.]. . .

The successor's ability to create new positions is, however, definitely limited. As a new manager he is especially hesitant to initiate anything that would require main office approval, particularly if it entails increased costs. Yet this is involved in opening up new supervisory positions.

An escape from the above difficulty is possible if new equipment and machinery are being installed in the plant. The simultaneous introduction of new machinery and new managers probably occurs with a frequency greater than that due solely to chance.

In this plant, about a million and a half dollars worth of new equipment was being installed in the board building, at just this time. With the anticipated increase in scope and speed of operations, a case was made out, in pure efficiency terms, to expand the supervisory staff. For example, it was pointed out that the increased speed of the new machines made for greater waste if a breakdown occurred, and thus more supervisors were needed to prevent this. The addition of "know how" and "do how" foremen was justified in this way.

It is not being suggested that the successor merely "rationalized" his status-generated needs for additional supervisors in terms made convenient by the technological innovations. Regardless of the new manager's motives for requesting additional supervisors, the introduction of new machinery did allow for the expansion of the supervisory staff, which consequently helped the successor to handle the "old lieutenants.". . .

Nor need he replace the entire group of "old lieutenants," even if this were feasible; for by firing some he creates anxiety among those who remain and extracts conformity from them. As Peele noted when asked:

> *"You had some difficulty with the supervisors. . . .?"*
>
> "Yes, I had some trouble straightening out shirkers. Some of them thought they were going to get fired. *I could work on these guys.* But others, who didn't expect to get fired, were. Each foreman is just a little bit *on edge* now. They don't know whether they're doing right. A new plant manager is going to make some changes—to suit my own way. I had to watch them. I made those changes."

In short, the use of replacements enables the successor to accomplish several things: (1) He gets rid of some of those who were "shirking"; (2) he silences others and forces acquiescence from them, and (3) he can create new lieutenants, from among those he brings up, who will be grateful and loyal to him. This can be seen from an interview with one of Peele's replacements:

> *"Who was the plant manager at the time you began working here?"*
>
> "Why, Fier was top man then and after him Farr, Doug Godfrey, and now Vincent."

"How would you compare the four men as bosses?"

"They were all good men if you did the job."

"Would you say any was a little more strict than the other?"

"Oh, maybe a little, one way or the other, but you expect that. Vincent comes around more than Godfrey did, but none of them was really strict."

"How would you say the men generally felt about them?"

"I don't think there was any feelings against any of them. I've never heard a word against Vincent."

"Would you say then that the men feel the same way about Vincent as they did about Doug?"

"I think that maybe the men think a little *more* of Vincent because he really sticks up for the men, and I don't mean only the foremen, but all the men."

Unlike his references to the preceding plant managers, this supervisor called Peele by his first name; he was reluctant to give voice to the near-universal criticisms of Peele's strictness; he imagined that Peele was better liked than Doug. Evidently his appointment to a supervisory position by the successor made him a staunch adherent of the new manager.

The new informal group

In obligating new lieutenants to himself, through the use of strategic replace-ments, the successor establishes extra-formal ties with them which he can draw upon to implement his goals. In effect, strategic replacement enables the new manager to form a new informal social circle, which revolves about himself and strengthens his status. It provides him with a new two-way communication network; on the one hand, carrying up news and information that the formal channels exclude; on the other hand, carrying down the meaning or "spirit" of the successor's policies and orders. Beyond its purely communication functions, the new informal group also enables the successor to control the plant more fully; for the new lieutenants can be depended on to enforce the new manager's changes and punish deviations from them.

Finally, the new informal group also served to ease Peele's personal anxieties. A new manager commonly becomes very friendly with one of his strategic replacements. This became Digger's role and, soon after his arrival, he was known to be Peele's confidant. Digger and Peele's relationship was widely resented in the plant and became one of the men's most outspoken grievances. Disturbed by Peele's failure to establish friendly connections with them, the workers, with more than a touch of envy, complained: "Digger and Peele are as thick as thieves."

Digger provided Peele with an opportunity to unburden himself at a time when few men wanted to have anything to do with him. Digger gave Peele support and approval when most of those near to him "hated his guts." In this way, Digger played an important cathartic function for Peele, serving to ease his fears and anxieties. Digger helped Peele, but at the cost of heightening the workers' awareness of Peele's impersonal and unfriendly behavior toward them. Moreover, since he felt confident of Peele's favor, Digger could behave in an "arrogant" manner, leading the workers to complain that "he acted as if he owned the plant." This, in turn, only swelled the workers' hostility toward Peele.

Succession and bureaucracy

Disposing of the "old lieutenants" takes time. If the new manager is at all sensitive to what is going on, he does not wish to be accused of failing to give the "old lieutenants" a "chance," nor of seeking to install his favorites with indecent haste. He has to spend some time looking for possible allies and lining up replacements. In the meanwhile, the breakdown of upward communications to the new manager grows more acute. It is, in part, as an outgrowth of this crisis that the successor elaborates the system of "paper reports," the better to "keep his finger on things," and to check up on the unreliable "old lieutenants."

At this time, he also began to introduce and emphasize adherence to the "rules." Barred from effective use of the informal system of controls, the successor was compelled to rely more heavily upon the formal system. As an observant main office executive noticed: "Peele will follow along in *organizational* lines, while Doug handled things on a *personal* basis." The comments of the Company's labor relations director provide a clue about the role of succession in this change:

> "*New* managers always tend to rely more on the rules. They call us up and ask us if we have lists of rules which they can use. *They are unsure of themselves and they need something to lean on.* After they're on the job somewhat longer they're less worried about the rules."

These remarks tend to reinforce the contention that there is a close connection between succession and a surge of bureaucratic development, particularly in the direction of formal rules.

To appreciate why this is so, it is necessary to consider another of the dilemmas in which the successor finds himself. It has been shown that the new manager's role disposes him to a great dependence on the main office. Yet his position is such that he must attempt to conceal this dependence, and attempt to act with a semblance of autonomy.

Some of the latter pressures stem from workers' feeling that a manager should "stand on his own feet." The main office staff, too, is ambivalent about the successor's dependence on them. The main office prefers a manager who will heed its advice on matters of major policy; but within these limits they want a manager to be independent. "We have about twenty-five plants to handle," explained a Lakeport administrator. "We just can't spend all of our time on any one plant." Nor does the main office especially esteem a manager who "doesn't talk back once in a while."

Thus the new manager must, somehow, seek techniques whereby he can be sure that his decisions are in conformity with main office expectations; techniques which will, at the same time, allow him to make these decisions with a minimum of contact with main office people, quickly, and with the appearance of independence. These appear, in part, to be the specific functions performed by the rules which the successor seeks from his main office. Once he has the rules, he need no longer telephone it about every problem that arises in the plant. The rules, further, provide a framework which he can use to justify his decisions should the main office ever examine or challenge them.

Nor are the rules useful only in the successor's dealings with the main office; they also help to make his behavior a bit more palatable to people in the plant. When Peele did something which he knew the workers would not like, he often justified it as due to main office requirements. The workers would then criticize the main office for the new pattern, blaming Peele only because he "didn't have guts enough to fight back." Thus one worker commented:

> ". . . it has always been the plant policy not to have men who are relations, especially father and son teams. But while Doug was here we did that quite a bit. He was pretty easygoing on that. But now that Vincent is here, it isn't being done."
> *"Why do you suppose that this is so?"*
> "Vincent is more strict on conforming to Company rules than Doug was."

In other words, Peele was seen as bringing the plant into line with established Company rules. Some of the aggression that would have been directed at Peele was thereby deflected onto the main office. In general, the Lakeport office was aware of this and accepted it as a way of relaxing relationships between plant workers and local management, encouraging the latter to "put the blame on us."

Like all other solutions which Peele adopted to handle the problems of his succession, the development of formal rules also had an anxiety-allaying function. The rules define the new situation into which the successor has entered, allowing him to make decisions with a minimum of uncertainty and personal responsibility. Moreover, there is reason to believe that the rules had, more specifically, a guilt-relieving role for Peele. Some of the things which Peele had done could not be easily condoned, even by himself. His failure to give Day a warning before he demoted him, or an explanation afterwards, involved the infraction of values which Peele had never deliberately set out to violate, and to which he was still oriented. The belief that he was only doing what he must, softened Peele's doubts about his own behavior. As he remarked:

> "Some of the men probably think I'm a mean cuss, but I've got to follow our Company policy like everyone else. If I don't, someone else will."

Underlying assumptions

[A section omitted indicates that since there was a high turnover rate of managers at the plant, the tensions of succession acting on Peele caused him to intensify bureaucratic methods.] . . . The assumptions underlying the analysis thus far can be summarized as follows: Bureaucratic behavior was conceived of as a problem-solving type of social action. This led to an inquiry about the nature of these problems; how were they conceived or formulated? We then had to specify who formulated these problems; that is, what was this person's status, and how did his status influence his formulation of problems and choice of problem-solutions?

Since groups possess forms of stratification, it cannot be tacitly assumed that all individuals, or all positions in the system of stratification, exert equal influence on those decisions from which bureaucratization emerges as planned or unanticipated consequence. Pedestrian as this point is, Weber's analysis of bureaucracy largely ignores it. But bureaucratic behavior in a factory must either be initiated by the manager, or at least finally ratified by him or his superiors. What has here been essayed is an analysis of some institutionally derived pressures, convergent on the position of a new plant manager, which made him accept and initiate bureaucratic patterns.

Thus relevance of *status*-generated tensions and perspectives is accentuated. Instead of assuming that bureaucracy emerged in direct response to threats to the *organization as a homogeneous whole,* the analysis proceeded from a different premise; namely, that the adaptation of an organization to a threat is mediated and shaped by powerful individuals. It was assumed, further, that to the degree these powerful individuals perceived the "needs" of the organization, they became "problems" which were molded in specific ways by status tensions. As a result, the adaptive efforts which are made may be divergent from the "needs" of the organization as a whole.

Peele's bureaucratic innovations cannot be understood in terms of their contribution to the stability of the plant as a whole. Nor were "strategic replacements" or "close supervision" mechanisms that brought the entire plant into equilibrium. At the very least, each of these three defense mechanisms did as much to disturb, as to defend, the integration of the plant.

These paradoxical consequences were explained by taking into account the dilemmas and tensions engendered by the peculiar role of a successor.

Growing points

If Peele's bureaucratic behavior, especially his development of bureaucratic rules, is usefully viewed as a problem-solution, what was the nature of the problem as he perceived it? A brief recapitulation of the plant situation, as Peele first came upon it, will reveal this. [Peele attempted to eliminate the workers' practices of early punch outs, unnecessary overtime, and unwarranted absenteeism.] . . . Analysis of the succession process also brought into view certain aspects of the organizational *situation* out of which the bureaucratic patterns grew. These, too, provide growing points for subsequent expansion, indicating a range of specific variables important in the later discussion.

From the standpoint of their effects on the plant as a social system, the following seem to be the most crucial tension-provoking features of the succession situation:

(1) *Interaction of Bearers of Different Values:* The successor was oriented to rational, efficiency-enhancing values, while workers were oriented mainly to the traditional, custom-honored sentiments of the indulgency pattern. The successor's outlook was structured by the main office's emphasis on rational administration; thus there was a value-cleavage emerging along status lines, that is, between top managers and the workers.

(2) *Ambiguous Canons of Legitimacy:* Whether or not the expectations held by workers were legitimate, or were properly applicable to the plant situation, was uncertain even in the workers' view. They were not so sure that their expectations were a solid and justifiable basis for action.

(3) *Unrequited Expectations:* The workers expected the new manager to conform to the indulgency pattern, even though unsure that this expectation was legitimate. The successor, though, was more concerned about his superiors' efficiency-centered expectations and, therefore, was not responsive to subordinates.

(4) *Decline of Informal Interaction Across Status Lines:* The new manager had fewer personal ties with workers.

(5) *Hiatus in the Chain of Command:* The successor could not rely upon the "old lieutenants" in supervisory positions to support and enforce his new policies.

(6) *Shortcircuited Communications:* Because of the inaccessibility of the informal system to the successor, as well as the hiatus in the chain of command, the new manager's sources of information were meager.

(7) *Challenge to Managerial Legitimacy:* Both the "old lieutenants" and the rank and file of workers doubted the legitimacy of the successor. They did

not merely resist him because they thought they could get away with it, that is, on purely expedient grounds, but because they felt that he was not a "proper" manager and did not *deserve* to be supported.

(8) *Degeneration of Motives for Obedience:* Both supervisors and workers had fewer sentiments of loyalty to Peele than they had to Doug. They resisted his program of changes and the policies he formulated.

NOTES

1. Peter Blau and Richard W. Scott say, "Since the distinctive characteristic of these [formal] organizations is that they have been formally established for the explicit purpose of achieving certain goals, the term 'formal organizations' is used to designate them" (Peter Blau and Richard W. Scott, *Formal Organizations,* p. 5).

2. Martin Albrow, *Bureaucracy,* pp. 18–19.

3. H. H. Gerth and C. Wright Mills, *From Max Weber,* pp. 50–51. *Rationalization* means ideas gained in systematic coherence and naturalistic consistency.

4. Ibid., pp. 197–216.

5. Peter Blau and Marshall W. Meyer, *Bureaucracy in Modern Society,* pp. 19–20.

6. Gerth and Mills, *From Max Weber,* p. 199.

7. Blau and Meyer, *Bureaucracy in Modern Society,* p. 20.

8. Gerth and Mills, *From Max Weber,* p. 241.

9. Albrow, *Bureaucracy,* p. 45.

10. Ibid., p. 47.

11. Cited in Reinhard Bendix, *Max Weber,* p. 464.

12. Albrow, *Bureaucracy,* p. 55.

13. Robert K. Merton, "Bureaucratic Structure and Personality," in *Reader in Bureaucracy,* ed. Robert K. Merton et al., pp. 361–71.

14. Carl Frederick, "Some Observations on Weber's Systematic Analysis of Bureaucracy," in Merton et al., *Reader in Bureaucracy,* p. 52.

15. Chester I. Barnard, *The Functions of the Executive* (Cambridge, Mass.: Harvard University Press, 1945), p. 127.

16. See Joseph La Palombara, *Bureaucracy and Political Development* (Princeton: Princeton University Press, 1966); cited in R. V. Presthus, "Weberian vs. Welfare Bureaucracy in Traditional Societies," *Administrative Science Quarterly* 6 (June 1961): 1–24.

17. Gerth and Mills, *From Max Weber,* p. 261.

18. Cited in Bruce Brugmann, ed., *The Ultimate Highrise* (San Francisco: San Francisco Bay Guardian, 1971), p. 64.

19. Samuel Haber, *Efficiency and Uplift* (Chicago: University of Chicago Press, 1964), p. ix.

20. Ibid., p. 7.

21. Sudhir Kakar, *Frederick Taylor: A Study in Personality and Innovation* (Cambridge, Mass.: M.I.T. Press, 1970), pp. 28–122.

22. Frederick W. Taylor, *Shop Management* (New York: Harper & Row, 1919), p. 35.

23. Frederick W. Taylor, *The Principles of Scientific Management* (New York: Harper & Row, 1911), p. 5.

24. Ibid., especially pp. 5–29.

25. Ibid., p. 7.

26. Ibid., p. 26.

27. Ibid., pp. 77–82.

28. Ibid., pp. 62–77, and Kakar, *Frederick Taylor,* pp. 55–74.

29. Taylor, *Shop Management,* p. 110.

30. Ibid., pp. 67, 102–4, 109–10, and 112–20.

31. Haber, *Efficiency and Uplift,* p. 33.

32. Kakar, *Frederick Taylor,* pp. 100–150.

33. Bertram M. Gross, *The Managing of Organizations,* 1:125.

34. Wilbert E. Moore, *Industrial Relations and the Social Order* (New York: Harper & Row, 1957), p. 190.

35. Hugh G. T. Aitkin, *Taylorism at the Watertown Arsenal* (Cambridge, Mass.: Harvard University Press, 1960), pp. 26–27.

36. Gross, *Managing of Organizations,* 1:128–36.

37. Luther Gulick and Lyndall Urwick, eds. *Papers on the Science of Administration.*

38. Luther Gulick, "Notes on the Theory of Organization," ibid., p. 13.

39. Ibid.

40. Gross, *Managing of Organizations,* 1:144.

41. Morris Schaefer, "Public Administration: Plumbing, Platonism, and Polygamy," *Public Administration Review* 27 (December 1967): 467–68.

42. Gross, *Managing of Organizations,* 1:146–48.

43. Ibid., p. 145.

44. Ibid.

45. Ibid., pp. 145–47.

46. Gulick, "Theory of Organization," pp. 15–30.

47. Gross, *Managing of Organizations,* 1:147–48.

48. John M. Pfiffner and Robert Presthus, *Public Administration,* 5th ed. (New York: Ronald Press Co., 1967), pp. 188–89.

49. Dwight Waldo, *The Administrative State* (New York: Ronald Press Co., 1948), pp. 74–79.

50. Ibid., p. 174.

51. Robert A. Dahl, "The Science of Public Administration: Three Problems," *Public Administration Review* 7 (winter 1947): 1–11.

52. Herbert A. Simon, *Administrative Behavior: A Study of Decision Making Processes in Administrative Organization,* 2d ed. (New York: Macmillan Co., 1957), pp. 20, 40.

53. Ibid., p. 23.

54. Emette Redford, *Ideal and Practice in Public Administration,* p. 1.

55. Luther Gulick, "Some Values in Public Administration," in Gulick and Urwick, *Papers on the Science of Administration.*

56. Frederick C. Mosher, "Some Notes on the Reorganization of Public Agencies," in *Public Administration and Democracy,* ed. Roscoe C. Martin, p. 138.

57. Frederick C. Mosher, *Governmental Reorganizations,* p. 498.

58. Harvey C. Mansfield, *Federal Executive Reorganizations.*

59. Herbert A. Simon, *Administrative Behavior: A Study of Decision Making Processes in Administrative Organization,* 1st ed. (New York: Macmillan Co., 1957), pp. 26–28.

60. James C. Worthy, "Organizational Structure and Morale," *American Sociological Review* 15 (April 1950): 169–79.

61. Rocco Corzo, Jr., and John N. Yanouzas, "Effects of Flat and Tall Organization Structure," *Administrative Science Quarterly* 14, no. 2 (June 1969): 178–91.

62. Blau and Scott, *Formal Organizations,* p. 172.

63. Melville Dalton, "Conflicts between Staff and Line Officers," *American Sociological Review* 15 (June 1950): 342–51.

64. James March and Herbert Simon, *Organizations* (New York: John Wiley & Sons, 1960), p. 33.

SELECTED BIBLIOGRAPHY

Albrow, Martin. *Bureaucracy.* New York: Praeger Publishers, 1970.

Bendix, Reinhard. *Max Weber: An Intellectual Portrait.* New York: Doubleday & Co., 1960.

Blau, Peter, and Meyer, Marshall W. *Bureaucracy in Modern Society.* 2d ed. New York: Random House, 1971.

Blau, Peter, and Scott, W. Richard. *Formal Organizations.* San Francisco: Chandler Publishing Co., 1962.

Gerth, H. H., and Mills, C. Wright. *From Max Weber.* New York: Oxford University Press, 1946.

Gouldner, Alvin W. *Patterns of Industrial Bureaucracy.* New York: Free Press, 1954.

Gross, Bertram M. *The Managing of Organizations.* Vol. 1. New York: Free Press, 1964.

Gulick, Luther, and Urwick, Lyndall, eds. *Papers on the Science of Administration.* New York: Institute of Public Administration, 1937.

Litterer, Joseph A. *Organizations.* 2d ed. New York: John Wiley & Sons, 1969.

Mansfield, Harvey C. *Federal Executive Reorganizations: Thirty Years of Experience.* Washington, D.C.: Brookings Institution, 1969.

March, James. *Handbook of Organizations.* Chicago: Rand McNally & Co., 1962.

Martin, Roscoe, ed. *Public Administration and Democracy.* Syracuse, N.Y.: Syracuse University Press, 1965.

Merton, Robert K.; Gray, Ailsa P.; Hockey, Barbara; and Selvin, Hanan C., eds. *Reader in Bureaucracy.* Glencoe, Ill.: Free Press, 1952.

Mosher, Frederick C. *Governmental Reorganizations.* Indianapolis: Bobbs-Merrill Co., 1967.

Redford, Emette. *Ideal and Practice in Public Administration.* Birmingham: University of Alabama Press, 1958.

Schaefer, Morris. "Public Administration: Plumbing, Platonism, and Polygamy." *Public Administration Review* 27 (1967): 467–73.

Sherman, Harvey. *It All Depends: A Pragmatic Approach to Organizations.* Birmingham: University of Alabama Press, 1966.

Taylor, Frederick W. *Scientific Management.* New York: Harper & Row, 1947.

Urwick, Lyndall F. "The Span of Control: Some Facts about the Fables." *Advanced Management* 21 (1956): 5–14.

Worthy, James C. "Organizational Structure and Morale." *American Sociological Review* 15 (1950): 69–179.

INFORMAL ASPECTS OF ORGANIZATIONS

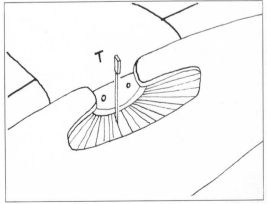

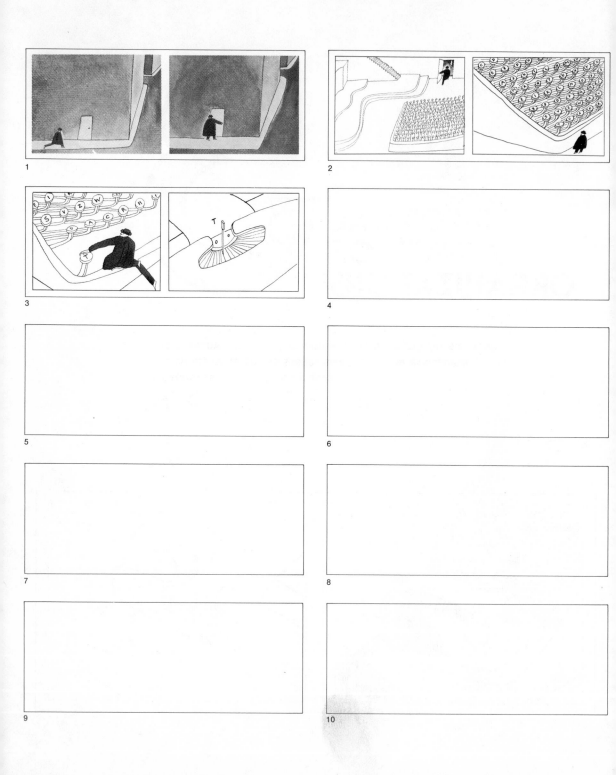

In a hierarchy every employee tends to rise to his level of incompetence. . . . In time, every post tends to be occupied by an employee who is imcompetent to carry out its duties. . . . Work is accomplished by those employees who have not yet reached their level of incompetence.

The Peter Principle
LAURENCE J. PETER and RAYMOND HULL

3 The legal-rational approach to the study of administration either entirely ignored, or gave short shrift to, the human dimension of the discipline. This situation began to change in the 1930s, largely in response to pressures from labor unions, which had begun to appear in the United States as early as 1792 but did not become a potent force in American life until the juncture of the nineteenth and twentieth centuries. With the passage of the Wagner Act in 1935, labor gained legal status, dignity, and power. Unions curbed paternalistic and authoritarian trends in management. As administrators began to recognize workers' contributions toward the realization of organizational goals, greater attention was given to considering and coordinating the human aspect of organizational behavior. Indeed, forcing attention toward the human element may be the American labor movement's greatest contribution to administrative theory and practice.[1]

The Great Depression also contributed to the need for, and acceptance of, a human relations approach to administration. Operating on the basis of laissez-faire principles and legal-rational administrative theory, the American economy soared during the 1920s; but the disastrous aftereffects of the 1929 Black Tuesday crash caused American administrators to become more susceptible to suggestions that might avert future economic catastrophe. Massive unemployment, economic insecurity, and public discontent called attention to many human problems that had previously been ignored. Public and private managers alike placed more emphasis on personnel departments and gave more of their attention to the human side of management.

Thus, human relations gained impetus and importance as a result of union agitation and the economic dislocations of the 1930s. As Harold Koontz has explained, the human relations approach to administration ". . . concentrates on the people part of management and rests on the principle that where people work together as groups in order to accomplish objectives, people understand people."[2]

Chester I.
Barnard
(1886–1961)

The term "behavioral science" denotes the scientific study of human behavior. Chester I. Barnard was an outstanding contributor to the effort to make public administration into a behavioral science and was one of the few highly successful practitioners to put his thoughts about administration onto paper.

Barnard had a rich and varied career as a chief executive. From 1927 to 1948 he was president of New Jersey Bell Telephone, a large public utility. During World War II he headed the USO, a nonprofit organization. From 1952 to 1954 he served as president of the Rockefeller Foundation, a large philanthropic organization, and he served on the boards of numerous profit and nonprofit organizations as well. His major work, *The Functions of the Executive* (1938), is a classic in the study of administration. Kenneth Boulding has stated that *The Functions of the Executive* is one of the three most influential books about organizations that he has read.[3] Herbert Simon has acknowledged his debt to Barnard in his own pioneering work, *Administrative Behavior*.[4]

Barnard's work is particularly useful because it is so broadly based, borrowing from economics, philosophy, political science, psychology, and the physical sciences as well as from his own experience. A seminal figure in pre–World War II administrative theory, he was the first to break away from the legal-rational school, the first to introduce the ideas of systems and decision making, and the first to emphasize the importance of the individual, the role of small groups, and the significance of psychological considerations in administration.[5]

Barnard regarded the traditional classical studies as overdescriptive and superficial.[6] "The thesis of this study," he stated in the preface to his book, "is that [law] arises from formal and especially the informal understandings of the people as socially organized, and that so far as these practices and understandings are formalized in substantive law and promulgated by law making authorities the 'law' is merely the formulation.[7] Formal organization he defined as " . . . a system of consciously coordinated activities or forces of two or more persons,"[8] emphasizing that it is people, not boxes on an organizational chart, that constitute the heart of an organization.

In sharp contrast to Weber and other formalists, Barnard argued that authority is not imposed from above but is granted to supervisors by employees, a useful concept in understanding the relation of subordinates to authority. Barnard was also the first major administrative theorist to develop the concept of the decision-making process, a contribution which alone assures his place in administrative theory. "The fine art of executive decision," he wrote, "consists in not deciding questions that are not pertinent, in not deciding prematurely, in not making decisions that cannot be made effective, and in not making decisions that others should make."[9] In Barnard's view, decision making involves searching for strategic factors that meet the organization's purposes.

Barnard's treatment of the importance to organizations of communication has been termed pioneering.[10] He regarded communications as a central function of the executive, emphasizing that only through effective communications can an organization's purposes be achieved; indeed, the very effectiveness of inducements depends on ability to communicate them.[11]

> The coordination of efforts essential to a system of cooperation requires . . . an organizational system of communication. Such a system of communication implies centers or points of interconnection and can only operate as these centers are occupied by persons who are called executives. It might be said, then, that the function of executives is to serve as channels of communication so far as communications must pass through central positions.[12]

He also believed that lines of communication should be verified and as short as possible.[13]

If an individual is to accept and obey a communication, Barnard believed, four conditions must be met: he must understand the communication, and he must believe that it is consistent with the organization's purposes, that it is compatible with his personal interest, and that he is mentally and physically able to comply with it.[14] Certain orders, depending on the individual affected, will be regarded as acceptable, others as unacceptable or perhaps viewed with relative indifference. This "zone of indifference" will widen or narrow depending on the inducements offered or the burdens and sacrifices involved in compliance.[15]

In Barnard's view, the individual is the strategic factor in any organization, and, regardless of his uniqueness, he must be induced to cooperate.[16] But human beings are dominated by egotistical drives, especially self-preservation and self-satisfaction, and organizations can exist only if they satisfy these needs. Barnard felt that the effectiveness of material inducements had been overemphasized; once minimum material needs are met, personal inducements in the form of opportunities for distinction, prestige, or personal power are more important in securing cooperative effort. Other personal inducements were called "ideal benedictions"; these included pride of workmanship, appeals to altruism or patriotism, and opportunities to satisfy religious needs. Barnard also believed that people need a satisfactory social situation in their work. Marked differences in education, race, or social status, for example, might adversely affect communications.[17]

Barnard was also a pioneer in recognizing the importance of small informal groups within the organization—groups which form without conscious, specific purpose but which nevertheless affect the knowledge, attitudes, and behaviors of their members.[18] While noting that they may be harmful insofar as they may make the individual more difficult to control,[19] for Barnard these informal groups facilitated communications (the "grapevine"), enhanced the organization's stability by increasing the individual's willingness to serve, and gave the individual a sense of self-respect and independent choice. This occurs because such groups are formed for personal reasons and not for the pursuit of impersonal goals.

In order to survive, an organization must achieve an equilibrium between the inducements it offers and the contributions that individuals are willing to make.[20] In Barnard's words: " . . . The efficiency of a cooperative system is its capacity to maintain itself by the individual satisfaction it affords. This may be called its capacity of equilibrium, the balancing of burdens by satisfactions which result in continuance."[21] The importance of system and equilibrium is emphasized throughout Barnard's work.

Mary Parker Follett (1868–1933)   Trained in economics and political science, Mary Parker Follett was active in many forms of community service, including vocational guidance and adult education. Although she was not an experienced administrator, few individuals have had greater influence on the theory and practice of administration. Follett helped to integrate psychology and administration, introduced questions of power conflict into the discipline, helped to break with the static principles approach and to move administration toward more realistic human concerns. She was among the first to recognize that conflict does occur within organizations, that it is a normal and even valuable way of allowing differences to be aired and recorded,[22] and that it can produce affirmative results. If compromise is to be reached, she believed, conflicting views should be integrated in such a way that neither side has to give in to the other; in this way both sides gain psychic satisfaction.[23]

Follett was one of the first major thinkers to address the problem of distinguishing between power (the ability to make things happen or to initiate change) and authority. The legal-rational school had assumed that organizational objectives were met by the giving of orders. Follett agreed, but observed that people resent being bossed; the more bossing, the more a pattern of opposition to being bossed is likely to emerge. More important than this, however, is the concept of the situational determination of power which Follett introduced to the study of administration; she also urged studies of how people interact in organizations.

In addition, Follett was keenly interested in national planning, believing that planning of the use of our various resources was pivotal in preventing waste and achieving material and spiritual enrichment. But national planning should stress coordination, not imposition; above all, it should enhance individualism, not destroy it.

The development of management as a profession owes much to this remarkable woman who spent much of her life writing and lecturing on the subject. In her view, the profession needed two major elements—a scientific basis and an ideal of service. By a scientific basis, she meant the application of scientific standards to a body of management knowledge. The major community service of the profession would be to provide people an opportunity for individual development through superior organizational methods.

Follett was not a systematic thinker who organized and summarized her thoughts. She was, however, a broad thinker, concerned with problems of psychology, leadership, motivation planning, power and authority, and one who never lost sight of democratic values.[24]

The Hawthorne Experiments (1927–1932)

At the Harvard Business School in the early 1920s, Elton Mayo (1880–1949), with several biochemists, was studying the effects of fatigue in industry but was particularly interested in studying the complexities of workers' behavior.[25] In 1923–24, under Mayo's leadership, a team of investigators attempted to ascertain the causes of a high rate of turnover among workers at a Philadelphia textile mill. Interviews and consultations with workers at the mill revealed that rest pauses improved employee morale and greatly reduced the rate of turnover.

As a result of this study, Mayo, F. J. Roethlisberger, and several other scholars from Harvard University were invited in 1927 by the National Research Council to study the effects of lighting on productivity at Western Electric's Hawthorne plant near Chicago. Although the results of the lighting study were inconclusive, the Hawthorne experiments were the first intensive, systematic attempts to explore the human factor in organization.[26] The data collected in resultant studies formed the starting point of a behavioral approach to the study of administration and the fount of the human relations school.

The Hawthorne experiments had several phases. The Second Relay and Mica Splitting Test Room experiments, which occurred over a two-year period, revealed wages to be an inconclusive factor as an incentive to increased production.[27] In another phase, 20,000 interviews were held with workers between 1928 and 1930. As direct questioning elicited stereotyped replies, nondirect questioning was attempted in which respondents were permitted to select the topics most interesting to them. This technique, which was found to have a therapeutic effect on workers, led to the final phase of the experiments—the Bank Wiring Room study of 1931—which would explore employee attitudes and group dynamics.

The major result of the Hawthorne experiments was to shatter the view of workers as responding solely to economic incentives and technological change. According to time and motion studies done at Western Electric, for example, workers were found to be able to do two and one-half "equipments" (completed works) per day. Although given group incentives to do so, they produced only two equipments per day because this was what group norms dictated. A proper day's work was acceptable; to do less was to be unfair to the company and perhaps to raise managerial questions; to do more might mean increased production and perhaps layoffs. There were strong social pressures on workers to adhere to these norms. Overproducers were sarcastically called "speedkings"; efforts were often made by workers to help their slower coworkers, but those who deliberately underproduced were termed "chiselers."

Production, then, was the result of social norms and not of such biogenetic factors as strength or intelligence. Noneconomic factors, especially group sanctions and rewards, greatly influenced the behavior of workers, who frequently reacted not as individuals but as groups. The Hawthorne experiments demonstrated that informal democratic leadership and participation can be more vital and important than formal leadership.

The human relations approach to administration became a fad after World War II. After the Hawthorne studies, workers were no longer regarded as mere appendages to their machines.[28] Human considerations became central to the study of administration as students grew increasingly interested in individual human needs, the impact of organization on human behavior, morale, leadership, and communication, and the influence of culture on bureaucratic behavior.

Yet the human relations approach was not without flaws. Much of the work of this school was based on the simplistic notion that a happy group is a productive group,[29] although Follett, among others, had demonstrated that conflict, too, can serve useful purposes. More important is the question of at whose expense a more harmonious organization is achieved. Gerald Caiden has argued that the human relations approach remained popular in the United States because it satisfied the American egalitarian ethic while cloaking the elitist assumptions of bureaucratic organization.[30]

HUMAN-CENTERED BUREAUCRACY

Fulfilling Human Needs

According to Abraham Maslow, people act to satisfy an ascending hierarchy of human needs. At the base of the hierarchy is the satisfaction of fundamental physiological and material needs—food, water, shelter, sex, survival. Next above this are the needs for personal safety and job security, superseded in turn by such social factors as the need for acceptance and friendship. Certain psychological needs, such as ego satisfaction, independence, and achievement, come next. Capping Maslow's hierarchy is the need for self-actualization, which means using one's creative abilities to the highest possible degree.[31] How well do America's bureaucratic organizations meet these human needs?

American workers employed in public and private enterprise have not only satisfied basic physical and material needs but have achieved a level of general economic prosperity that Marx would not have believed possible in a capitalistic society. At the same time, however, social psychologist Chris Argyris believes that the objectives of organizations and of the individuals in organizations are diametrically opposed. Formal organizations tend to create situations in which people become passive, dependent, and inhibited from using their full capacities for self-actualization. The employee who encounters frustration and conflict on the job has few alternatives. He can quit; he can rise higher in the organization; or he may choose to defend his concept of self by adopting defense mechanisms, such as becoming apathetic or placing more emphasis on the acquisition of material goods.[32] The basic contradiction can be overcome, Argyris argues, only when management believes that satisfying workers' needs for self-actualization is as important as production.[33]

In 1947, under the auspices of the University of Michigan Survey Research Center, Renis Likert conducted a study of the Prudential Life home office in Newark, New Jersey. On the basis of nondirective questionnaires given to more than four hundred clerical workers, it was found that workers preferred general rather than close supervision and employee-centered rather than production-centered supervisors.[34] Hundreds of similar studies administered in industrial and government organizations have found that farm managers, for example, are more concerned with the feeding of animals and care of crops than with farm hands; likewise factory managers tend to give more attention to machinery than to those who operate it. Likert believes that this imbalance between organizational and personal objectives is encouraged by traditional management concepts which base promotion on production, cost reduction, and other goals that have the effect of reducing the organization's investment in human concerns.[35]

In a classic study of the motivations of accountants, engineers, and certain nonprofessional workers, Frederick Herzberg and his associates found that inadequate pay, unenlightened personnel policy, and poor working conditions might generate unhappiness but that correcting these factors was not enough to produce a contented employee. Contented workers, the study showed, are those who find happiness in the intrinsic nature of the work. Vital and rewarding work alone allows for self-actualization.[36]

In another study, the Human Relations Program of the University of Michigan Survey Research Center undertook to test two hypotheses relating to self-actualization: (1) that an increased role in the decision-making process would increase the job satisfaction of rank and file groups; and (2) that an increased role in the decision-making process would increase worker productivity. The experiment was conducted in one department of a non-unionized industrial organization that had four parallel divisions, all concerned with clerical activities.

Two of the divisions participated in the program giving the rank and file authority to make decisions in matters that were important to them, including work methods and processes, the scheduling of recess periods, and punctuality. In the other two divisions, the decision-making role of upper management was increased. Study results showed substantial increases in the job satisfaction of participants in the first units and decreased satisfaction on the part of participants in the more hierarchically controlled units. Productivity increased in both groups, the more hierarchically controlled divisions reporting the greater increases.[37]

In spite of the layoff of 78,000 people and massive job insecurity in the automobile industry in 1974, auto manufacturers and union officials attributed the high rate of worker absenteeism, estimated at 5 percent of the work force, in part to the greater sense of alienation felt by younger workers on the assembly line.[38] In *The Greening of America* (1970), Charles Reich argues that young people who are turning to craft work in leather, sculpture, and jewelry making are motivated by the need for self-actualizaton to shun more confining employment. Yet few people have the talent to support themselves in this way; most have still to find economic and personal fulfillment in organizations.

To be sure, self-actualization is not a pressing concern of all workers; people respond to a variety of motivations in their work behavior. One study has reported that only 9 percent of the workers interviewed preferred informal job-centered groups in an industrial setting.[39] Some workers continue to prefer higher wages to a greater sense of achievement.[40] Nevertheless, self-actualization is a vital element in resolving organizational discontent, and the need for it challenges the human relations approach which had assumed that humane treatment and awareness of social needs were all that was needed to increase production.[41]

Controls and incentives are not enough; management must arrange work so that it will be more interesting and challenging to the worker. Composite work teams may provide a partial answer. In place of the traditional method in which each employee places one part on a car moving down an assembly line, Swedish auto companies have permitted groups of workers to assemble an entire car so that they can feel pride and fulfillment on seeing the completed product come to fruition before their eyes. This effort has reportedly had positive results in terms of worker morale and self-actualization.[42]

Every group in a bureaucracy, public or private, tends to regard its own activities and responsibilities as more important and, in general, superior to those of other groups.[43] There are few studies analyzing the mutual perceptions of politicians and public bureaucrats, but a 1969 study of sixty legislators and bureaucrats in India found considerable misperception and conflict between them. Although policy making and policy execution were believed to overlap, each group thought itself more important than the other.[44]

Bureaucratic Perception

James Burnham has shown that a similar attitude is to be found between bureaucrats and legislators in the United States.[45] A ranking bureaucrat recently transferred from the Department of State to the Department of Agriculture explained that a bureaucrat never takes action without the support and consensus of bureaucratic colleagues who might have an interest in the matter, but then forges a program he believes in, assuming that Congress would agree if Congress had all the facts. Another bureaucratic official complained that bringing legislation in the nation's interests to Congress was like sending the Christians among the heathen. Congress seldom works in a well-informed way to pass legislation. In his view, congressmen were on the whole a dumb bunch, voicing opinions on issues about which they knew very little. Most public administrators, on the other hand, were well qualified for the work assigned to them; consequently, administrators are forced to spend a great deal of time attempting to chart courses of action that do not require congressional assent.

A postal official was indignant that his department had to employ personnel for the purpose of maintaining contact with congressmen and answering their questions. He complained that most congressional activity revolves around votes and that congressmen seldom vote in the national interest because, unlike bureaucrats, they must concern themselves with being reelected. Congress, he said, lacked the competence to supervise the bureaucracy; the legislature was always passing laws without considering their impact on the operations of the postal system.[46]

In an attempt to deal with the question of role perception, in the early 1970s Robert N. Spadaro interviewed twenty politicians and twenty public administrators in Minnesota, Pennsylvania, and South Carolina—states selected for their contrasting political styles. It was generally agreed that the major problems of their respective states were the common concern of both groups; both groups agreed that policy formulation should be left to the politicians and program implementation to the administrators. The politicians believed that administrators were motivated in general by security; administrators believed that most politicians were primarily motivated by civic consciousness. But when asked which group best represented the public, politicians overwhelmingly selected politicians, and administrators overwhelmingly selected administrators. Each group held a fairly low opinion of, and felt that it was misunderstood by, the other group.

Politicians felt that administrators distrusted them, failed to give equitable treatment to all people, were neither better trained, more efficient, nor better able to run the bureaucracy than politicians, were aloof from the public, and were often too rigid in their attitudes and application of bureaucratic rules. Administrators viewed politicians as inefficient, partial to more articulate groups, neither fair nor just, neither better trained nor better able to run the government than they were. In terms of policy preferences, politicians preferred short-term decision making while administrators preferred longer-range alternatives.

Although the scope of this study is limited, it does show that the degree of mutual confidence between politicians and administrators leaves something to be desired and that that and individual's view of other people and other organizations is colored by identification with his own role and organization.[47] There can be no question that these attitudes have unfortunate consequences for the formulation and pursuit of public policy.

Dearborn and Simon have noted that the private executive, too, regards the problems and goals of his own department as those most important to the organization as a whole. To test this proposition, twenty-three executives employed by a large manufacturing concern were asked to read a case study widely used in business schools—the study described a company of moderate size engaged in the manufacture of seamless steel tubes—to view the problem from a company-wide rather than from a departmental point of view, and to write brief opinions concerning which problems should occupy the new president of the company first.

The twenty-three executives were similar in social and educational background, and all were selected from middle-management positions, including sales, production units, accounting, and miscellaneous areas (research and development, legal, and so forth). The results supported the proposition that each executive will perceive those matters that relate specifically to his own area as being the most important to the entire organization. The authors concluded that criteria for selecting the most significant problems had become internalized and that the men saw the company through the eyes of their own departments.[48]

For a final example of how bureaucratic perception can color reality, in 1974 Mayor Pete Wilson of San Diego stated that effluent from the city passes a mile from the shore, where it causes no harm to beaches or marine life, and that San Diego Bay had been sufficiently restored so that people could swim in it. Yet officials of the Environmental Protection Agency insisted that $50 million be spent to treat the effluent. Wilson believed that the money would be better spent on unemployment and housing, serious problems in San Diego, and complained correctly that the EPA officials had "tunnel vision."[49]

Robert Presthus, Anthony Downs, and Alvin Gouldner have described models of personality modification to organizational life, each of which attempts to explain how human beings cope with problems of organizational life. Presthus divides employees into three types: upward mobiles, indifferents, and ambivalents. The upward mobiles are optimistic, enjoy high morale and a high degree of job satisfaction, strongly identify with the organization, derive strength from their involvement in it, and are rewarded with a disproportionate share of money, power, and ego reinforcement.

People in Organizations

upward mobiles

indifferents

The indifferents, according to Presthus, do not identify with the organization but seek their satisfactions outside the work environment. Eschewing success and power, the indifferent desires the security that organizational life can give but is content to preserve that security with little expenditure of effort on his part.

The ambivalent, who falls between these two types, also wants the dividends that organizations can give but is unwilling to play the games necessary to get them because he fears surrendering his individuality to the organization. Chronically dissatisfied, the ambivalent is sharply critical because he cannot accept the charismatic or traditional bases of authority. For him, rationality alone is the basis for organizational activity.[50]

ambivalents

Downs believes that bureaucratic types arise from a combination of psychological predisposition, the position occupied, and the likelihood of achieving goals that the individual regards as psychologically important. For Downs, people are either purely self-interested types (climbers or conservers) or mixed-motivated types (zealots, advocates, or statesmen).

Self-interested officials are primarily motivated by goals that benefit themselves more than they benefit the organization or society. Of the two self-interested subtypes, "climbers" seek income, power, and prestige; "conservers" place paramount importance on their own convenience and security. The latter are usually found in the middle ranks of organization where, having reached their own peak, they oppose change that might endanger their positions.

Of the three mixed-motivated subtypes, "zealots" are loyal to narrow policies or concepts, desire power both for its own sake and to achieve the policies they favor, and will vigorously campaign for change, even at the risk of antagonizing their superiors. "Advocates" are loyal to broader sets of functions or organizational goals and seek power in order to exercise greater influence on policies or functions within the organization. "Statesmen" are loyal to society as a whole and seek power to effect the betterment of society. In their altruism and regard for the general welfare, statesmen most closely resemble the model "textbook" bureaucrat. But in all established bureaucracies, Downs asserts, most officials will eventually reach their peak and hence become conservers in the long run.[51]

Alvin Gouldner divides members of organizations into "cosmopolitans" and "locals." Cosmopolitans are loyal to a broader set of policies or to the larger cultural or political community. In a college community, for example, the cosmopolitan is loyal to his discipline, not to his department. Locals are more rooted in the local community and will achieve upward mobility, if they desire it, within that community.[52]

To accede to every whim of the organization, to surrender one's individuality to it, is another form of adaptation described by William H. Whyte in *The Organization Man* (1956).[53] In the mid-1950s Whyte saw a new American ethic developing, one that emphasized conformity and belonging, in contrast to the traditional Protestant ethic, which had emphasized individuality and risk taking. Among the fiction of the period, even Herman Wouk's popular *Caine Mutiny* (subsequently made into a motion picture) glorified those who obeyed the system. The Organization Man belonged to the organization body and soul and was imprisoned in its brotherhood.[54] The choice of home, suburb, church, and club, the type of married life, and the raising of children—all were influenced by the demands and desires of the organization.[55] Although Whyte urged that people should fight for their individuality, he believed that one had to gain access to the organization before it could be changed and therefore concluded his book with a note on how to cheat on personality tests.

According to two eminent anthropologists, culture consists of those explicit and implicit patterns of behavior, acquired and transmitted by means of symbols, which collectively constitute the distinctive achievements of human groups, including their embodiment in artifacts. That is, ideas, values, and patterns arise from a selective historical process and are learned by means of their transmittal as symbols. Culture is both abstracted from, and a product of, learned behavior.[56] Insofar as organizations are themselves manifestations of learned behavior, how effectively they can perform their functions depends on their ability to comprehend the culture to which they are supposed to relate. No organization can succeed unless it understands and is congruent with the culture it seeks to serve.

Culture and Bureaucracy

Behavioral scientists have emphasized the necessity of recognizing and understanding the various subcultures that exist within the culture as a whole—within the American culture, for example, the black, Jewish, Latino, and native Indian subcultures. (It has been suggested that, because of their pervasive influence on learning and behavior, contemporary large organizations themselves constitute a subculture.) The inability of relevant organizations to understand the cultural norms of such subgroups has been a signal factor in the failure of programs aimed at helping these people.

To enhance their prospects of survival in a harsh desert environment, for example, the Hopi Indians developed a culture that eschewed individualism in favor of mutual cooperation. But the organization that sought to aid the Hopi attempted to inculcate into their culture the American values of individualism and competitiveness. To reward fast learners, in one instance, a teacher asked students to turn their backs as they completed their assignments, but the students refused this competitive honor.[57] Thus, although change is essential if cultures are to survive, it must be fostered within the context of prevailing cultural values. The dramatic demonstrations at Wounded Knee, South Dakota, in 1973 were manifestations of the failure of the Bureau of Indian Affairs, especially, to understand Native American culture.

To enchance his understanding of the black urban ghetto and to investigate the attitudes of ghetto blacks toward work, anthropologist Elliot Liebow decided in the mid-1960s to live in Tally's Corner, an area of overcrowded, broken-down dwellings in Washington, D.C., within walking distance of the Capitol and the Smithsonian Institution.[58] In response to the question of whether they want to work, a number of men in Tally's Corner said no.

One man with a gnarled arthritic hand wondered whether he would live long enough to collect social security but did not care in any case. Another exhibited his left leg, which had withered in childhood. Another, who appeared strong, coughed blood if he bent over or moved suddenly. Still another feared that his wife would be unfaithful if he went out to work. Men who had been laid off jobs and were receiving unemployment compensation felt there was no advantage in accepting jobs that paid little more than they were already drawing. Construction jobs paid well but often required references, union membership, skills, experience, or transportation to the suburbs, job criteria which the experiences and conditions of the ghetto precluded them from meeting. Moreover, construction work was often seasonal, while more permanent jobs, such as washing dishes, janitorial or restaurant work, did not pay enough money for them to support their families.[59] One man who said that he had graduated from a Baltimore high school claimed nevertheless to know nothing.[60]

In short, low self-esteem coupled with a sense of personal and group failure generates fear and defeat and prevents many from seeking jobs with greater responsibility. Middle-class jobs may be sources of pride and prestige to those who hold them; to the inhabitants of Tally's Corner, however, who meet self-fulfilling prophecies everywhere, jobs are not stepping stones to something better but only dead ends promising nothing better for tomorrow than for today. In Tally's Corner the sense of foredoomed failure was so pervasive as to constitute a major cause of marital failure.

> He carries this failure home when his family life is undergoing a parallel deterioration. His wife's adult male models also failed as husbands and fathers and she expects no less from him. . . . But his failure to do these things does not make him easier to live with because it was expected. . . . Her demands mirror the man both as society says he should be and as he really is, enlarging his failure in both their eyes. Sometimes he sits down and cries at the humiliation of it all.[61]

Although there may be many possible ways to ameliorate the plight of the variously troubled cultural substrata in the United States, no organization or program will succeed in breaking this cycle unless it understands the basic attitudes and values that reinforce it.

LEADERSHIP

Some men are born to greatness, Shakespeare wrote; others achieve greatness, while others have greatness thrust upon them. The question of what constitutes a good leader has been much researched and debated. The following discussion explores three basic concepts of leadership: trait theory, behavioral theory, and situational theory.

Trait theory. Max Weber believed that one of the fundamental types of leadership is that which is called charismatic and that "charisma" is:

> . . . a certain quality of individual personality by virtue of which he is set apart from ordinary men and treated as endowed with supernatural, superhuman, at least specially exceptional powers or qualities. These are not accessible to the ordinary person, but are regarded as divine in origin, or as exemplary, and on the basis of them the individual concerned is treated as a leader.[62]

Historian James Parton suggests that Daniel Webster's charisma was attributable to a number of factors, including his ability as an orator, lawyer, and statesman, and also owing to his appearance, especially his massive chest, leonine head, and furnacelike black eyes.[63] According to Parton:

> Fidgety men were quieted in his presence, women were spellbound by it, and the busy, anxious public contemplated his majestic calm with a feeling of relief as well as admiration. Large numbers of people in New England for many years reposed in Daniel Webster. He represented to them the majesty and strength of the government of the United States. He gave them a sense of safety amid the flights of politics of the times.[64]

But charisma is a fleeting, elusive force. For almost a decade the African leader Kwame Nkrumah was said to possess charisma; yet he was ignobly deposed and exiled in 1966. Although documentation abundantly indicates that Hitler exercised a powerful sway over certain individuals, his mass support was not based on charisma but on appeal to class and to economic improvement.[65] If President John F. Kennedy's personal magic evoked Camelot, the force of the magic was not reflected in his dealings with Congress. Freud saw leaders as the personification of father images, and such a concept has some utility because many people find psychic comfort in submission to leaders who might be viewed as protectors.[66]

Many studies have sought to determine whether leaders and followers differ significantly in one or more characteristics. One early study found that, in the previous studies reviewed, only 5 percent of the leadership characteristics identified were common to leaders and followers.[67] K. M. Stogdill's work (1948) revealed that intelligence, scholarship, dependability, responsibility, social participation, and socioeconomic status differentiated leaders from nonleaders.[68] Later studies, however, failed to find any traits or characteristics that set leaders apart from nonleaders.[69]

More recent research indicates several traits that correlate significantly with managerial effectiveness. Keith Davis suggests that intelligence, social maturity and breadth, inner motivation and achievement drives, and human relations attitudes bear a high correlation to successful organizational leadership.[70] This means that leaders usually have higher intelligence than followers (though they cannot be conspicuously more intelligent), tend to be more emotionally stable and self-respectful and to enjoy a broader range of interests and activities, tend to display intense motivational drives and to strive for intrinsic rather than extrinisic rewards. Successful leaders are able to empathize with their followers and, according to Michigan and Ohio State studies, are employee centered rather than production centered.[71] This list of possible leadership traits has yet to be completely validated, however. The traits approach has yielded some important descriptive insights, but its predictive value is not yet established.

Behavioral theory. The question of whether democratic or autocratic leaders are the more effective has also been the subject of much research—the democratic leader being one who believes in consultative or participatory decision making, who is considerate toward his subordinates, and who supervises in a general rather than in a close way, allowing his subordinates considerable latitude of choice and action.

The first study to address itself to this question indicated that autocratic leadership aroused discontent and hostility and that work was performed only when the leader was watching; however, no objective touchstone was used in this study. [72] Several studies suggest that democratic-supportive leadership enhances production. Schacter and his associates found that workers closely supervised and treated in a punitive manner exhibited poorer performance records than those under general, nonpunitive supervision.[73] Shaw's study of small problem-solving groups found that autocratically supervised groups required less time to solve problems and made fewer errors.[74] Still another study alternated supportive and nonsupportive styles of leadership on the assembly line and found no significant difference in production.[75]

A summary of various studies suggests that democratic-supportive leadership is most effective where information is not standardized and decisions are not routine, and where decisions do not have to be made rapidly —in other words, in circumstances that allow for participatory decision making. This style will also be more effective where subordinates feel a need for independence, see themselves as able to contribute to the decision-making process, and are confident of their ability to work without close supervision.[76]

Ohio State studies administered in a variety of situations and populations have confirmed that planning, organizing, coordinating, directing, and controlling the work of subordinates constitutes leadership.[77] Studies carried out by the University of Michigan in 1950 revealed that managers rated most effective by their superiors spent more time planning and organizing the work of their subordinates.[78] Later studies have confirmed that task-oriented supervisors contribute more to working organizations than self-oriented or interaction-oriented supervisors.[79]

Thus there is considerable evidence to support the traditional view that a good leader organizes, plans, and controls the work of his subordinates. Yet other research substantiates the view that the most effective leader combines the democratic-supportive with the instrumental approach. In a 1952 study, servicemen rated noncommissioned officers highly if the latter were considerate, while officers rated NCOs highly if they performed well in instrumental values.[80] This suggests that if the middle manager can somehow rank highly in both areas, his effectiveness to subordinates, superiors, and to the organization is enhanced.

Situational theory. Mary Parker Follett was the first to suggest that the situation determines what is effective leadership, and a good deal of research has been done since the 1940s to ascertain the validity of this hypothesis. After reviewing this literature, two scholars found the following variables to be the most significant:

1. The previous history of the organization, including the experience of its chief executives
2. The community in which the organization operates
3. The specific requirements of the organization
4. The psychological climate of the particular group being led
5. The kind or type of position the group leader enjoys
6. The size of the group being led
7. The degree to which cooperation within the group is necessary
8. Subordinate cultural expectations
9. The nature of the individual personalities that compose the group
10. The amount of time needed and allowed for decision making[81]

Since 1951 Fred Fiedler has done twenty-five major studies on the importance of situational leadership[82] Fiedler operationalized his measurement of leadership style by means of two analytical concepts which he termed Assumed Similarity between Opposites (ASO) and Least Preferred Coworkers (LPC). ASO attempts to determine the degree to which a leader perceives similarities between most and least preferred coworkers. A perception of great similarity between them indicates that the leader is not discriminating in his preferences among coworkers. LPC measures the degree to which a leader sees even a weak worker in a relatively favorable light.

A permissive or democratically styled leader would not see much difference between a most and least preferred situation (ASO) and is likely to give fairly high ratings even to least preferred coworkers (LPC). A more task-oriented leader, on the other hand, would perceive great differences between workers (ASO) and render very unfavorable ratings to the least preferred coworker (LPC). Fiedler was convinced that a combination of the situation and style of leadership determined leadership effectiveness.

Two examples may illustrate. In some situations the group is willing to be directed and expects to be told what to do. When an aircraft captain is making a final approach to the runway, the passengers do not expect him to ask his crew how to land. In other situations, Fiedler suggests, one of the most important things management can do is to train leaders to diagnose the group-task situation to determine which strategy or style is most appropriate. For example, a directive, low-LPC (hard-nosed) leader confronting a relatively unstructured task should move to structure and clarify the task so that he can operate more effectively.[83]

Motivation and Leadership

Paul Goodman has observed that there is little job satisfaction to be found in pushing a button that makes a machine punch a hole in a piece of metal that ultimately becomes part of a car body. In Goodman's view, there were few interesting or fulfilling jobs in mid–twentieth-century America.[84] In a recent book entitled *Working,* Studs Terkel interviewed more than two hundred people, of whom a great many disliked their work, one receptionist complaining that a monkey could do what she does. "This fear of not being needed in a world of needless things," wrote Terkel, "most clearly spells out the unnaturalness, the surreality of so much that is called work today."[85]

Frederick Herzberg has found that people who are happy in their work find their satisfaction directly related to job *content* (job satisfiers), while those unhappy with their work derive dissatisfaction from the job *context* (job dissatisfiers). Herzberg termed the job satisfiers "motivators" and the job dissatisfiers "hygiene factors," and these two factors became the prime ingredients in Herzberg's two-step theory of motivation.[86]

Motivators include the work itself, responsibility, achievement, recognition, advancement, and growth. Hygiene factors include such elements as company policy and administration, supervision, working conditions, interpersonal relationships with superiors, peers, and subordinates, salary, status, job security, and personal life. The hygiene factors relate roughly to Maslow's lower levels of needs. They prevent dissatisfaction but do not lead to satisfaction; they put a limit on negative motivation, but they cannot themselves motivate—only the motivators can do that. In order to be genuinely motivated, Herzberg concluded, a person must have a job with challenging content, a theory he has validated in sixteen subsequent studies as well as in cross-cultural contexts.[87] But some critics have argued that similar tests have yielded different results and that Herzberg's work ignores personality development and individual differences.[88]

Victor Vroom, one of Herzberg's critics, devised a theory that would take individual differences into consideration. This theory emphasized "valence" vis-à-vis "expectancy."[89] By valence Vroom refers to the employee's values; expectancy refers to the employee's assessment of the probability of attaining a desired outcome. If an employee highly values money (valence) and feels that his increased performance will yield additional income (expectancy), he will probably work harder. If he highly values promotion (valence) but feels that despite greater personal efforts he will not be promoted (expectancy), he will not be motivated to produce more. Thus an individual's valence and expectancy determine his motivation. Vroom's theory does not categorize people, and limited research has been undertaken to validate it;[90] yet it does enable us to understand some key variables in worker motivation.

Management by Objective (MBO) attempts to define an individual's area of responsibility, determined jointly with his superior, followed by appraisal of the results. The assumption is that this process will improve the subordinate's understanding of what is expected of him, will enhance superior-subordinate communication, and will reduce anxiety arising from ambiguity about job expectation. Theoretically, this enhanced involvement in goal setting will increase the individual's motivation and help to integrate his goals with those of the organization. The very act of communicating the purposes and objectives of the organization helps to enhance the commitment to achieve them.

MBO is compatible with other modern behavioral techniques, such as job enrichment, improved communications, and participatory decision making, all of which aim at improving employee motivation.[91] Sensitivity training is still another behavioral technique whose object is to make an individual more aware of his conscious and unconscious motivations and how his behavior affects and is perceived by others.

Sensitivity training evolved from Kurt Lewin's group dynamics concepts pioneered before World War II. Most of its organizational applications can be traced to the National Leadership Training Laboratory in Bethel, Maine, which began in 1947. The process is called training because it is meant to be a learning experience, with emphasis on exchange of information about actual human behavior on the basis of sometimes emotional personal confrontation. Through sensitivity training it is hoped that the individual will learn to observe and react to the behavior of others, develop increased awareness of other people's feelings, learn to evaluate his own behavior on the spot, and become more in tune with group communication, cohesiveness, and effectiveness.[92]

Frustration is used as part of the learning process. A training group, or T-group, is composed of ten strangers who are told by a trainer that they are there to learn about themselves and about group dynamics by becoming involved with one another. The trainer then moves to the sidelines without telling the group what to do. Managers, who are normally very task oriented, find themselves in a nonstructured situation, which is frustrating to them but which has the effect of focusing their attention squarely on the group, its individual members, and their interaction because these are the only phenomena they have to deal with.[93]

Since the 1960s many organizations have introduced an approach known as "grid training" to achieve the same results. This consists of the use of self-administered instruments (i.e., given by an individual to himself) which provide feedback to aid in individual and group learning.[94] In still another approach, several organizations have made use of seminars offered by the Menninger Foundation. These seminars aim at mobilizing all members of an organization to achieve the organization's goals by increasing the effectiveness of management and others, by furthering an understanding of human motivation, and by improving communication skills. The seminars last one week, are limited to twenty-one participants, and are conducted by psychologists, psychiatrists, and psychiatric social workers.[95] By the mid-1970s, however, many of these efforts had been discontinued. Many organizations are today encouraging their managers to study transactional analysis and transcendental meditation. Transactional analysis is concerned with understanding human behavior at the adult, parent, and child levels and how these behavioral levels influence the individual and his relations with others.[96] Meditation encourages better understanding and control between mind and body.

W. H. Auden has observed that behavioral science works, but so does torture. Although behavioral science has enriched our understanding of motivational and leadership problems, how organizations will use the fruits of this research is a vital question. The Nixon transcripts, for example, showed that presidential aide H. R. Haldeman had used transactional analysis concepts (e.g., "strokes") to "stonewall" the administration's efforts to withhold information from Congress, the press, and the public.[97] That behavioral science has also enhanced the possibilities of organizational manipulation must be taken into account in any responsible assessment of its many positive contributions to the study and practice of administration.

USES AND ABUSES OF PUBLIC RELATIONS

If they are to survive, all organizations, public and private, need good public relations and a climate of supportive public opinion; and, as Francis E. Rourke has noted, public opinion plays a uniquely central role in American

life. Quoting such diverse figures as de Tocqueville, Lord Bryce, and David
Riesman, he writes:

> For De Tocqueville, public favor in a democracy seems as
> necessary as the air we breathe, and to live at variance with the
> multitude is, as it were, not to live. In Bryce's view the sovereignty
> of public opinion in American society is no less than total. "He
> whom the multitude condemns . . . has no further court of appeal
> to look to. Rome has spoken. His cause has been heard and
> judgment has gone against him." Finally, Riesman, in an analysis
> of contemporary American society writes, "Approval itself,
> irrespective of content, becomes almost the unequivocal good. . . .
> One makes good when one is approved of. Thus all power, not
> merely some power, is in the hands of the actual or imaginary
> approving group."[98]

Perhaps the most radical shift in private organizational behavior during this
century has been the abandonment of the "public be damned" attitude for
a preoccupation with public sentiment. Billions of dollars are spent annually
in an attempt to curry public good will. American public administration is
likewise not oblivious to the importance of public opinion.

There are some sound reasons for government to maintain active and
extensive public relations programs. The dissemination of information on
such topics as school organization, child labor, and improved methods of
agriculture, for instance, has been a central mission of the Office of Education, the Children's Bureau, and the Department of Agriculture's Extension
Service since their inception. The Surgeon General's Report of 1964 helped
to educate Americans about the dangers of smoking; the Food and Drug
Administration's 1962 report on thalidomide helped to alert the public to
the tragic effects of that drug. Indeed, the mere threat of adverse publicity
can be used as a weapon; hence the Securities and Exchange Commission
has seldom to resort to formal litigation because the fear of adverse public
opinion is usually enough to win adherence to the SEC's suggestions.[99]

Public agencies are often required by law to inform the public about
their activities. The Department of Agriculture, for example, was established in 1862 to "acquire and diffuse among the people of the United States
information on such subjects connected with agriculture in the most general
and comprehensive sense of the word."[100] The Civil Aeronautics Board
likewise is "empowered to collect and disseminate information relative to
civil aeronautics."[101]

In general, however, the New Deal marked the beginning of an effort
by federal agencies to inform the public of their doings. Investigating these
growing public relations efforts in 1936, Congress found that the executive
branch alone had issued 4,900 news releases, 7 billion copies of printed

materials, had mailing lists containing more than 2 million names, and had produced 533 films—the materials ranging from unobjectionable releases to self-congratulatory statements about agency efficiency. In 1948 the Bureau of the Budget estimated that 4,500 federal government employees were engaged in public relations work. In 1951 a House committee expressed the view that the administrative lobby was the most influential in Washington.[102]

The FBI has probably made the most effective use of public relations. J. Edgar Hoover, who never held a news conference, built the bureau's image by personally authorizing books, movies, and television shows that had been created by carefully selected admirers. In 1940 Nebraska Senator George Norris called Hoover the greatest publicity hound in the country.[103] Mr. Hoover's immediate successor, Clarence M. Kelly, held regular news conferences, however, and also doubled the FBI's public information staff.[104]

The bureaucratic passion for secrecy was noted early by no less an astute observer than Max Weber. Military organizations, he wrote, must conceal their most important activities in order to maintain a competitive advantage over rival administrative units.[105] In private organizations, too, the safeguarding of trade secrets might be vital to survival in a competitive business climate. Weber postulates that bureaucrats like secrecy because it insulates them from public scrutiny: "The bureaucracy, out of a sure power instinct, fights every attempt of the parliament to gain knowledge by means of its own experts or for interest groups."[106]

The so-called "housekeeping" power of America's public bureaucracy enables department heads to prescribe regulations concerning the custody and use of departmental records, papers, and property, and these regulations have been used to maintain secrecy and to withhold information.[107] In 1960 a House Subcommittee on Governmental Information listed 172 statutes permitting government to withhold information but only 75 requiring it to do so.[108]

The power to classify documents has enabled bureaucrats to withhold vast amounts of information from the public. The Assistant Secretary of Defense (Administration) testified in 1970 that 17 percent of the department's documents were classified—an amount equal to eighteen stacks and as high as the Washington Monument.[109] Executive privilege, too, has been used by every president since George Washington to withhold information whose disclosure was believed to be inimical to the national interest. It has also enabled presidents to refuse to permit their intimate advisers to testify before Congress on the grounds that such testimony would defeat free and candid discussions among the presidential cabal.

A number of measures have been introduced to limit the scope of governmental secrecy. The 1966 Freedom of Information Act was an abortive step in this direction, although Congress revised this act in 1974 in the hope of enabling citizens to have greater access to governmental documents. Perhaps more effective is the executive order issued by President Nixon on 9 March 1972 declaring that documents may be classified as secret only if they can reasonably be expected to harm the national interest (before this, documents could be classified as secret even if the possibility of harm was remote). This order should also reduce the number of individuals and departments that can use secret and top secret classifications. In July 1974 the Supreme Court for the first time challenged the constitutionality of executive privilege, declaring that the concept was not unlimited, that neither executive privilege nor the need for confidentiality were reason enough to withhold information relevant to a criminal trial, and that executive considerations ". . . cannot prevail over the fundamental demands for due process of law in the fair administration of criminal justice."[110]

The American press has too often in the past accepted White House briefings and governmental pronouncements as truth unalloyed.[111] More than any other event of recent years, however, Watergate has revealed the potentialities for the misuse of governmental publicity for self-serving ends, and a few enterprising reporters have demonstrated how valuable the press can be in breaking through the veil of governmental secrecy.

Columnist Jack Anderson disclosed in 1971, for example, that Secretary of State Henry Kissinger had lied to the American people about U.S. neutrality in the India-Pakistan war over Bangladesh. According to Anderson, Kissinger had told his minions that he was catching hell from Nixon every half-hour because we were not being tough enough on India.[112] The publication of the *Pentagon Papers* (which the Justice Department sought to prevent being published in 1971) revealed that much valuable information had been withheld and much false information disseminated about U.S. intentions and actions in Indochina from 1945 to 1970. Two tenacious *Washington Post* reporters, Carl Bernstein and Bob Woodward, refused to dismiss the break-in at Democratic National Headquarters in Washington, D.C., as a "third-rate burglary" that was "not worthy of White House comment."[113] It was largely their investigations that ferreted out the trail of deception and fraud that led ultimately to Richard Nixon's resignation in 1974.[114]

Because government agencies have an obligation to inform the public they are supposed to serve, public relations is an essential part of public administration. But it also has great potential for harm and has been badly abused, and its abuse poses grave problems for a democratic society. As one of the most acute commentators on the subject has observed:

. . . The ability to manipulate opinion has given democratic government a powerful new weapon for controlling the electorate to which it is in theory subordinate. Through the skillful use of techniques of publicity, along with the suppression of information by practices of the official secrecy, the rulers in a democratic state can go a long way toward shaping the contours of majority opinion. At the same time, the threat of adverse publicity initiated by governmental action can be used to intimidate a minority or to discourage, if not silence, dissent. To the extent that these efforts are successful, public opinion becomes the servant rather than the master of government, reversing the relationship which democratic theory assumes and narrowing the gap between democratic and totalitarian societies.[115]

Thus social science has taught us much about the informal workings of bureaucracies. The question today is whether this increased knowledge and awareness will be used to create a more open society or whether it will be used to manipulate and enslave.

CASE STUDY 1

The Peter Principle
LAURENCE J. PETER and RAYMOND HULL

The authors of this engaging work, subtitled "Why Things Always Go Wrong," observed that occupational incompetence is rampant and triumphant because most people habitually bungle their work. A three-quarter-mile highway bridge collapses into the sea because, despite repeated checks and rechecks, someone has botched the design of a supporting pier. At a British power station, three giant cooling towers, costing $1 million each, collapse because they cannot withstand a vigorous gust of wind. One-fifth of all recently produced cars have to be recalled because of potentially dangerous production defects. On completion, the Houston Astrodome baseball stadium is found to be ill-suited for baseball because on bright days fielders cannot see fly balls against the glare of the skylights.

The Peter Principle—which asserts that in a hierarchy, every employee tends to rise to his level of incompetence—is in robust operation in many organizations, though it will not be found on formal organizational charts. Professor Peter's view of leadership and of the types who aspire to it differs markedly from that of Vroom, Presthus, and Downs. The Peter Principle also adds a new dimension to motivational theory, especially compared with the theories of Follett and Herzberg. As you read this selection, consider the following questions:

1. *How does the Peter Principle accord with the discussions of leadership and motivation in this chapter?*
2. *How does the Peter Principle apply to your life? Do your professors, dean, or employer fill the mold?*
3. *Is there any future for society if the Peter Principle is valid?*

"I begin to smell a rat."

CERVANTES

When I was a boy I was taught that the men upstairs knew what they were doing. I was told, "Peter, the more you know, the further you go." So I stayed in school until I graduated from college and then went forth into the world clutching firmly these ideas and my new teaching certificate. During the first year of teaching I was upset to find that a number of teachers, school principals, supervisors and superintendents appeared to be unaware of their professional responsibilities and incompetent in executing their duties. For example my principal's main concerns were that all window shades be at the same level, that classrooms should be quiet and that no one step on or near the rose beds. The superintendent's main concerns were that no minority group, no matter how fanatical, should ever be offended and that all official forms be submitted on time. The children's education appeared farthest from the administrator's mind.

At first I thought this was a special weakness of the school system in which I taught so I applied for certification in another province. I filled out the special forms, enclosed the required documents and complied willingly with all the red tape. Several weeks later, back came my application and all the documents!

No, there was nothing wrong with my credentials; the forms were correctly filled out; an official departmental stamp showed that they had been received in good order. But an accompanying letter said, "The new regulations require that such forms cannot be accepted by the Department of Education unless they have been registered at the Post Office to ensure safe delivery. Will you please remail the forms to the Department, making sure to register them this time?"

I began to suspect that the local school system did not have a monopoly on incompetence.

As I looked further afield, I saw that every organization contained a number of persons who could not do their jobs.

A universal phenomenon

Occupational incompetence is everywhere. Have you noticed it? Probably we all have noticed it.

We see indecisive politicians posing as resolute statesmen and the "authoritative source" who blames his misinformation on "situational imponderables." Limitless are the public servants who are indolent and insolent; military commanders whose behavioral timidity belies their dreadnaught rhetoric, and governors whose innate servility prevents their actually governing. In our sophistication, we virtually shrug aside the immoral cleric, corrupt judge, incoherent attorney, author who cannot write and English teacher who cannot spell. At universities we see proclamations authored by administrators whose own office communications are hopelessly muddled; and droning lectures from inaudible or incomprehensible instructors.

Seeing incompetence at all levels of every hierarchy—political, legal, educational and industrial—I hypothesized that the cause was some inherent feature of the rules governing the placement of employees. Thus began my serious study of the ways in which employees move upward through a hierarchy, and of what happens to them after promotion.

For my scientific data hundreds of case histories were collected. Here are three typical examples.

MUNICIPAL GOVERNMENT FILE, CASE NO. 17   J. S. Minion* was a maintenance foreman in the public works department of Excelsior City. He was a favorite of the senior officials at City Hall. They all praised his unfailing affability.

"I like Minion," said the superintendent of works. "He has good judgment and is always pleasant and agreeable."

This behavior was appropriate for Minion's position: he was not supposed to make policy, so he had no need to disagree with his superiors.

The superintendent of works retired and Minion succeeded him. Minion continued to agree with everyone. He passed to his foreman every suggestion that came from above. The resulting conflicts in policy, and the continual changing of plans, soon demoralized the department. Complaints poured in from the Mayor and other officials, from taxpayers and from the maintenance-workers' union.

Minion still says "Yes" to everyone, and carries messages briskly back and forth between his superiors and his subordinates. Nominally a superin-

*Some names have been changed, in order to protect the guilty.

tendent, he actually does the work of a messenger. The maintenance department regularly exceeds its budget, yet fails to fulfill its program of work. In short, Minion, a competent foreman, became an incompetent superintendent.

SERVICE INDUSTRIES FILE, CASE NO. 3   E. Tinker was exceptionally zealous and intelligent as an apprentice at G. Reece Auto Repair Inc., and soon rose to journeyman mechanic. In this job he showed outstanding ability in diagnosing obscure faults, and endless patience in correcting them. He was promoted to foreman of the repair shop.

But here his love of things mechanical and his perfectionism become liabilities. He will undertake any job that he thinks looks interesting, no matter how busy the shop may be. "We'll work it in somehow," he says.

He will not let a job go until he is fully satisfied with it.

He meddles constantly. He is seldom to be found at his desk. He is usually up to his elbows in a dismantled motor and while the man who should be doing the work stands watching, other workmen sit around waiting to be assigned new tasks. As a result the shop is always overcrowded with work, always in a muddle, and delivery times are often missed.

Tinker cannot understand that the average customer cares little about perfection—he wants his car back on time! He cannot understand that most of his men are less interested in motors than in their pay checks. So Tinker cannot get on with his customers or with his subordinates. He was a competent mechanic, but is now an incompetent foreman.

MILITARY FILE, CASE NO. 8   Consider the case of the late renowned General A. Goodwin. His hearty, informal manner, his racy style of speech, his scorn for petty regulations and his undoubted personal bravery made him the idol of his men. He led them to many well-deserved victories.

When Goodwin was promoted to field marshal he had to deal, not with ordinary soldiers, but with politicians and allied generalissimos.

He would not conform to the necessary protocol. He could not turn his tongue to the conventional courtesies and flatteries. He quarreled with all the dignitaries and took to lying for days at a time, drunk and sulking, in his trailer. The conduct of the war slipped out of his hands into those of his subordinates. He had been promoted to a position that he was incompetent to fill.

An important clue!

In time I saw that all such cases had a common feature. The employee had been promoted from a position of competence to a position of incompetence. I saw that, sooner or later, this could happen to every employee in every hierarchy.

HYPOTHETICAL CASE FILE, CASE NO. 1   Suppose you own a pill-rolling factory, Perfect Pill Incorporated. Your foreman pill roller dies of a perforated ulcer. You need a replacement. You naturally look among your rank-and-file pill rollers.

Miss Oval, Mrs. Cylinder, Mr. Ellipse and Mr. Cube all show various degrees of incompetence. They will naturally be ineligible for promotion. You will choose—other things being equal—your most competent pill roller, Mr. Sphere, and promote him to foreman.

Now suppose Mr. Sphere proves competent as foreman. Later, when your general foreman, Legree, moves up to Works Manager, Sphere will be eligible to take his place.

If, on the other hand, Sphere is an incompetent foreman, he will get no more promotion. He has reached what I call his "level of incompetence." He will stay there till the end of his career.

Some employees, like Ellipse and Cube, reach a level of incompetence in the lowest grade and are never promoted. Some, like Sphere (assuming he is not a satisfactory foreman), reach it after one promotion.

E. Tinker, the automobile repair-shop foreman, reached his level of incompetence on the third stage of the hierarchy. General Goodwin reached his level of incompetence at the very top of the hierarchy.

So my analysis of hundreds of cases of occupational incompetence led me on to formulate *The Peter Principle:*

IN A HIERARCHY EVERY EMPLOYEE TENDS
TO RISE TO HIS LEVEL OF INCOMPETENCE

A new science!

Having formulated the Principle, I discovered that I had inadvertently founded a new science, hierarchiology, the study of hierarchies.

The term "hierarchy" was originally used to describe the system of church government by priests graded into ranks. The contemporary meaning includes any organization whose members or employees are arranged in order of rank, grade or class.

Hierarchiology, although a relatively recent discipline, appears to have great applicability to the fields of public and private administration.

This means you!

My Principle is the key to an understanding of all hierarchal systems, and therefore to an understanding of the whole structure of civilization. A few eccentrics try to avoid getting involved with hierarchies, but everyone in business, industry, trade-unionism, politics, government, the armed forces, religion and education is so involved. All of them are controlled by the Peter Principle.

Many of them, to be sure, may win a promotion or two, moving from one level of competence to a higher level of competence. But competence in that new position qualifies them for still another promotion. For each individual, for *you,* for *me,* the final promotion is from a level of competence to a level of incompetence.*

So, given enough time—and assuming the existence of enough ranks in the hierarchy—each employee rises to, and remains at, his level of incompetence. Peter's Corollary states:

In time, every post tends to be occupied by an employee who is incompetent to carry out its duties.

Who turns the wheels?

You will rarely find, of course, a system in which *every* employee has reached his level of incompetence. In most instances, something is being done to further the ostensible purposes for which the hierarchy exists.

Work is accomplished by those employees who have not yet reached their level of incompetence.

CASE STUDY 2

Inside the Oval Office
JEB STUART MAGRUDER

In 1974 Jeb Stuart Magruder was sentenced to a term of imprisonment ranging from ten months to four years for his part in planning the Watergate wiretaps, illegal entry, and burglary and for subsequent repeated perjury. The following selection—an account of, and apologia for, one of his exploits—illustrates a number of informal aspects of administration, especially the motivation of certain aides in the Nixon administration. With few significant exceptions, the men who came to power with Richard Nixon were prepared willingly to adopt Magruder's advice to himself: "Jeb, you like this job and you're going to do what they tell you."

Some of the activity that characterized the inner workings of the Nixon administration is not unusual in large organizations, whether public or private. It should be remembered, however, that the types of administrative

*The phenomena of "percussive sublimation" (commonly referred to as "being kicked upstairs") and of "the lateral arabesque" are not, as the casual observer might think, exceptions to the Principle. They are only pseudo-promotions. . . .

personnel to be found in this case had not been envisioned by the U.S. Constitution, nor can they be found in the organizational charts of presidency featured in many textbooks. Magruder has much to say about motivation and the situational theory of leadership. Of special relevance to this case are Barnard's concepts of informal organization. As you read this selection, ask yourself the following questions:

1. *How did the current political culture support Magruder's attitudes?*
2. *What was President Nixon's leadership role in initiating Magruder's activities?*
3. *How do you assess Magruder's motivation?*
4. *What would you have done in Magruder's place?*
5. *Was it inevitable that a bright, ambitious man should end as Magruder did?*

On the morning of November 5, 1969, after I had been working in the White House for a month, I was sitting in the President's office listening spellbound as an exultant Richard Nixon savored his most recent political victory.

We've got those liberal bastards on the run now, he was telling us in a proud monologue; we've got them on the run and we're going to keep them on the run.

Two nights before, he had gone on television to announce his plan for U.S. troop withdrawals from Vietnam and a larger military role for the South Vietnamese armed forces. The speech had been intended to deflate the resurgent antiwar movement, and the press and public reaction had been excellent. Now, as a way of saying thanks to the people who had helped him meet the crisis, Nixon had invited several members of his staff in for coffee.

Bob Haldeman was there, and Henry Kissinger, Ron Ziegler, Herb Klein, Dwight Chapin, speechwriters Pat Buchanan and Ray Price, and myself, the only newcomer in the group.

Nixon slumped contentedly in his chair, his feet up on his desk, a pleased smile on his face, as his monologue continued. In politics, he said, the best defense was a good offense; we'd floored those liberal sons of bitches with the TV speech and we'd never let them get back on their feet. His language was rough, but his tone was one of satisfaction, not anger. We'd won a big battle, he stressed, and we had the team now to keep on winning.

We all shared his satisfaction and his relief. The tension had been building in the White House for weeks. The antiwar movement had staged its nationwide moratorium rallies on October 15 and was holding a massive demonstration in Washington on November 15. But the President, with his announcement of troop withdrawals, had cut them off at the ankles, or so it seemed.

Nixon went around the room with a word or two for everyone. When he praised Kissinger, his foreign affairs adviser cautioned that, while we had indeed turned a corner, a satisfactory settlement to the war might still be a long way off. Nixon praised the speechwriters for their work on his speech. Then he turned to me and Chapin and recalled the stacks of telegrams we'd had waiting on his desk the previous morning, and the excellent wire-service picture they'd made.

"Those telegrams were great," he said to Chapin. "You and Jeb got those, didn't you? I heard you had a little trouble."

"At first, the Western Union people said it wouldn't be possible to get them delivered the next morning," Chapin explained. "Then I called the president of Western Union and he said it *would* be possible."

Nixon grinned and turned to Pat Buchanan, the very conservative, very combative ex-newspaperman who prepared his daily news summary as well as writing speeches.

"Pat, how were the television reports last night?" he asked.

"They were all good except one," Buchanan said, and named a network correspondent who we felt often showed an anti-Administration bias.

Henry Kissinger broke in.

"Well, Mr. President, that man is an agent of the Rumanian government."

He explained that the correspondent was on a retainer to provide Washington reports to the Rumanian government, which is, of course, a Communist government.

"That's right," the President said angrily. "That guy is a Communist."

He looked at me.

"Jeb, you're our new ramrod around here. Get the word out on that guy."

I saw Herb Klein turning white.

"Yes sir, Mr. President," I said.

The talk passed to other matters, the butler moved among us with hot coffee, and a little later, the President stood up, the signal that the meeting was over. I returned to my office in the White House basement, across from the Mess and around the corner from Kissinger's suite of offices. Everyone else may have forgotten the matter, but I had received a direct order from the President to get the word out on the television correspondent's alleged ties to the Rumanian government. I didn't waste any time in soul-searching—I'd already seen, in one month in the White House, that those assistants who tried to second-guess the President's judgments didn't last long in his favor. So I passed the word about the correspondent to some friendly reporters.

The next thing we knew, the correspondent was in Herb Klein's office demanding to know the whereabouts of this son of a bitch Magruder who was calling him a Communist. Klein, who often found himself in jams like that, apologized profusely; Magruder, he explained, was a new man who'd made a mistake, and it would never happen again.

Other things would happen, however, for if there was any one lesson I took away from that meeting it was that the tough antimedia line I'd been hearing from Haldeman for a month didn't originate with Haldeman, it came straight from the President himself.

I had no bias against the media at that point. I'd had very little dealing with the national media. I thought a disproportionate number of reporters and commentators were liberals, but I realized that we Republicans had our friends in the media too. But the important point was my realization that if I wanted to do well, I'd better take the line that Nixon and Haldeman took. There just wasn't any room for debate on the issue. The media were out to get us, so we'd get them first. In my early days, I'd sometimes tell people like Dwight Chapin or Larry Higby, "You guys are paranoid. Look what the media did to Teddy after Chappaquiddick. They do it to everybody, not just us." But that kind of argument fell on deaf ears.

When I arrived at the White House, a shakedown was in progress. Some of the staff's influence was increasing, and that of others' was lessening. I saw that those who were losing influence were those who were seen as "soft" on the media or on liberals in general, including Herb Klein, whose future as Director of Communications was in doubt, and Bob Finch, who was on his way out as Secretary of Health, Education, and Welfare. Those whose influence was intensifying were the hard-liners—Bob Haldeman, Attorney General John Mitchell, and soon, Presidential counsel Charles Colson—men whose contempt for the media and for our liberal critics equaled Nixon's own.

For my own part, the choice was clear. I had bounced around for several years, not having a job I really liked since I'd left Jewel [Tea Company], and now I had a job I loved, one that might be a springboard toward unlimited success.

"Jeb," I told myself, "You're not going to screw this one up. You like this job and you're going to do what they tell you."

. . . Why did it happen?

I've tried, throughout this book, to suggest some of the personal and political factors that led to Watergate. In summary, I think there were three major causes.

First, the fact that over the past third of a century too much power has accumulated in the White House. There are too many people working there who are not confirmed by the Senate and are not responsible to anyone but the President. In recent months I have seen this view expressed in several articles. I can only add that I have observed the Imperial Presidency up close, as a member of the royal court, and while life there is pleasant, it is also unreal. People with vast power at their disposal get cut off from reality, and their power is inevitably misused. One Administration will have its Watergate, another its Vietnam. Clearly, there is a need for the Congress, the courts, the media, and the general public, each in its own way, to work to lessen both the power and the aura of divine right that now surround our President. I agree with Professor Philip Kurland, who wrote in the *Wall Street Journal,* "It was exactly when the White House became what it is now, a fourth branch of government, that we started down the road to Watergate."

I think the second cause of Watergate was the peculiar nature of Richard Nixon, a man of enormous talents and enormous weaknesses. Without question, Nixon had the potential to be the greatest conservative political leader of his time; he knew his goals and he had the skills required to achieve them. Yet he had a fatal flaw, too, an inability to tolerate criticism, an instinct to overreact in political combat.

I don't know which came first, the liberals' loathing of Nixon or Nixon's loathing of the liberals, but the passions fed on one another, grew more and more bitter, until once he achieved the Presidency, Nixon could not resist the urge to use his awesome powers to "get" his enemies. A President sets the tone for his Administration. If President Nixon had said, "I want each of you to do his job, to obey the laws, and not to worry about our critics," there would have been no Watergate. Instead, the President's insecurities, aggravated by the constant opposition of the media, liberal politicians, and the antiwar activists, led to an atmosphere in the White House that could create the plumbers, the enemies lists, and Watergate.

Finally, Watergate happened because some of us who served the President served him poorly. It is not enough to blame the atmosphere he created. No one forced me or the others to break the law. Instead, as I have tried to show, we ignored our better judgment out of a combination of ambition, loyalty, and partisan passion. We could have objected to what was happening or resigned in protest. Instead, we convinced ourselves that wrong was right, and plunged ahead.

There is no way to justify burglary, wiretapping, perjury, and all the other elements of the cover-up. In my own case, I think I was guilty of a tremendous insensitivity to the basic tenets of democracy. I and others rationalized illegal actions on the grounds of "politics as usual" or "intelligence gathering" or "national security." We were completely wrong, and only when we have admitted that and paid the public price of our mistakes can we expect the public at large to have much faith in our government or our political system.

Too often, we view our Constitutional rights as abstractions. I must admit that I did not fully consider just how wrong our act of wiretapping was until I learned that Haldeman, Dean, and Ehrlichman—my *friends*—had secretly taped their talks with me. I went into a rage. Those were *private talks.* They had no *right* to do that. Finally I realized, not just intellectually, but in my gut, that we had no right to wiretap Larry O'Brien's phone, either. Nor, I eventually came to see, can society tolerate the act of perjury, which strikes at the heart of our system of justice.

I have sometimes been asked if I think I have a flaw of character that led me to make the mistakes I made. Obviously, someone who knowingly breaks the law has some flaw of character or of judgment or of sensitivity to right and wrong. Yet I think, too, that if we consider how many people broke the law in the Watergate affair, men who were usually model citizens in their private lives, we must ask if our failures do not somehow reflect larger failures in the values of our society.

I think that, as Bill Coffin suggested, I am a fairly representative member of my generation. And, looking back over my life, I think that I and many members of my generation placed far too much emphasis on our personal ambitions, on achieving success, as measured in materialistic terms, and far too little emphasis on moral and humanistic values. I think that most of us who were involved in Watergate were unprepared for the pressures and temptations that await you at the highest levels of the political world. We had private morality but not a sense of public morality. Instead of applying our private morality to public affairs, we accepted the President's standards of political behavior, and the results were tragic for him and for us.

One of the great misfortunes of Watergate is that it has wiped out a generation of men who had the ability and the commitment to be future leaders of the Republican Party; men like Bud Krogh, who has already entered prison, and Dean, Porter, and myself, who are awaiting sentencing, and Chapin, who is awaiting trial on a perjury charge. Other men who had no involvement in the scandal have been injured as well; one example is Rob Odle, who lost a job because a particular Cabinet member didn't want a person on his staff whose name had in any way been mentioned in connection with Watergate.

I have described many things I did that I'm now deeply ashamed of. I've tried to relate them candidly, and I've not attempted, as I detailed each wrongdoing, to express to the reader my retrospective shame and sorrow. But the reader is assured that there has been a great deal of shame and sorrow. I've damaged my own life, I've hurt those I love most, and I've helped deal a terrible blow to the political cause I believe in. I hope that young people who are in politics, or who may enter politics, may view this book as a cautionary tale. I won't tell them, as Gordon Strachan did, to stay away from politics. I would tell them, rather, to play the game hard but clean, and to bring to public life the same high standards they would apply in private life. I didn't do that, and I feel that I owe an apology to the American people for having abused the position of public trust that I was given.

I have no regrets about anything that has happened since I began cooperating with the prosecutors. I think the agreement I reached with the prosecutors was a reasonable one. John Dean fought for months to trade his testimony for immunity from prosecution, but in the end he accepted a one-count indictment, just as I did. Other of my colleagues, as I write this, have been indicted and are awaiting trial. Perhaps, by one legal means or another, they may escape punishment. Even if they do, even if I might have done the same, I still think I made the right decision in pleading guilty and accepting the consequences. Better to admit the truth and pay the penalty.

Others can make their own decisions; I've made mine. As I write this, it appears that Judge Sirica will soon pass sentence on me. I wouldn't be honest if I said I expect to benefit from prison. If I never went to prison, I would have been changed by this experience. I've been living in a kind of prison for almost two years, ever since the day the burglars were arrested in the Watergate. Yet if society's laws are to be respected, people who break them must be punished, and prison is one tangible form of punishment. I hope that my prison term will, in society's eyes, wipe my record clean and give me a chance to start anew. As I told the senators, I don't intend to be destroyed by this experience. I will still have a long life ahead of me, and I think it can be a good life, for me and my family.

NOTES

1. Harold Koontz and Cyril O'Donell, *Principles of Management,* 2d ed. (New York: McGraw-Hill, 1959), pp. 31–32.

2. Harold Koontz, "The Management Theory Jungle," *Academy of Management Journal* 4, no. 3 (1961): 178.

3. Kenneth Boulding, *The Image* (Ann Arbor, Mich.: University of Michigan Press, 1956), p. 53.

4. Herbert Simon, *Administrative Behavior* (New York: Macmillan Co., 1948), pp. xv–xvi.

5. See also William B. Wolf, *How to Understand Management: An Introduction to Chester I. Barnard* (Los Angeles: Lucas Brothers Publishers, 1968); and idem., *Conversations with Chester I. Barnard* (Ithaca, N.Y.: Cornell University Press, 1972).

6. Chester I. Bernard, *The Functions of the Executive,* pp. viii–ix.

7. Ibid., p. x.

8. Ibid., p. 73.

9. Ibid., p. 194.

10. Bertram M. Gross, *The Managing of Organizations,* vol. 1 (New York: Free Press, 1964), p. 178.

11. Barnard, *Functions of the Executive,* p. 89.

12. Ibid., p. 215.

13. Ibid., pp. 82–95, 161–84.

14. Ibid., pp. 168–69.

15. Ibid.

16. Ibid., p. 138.

17. Ibid., pp. 146–47.

18. Ibid., pp. 114–15.

19. Ibid., p. 122.

20. Ibid.

21. Ibid., p. 57.

22. Mary Parker Follett, *Creative Experience* (London: Longmans, Green & Co., 1924), p. 300.

23. Mary Parker Follett, *Constructive Conflict in Dynamic Administration: The Collected Papers of Mary Parker Follett,* ed. Harvey Metcalf and Lyndall Urwick (New York: Harper & Row, 1942).

24. Gross, *Managing of Organizations,* 1:150–60.

25. For details of his life, see Lyndall Urwick, *The Life and Work of Elton Mayo* (London: Urwick Jorr & Partners, 1960).

26. The work is treated in F. J. Roethlisberger and William J. Dickson, *Management and the Worker.*

27. Ibid., p. 160.

28. C. Wright Mills, *The Power Elite* (New York: Oxford University Press, 1956).

29. Alan C. Filley and Robert J. House, *Managerial Process and Organizational Behavior* (Glenview, Ill.: Scott, Foresman & Co., 1969), p. 22.

30. Gerald E. Caiden, *The Dynamics of Public Administration* (New York: Holt, Rinehart & Winston, 1971).

31. Abraham Maslow, *Motivation and Personality;* for an update, see idem., *Eupsychian* Management (Homewood, Ill.: Richard D. Irwin, 1965).

32. Chris Argyris, *Personality and Organization.* Argyris somewhat revised his views in subsequent books; see idem., *Integrating the Individual and the Organization* (New York: John Wiley & Sons, 1964).

33. Ibid., p. 74.

34. Renis Likert, *New Patterns of Management;* for his later views, see idem., *The Human Organization* (New York: McGraw-Hill, 1967).

35. Ibid., p. 73; see also Carey McWilliams, *Factories in the Field* (Boston: Little, Brown & Co., 1974).

36. Frederick Herzberg, Bernard Mausner, and Barbara Bloch Snyderman, *The Motivation to Work,* 2d ed. (New York: John Wiley & Sons, 1959).

37. Nancy C. Morse and Everett Reimer, "The Experimental Change of a Major Organizational Variable, *Journal of Abnormal and Social Psychology* 52 (1956): 120–29.

38. "Job Pinch Fails to Slow Detroit Absenteeism," *San Francisco Examiner,* 23 June 1974.

39. Charles R. Walker and Robert H. Guest, *The Man on the Assembly Line* (Cambridge, Mass.: Harvard University Press, 1952), p. 91.

40. Robert Dubin, "Industrial Workers' Worlds: A Study of the 'Central Life Interests' of Industrial Workers," *Social Problems* 3, no. 3 (January 1956): 136–40.

41. Ibid.

42. See Keith Davis, *Human Relations and Organizational Behavior,* 4th ed. (New York: McGraw-Hill, 1974), pp. 79–109.

43. It should be remembered that in order to transact their business, legislatures are organized bureaucracies.

44. Shanti Kothari and Ramashray Roy, *Relations between Politicians and Administrators at the District Level* (New Delhi: Administrative Reforms Commission of the Government of India, 1969).

45. James Burnham, *Congress and the American Tradition* (Chicago: Henry Regnery Co., 1959), pp. 157–66.

46. Ibid.

47. Robert N. Spadaro, "Role Perceptions of Politicians vis-à-vis Public Administrators: Parameters for Public Policy," *Western Political Quarterly* 26, no. 4 (December 1973): 717–25.

48. DeWitt C. Dearborn and Herbert A. Simon, "Selective Perception: A Note on the Departmental Identifications of Executives," *Sociometry* 21, no. 2 (June 1958): 140–44.

49. "A Mayor Talks about Squeaky Wheel Spending," *San Francisco Chronicle,* 3 July 1974.

50. Robert V. Presthus, *The Organizational Society,* pp. 167–281.

51. Anthony Downs, *Inside Bureaucracy* (Boston: Little, Brown & Co., 1967), pp. 79–111.

52. Alvin W. Gouldner, "Cosmopolitans and Locals: Towards an Analysis of Latent Social Roles," *Administrative Science Quarterly* 2 (September 1957–58): 281–306, 440–80.

53. William H. Whyte, *The Organization Man.*

54. Ibid., p. 6.

55. Ibid., pp. 267–393.

56. Alfred L. Kroeber and Clyde Kluckholm, "Culture: A Critical Review of Concepts and Definitions," in *Organizational Behavior,* ed. Fred Luthans (New York: McGraw-Hill, 1973).

57. Felix A. Nigro, *Modern Public Administration,* 3d ed. (New York: Harper & Row, 1973), pp. 60–62.

58. Elliot Liebow, *Tally's Corner.*

59. Ibid., pp. 28–36.

60. Ibid., p. 52.

61. Ibid., p. 212.

62. Weber, cited in D. L. Cohen, "The Concept of Charisma and the Analysis of Leadership," *Political Studies* 20, no. 3 (September 1972): 299.

63. James Parton, cited in Irving H. Bartlett, "Daniel Webster as a Symbolic Hero," *New England Quarterly* 29 (December 1972): 484–507.

64. Ibid., p. 484.

65. Cohen, "Concept of Charisma," pp. 300–305.

66. John M. Pfiffner and Robert Presthus, *Public Administration,* 5th ed. (New York: Ronald Press, 1967), pp. 92–93.

67. C. Bird, *Social Psychology* (New York: Appleton-Century-Crofts, 1940).

68. K. M. Stogdill, "Personality Factors Associated with Leadership: A Survey of the Literature," *Journal of Psychology* 25 (1948): 35–71.

69. Cecil Gibb, "Leadership," *Handbook of Social Psychology,* vol. 2, ed. Gardner Lindzey (New York: Addison-Wesley Publishing Co., 1954), pp. 877–920.

70. Keith Davis, *Human Relations at Work,* 4th ed. (New York: McGraw-Hill, 1972), pp. 103–4.

71. Ibid.; see also Edwin F. Ghiselli, "Managerial Talent," *American Psychologist* 18 (October 1963): 631–41.

72. Kurt Lewin, Robert Lippitt, and Ralph K. White, "Patterns of Aggressive Behavior in Experimentally Created Social Climates," *Journal of Social Psychology,* May 1939, pp. 271–76.

73. Stanley Schacter, Ben Willerman, Leon Festinger, and Ray Hyman, "Emotional Disruption and Industrial Productivity," *Journal of Applied Psychology,* 45, no. 4 (August 1961): 201–13.

74. Marvin E. Shaw, "A Comparison of Two Types of Leadership in Various Community Nets," *Journal of Abnormal and Social Psychology* 50 (1955): 127–34.

75. R. de Charms and W. Bridgeman, *Leadership Compliance and Group Behavior* (Technical report W–93, Contract, Washington University, St. Louis, Mo., 1961).

76. Filley and House, *Managerial Process and Organizational Behavior,* pp. 404–5.

77. K. M. Stogdill and A. E. Coons, *Leader Behavior: Its Description and Measurement,* Bureau of Business Research Monograph 38, Ohio State University (1957).

78. Daniel Katz and Robert L. Kaln, *Productivity, Supervision, and Morale in an Office Situation* (Ann Arbor, Mich.: University of Michigan Survey Research Center, 1950).

79. Bernard M. Bass and George Dunteman, "Behavior in Groups as a Function of Self, Interaction, and Task Orientation," *Journal of Abnormal and Social Psychology* 66 (1963): 419–28.

80. J. V. Moore and R. J. Smith, Jr., "Aspects of Non-Commissioned Officers' Leadership," (Technical report, U.S. Air Force, Human Resources Research Center, 1952).

81. H. Oaklander and E. A. Fleishman, "Patterns of Leadership related to Organizational Stress in Hospital Settings," *Administrative Science Quarterly* 8 (March 1964): 520–32.

82. Fred E. Fielder, *A Theory of Leadership Effectiveness* (New York: McGraw-Hill, 1967).

83. Ibid., pp. 133–34, 184–85; see also Fred E. Fielder, "Personality Motivational Systems and Behavior of High and Low LPC Persons," *Human Relations* 25, no. 5 (November 1972): 391–412.

84. Paul Goodman, *Growing Up Absurd* (New York: Random House, 1960).

85. Studs Terkel, *Working* (New York: Random House, 1972), p. xviii; see also Luthans, *Organizational Behavior,* p. 488.

86. Herzberg, Mausner, and Snyderman, *Motivation to Work.*

87. Frederick Herzberg, *Work and the Nature of Man.*

88. George Graen, "Motivator and Hygiene Dimensions for Research and Development Engineers," *Journal of Applied Psychology* 50, no. 6 (December 1966): 551–55; see also Victor H. Vroom, *Work and Motivation,* p. 128.

89. See Victor H. Vroom, *Motivation and Modern Society* (New York: John Wiley & Sons, 1964); and idem., *Motivation and Morale* (New York: John Wiley & Sons, 1964).

90. Jay Galbraith and L. L. Cummings, "An Empirical Investigation of the Motivational Determinants of Task Performance: Interactive Effects between Instrumentality-Valence and Motivation-Ability," *Organizational Behavior and Human Performance* 2, no. 3 (August 1967): 237–57.

91. Luthans, *Organizational Behavior* pp. 516–21; see also John M. Ivancevich, "A Study of the Impact of Management by Objectives on Perceived Need Satisfaction," *Personnel Psychology,* summer 1970, pp. 139–51.

92. "Sensitivity Training," *Behavior Science: Concepts and Management Applications,* New York Conference Board Studies in Personnel Policy no. 216 (1970), p. 42.

93. Ibid., p. 46.

94. Robert R. Blake, Jane S. Mouton, Louis B. Barnest, and Larry E. Greiner, "Breakthrough in Organizational Development," *Harvard Business Review* 42, no. 6 (November–December 1964): 134–55.

95. Conference Board, *Behavioral Science: Concepts and Management Applications* (New York: Conference Board, 1969), pp. 56–58.

96. See Eric Berne, *What Do You Say after You Say Hello?* (New York: Bantam Books, 1974).

97. See Washington Post Staff, *The Presidential Transcripts* (New York: Dell Publishing Co., 1974).

98. Cited in Francis E. Rourke, *Secrecy and Publicity,* p. 213.

99. Kenneth C. Davis, *Administrative Law Treatise,* vol. 1 (St. Paul, Minn: West Publishing Co., 1958).

100. Nigro, *Modern Public Administration,* p. 220.

101. Cited in Pfiffner and Presthus, *Public Administration,* p. 154.

102. Rourke, *Secrecy and Publicity,* p. 192.

103. Ibid.

104. "New FBI Story," *Newsweek,* 15 July 1974, p. 55.

105. H. H. Gerth and C. Wright Mills, *From Max Weber* (New York: Oxford University Press, 1946), pp. 196–244.

106. Ibid., pp. 233–34.

107. Rourke, *Secrecy and Publicity,* p. 48.

108. Ibid., p. 57.

109. Nigro, *Modern Public Administration,* p. 227.

110. *Newsweek,* 5 August 1974, p. 23.

111. See, for example, Warren Weaver, *Both Your Houses* (New York: Praeger Publishers, 1972), pp. 8–24.

112. Jack Anderson and George Clifford, *The Anderson Papers* (New York: Ballantine Books, 1974), pp. 253–326.

113. Cited in "Fine Print," *New Republic,* 22 June 1974, p. 29.

114. Carl Bernstein and Bob Woodward, *All the President's Men.*

115. Rourke, *Secrecy and Publicity,* p. xi.

SELECTED BIBLIOGRAPHY

Argyris, Chris. *Personality and Organization: The Conflict between System and the Individual.* New York: Harper & Row, 1957.

Barnard, Chester I. *The Functions of the Executive.* Cambridge, Mass.: Harvard University Press, 1938.

Bernstein, Carl, and Woodward, Bob. *All the President's Men.* New York: Simon & Schuster, 1974.

Carey, William D. "Leadership and Management in the Federal Government." *Public Administration Review* 33 (1973): 456–60.

Cleveland, Harlan. *The Future Executive.* New York: Harper & Row, 1972.

Dubin, Robert; Homans, George C.; Mann, Floyd C.; and Miller, Delbert C. *Leadership and Productivity.* San Francisco: Chandler Publishing Co., 1965.

Dunn, Delmer. *Public Officials and the Press.* Reading, Mass.: Addison-Wesley Publishing Co., 1969.

Etzioni, Amitai. *Complex Organization: A Sociological Reader.* New York: Holt, Rinehart & Winston, 1961.

Follett, Mary Parker. *Dynamic Administration.* Edited by H. C. Metcalf and L. Urwick. New York: Harper & Row, 1940.

Fox, Elliot M. "Mary Parker Follett: The Enduring Contribution." *Public Administration Review* 28 (1963): 520–29.

Herzberg, Frederick. *Work and the Nature of Man.* Cleveland: World Publishing Co., 1966.

Katz, Daniel, and Kaln, Robert L. *The Social Psychology of Organizations.* New York: John Wiley & Sons, 1966.

Liebow, Elliot. *Tally's Corner: A Study of Negro Streetcorner Men.* Boston: Little, Brown & Co., 1967.

Likert, Renis. *New Patterns of Management.* New York: McGraw-Hill, 1961.

Magruder, Jeb Stuart. *An American Life: One Man's Road to Watergate.* New York: Atheneum Publishers, 1974.

Marchelli, Victor, and Marks, John D. *The CIA and the Cult of Intelligence.* New York: Alfred A. Knopf, 1974.

Maslow, Abraham. *Motivation and Personality.* New York: Harper & Row, 1954.

Meyer, Marshall. *Bureaucratic Structure and Authority Coordination in 254 Government Agencies.* New York: Harper & Row, 1972.

Morse, Nancy C., and Reimer, Everett. "The Experimental Change of a Major Organizational Variable." *Journal of Abnormal and Social Psychology* 52 (1957): 120–29.

Peter, Laurence, and Hull, Raymond. *The Peter Principle.* New York: Bantam Books, 1970.

Presthus, Robert V. *The Organizational Society: An Analysis and a Theory.* New York: Alfred A. Knopf, 1962.

Roethlisberger, F. J., and Dickson, William J. *Management and the Worker.* Cambridge, Mass.: Harvard University Press, 1939.

Rourke, Francis E. *Secrecy and Publicity.* Baltimore: Johns Hopkins Press, 1966.

Sapolsky, Harvey M. *The Polaris System Development: Bureaucratic and Programmic Success in Government.* Cambridge, Mass.: Harvard University Press, 1972.

Thompson, Victor A. *Modern Organization: A General Theory.* New York: Alfred A. Knopf, 1972.

Vroom, Victor H. *Work and Motivation.* New York: John Wiley & Sons, 1974.

Whyte, William H. *The Organization Man.* New York: Simon & Schuster, 1956.

Wilson, James Q. *Political Organization.* New York: Basic Books, 1972.

DECISION
MAKING AND
COMMUNICATION

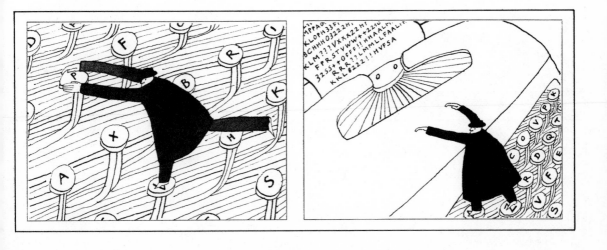

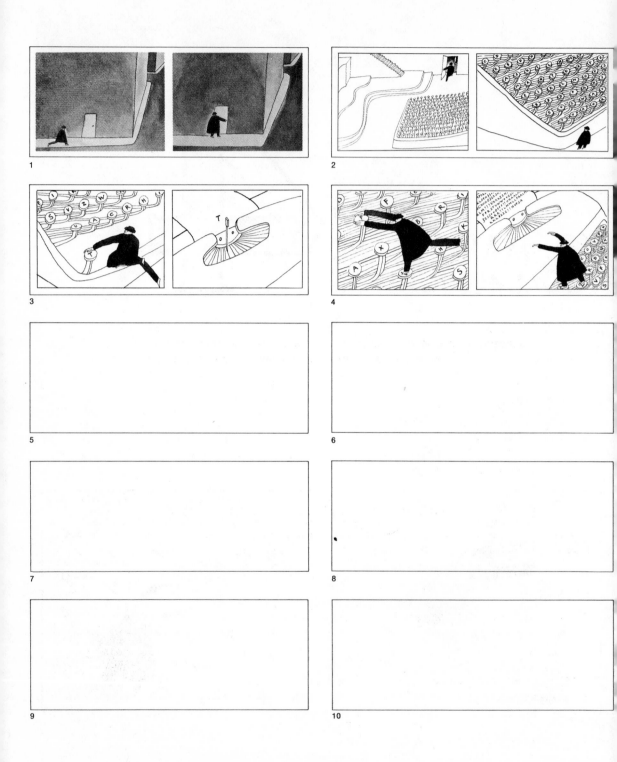

1

2

3

4

5

6

7

8

9

10

P[resident]: *Well, not sure of their analysis, I'm not going to get that involved. . . .*
H[aldeman]: *No, sir. We don't want you to. . . .*
P[resident]: *Play it tough. That's the way they play it and that's the way we are going to play it.*

Los Angeles Times
6 August 1974

4 In modern organizations, decision making is a collective, hierarchical, sequential process. To varying degrees, all participants in an organization become involved in determining operating policies and implementing programs, but the authority and complexity of decisions generally increase toward the higher levels of organization. Top-level executives focus on overall policies, on ends rather than on means; at this level, decisions may be based more on political than on technical considerations. Middle-level personnel tend to refine and direct top-level policy, help to carry it out and to oversee its implementation. Lower-level personnel are primarily concerned with effectively implementing policies communicated to them from above, and it is at this level that weaknesses in the making and communicating of decisions can become most important. A wrong decision made by a clerk can cause the objectives of the top executive to fail.

Authority has been defined as "the power to make decisions which guide the actions of another."[1] Max Weber and Robert Michels have noted that in modern organizations authority is generally characterized by highly centralized "oligarchic" control.[2] Formal authority should not automatically be equated with power at the top, however. Trusted subordinates with technical or other special expertise can exercise considerable influence over top administrators who, by abstracting the main points of a problem to meet

93

their own purposes, tend to oversimplify complex decisions. In addition, the informal structure of an organization often gives more power to certain individuals than their formal job descriptions might indicate—to the department secretary, for example, whose direct communication with a department head enables her to know more about what is going on and to exercise greater influence than would seem likely at her level in the organizational hierarchy.

This chapter will examine the theory and practice of decision making, its various elements and errors, and its importance to the organization, as well as the formal and informal means by which decisions are communicated, and some of the obstacles to effective communication. The two case studies at the end of the chapter illustrate elements of the decision-making process. The Nixon-Haldeman conversation deals with the fatal decision to further the Watergate cover-up. "The Carbondale Story" by C. William Norman demonstrates the dangers of faulty communication between management and city employees.

THE DECISION-MAKING PROCESS

Decision making involves collecting information and weighing alternatives in order to achieve a maximum goal with minimum risk to the goal sought. The elements of the process generally include: a situation that demands (or seems to demand) action; time pressure created by worsening circumstances; an absence of complete information; uncertainty about the risks inherent in any decision; the likelihood of costly consequences in the event of a wrong decision; the likelihood of benefits accruing from an effective decision; and the existence of two or more alternative actions.[3]

According to Herbert Simon, every decision involves both "factual" and "value" elements, the latter reflected in such terms as "ought," "good," and "preferable."[4] Factual propositions cannot be derived from value judgments which emphasize the "ought to be" rather than the facts. But an administrator is often torn between his personal values and existing facts, and his decisions may be more influenced by the former than by the latter. Decisions may also be spontaneous, or nonprogrammed, insofar as they may be based on instinct, but instinct alone is not enough for deciding complex organizational policies that may have substantial consequences for a great many people.

Decision making can be approached by means of a variety of methods. Those surveyed in this chapter include: (1) rational decisions based on comprehensive information, or the "rational-comprehensive approach," (2) decisions based on available partial information to satisfy immediate goals and competing interests, or "satisficing," and (3) partial decisions designed to achieve an objective in a piecemeal or incremental fashion, or "incrementalism."[5]

In his study of "Administrative Rationality," John Pfiffner describes rational-comprehensive decision making as a logical progression of steps involving identification and examination of the problem, clarification of all possible alternatives, examination and analysis of each alternative, comparison of the consequences of each alternative, and selection of the best alternative to solve the problem or to meet the intended goal.[6] To these should be added the establishment of one or more clear objectives, a major step in any systems analysis, which may be broadly defined as a method designed to resolve organizational problems by means of effective decision-making techniques.[7]

Rational-Comprehensive Approach

The rational-comprehensive approach should be regarded as an optimal procedure, or one that would be desirable in most conditions. In reality, the effective use of this approach is inhibited by the facts that decisions are not always made logically and that it is difficult, if not impossible, for decision makers to be completely informed about, or able to anticipate, all the consequences of any given decision.

Faults and fallacies. The unwillingness or inability to make decisions, the tendency to make snap decisions on the basis of incomplete or superficial evidence, accepting the most readily available short-range solutions, making false analogies between old and new experiences or overrelying on past experience, oversimplifying, relying on preconceived assumptions, and "groupthink"—all number among the common faults and fallacies that may impede the exercise of rational choice.

It can be argued, as Robert Dahl and Charles Lindblom have pointed out, that passing the buck in some instances increases participation in a decision and enhances coordination and cooperation in the organization.

> Specialization helps the specialist to make competent decisions within his domain of enterprise, but it also means that he may be incompetent outside it. What appears to be a weak-kneed refusal to come to the point may actually be a healthy limitation of the specialist's power. Hierarchy operates in the same direction, for one of the major purposes of hierarchy is to prevent subordinates from making decisions they ought not to make. In a complex organization, coordination would be impossible if the members did not know when to "pass the buck."[8]

Committing a government agency to a course of action carries significant risks and arouses considerable anxiety, and it is therefore not surprising that many might prefer to delegate authority in such a case to another person. At the same time, however, it cannot be denied that for many people it is far easier to analyze a problem and to procrastinate in general than to make a commitment to specific course of action, and such indecisiveness must be taken into account in any consideration of the effectiveness of the rational-comprehensive approach to decision making.

Some people err in making sudden decisions based only on such information as may be available at the time, without pursuing further inquiry into the possible consequences of the decision. The compulsive decision maker may be imprecise in his understanding of a problem, accepting near-sighted expedient solutions which may create more difficult long-range problems for the future. City council decisions to restrict growth, for example, may underestimate the long-range economic impact on the city or the subsequent pressure to overbuild on remaining available land. As a result of the National Environmental Policy Act of 1969, however, environmental impact reports have aided city policymakers in anticipating future consequences of local government decisions about urban development.

People who place excessive faith in past experience tend to search for analogies between old and new situations, mistakenly viewing each situation not as unique but as a reflection of an earlier event. During periods of stability, for example, organization personnel will generally behave as they have in the past. But forecasting public employee reaction is highly unreliable today when strikes by public workers are breaking precedents. Most policymakers can no longer depend on experience to anticipate employee needs, especially in times of inflation.

Oversimplified decisions are often directed toward short-range solutions to problems rather than toward the problems themselves. The reaction of the city of Detroit to the bloody racial violence of 1967, for example, was not to treat the injustices in labor, employment, and housing which led to outbreaks of racial violence but rather to spend close to a million dollars on riot equipment. Although no one decision can resolve all the problems that create riots, such problems cannot be considered "unsolvable."[9] Rather a series of less complicated steps covering both long- and short-range solutions will help to avoid oversimplification and generate a series of decisions aimed at resolving the major problems.

Alexander Leighton has noted that those who make decisions may appear to follow a logical sequence of steps to arrive at a conclusion but that all too often the conclusion is arrived at first and facts then selected to fit the conclusion.[10] The danger in selective bias is that facts in disagreement with the decision may be regarded as inaccurate, irrelevant, or invalid. Thus, in the case of the Detroit riots, the government of Detroit did not rely on the National Advisory Commission on Civil Disorders to justify its purchase of arms to suppress subsequent riots.[11] The commission had argued for new jobs in the ghetto, elimination of de facto segregation, construction of new housing, and more liberal welfare benefits—goals that require far more complicated decisions than the arming of city police, which involved a relatively short-range plan, a simple decision, and a capital outlay of money.

Irving Janis, who has studied the faults of group decision making, notes at least six major defects contributing to failure in problem solving.[12]

1. Limitation of group discussions to a few alternative courses of action (usually two)
2. Failure to reexamine the course of action initially preferred by the group for hidden flaws
3. Failure to reconsider discarded plans for hidden benefits
4. Little or no effort to obtain expert professional opinion on matters about which the group is not fully knowledgeable
5. Selective bias, or ignoring that information which does not support their preferred policy
6. Failure to spend time considering how the chosen plan could be hindered by political opponents, bureaucratic inertia, or just simple derailment by common accidents; hence, failure to work out contingency plans to cope with foreseeable setbacks that could endanger the overall success of the chosen course of action[13]

Janis attributes some of these features of poor decision making to "groupthink": "The more amiability and espirit de corps among the members of a policy-making in-group, the greater is the danger that independent critical thinking will be replaced by groupthink, which is likely to result in irrational and dehumanizing actions directed against out-groups." The groupthink leader does not transform his advisers into yes men but may inadvertently employ certain subtle constraints that inhibit members of the group from speaking their minds fully or from criticizing in depth when they perceive that most others in the group have reached a consensus. Thus groupthink leads to a "deterioration of mental efficiency, reality testing, and moral judgment that results from in-group pressures."[14]

A sense of collective invulnerability that breeds excessive optimism and encourages extreme risk taking is one of the major characteristics of groupthink, as exemplified by the disastrous Bay of Pigs decision (1961), which arose in part from the conviction among Kennedy men that "New Frontiersmen" could overcome all challenges. Another characteristic is a collective rationalization that plays down the necessity of reconsidering faulty old assumptions. Perhaps the major stumbling block for the Watergate defendants, and a third characteristic of groupthink, was their unquestioning belief in the moral rectitude of the group, a belief so absolute as to preclude examination of the ethical consequences of the group's decisions.

A fourth characteristic—the tendency to view enemy leaders from an ideological rather than from a factual or realistic standpoint—was the primary error in the decision of the Truman administration to escalate the war in Korea. The removal of Secretary of Defense Robert McNamara from the Johnson cabinet in 1968 because of his dissenting view of Vietnam War policy illustrates a fifth characteristic of groupthink—the application of direct pressure to any member who argues strongly against the group's illusions, stereotypes, or plans. A shared illusion of unanimity of judgment conforming to the majority view (silence means consent) arises from this characteristic, as does the self-censorship of deviations from the apparent group consensus to minimize an individual's self-doubts. Finally, groupthink is characterized by the emergence of "mindguards," members who protect the group from contrary information that might disrupt group unanimity.

Other limitations. From this discussion of faults and errors it can be seen that decision making is not always a logical process that lends itself effectively to the rational-comprehensive approach. In his study of bureaucracy, Anthony Downs has suggested several reasons why decision making cannot be entirely comprehensive either.

1. Each decision maker can devote only a limited amount of time to decision making.
2. Each decision maker can mentally weigh and consider only a limited amount of information at one time.
3. The functions of most officials require them to become involved in more activities than they can consider simultaneously; hence they must normally focus their attention on only part of their major concerns while the rest remain latent.
4. The amount of information initially available to every decision maker about each problem is only a small fraction of all the information potentially available on the subject.
5. Additional information bearing on any particular problem can usually be procured, but the costs of procurement and utilization may rise rapidly as the amount of data increases.
6. Important aspects of many problems involve information that cannot be procured at all, especially concerning future events; hence many decisions must be made in the face of some ineradicable uncertainty.[15]

Other factors affecting the comprehensive aspect of this approach include the impact of the organization on decision making, the problem of sunk costs, and the uncertainty factor.

The organization itself can greatly increase the complexity of the rational-comprehensive approach by limiting acquisition of information, by discouraging creativity and originality, and by imposing restraints on decision makers. President Nixon's limited access to independent sources of information regarding the consequences of using the CIA to curb the FBI investigation of campaign money illustrates how the informal organization can limit the acquisition of suggestions for alternate courses of action.

Creativity and innovation may be discouraged particularly if major change offers a threat to existing personnel. In their study of New York City, for example, Sayre and Kaufman conclude:

> The major consequences of the participation in the city's political process by the leaders of the organized bureaucracies may be summed up in their habit of strong resistance to change. Their influence is most often exercised against innovations in public policy, in technology, in jurisdictional arrangements, in the organizational structure of departments and agencies, and in the administrative procedures of the city government. Their strongest drives are toward higher salaries and wages and toward the other elements of the personnel system which enhance tenure protections, limit competition for advancement, and resist the interventions of other participants. Accordingly, when Mayors and department heads attempt to lead and direct the bureaucrats of the city government, they do so with few realistic expectations that the response will be prompt and affirmative.[16]

In New York, leaders of the organized bureaucracies were very reluctant to accept change. Innovative decisions were achieved as a result of continual bargaining and of fluctuating alliances among major centers of decision making, such as the powerful borough representatives, department heads, and labor leaders. Some departments, reluctant to assume responsibility for new programs and problems, attributed the responsibility to another department.[17]

In addition to internal restraints, outside controls can limit those who make decisions; these include state and federal laws requiring, for instance, new minimum wages or minority group hiring programs. As illustrated by the Carbondale case appended to this chapter career officials may become entrenched and unwilling to respond to outside pressures from appointed or elected leaders committed to new changes in the organization.[18]

"Sunk costs" denote commitments of time, money, and other resources that may limit the potential range of a decision maker's future adaptability. If considerable money has been invested in a project, there is a tendency toward conservatism in subsequent decisions affecting the project, even if the decision to initiate the project had been a poor one in the first place. Having once made a sizable investment, an administrator continues to think that with a little more money and effort the desired result may yet be achieved.

Any new departmental administrator in government will find evidence of sunk costs in capital budget determinations. Attempts to limit expenditures will generate opposition because of financial commitments previously made to a program. Thus the Pentagon's commitment and expenditures on the C-5A aircraft program brought considerable opposition to a Pentagon official, A. Ernest Fitzgerald, who, by exposing a $2 billion cost overrun outside normal administrative channels, was forced out of his $32,000 a year job in December 1968. Fitzgerald was reinstated three years later largely as a result of the Senate Watergate hearings, in which it was disclosed that a White House aide had objected in a memorandum that "only a basic no-goodnik would take his official business grievances so far from channels."[19] Sunk costs in areas such as social welfare programs and veterans' benefits considerably restrict the flexibility of any new administrator to take risks and often result in decisions similar to those made in the past.

Because administrators inherit sunk costs, it is awkward and politically unwise to criticize one's predecessors openly. An official who takes over a post may prefer to perpetuate poor policies because he will himself soon retire. A younger official may continue an inadequate policy because of politically undesirable results that may jeopardize his future career. On controversial issues, such as those involving congressional dissatisfaction with a program, policies may be changed regardless of any sunk costs involved. In 1971, for example, the decision was made to terminate the SST, or Supersonic Transport plan, even though nearly a billion dollars had already been put into the project,[20] and even though proponents of the SST argued that the cancellation penalties would cost the government as much as if the project were to be completed.

Sunk costs may also take the form of legal precedents. The precedents established by Chief Justice Earl Warren on the United States Supreme Court, for example, cannot be completely changed for successive justices. One scholar has noted: "No justice is ever completely free to ignore what the court did in the past. Out of respect for the court itself, the justices have to pay homage to precedent, whatever their personal feelings about the wisdom of that precedent."[21] This may also be true in administrative agencies where staff regards long-standing accepted policies as precedent.

Finally, because decision making deals with a future that cannot be fully anticipated, the process of deciding can never be completely rational-comprehensive. Few administrators are able to gather all the facts for a decision; although the outcome of an event can be assessed and influenced at the same time by the selective acquisition of information,[22] and an administrator can also test the consequences of a decision in advance.

Some people oppose political survey polls on the grounds that they may influence election outcomes. The report by a major poll in the summer of 1974 that 66 percent of the voters favored impeachment of the president could, it was believed, influence other voters as well as members of Congress.[23] Voting on the passage of the three articles of impeachment, the thirty-eight members of the House Judiciary Committee all struggled with the facts and took certain risks in so doing, as all had to weigh the political consequences of their decision in terms of reelection prospects, public and press reaction, concern about partisanship, and voting on a question of impeachment based on some but not all transcripts.[24]

The Supreme Court had decided to require the president to release sixty-two additional tapes, and several Republican members wished to delay the Judiciary Committee proceedings for any additional facts bearing on the president's innocence or guilt.[25] But such was the preponderance of evidence of President Nixon's wrongdoing from already subpoenaed presidential tapes, together with current publicity and some partisanship, that several members had already made up their mind about Nixon's guilt in the matters of abuse of power, covering up evidence, and refusing to respond to congressional subpoenas. Certainly their collective decision was a major factor in forcing the president's resignation on 8 August 1974.

Having made his decision, an administrator can pretest for consequences in two ways. First, he can make a trial run, or try out the decision short of full implementation. The president, for example, can make known what he is considering to test public and legislative opinion before formally announcing a new policy. In the event of a negative reaction, he can rethink his decision and possibly benefit from new input. Second, an administrator can implement a policy in stages. A new training program may be instituted using two groups of ten people each in order to compare results and to adopt those elements most appropriate for all trainees; then the new training program will be expanded as needed.

Obstacles to implementation. The rational-comprehensive approach is also limited by certain obstacles to implementation; these include poor communication, personnel problems (such as conflicting interests, inadequate knowledge or skill), inadequate facilities, inadequate funding, unrealistic deadlines, and unclear delegation of responsibility.

Once a commitment to action is made, its acceptance and viability will depend on how effectively it is communicated to staff. A decision communicated with confidence and determination will naturally have greater success than one communicated with doubt, hesitation, or pessimism. The number and quality of personnel who will carry out the decision are essential factors in its effective implementation; necessary facilities and funding must also meet the needs of implementation. Policy makers must determine the amount of funding required for a project and anticipate possible overruns so that costs do not get completely out of hand.

In order not to initiate a project prematurely or delay it unnecessarily, decisions should include directives concerning when to begin, what pace to observe, and a deadline for completion—the pace depending on whether the project will have top priority or be extended over a longer period of time. To ensure effective implementation of a decision, the policymaker may wish to oversee it himself; but delegation of responsibility may make better use of his time and also provide an opportunity for staff to gain experience through participation. Finally, if a decision appears to have been a wrong one, it is best to accept the losses, analyze the causes, and attempt to reformulate before proceeding again.

Satisficing and Incrementalism

As the foregoing discussion suggests, the rational-comprehensive approach is difficult, if not impossible, to practice. For most administrators it is necessary to "satisfice," or to make do with satisfactory decisions. Herbert Simon has noted that "while economic man maximizes—selects the best alternatives from among all those available to him—his cousin, whom we shall call administrative man, satisfices—looks for a course of action that is satisfactory or 'good enough.'"[26]

There are three fundamental satisficing techniques available to the administrator who must clarify problems and establish policies and goals. First, he can make use of those basic existing agency resources that his superiors would expect him to use in the process of making a decision. An administration will generally not attempt a broad departure in policy to avoid opposition within or outside the organization.

Second, he may arrange compromises among the various elements that affect the working of the organization. Bargaining over policy and goals is not a feature of the rational decision-making model, but it is essential in democratic theory and also necessary to preserve organizational unity and support. Third, he can avoid formulating explicit goals and policies in order to avoid the unnecessary conflict that such explicitness may generate. For an official to make a unilateral announcement of policy before consulting with those around him or those affected by the policy is to inhibit the necessary feedback that tells him whether the policy is acceptable. An official will profit by consulting the views and experiences of his colleagues, and the sharing of opinions often makes for wiser, more acceptable decisions.

Ira Sharkansky has observed that satisficing is appropriate when information is limited or difficult to obtain.

> Administrators often cut off their search for information about problems, goals, or policies when they discover a mode of operation that will involve the least profound change in their established programs. They do not search all possible alternatives until they find "the one best" way. Instead, they search until they find something which "will work," i.e., provide satisfactory relief from the perceived difficulties without threatening undesirable unrest within the agency and among the legislators, executives, and interest groups who involve themselves in its affairs.[27]

Most decisions tend to be incremental in character as a result of satisficing, and incrementalism may be described as follows:

1. Rather than attempting a comprehensive survey and evaluation of all alternatives, the decision maker focuses only on those policies that differ incrementally from existing policies.
2. Only a relatively small number of policy alternatives are considered.
3. For each policy alternative, only a restricted number of "important" consequences are evaluated.
4. The problem confronting the decision maker is continually redefined: incrementalism allows for countless ends-means and means-ends adjustments that, in effect, make the problem more manageable.
5. Thus there is no one decision or "right" solution, but a "never-ending series of attacks" on the issues at hand through serial analyses and evaluation.
6. As such, incremental decision making is described as remedial, geared more to the alleviation of present, concrete social imperfections than to the promotion of future social goals.[28]

Amitai Etzioni has criticized incrementalism on the grounds that "the number and role of fundamental decisions are significantly greater than incrementalists state, and when the fundamental ones are missing, incremental decision making amounts to drifting—action without direction."[29] Certainly incremental decision making is more appropriate to some types of decisions than to others. It has been suggested that the budgetary process is uniquely incremental in nature because of its step-by-step formulation;[30] a study of Detroit, Cleveland, and Pittsburgh has shown how incremental budget makers distributed yearly increases in revenues without regard for program values.[31] Money is distributed on the basis of a priority unrelated to program—that is, salaries come first, equipment next, and maintenance last.

Also, a policymaker may become more incremental in his decision making the more risk is involved; instead of initiating change in a rational priority, he may wait until it is necessary to make a decision. The process of accommodating demands (compromise and negotiation) has been referred to as "mutual adjustment," while decision making by mutual adjustment has been termed "muddling through"—following a lethargic path in policymaking by detouring around hard decisions rather than meeting them forthrightly.[32]

As an alternative to incremental decision making, Etzioni offers a "mixed-scanning" approach which combines rational-comprehensive and incremental strategy to achieve the implementation of overall policy.[33] The first approach would scan the elements of the decision in general; the second would concentrate on specific items requiring investigation as perceived necessary by the administrator. By investigating only selective points, the administrator is not so overwhelmed by detail as to lose sight of the fundamental policy objectives. Etzioni notes: "Fundamental decisions are made by exploring the main alternatives the actor sees in view of his conception of his goals, but—unlike what rationalism would indicate—details and specifications are omitted so that an overview is feasible. Incremental decisions are made but within the contexts set by fundamental decisions."[34]

Louis Gawthrop has questioned the overall value of incrementalism, suggesting that it is neither effective nor operational.

> The incremental process is not designed to achieve maximum problem-solving effectiveness in the face of a rapidly expanding growth rate, be that growth rate defined in terms of population expansion, facility utilization increase, or the development of scientific knowledge. Insofar as the critical needs for basic, hard-core, technical and logistical solutions are concerned, the incremental process is inadequately designed to stem the mounting anxieties within the body politic that this situation is creating. Some form of rational-comprehensive analysis seems imperative.[35]

Basically, Gawthrop argues for decentralized, nonincremental decisions—the administrator could apply the rational-comprehensive analysis to his own areas of specialty[36]—and suggests a division of duties between policy makers and policy implementers.

Thus the decision-making process may arise from a variety of models. Simon suggests, for example, nonprogrammed decisions based on instinct, intuition, or other extrarational factors, pure rational-comprehensive decisions, and satisficing decisions. Lindblom has suggested a "muddling through" model in which decisions develop incrementally. Etzioni has recommended mixed scanning, which combines fundamental policymaking with incremental strategies to help implement fundamental decisions. Other models exist, but the emphasis in decision making today is more on practical application than on theory.[37]

COMMUNICATION: THE INDISPENSABLE CONNECTION

Once a decision has been made it must be effectively communicated to those responsible for its implementation, but as Herbert Simon has observed:

Formal Communication

> No step in the administrative process is more generally ignored or poorly performed than the task of communicating decisions. All too often, plans are "ordered" into effect without any consideration of the manner in which they can be brought to influence the behavior of the individual members of the group. Procedural manuals are promulgated without follow-up to determine whether the contents of the manuals are used by the individuals to guide their decisions. Organization plans are drawn on paper, although the members of the organization are ignorant of the plan that purports to describe their relationships.[38]

Formal communications can flow downward from the top to the lowest ranking persons in the organizational hierarchy, upward from subordinates to top management, and laterally between organizations and among persons at the same or similar levels in the hierarchy.[39]

Downward communication. As the Hawthorne studies at Western Electric demonstrated, downward communication is not a simple matter.[40] One experiment revealed that members of a small group engaged in making telephone switches, having agreed among themselves on a certain daily output, would not increase production, fearing that this would threaten job security or wage increase demands. Assured by management that this was not the case, they nevertheless rejected those who did too much work as "rate busters," those who did too little as "chiselers," and those who reported information harmful to them as "squealers." It eventually became clear to management that if downward decisions were to be accepted, upward communication would have to be encouraged.[41]

When communications pass downward through several levels of management, the possibility of misapprehension increases and may lead to diminished efficiency, even to employee disturbances such as strikes. Confused communication can result in misunderstanding of the purpose of programs or of the method of evaluating worker performance and projects. Inadequate communication can diminish organization goals and commitment, while the communication of ambiguous objectives can create management problems concerning which group is responsible for integrating or completing a job. Indeed, the end result of confused downward communication may not be that which management had sought to achieve.

Upward communication. Organizational distance or the physical inaccessibility of management, psychological barriers between supervisor and subordinate, the barriers imposed by technical specialization, and the force of organizational custom or tradition—all affect an employee's ability to communicate upward.[42]

Physical inaccessibility may cause top management in a large organization to be out of touch with lower ranking workers who can communicate with them only through "channels" or a series of supervisors. In addition, communications from workers to top management may become distorted in their course through these channels; a message may be altered or even blocked by intermediaries between sender and receiver.[43] As upward communications tend to reflect on the performance of subordinates, the latter may wish to screen problems from upper management in order to minimize negative flak from above, and this in turn will limit the ability of upper management to be aware of problems or to know what is going on below.

Some observers believe that close aides and advisers isolated President Nixon in this way from knowing plans and details of the Watergate break-in, thereby placing him in the position of having either to dismiss key members of his administration or to cover up their wrongdoing. Others believe that a president, like any administrator, can isolate himself from upward communications whose substance he prefers not to know, especially if he should be called on to testify under penalty of perjury. Some administrators prefer to delegate nearly total responsibility to assistants in order that they may themselves be free to concentrate on specific problems and issues.

An administrator who holds strong views on a given subject may discourage upward communication by making it psychologically difficult for subordinates to advance new ideas. In general, however, the type of relationship that exists between supervisor and subordinate will be influenced by the type of organization they serve. Formal communications, both downward and upward, will be tense and restricted, for example, where the communication of classified military secrets is confined exclusively to those who "need to know" and to those authorized to receive such information. If a security leak should bring about reorganization, employees will be apprehensive about their jobs.

In Charles Redfield's view, a fear of authority greatly affects upward flow of communication.[44] A subordinate might fear his supervisor, while the supervisor himself might be reluctant to seek advice for fear of losing face by admitting to a lack of knowledge or to a mistake. But a supervisor should have some face-to-face contact with all levels of the organization. It has been estimated that 75 percent of all communications are vocal.[45] Thus the larger the organization, the more important it is for top management to allow for personal communication at every level.

But no amount of personal communication will benefit an administrator who is not skilled in receiving as well as in giving information. A top official must not always present ideas without allowing feedback or response from others. Researchers have noted that "the biggest block to personal communication is man's inability to listen intelligently, understandingly, and skillfully to another person."[46] Social psychologists emphasize the importance of spelling out the meanings we wish to communicate, the dangers of inference, and the dangers in assuming that the technical language in which professional specialists express themselves will be commonly understood.

Finally, there is a far greater tradition of downward than of upward communication in most organizations because it is more difficult, and also less natural, to make upward demands on management, such as those concerning wages or working conditions. Employees addicted to upward demands may be regarded as troublemakers; whether they choose to take this risk will depend on their feeling of job security.

Lateral communication. Lateral relationships within and between organizations are difficult to develop and maintain, especially among government agencies in which specialization and rivalry may impede effective communication. Specialists often disagree with general administrators who do not understand their problems and concerns. Scientists and engineers, for example, employ different research methods. A scientist freely proposes ideas and plans to which an engineer may object on the grounds of their infeasibility or because of the difficulty of implementing them.

Rivalry for funds and other types of interagency competition also inhibit communication with colleagues performing similar functions in other organizations. An administrator who encounters this problem should attempt to improve interpersonal relations among his subordinates and with administrators of other agencies as well. The success of any lateral communication depends on the motivation of executives as well as on the timing and strategy of the administrator.[47]

Informal Communication

Informal communications coexist with formal communications and do not necessarily follow a hierarchical pattern but may flow along upward, downward, or lateral paths for both harmful and beneficial purposes. In order not to endanger their job security, employees may complain anonymously to fellow workers who pass the information by indirect means to management, perhaps through the chief administrative officer's executive secretary. A manager may wish to tell a subordinate informally how to improve poor job performance. Administrators from different agencies may meet at the country club to discuss the means of coordinating a larger program for their mutual benefit. Informal communication should not be allowed to replace formal channels, although the "grapevine," with all its incomplete and inaccurate rumor mongering, will almost certainly always exist.

Feedback. Information placed into an organization, whether formally or informally, will evoke a response which, by changing the behavior of those involved, will influence the decision-making process. The importance of administrators as recipients of communications must therefore not be obscured by overemphasis on the transmitter. Considerable influence and control can be exercised through a knowledge of how proposals will be accepted and by using this knowledge to improve an administrator's performance.

"Feedback" is information or response that is transmitted back to the initiator in the larger organizational system, and "cybernetics" (from the Greek *kubernētēs,* "steersman") has basically to do with the role of feedback in communication and decision making. In the words of Stafford Beer, "Cybernetics is the scientific study of the nature of control, not in the narrow sense of command and the giving of orders, but in the subtle sense of self-regulation and adaptability."[48] The nature of feedback will often depend on how a policy has been received, regardless of whether the communication has been informal or formal, upward, downward, or lateral.

Thus the quality of the decision-making process determines the effectiveness of communication, which is the vital link in transmitting information throughout the organization. Having explored the formal and informal elements of organization, decision making, and communication, we are now prepared to see how these apply to such administrative functions as the budgetary process, personnel administration, and bureaucratic growth and responsibility.

CASE STUDY 1

Transcripts of Richard M. Nixon's Talks with H. R. Haldeman

The following case study consists of selections from a thirty-four–page transcript of taped conversations in which White House Chief of Staff H. R.

From *Los Angeles Times*, 6 August 1974.

Haldeman informs President Nixon that the Watergate burglary had been financed by Nixon campaign money. In one of the most fatal decisions of his administration, the president orders Haldeman to use the CIA, especially Director Richard Helms and Deputy Director Vernon A. Walters, to stop the FBI and former Acting Director L. Patrick Gray from investigating the money.

Haldeman admits his belief that former Attorney General John Mitchell (whom the president had previously helped to resign as campaign chief "for personal reasons") had had advance knowledge of the Watergate break-in. In one of the transcripts Mr. Nixon expresses concern that E. Howard Hunt, Jr., a White House aide who at the time of the conversation was being sought as one of the Watergate conspirators, would "uncover a lot of things." (For further clarification, Bernard L. Barker was one of the burglars arrested along with Hunt in the Watergate break-in; Maurice Stans was chairman of the Finance Committee to Re-elect the President.)

The transcript, released on 6 August 1974, had, with the exception of a few top aides, been concealed from Nixon's own staff and legal counsel. James D. St. Clair, chief counsel for the president, was embarrassed that his client had withheld pertinent information from him and had threatened to resign unless the transcript was released. On its release, the president said that the transcript "may further damage my case especially because attention will be drawn separately to it rather than to the evidence in its entirety." Nixon also observed: "At that time I did not realize the extent of the implications which those conversations might now appear to have. As a result, those arguing my case, as well as those passing judgment on the case, did so with information that was incomplete and in some respect erroneous. This was a serious act of omission. . . ."

This case study illustrates some of the problems of incremental decision making—the cutting off of open communications by the president's confinement to a limited group of top advisers and especially the limiting of access to independent sources of information that might have enabled the president (assuming his willingness in this regard) to assess the alternatives to, and consequences of, his decision. The reader may benefit at this point by reexamining the problems of the rational-comprehensive approach to decision making and particularly the discussion of "groupthink." As you read this selection, ask yourself the following questions:

1. *What were the president's errors in decision making?*
2. *Was the president's decision entirely incremental? satisficing?*

10:04 a.m. to 11:39 a.m.

H: Now, on the investigation, you know the Democratic break-in thing, we're back in the problem area because the FBI is not under control, because Gray doesn't exactly know how to control it and they have—their investigation is now leading into some productive areas—because they've been able to trace the money—not through the money itself— but through the bank sources—the banker. And, and it goes in some directions we don't want it to go. Ah, also there have been some things—like an informant came in off the street to the FBI in Miami who was a photographer or has a friend who is a photographer who developed some films through this guy Barker and the films had pictures of Democratic National Committee letterhead documents and things. So it's things like that that are filtering in. Mitchell came up with yesterday, and John Dean analyzed very carefully last night and concludes, concurs now with Mitchell's recommendation that the only way to solve this, and we're set up beautifully to do it, ah, in that and that—the only network that paid any attention to it last night was NBC—they did a massive story on the Cuban thing.

P: That's right.

H: That the way to handle this now is for us to have Walters call Pat Gray and just say, "Stay to hell out of this—this is, ah, business here we don't want you to go any further on it." That's not an unusual development, and, ah, that would take care of it.

P: What about Pat Gray—you mean Pat Gray doesn't want to?

H: Pat does want to. He doesn't know how to, and he doesn't have, he doesn't have any basis for doing it. Given this, he will then have the basis. He'll call Mark Felt in, and the two of them—and Mark Felt wants to cooperate because he's ambitious—

P: Yeah.

H: He'll call him in and say, "We've got the signal from across the river to put the hold on this." And that will fit rather well because the FBI agents who are working the case, at this point, feel that's what it is.

P: This is CIA? They've traced the money? Who'd they trace it to?

H: Well they've traced it to a name, but they haven't gotten to the guy yet.

P: Would it be somebody here?

H: Ken Dahlberg.

P: Who the hell is Ken Dahlberg?

H: He gave $25,000 in Minnesota and, ah, the check went directly to this guy Barker.

P: It isn't from the committee though, from Stans?

H: Yeah. It is. It's directly traceable and there's some more through some Texas people that went to the Mexican bank which can also be traced to the Mexican bank—they'll get their names today.

H: —And (pause)

P: Well, I mean, there's no way—I'm just thinking if they don't cooperate, what do they say? That they were approached by the Cubans. That's what Dahlberg has to say, the Texans, too, that they—

H: Well, if they will. But then we're relying on more and more people all the time. That's the problem and they'll stop if we could take this other route.

P: All right.

H: And you seem to think the thing to do is get them to stop?

P: Right, fine.

H: They say the only way to do that is from White House instructions. And it's got to be to Helms and to—ah, what's his name. . . .? Walters.

P: Walters.

H: And the proposal would be that Ehrlichman and I call them in, and say, ah—

P: All right, fine. How do you call him in—I mean you just—well, we protected Helms from one hell of a lot of things.

P: That's what Ehrlichman says.

P: Of course, this Hunt, that will uncover a lot of things. You open that scab there's a hell of a lot of things and we just feel that it would be very detrimental to have this thing go any further. This involves these Cubans, Hunt, and a lot of hanky-panky that we have nothing to do with ourselves. Well what the hell, did Mitchell know about this?

H: I think so. I don't think he knew the details, but I think he knew.

P: He didn't know how it was going to be handled though—with Dahlberg and the Texans and so forth? Well who was the asshole that did? Is it Liddy? [former White House aide]. Is that the fellow? He must be a little nuts!

H: He is.

P: I mean he just isn't well screwed on is he? Is that the problem?

H: No, but he was under pressure, apparently, to get more information, and as he got more pressure, he pushed the people harder to move harder—

P: Pressure from Mitchell?

H: Apparently.

P: Oh, Mitchell. Mitchell was at the point (unintelligible).

H: Yeah.

P: All right, fine. I understand it all. We won't second-guess Mitchell and the rest. Thank God it wasn't Colson [former White House special counsel].

H: The FBI interviewed Colson yesterday. They determined that would be a good thing to do. To have him take an interrogation, which he did, and that—the FBI guys working the case concluded that there were one or two possibilities—one, that this was a House—they don't think that there is anything at the Election Committee—they don't think it was either a White House operation and they had some obscure reasons for it—nonpolitical, or it was a—Cuban and the CIA. And after their interrogation of Colson yesterday, they concluded it was not the White House, but are new convinced it is a CIA thing, so the CIA turnoff would—

P: Well, not sure of their analysis, I'm not going to get that involved. I'm (unintelligible).

H: No, sir. We don't want you to.

P: You call them in.

H: Good deal.

P: Play it tough. That's the way they play it and that's the way we are going to play it.

H: O.K.

P: When I saw that news summary, I questioned whether it's a bunch of crap, but I though er, well it's good to have them off us awhile, because when they start bugging us, which they have, our little boys will not know how to handle it. I hope they will though.

H: You never know.

P: Good.

P: I don't know—maybe it isn't working out and (unintelligible) maybe it is.

H: Well, it's a close call. Ehrlichman thought you probably—

P: What?

H: Well he said you probably didn't need it. He didn't think you should—not at all. He said he felt fine doing it.

P: He did? The question, the point, is does he think everybody is going to understand the busing?

H: That's right.

P: And, ah, well (unintelligible) says no.

H: Well, the fact is somewhere in between, I think, because I think that (unintelligible) is missing some—

P: Well, if the fact is somewhere in between, we better do it.

H: Yeah, I think Mitchell says, "Hell yes. Anything we can hit on at anytime we get the chance—and we've got a reason for doing it—do it."

P: When you get in—when you get in (unintelligible) people, say, "Look the problem is that this will open the whole, the whole Bay of Pigs thing, and the President just feels that ah, without going into the details—don't don't [sic] lie to them to the extent to say there is no involvement, but just say this is a comedy of errors, without getting into it, the President believes that it is going to open the whole Bay of Pigs thing up again. And, ah, because these people are plugging for (unintelligible) and that they should call the FBI in and (unintelligible) don't go any further into this case period!

P: (Inaudible) our cause—

H: Get more done for our cause by the opposition than by us.

P: Well, can you get it done?

H: I think so.

P: (unintelligible) moves (unintelligible) election (unintelligible) said it in its lead editorial today. Another "McGovern's got to change his position." That that would be a good thing, that's constructive. Ah, the white wash for change.

P: (unintelligible) urging him to do so—say that is perfectly all right?

H: Cause then they are saying—on the other hand—that he were not so smart. We have to admire the progress he's made on the basis of the position he's taken and maybe he's right and we're wrong.

P: (Inaudible) I just, ha ha

P: (unintelligible) I spend an hour—whatever it was—45 minutes or so with television executives (unintelligible) all in and outs (unintelligible). "Look, we have no right to ask the President anything (unintelligible) biased." (unintelligible) says I'm going to raise hell with the networks. And look, you've just not got to let Klein [Herbert G. Klein, former director of communications in the Nixon administration] ever set up a meeting again. He just doesn't have his head screwed on. You know what I mean. He just opens it up and sits there with eggs on his face. He's just not our guy at all is he?

H: No.

P: Absolutely, totally, unorganized.

H: He's a very nice guy.

P: People love him, but damn is he unorganized.

H: But, I don't think you have to be there until Tuesday.

P: I don't want to go near the damned place until Tuesday. I don't want to be near it. I've got the arrival planned (unintelligible) my arrival of, ah—

H: Now we're going to do, unless you have some objection, we should do your arrival at Miami International not at Homestead.

P: Yes, I agree. . . .

1:04 p.m. to 1:13 p.m.

P: O.K. just postpone (scratching noises) (unintelligible) Just say (unintelligible) very bad to have this fellow Hunt, ah, he knows too damned much, if he was involved—you happen to know that? If it gets out that this is all involved, the Cuba thing would be a fiasco. It would make the CIA look bad, it's going to make Hunt look bad, and it is likely to blow the whole Bay of Pigs thing which we think would be very unfortunate—both for CIA and for the country, at this time, and for American foreign policy. Just tell him to lay off. Don't you?

H: Yep. That's the basis to do it on. Just leave it at that.

P: I don't know if he'll get any ideas for doing it because our concern political (unintelligible). Helms is not one to (unintelligible) I would just say, lookit, because of the Hunt involvement, whole cover basically this—

H: Yep. Good move.

P: Well, they've got some pretty good ideas on this Meany thing. Shultz did a good paper. I read it all (voices fade).

2:20 p.m. to 2:45 p.m.

H: No problem.

P: (Unintelligible)

H: Well, it was kind of interesting. Walters made the point and I didn't mention Hunt, I just said that the thing was leading into directions that were going to create potential problems because they were exploring leads that led back into areas that would be harmful to the CIA and harmful to the government (unintelligible) didn't have anything to do (unintelligible). . . .

H: Gray called Helms and said I think we've run right into the middle of a CIA covert operation.

P: Gray said that?

H: Yeah. And (unintelligible) said nothing we've done at this point and ah (unintelligible) says well it sure looks to me like it is (unintelligible) and ah, that was the end of the conversation (unintelligible) the problem is it tracks back to the Bay of Pigs and it tracks back to some other [*sic*] the leads run out to people who had no involvement in this, except by contracts and connection, but it gets to areas that are liable to be realized? The whole problem (unintelligible) Hunt. So at this point he kind of got the picture. He said, he said we'll be very happy to be helpful (unintelligible) handle anything you want. I would like to know the reason for being helpful, and I made it clear to him he wasn't going to get explicit (unintelligible) generality, and he said fine. And Walters (unintelligible) is going to make a call to Gray. That's the way we put it and that's the way it was left.

CASE STUDY 2

The Carbondale Story

C. WILLIAM NORMAN

> The following case history, in which a city administrator is confronted with a strike by police and fire protection employees, demonstrates how faulty

C. William Norman, "The Carbondale Story," PUBLIC EMPLOYEE RELATIONS LIBRARY, No. 20, Keith Ocheltree (ed.), Chicago, Ill.: Public Personnel Association, 1969.

communications between city officials and others can result in serious labor problems. The communications problem greatly complicated the work of the personnel consultant in this case because employees misunderstood his purposes and feared that their jobs and positions would be threatened by his actions.

Communication was also a problem in determining the relationships between the city and various state agencies. When the city needed help, the function of state agencies was not clear, and the actions of these agencies were not always understood by either labor or management. The lack of state legislation and statutes clarifying the roles and authority of labor and city management added to the confusion over what the rights of the opposing parties were. Communications and solidarity were much stronger among city management officials. The city council continued to support the city manager and public safety director in spite of continued demands for their resignation. As you read this selection, ask yourself the following questions:

1. *As city manager, how would you have acted against the chief of police?*
2. *What errors in decision making did the city manager and police chief make?*
3. *How would you have used communication methods to end employee misunderstandings?*

Background

In September 1966, Carbondale, Illinois, acquired a council-manager form of city government. The city manager believed that it was in the best interests of city employees to have uniform pay policies and formally adopted merit personnel procedures, and his efforts toward these ends received strong support from the city council in early 1967.

Labor trouble developed when a personnel consultant was hired to prepare a position classification plan covering all city jobs. One employees' union feared that this was part of a scheme to eliminate people for inefficiency and to make their jobs less desirable; thus, union members refused to complete the usual forms describing their jobs. At the same time, the city was introducing new administrative personnel to head several departments and to reorganize the structure of city government, particularly the public works divisions. A new pay plan was implemented for all employees except those union members who refused to accept the seniority pay steps provided for in the plan. Several employees feared that the pay plan and city administrative changes threatened their job security.

In the fall of 1967 a new police administrator was hired to serve as director of public safety, with police, fire protection, and civil defense as his responsibilities. For a variety of reasons, this administrator did not receive employee acceptance, and his programs were not carried out. When he tried to enforce compliance, the chief of police sent a nine-page letter of grievances against him to the new director, the city manager, and the newspapers. The city manager believed that the chief was wrong in refusing to implement changes or to comply with revised department-head duties and, most of all, in having sent the letter to the newspapers. As a result, he instructed the new director to fire the police chief.

The pace quickens
Following delivery of the letter terminating the Police Chief's services, subsequent events occurred with such rapidity and increasing seriousness that we [city officials] were almost constantly kept off balance:

Wednesday, March 6
9:30 a.m.—Chief was fired effective immediately.

3:30 p.m.—The Director was presented with a letter signed by all but one civilian member of the 26 employees of the Police Department to the effect that unless both the City Manager and the Police Chief resigned immediately, all employees would resign one-half hour later.

4:00 p.m.—All Police personnel left their jobs and the county sheriff and one deputy arrived to provide police protection.

Prior to 4:00 p.m. the Director of Public Safety and the City Manager, in their efforts to find substitute police protection, discovered that the sheriff had been previously requested by "a police officer" to take over at 4:00 p.m. The Southern Illinois University security force and the state police agreed to help with patrol upon our request.

7:30 to 12:00 p.m.—City Council met and declared the "resignations" to be an illegal strike and indicated council willingness to discuss grievances with police personnel the following morning. At this time and in subsequent statements the employees were assured that no disciplinary action would be taken if they voluntarily returned to work.

Thursday, March 7
10:00 a.m.—City Firemen advised the Council by letter that they were joining the police officers and would not return to work until the Director of Public Safety and City Manager resigned. They agreed to maintain a skeleton force on duty and to receive alarms and to respond to actual fires. The Fire Chief and all Captains included themselves in the department's action.

10:30 a.m.—With the exception of the Director of Public Works, three
superintendents, a draftsman and a secretary, all public works
employees met and agreed to join a sympathy walkout. Plant operators
at the two sewage plants and the water plant later agreed to have one
man available at each plant to "supervise" efforts by the 5 "supervisory"
personnel of the department who remained on duty.

Thus by noon on March 7 only about 25 out of 124 city employees remained
on duty. Efforts to recruit male employees of the Building and Zoning
Department to assist in keeping the water and sewage plants in operation
were unsuccessful.

Council gives support

The events of the remainder of the week were dominated by attempts to find
a way to bring public service functions back to normal, short of removal of
the City Manager and Director of Public Safety. At no time did any member
of Council indicate any lack of support for these men, nor any willingness
to allow employees to dictate Council policy. While it was recognized that
an illegal strike of public employees was subject to court action, both Council
and staff were of the opinion that this should be a last resort—that surely a
solution to this basically administrative problem could be found within the
framework of orderly government.

Two public meetings were held by Council on Thursday—one in the
morning, the other in the evening. Employees who attended these meetings,
mostly police officers, expressed no willingness to discuss grievances or
negotiate. A mass meeting for city employees, held Thursday afternoon in a
local lodge hall was according to newspaper accounts, completely dominated
by candidates defeated at the prior year's election, or their friends.

Just before noon on Friday, March 8, the city was granted a temporary
injunction by a circuit judge, ordering employees to return to work and calling
for a hearing on a permanent injunction at 9:00 a.m. on the following Monday.
The sheriff was ordered to serve copies of this order personally on each of
the 99 non-working employees. By 9:00 p.m. Friday only five had been served.
However, by Saturday morning the utility plant and Fire Department personnel
who would normally work on Saturday, had returned. Police officers returned
later on Saturday.

Management effectiveness hampered

The following factors, which developed during the mass walkout, had an
important bearing on the final settlement:

1. Since the City Manager's resignation was continuously repeated as a
   condition of settlement, his effectiveness as a negotiator was
   seriously hampered.

2. While the Director of Public Safety was formally appointed Acting Chief of Police upon the Chief's being fired, he was for all practical purposes without power for three reasons—
   a. All area law enforcement personnel operated under the theory that state law makes the sheriff "chief law enforcement officer" during times of crisis and completely ignored the Acting Chief in their efforts to provide police protection to the City.
   b. Because of the natural fraternal feeling among all police personnel, the substitute police had an obvious feeling of sympathy for the city employees, and an equally obvious distrust for the "foreigners"—the Public Safety Director and City Manager.
   c. While power to recruit temporary or permanent replacements for the striking employees did exist, the unanimity of the strike, and a concern for possible reprisals against "strike breakers" accompanied by strong traditions in the region, made this approach seem undesirable.
   The City Council and City administration were thus removed from any control of the City's law enforcement.

3. Contacts with appropriate state officials, including the Governor's Office, indicated that help from the National Guard would only follow a complete breakdown in local efforts to maintain control. Our concern for potential violence to persons or property which might precede arrival of the Guard, prevented us from viewing this as a logical means for assuring the control of the City Council and City Manager over the city government. This concern for potential violence was fostered by—
   a. repeated threats to the life and family of the Public Safety Director,
   b. actions and statements by a few employees during contacts with various City officials,
   c. a history of violent strikes by coal miners of the area, which the complete solidarity of the city employee actions seemed to emulate, and
   d. actual occurrences due to racial or university unrest which had developed during the prior year and threatened to be renewed in the spring of 1968.

4. Calls to the State Health Department resulted in our being informed that the state would assume responsibility for treating sewage or taking over water plant operation only *after* these vital functions became inoperative, and treated water in storage (about one day's supply) had been exhausted. On two occasions officials of the State warned that if pollution occurred because of inoperative sewage plants, the City would be fined $500 per day. Of the five employees available to operate our three plants on a 24-hour basis, only two had any prior operating knowledge. After three days of keeping the plants going, the threat of exhaustion or operating breakdown became serious.

5. Although no public statements were made, responsible officials of each of the law enforcement agencies providing police protection to the City, except the Sheriff, made statements to the City Manager

or Director of Public Safety such as, "we are not sure we can have anyone available after 4:00 this afternoon . . . or after 8:00 tomorrow morning." On at least one occasion the Mayor had to make a personal appeal to the state Director of Public Safety to have state patrol cars moved from patrol outside the City to patrolling state highways within the city where they would be available for more immediate response. With only five permanent deputies to provide police protection to the entire county and also to operate a jail, the Sheriff was obviously handicapped in what he could personally accomplish.

6. While there were reports that employees had many grievances, there developed no employee leadership to assume responsibility for discussing any specific grievance. Several attempts by interested, non-participating citizens to initiate negotiations or to mediate failed for this reason—as did attempts by city officials.

Mass meeting held

A mass meeting attended by almost all affected employees was held in the courthouse immediately prior to the Monday morning hearing. At this meeting the employees agreed that three respected attorneys from another city would be retained to represent the employees. The attorneys then obtained a signed statement from each employee present that if the court ruled that their "resignation" was in fact an illegal strike and assessed penalties if they refused to return to work, they would each submit individual letters of resignation.

There seemed to be little likelihood that the judge could rule otherwise. If they followed through, we would thus lose the "volunteer" services of the firemen and utility plant operators. We were also becoming increasingly concerned about how to provide continuing police protection because of increasing resistance from local law enforcement agencies to the established governmental authority of the city, and a growing threat of violence. To consider recruiting a sufficient number of new employees with necessary skills to provide essential services from our relatively sparsely populated area did not seem to be practical.

It was with these considerations that I asked for a recess of the hearing and sought and received from the City Council full authority to negotiate a settlement. The results of this negotiation with the employees' attorneys were that, in return for the employees' return to work, the Chief of Police would be reinstated "without recriminations" and the Manager would accept the Public Safety Director's resignation which had been tendered during negotiations. Demands for the Manager's removal were withdrawn.

The crisis was settled with probably a minimum of individual or community sacrifice—except for the ruined career of a very competent police administrator. The scars of the battle, however, remain and are particularly visible in relations between the Manager and Council and the Police Department. Whether or not the climate of local politics was materially affected is difficult to determine. The ability of the Council to make policy and of the Manager to administer that policy has, at the very least, not been improved.

Wage strike

Our city's second and only other experience with an employee strike, while affected by overtones of the previous strike, was far more traditional, both in terms of cause and results.

On May 1, 1969, when the Plumbers and Pipefitters Union and the Manager and Council failed to reach agreement on a wage package, all water and sewage employees walked off the job at midnight, upon expiration of their contract. The next morning the City Attorney sought a court injunction declaring the strike illegal and ordering employees back to work. Instead of granting a temporary injunction immediately, the judge scheduled a hearing for the following morning.

Just prior to the hearing the judge invited representatives from the city and the union into his chambers for a final effort at conciliation. The union's attorney indicated that if the City could make a "token" offer to permit a "saving of face," he felt the membership could be persuaded to settle. As a result, the number of years required for 3 weeks' paid vacation was reduced from 10 to 8, agreement was reached, and the strike was settled.

In this instance the City was in a much more favorable position to deal with the strike. First, we were prepared. Key employees had been trained to operate the water and sewage plants, and arrangements had been made for supervisory and staff personnel to be available to keep the water supply going for an almost indefinite period of time, barring major line or equipment failures. It was agreed that our efforts would be concentrated on water supply with secondary priority given to sewage treatment. The first day of the strike, when we officially notified the State Sanitary Water Board of the possible failure of our sewage treatment facilities, they responded in true form by sending the City Council a telegram warning of fines if our plants caused serious pollution —still no offers of help or recognition of the state's responsibilities in such matters.

The second important difference was that the striking employees did not receive any apparent sympathy from the other employees, who remained on the job despite rumors that they would walk out.

With the memories of the previous strike still fresh in their minds, the City Council was led to be more generous with these employees than they had previously been with all other employees in the general pay plan—even though the increase in wages finally agreed to was less than half the union's initial demands. This made a strike settlement easier to accomplish, but will

undoubtedly cause greater difficulty in achieving general acceptance during
the coming year. Even a second-round increase for all other employees of
2½ per cent, granted in recognition of firemen's demands, has fallen short of
equalling the plumbers' and pipefitters' new contract.

During a three-year period in which the cost of living increased less than
15 percent, city employees received wage increases varying from 32 to 52
percent, depending on job classification and seniority. The pay increases
were justified on the basis of pay rates of area employers, such as Southern
Illinois University; yet employee dissatisfaction increased. Why? The city
manager concluded that city employees, having seen the result of union and
minority-group efforts, want to have similar success.

Conclusion

    The city manager also argues that cities need state assistance in pro-
tecting them from certain labor problems. He suggests that: (1) strikes
against essential public services, such as police and fire protection and
sewage treatment plants, should be forced to submit to compulsory arbitration; (2) state agencies should have a program that helps cities to handle
strikes, such as a policy that would make state police and national guard
more readily available to restore or ensure peace; and (3) state health departments should develop a plan of action guaranteeing continuation of
essential water and sewerage services in the event of strikes.

NOTES

1. Herbert A. Simon, *Administrative Behavior*, p. 125.

2. Max Weber, *The Theory of Social and Economic Organization*, and Robert Michels, *Political Parties*. For a discussion of organizational authority, see Robert L. Peabody, *Organizational Authority*.

3. Auren Uris, *The Executive Deskbook*, chap. 3.

4. Simon, *Administrative Behavior*, p. 46.

5. Charles E. Lindblom, "The Science of Muddling Through," *Public Administration Review* 19 (spring 1959): 79–88; and Charles E. Lindblom, *The Policy Making Process*, pp. 12–20.

6. John M. Pfiffner, "Administrative Rationality," *Public Administration Review* 20 (summer 1960): 129.

7. For a comprehensive discussion of systems analysis, particularly as applied to the budgetary process, see John B. Benton, *Managing the Organizational Decision Process*, pp. 43–54.

8. Robert A. Dahl and Charles E. Lindblom, *Politics, Economics and Welfare*, p. 249. The argument that decisions not made can be as important as those that are made, particularly with regard to environmental pollution, is presented in Matthew A. Crenson, *The Un-Politics of Air Pollution*, pp. 177–84.

9. Morris Davis, "Some Aspects of Detroit's Decisional Profile," *Administrative Science Quarterly* 12 (September 1967): 209–24; see also Robert J. Mowitz and Neil S. Wright, *Profile of a Metropolis,* which covers several case studies concerning major urban decisions between 1945 and 1960.

10. Alexander Leighton, *Human Relations in a Changing World,* pp. 150–55.

11. National Advisory Commission on Civil Disorders, *Report,* pp. 110–12.

12. Irving L. Janis, *Victims of Groupthink,* pp. 10–11.

13. Ibid., p. 10. The discovery of the Watergate burglary of Democratic National Headquarters is a classic example of number 6 on the list of errors in decision making. The White House advisers had simply not counted on the impact of bureaucratic inertia and sabotage by political opponents and errors in strategy.

14. Ibid., p. 9.

15. Anthony Downs, *Inside Bureaucracy,* p. 75.

16. Wallace S. Sayre and Herbert Kaufman, *Governing New York,* p. 446.

17. Ibid., see chap. 19, pp. 709–38.

18. The organization can enforce rationality by its structure and assigned responsibilities and at the same time limit any innovation in decisions because of a closed hierarchy. See Herbert Kaufman, *The Forest Ranger;* also Ashley L. Schiff, "Innovation and Administrative Decision Making," *Administrative Science Quarterly* 2 (June 1966): 1–30.

19. Jethro K. Lieberman, *How the Government Breaks the Law,* pp. 29–33.

20. Louis C. Gawthrop, *Administrative Politics and Social Change,* pp. 79–80.

21. Linda Mathews, "Supreme Court 1973–74 theme: Inconsistency," *Los Angeles Times,* 4 August 1974. For a discussion of the costs of uncertainty in administrative decision making, see Ruth P. Mack, *Planning on Uncertainty.*

22. Robert Merton argues that committing ourselves to one objective tends to shape that objective (Robert K. Merton, "The Unanticipated Consequences of Purposive Social Action," *American Sociological Review* 1 [December 1936]: 898–90).

23. *Los Angeles Times,* 6 August 1974.

24. "Pressure on the 'Persuadables,'" *Newsweek,* 29 July 1974, pp. 18–19.

25. United States v. Richard M. Nixon, 94 Supreme Court Reporter, p. 3090, decided 24 July 1974.

26. Robert T. Golembiewski, William A. Welsh, and William J. Crotty, *A Methodological Primer for Political Scientists,* p. 208.

27. Ira Sharkansky, ed., *Policy Analysis in Political Science,* p. 55; Downs, *Inside Bureaucracy,* p. 173.

28. Charles E. Lindblom, *The Intelligence of Democracy,* pp. 144–48, as summarized by Amitai Etzioni, "Mixed Scanning," *Public Administration Review* 27 (December 1967): 386–87.

29. Etzioni, "Mixed Scanning," p. 388.

30. See Aaron Wildavsky, *The Politics of the Budgetary Process,* chap. 3; and Ira Sharkansky, *The Routines of Politics.*

31. John P. Crecine, "A Simulation of Municipal Budgeting," in Sharkansky, *Policy Analysis in Political Science,* pp. 270–303.

32. Lindblom, "Science of Muddling Through," pp. 79–88.

33. Etzioni, "Mixed Scanning," pp. 358–92.

34. Ibid., pp. 389–90.

35. Gawthrop, *Administrative Politics and Social Change,* pp. 82–83.

36. Ibid., p. 94.

37. See, for example, Thomas P. Ference, "Organizational Communications Systems and the Decision Process," *Management Science* 17, no. 2 (October 1970): B83–96; also Matthew Tuite, Roger Chisholm, and Michael Radnor, *Interorganizational Decision Making,* pp. 127–221.

38. Simon, *Administrative Behavior,* p. 108.

39. This discussion relies on the work of Lloyd G. Nigro, *Modern Public Administration,* chap. 10.

40. F. J. Roethlisberger and William J. Dickson, *Management and the Worker,* chap. 3.

41. Ibid., p. 522.

42. For more information on barriers to communication, see Carl Rogers and Fritz Roethlisberger, "Barriers and Gateways to Communication," *Harvard Business Review* 30, no. 4 (July–August 1952): 46.

43. Harold L. Wilensky, *Organizational Intelligence,* p. 41. During the Cuban Missile crisis the need to avoid confusion was critical. A "hot line" was established between Moscow and Washington for this purpose (see Graham T. Allison, *Essence of Decision Explaining the Cuban Missile Crisis,* pp. 216–18).

44. Charles E. Redfield, *Communication in Management,* p. 131.

45. Harold P. Zelko, "How Effective Are Your Communications," *Advanced Management* 17 (February 1956): 10.

46. Rogers and Roethlisberger, "Barriers and Gateways to Communication," p. 46.

47. For a survey of communication in public administration, see Robert B. Highsaw and Don L. Bowen, eds., *Communication in Public Administration;* see also Chester I. Barnard, "Education for Executives," in *Human Relations in Administration,* ed. Robert Dubin, pp. 16–23; and T. Hardwick and B. F. Landuyt, *Administrative Strategy and Decision Making,* chap. 14, especially pp. 417–30.

48. Stafford Beer, *Cybernetics and Management,* pp. 7, 11; see also Norbert Wiener, *The Human Use of Human Beings;* and Richard F. Ericson, "Organizational Cybernetics and Human Values," *Academy of Management Journal* 50 (March 1970): 49–65.

SELECTED BIBLIOGRAPHY

Allison, Graham T. *Essence of Decision Explaining the Cuban Missile Crisis.* Boston: Little, Brown & Co., 1971.

Barnard, Chester I. "Education for Executives." In *Human Relations in Administration,* edited by Robert Dubin, pp. 16–23. Englewood Cliffs, N.J.: Prentice-Hall, 1961.

Beer, Stafford. *Cybernetics and Management.* 2d ed. London: English Universities Press, 1967.

Benton, John B. *Managing the Organizational Decision Process.* Lexington, Mass.: D. C. Health & Co., Lexington Books, 1973

Crecine, John P. "A Simulation of Municipal Budgeting: The Impact of Problem Environment." In *Policy Analysis in Political Science,* edited by Ira Sharkansky, pp. 270–303. Chicago: Markham Publishing Co., 1970.

Crenson, Matthew A. *The Un-Politics of Air Pollution: A Study on Non-Decision Making in the Cities.* Baltimore: Johns Hopkins Press, 1971.

Dahl, Robert A., and Lindblom, Charles E. *Politics, Economics and Welfare.* New York: Harper & Row, 1953.

Davis, Morris. "Some Aspects of Detroit's Decisional Profile." *Administrative Science Quarterly* 12 (1967): 209–24.

Downs, Anthony. *Inside Bureaucracy.* Boston: Little, Brown & Co., 1967.

Ericson, Richard F. "Organizational Cybernetics and Human Values." *Academy of Management Journal* 50 (1970): 49–65.

Etzioni, Amitai. "Mixed Scanning: A 'Third' Approach to Decision Making." *Public Administration Review* 27 (1967): 386–87.

Ference, Thomas P. "Organizational Communications Systems and the Decision Process." *Management Science* 17 (1970): B83–96.

Gawthrop, Louis C. *Administrative Politics and Social Change.* New York: St. Martin's Press, 1971.

Golembiewski, Robert T.; Welsh, William A.; and Crotty, William J. *A Methodological Primer for Political Scientists.* Chicago: Rand McNally & Co., 1969.

Hardwick, T., and Landuyt, B. F. *Administrative Strategy and Decision Making.* Cincinnati: South-Western Publishing Co., 1966.

Highsaw, Robert B., and Bowen, Don L., eds. *Communication in Public Administration.* Montgomery, Ala.: University of Alabama Press, 1965.

Janis, Irving L. *Victims of Groupthink.* Boston: Houghton Mifflin Co., 1972.

Kaufman, Herbert. *The Forest Ranger: A Study in Administrative Behavior.* Baltimore: Johns Hopkins Press, 1960.

Leighton, Alexander. *Human Relations in a Changing World.* New York: E. P. Dutton & Co., 1949.

Lieberman, Jethro K. *How the Government Breaks the Law.* New York: Stein & Day, 1972.

Lindblom, Charles E. *The Intelligence of Democracy.* New York: Macmillan Co., 1965.

––––––. *The Policy Making Process.* Englewood Cliffs, N.J.: Prentice-Hall, 1968.

––––––. "The Science of Muddling Through." *Public Administration Review* 19 (1959): 79–80.

Mack, Ruth P. *Planning on Uncertainty: Decision Making in Business and Government Administration.* New York: John Wiley & Sons, 1971.

Mathews, Linda. "Supreme Court 1973–74 Theme: Inconsistency." *Los Angeles Times,* 4 August 1974.

Merton, Robert K. "The Unanticipated Consequences of Purposive Social Action." *American Sociological Review* 1 (1936): 898–904.

Michels, Robert. *Political Parties: A Sociological Study of the Oligarchical Tendencies of Modern Democracy.* Glencoe, Ill.: Free Press, 1949.

Mowitz, Robert J., and Wright, Neil S. *Profile of a Metropolis.* Detroit: Wayne State University Press, 1962.

National Advisory Commission on Civil Disorders. Report. Washington, D.C.: Government Printing Office, 1968, pp. 110–12.

Nigro, Lloyd G. *Modern Public Administration.* 3d ed. New York: Harper & Row, 1973.

Peabody, Robert L. *Organizational Authority: Superior-Subordinate Relations in Three Public Service Organizations.* New York: Atherton Press, 1964.

Pfiffner, John M. "Administrative Rationality." *Public Administration Review* 20 (1960): 129.

"Pressure on the Persuadables." *Newsweek,* 29, July 1974, pp. 18–19.

Redfield, Charles E. *Communication in Management: A Guide to Administrative Communication.* Chicago: University of Chicago Press, 1953.

Roethlisberger, F. J., and Dickson, William J. *Management and the Worker.* Cambridge, Mass.: Harvard University Press, 1959.

Rogers, Carl, and Roethlisberger, Fritz. "Barriers and Gateways to Communication." *Harvard Business Review* 30 (1952): 46.

Sayre, Wallace S., and Kaufman, Herbert. *Governing New York City: Politics in the Metropolis.* New York: Russell Sage Foundation, 1960.

Schiff, Ashley L. "Innovation and Administrative Decision Making: The Conservation of Land Resources." *Administrative Science Quarterly* 2 (1966): 1–30.

Sharkansky, Ira, ed. *Policy Analysis in Political Science.* Chicago: Markham Publishing Co., 1970.

_____. *The Routines of Politics.* New York: Van Nostrand Reinhold Co., 1970.

Simon, Herbert A. *Administrative Behavior: A Study of Decision Making Processes in Administrative Organization.* 2d ed. New York: Macmillan Co., 1957.

Tuite, Matthew; Chisholm, Roger; and Radnor, Michael. *Interorganizational Decision Making.* Chicago: Aldine Publishing Co., 1972.

United States v. Richard M. Nixon. 94 Supreme Court Reporter, 24 July 1974, p. 3090.

Uris, Auren. *The Executive Deskbook.* New York: Van Nostrand Reinhold Co., 1970.

Weber, Max. *The Theory of Social and Economic Organization.* Glencoe, Ill: Free Press, 1947.

Wiener, Norbert. *The Human Use of Human Beings.* Boston: Houghton Mifflin Co., 1954.

Wildavsky, Aaron. *The Politics of the Budgetary Process.* Boston: Little, Brown & Co., 1964.

Wilensky, Harold L. *Organizational Intelligence: Knowledge and Policy in Government and Industry.* New York: Basic Books, 1967.

Zelko, Harold P. "How Effective Are Your Communications," *Advanced Management* 17 (1956): 10.

THE BUDGETARY PROCESS

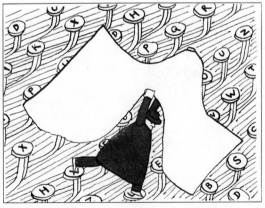

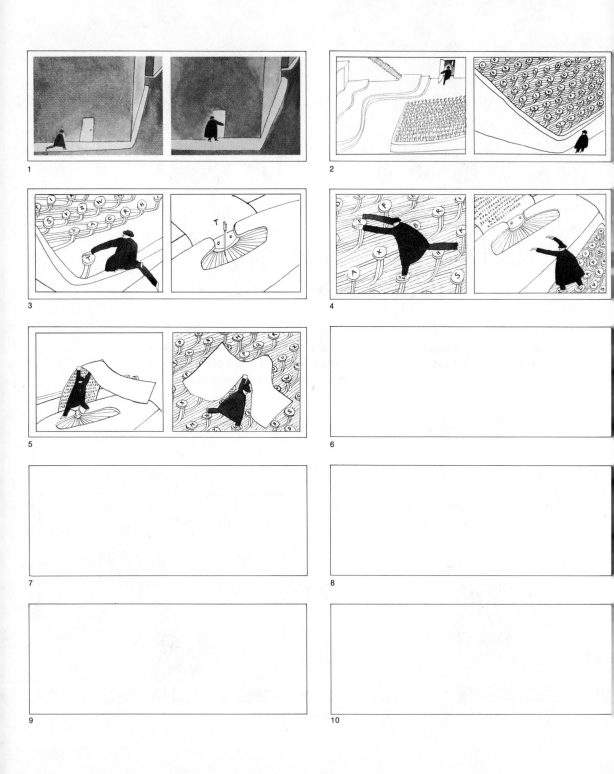

5 Public finance management, one of the most important aspects of stable government, determines where great sums of money come from, the purposes for which this money is spent, and how it is managed and accounted for. Broadly defined, it includes taxation and taxing policies (to which congressional constituents are sensitive, especially in times of inflation), as well as debt management, budgeting, accounting, treasury operations, and auditing.

All governments must exercise such functions, and, as there is only so much money to go around, the concern with priorities—who gets how much for what—is of paramount importance. It is embarrassing when an investigation by the National Taxpayers Union reveals that $375,000 was spent for a Pentagon study of the Frisbee, that $159,000 was spent to teach mothers how to play with their babies, or that $121,000 was spent to find out why some people say "ain't."[1] Clearly, congressmen are hard put to justify such federal projects. On another level, it will be seen that the more money is spent on defense and overseas activities, the less there will be for domestic problems and programs, while a significant reduction in defense spending will impact on a large segment of the overall economy insofar as it affects defense-related jobs and industries. In short, distribution of resources is greatly concerned with human consequences.

But the rising cost of government frequently exceeds government's ability to pay for numerous and expanding programs. National congressional leaders, who hold much of the power of the purse through significant appropriations committees, may be aware of the problem but take little action to control government spending. The public bureaucracies, too, make major demands for money. Once formed, agencies, like programs, are difficult to terminate because affected employees fight for their survival.

Government involvement in control of the economy is increasing rapidly. From the laissez-faire days of Harding and Coolidge, we have moved to acceptance of the legitimacy of government manipulation of wages, prices, and taxes under presidents Kennedy, Johnson, Nixon, and Ford. The British economist and civil servant John Maynard Keynes held in 1930 that governments could stabilize prices and unemployment by adopting a fiscal policy of adjusting government expenditures to prevent inflation, recession, or depression. The Full Employment Act of 1946, by establishing government's responsibility to maintain full employment, sought to stabilize the economy by providing stimuli when economic expansion slowed and by applying brakes when inflation developed.[2]

The Keynesian concept of economic policy also emphasized government's role in balancing the amount of money in circulation. Today this is done largely by the Federal Reserve System.[3] Economist John Kenneth Galbraith would have government go even further and make most wage and price decisions as well. Abandoning the Keynesian theories which have been standard liberal economic dogma for more than forty years, Galbraith argues that only permanent government controls can break the power of big business and big labor unions to force inflation and its resulting unemployment on the economy.[4]

Except for its awareness of rising taxes and a general knowledge of the nature of federal, state, and local expenditures, the public demonstrates only a marginal understanding of financial policy determination. For most people, government budgeting, with its elaborate statistics, is overwhelming because of the amounts of money involved. The Defense Department, for example, rounds off estimates to the nearest $50 million, which is barely comprehensible to people who will never handle more than a fiftieth of that sum in the whole of their lives.[5] Thus the public tends to become frustrated and distrustful of government when it encounters occasional mismanagement or underestimations of a major governmental project.

Moreover, with Arab oil quotas and prices, the world food problem, and the coming of the European Common Market, international economies are more closely bound together, so that a major fiscal decision in the United States may now have worldwide implications. A huge sale of American grain to the Soviet Union in 1974, for example, resulted in rising food prices in the United States and less surplus grain for foreign aid programs in other countries such as India.

In addition, currency itself is influenced by international money markets, central banks, other financial institutions, and money speculators. Decisions determining the extent of a trade deficit may have a direct effect on the value of the dollar, domestically and internationally. The American dollar is no longer an independent or necessarily sought-after currency.

This selective chapter on public finance begins by exploring the reasons for the rising costs of government, considers various concepts in money management related to the budgeting process, attempts a more detailed explanation of the techniques of budgeting, accounting, and auditing, and concludes with an example of budgetary debate over defense preparedness and weapons procurement and a budgetary example of Parkinson's Law. The appended case studies illustrate some of the kinds of decision-making problems and conflicts that may arise during the budgetary process.

HIGH COSTS OF GOVERNMENT

Government expenditure policies are more susceptible to inept management than they are to problems of corruption. The marked increase in public expenditures among the affluent nations during the past century can often be attributed to increased public demands coupled with poor administrative practices, including overstaffing, inept accounting, incompetent personnel, unimaginative leadership, and pork barrel appropriations. Poor administrative practices can occasionally result in cost overruns in projects. Establishing objectives and standards of performance in advance of implementation might help to correct such problems. Cost-benefit analysis, for example, is a basic element of program budgeting that measures the cost of a project against the amount of benefit, in terms of money or material saved or earned, that the government agency or department can expect in return. This approach helps to determine priorities and amount of expenditures by its ability to show the positive result of an administrative practice before it is implemented.

War, too, creates a tremendous need for revenues; during national military engagements, defense becomes a bottomless pit. The new agencies and departments that are formed to meet a war effort are difficult to eliminate later. There is nothing more permanent than a temporary agency of the government. As Professor Aaron Wildavsky has commented, "A temporary adjustment to a passing situation results in an emergency appropriation for a fixed period, which turns out to be a permanent expenditure."[6] A congressman put it another way: "Of course, [the agency] said it would take them about two years to clear it up, and then they would be off the payroll. Since then, I think you have added 30 [people] to this group." New forms of taxation, such as the federal excise tax and the excess profits tax, are not later abandoned any more than war debts are abandoned.

As population grows, the need for new and expanded government services and economic help at the federal, state, and local levels grows accordingly. Examples include benefits for Vietnam veterans who wish to continue their education, public welfare programs, increases in social security payments to senior citizens to compensate for the rising cost of living, and lower home mortgage loans for those (particularly recently graduated students) who want to own their own homes. In 1974 the interest rates for some home loans exceeded 12.5 percent, the highest in our history. In 1975 home loans were declining but were still at record highs. Through the Federal Housing Administration and legislation signed by President Ford, the federal government has poured millions into the mortgage market to bring down interest rates.

The famous, or infamous, Internal Revenue Service form 1040 is the reporting form for the federal government's major source of revenue, the income tax. State and local governments rely primarily on sales and property taxes for revenue. Increases in these compulsory taxes generate public resentment of the larger sum withheld from the paycheck to pay for federal income tax, and, in many cases, social security taxes and state income taxes as well. In addition, working men and women may be paying property taxes on their homes and other possessions, motor vehicle registration fees, and other service charges.

Public reaction against certain government expenditures acts to some extent as a restraint on government. The public can react against higher property taxes by rejecting school bonds and other legislative proposals submitted for voter approval. But more often government costs are not submitted to the electorate. They may become such fixed items in the budget as welfare programs, education, and public works projects.

Occasionally, odd taxing practices develop to which the public does not react. In California, for example, a particular proposition on the ballot would at one time have allowed the state to use gasoline tax monies for highway construction and maintenance, as well as for mass transit programs. The ballot measure failed, and, as a result of subsequent special interest demands in the state legislature, the state 6 percent sales tax was applied to gasoline in order to provide for transit uses throughout the state. But motorists soon found themselves paying a cumulative tax on a tax, or the 6 percent sales tax on top of a seven-cent–per-gallon state tax on top of another four-cent–per-gallon federal tax.[7] Furthermore, pressure was applied by state legislators and administrative advisers to President Ford during the Arab oil crisis to add an additional tax as an energy conservation measure. Legislatures, of course, may not approve additional taxes and may thus act also as a restraint on government spending.

The government may also raise money through the sale of public land, since it is the largest landowner in the United States. The Alaskan state government, for example, raised almost a billion dollars by leasing state-owned land to private oil companies in 1969. The federal government did the same thing in oil leases along the cost of California near Santa Barbara and the Gulf Coast of Mexico.

Government can also raise money by borrowing. The government is always borrowing from its citizens by means of loans, savings bonds, and the like. Most of our public debt is the result of war expenditures and major building projects. By 1967 the public debt towered over private debt. From 1929 to 1967 public debt increased fourteen times while private debt increased only six times.[8] Of course, the federal government could easily pay the public debt by simply printing more money, but this would result in economic chaos.

Public loans are particularly attractive because there is little chance of default by the government in payment of U.S. Treasury notes, bonds, and bills. This is because they are backed by the U.S. Treasury and the power of the federal government to tax in order to raise revenue. City governments offer municipal bonds to the public to obtain capital for building projects. Not only are these bonds secured by the guarantee that city government will pay them off with taxes and service charges, but the investor pays no federal or local taxes on the interest earned from them. Only during the 1975 budget crisis in New York City was there a threat that the city could not meet its bonded indebtedness payments. Further, the number and size of government loans and use of bonds per year has an impact on the money market. The offering of high-interest Treasury notes and bonds by the federal government, for example, attracts a great deal of consumer money away from savings and loan institutions and banks paying lower interest, resulting in part in a rapid increase in home mortgage interest rates. Finally, private business is occasionally successful in borrowing from the federal government, as Lockheed Aircraft Corporation did to back up a loan in 1971.

Faced with threatened taxpayer revolts and the need to reduce numbers of employees because of the rising costs of government, some state governments have recently adopted lotteries as fund-raising devices. In a state lottery, several thousand people may purchase tickets, and the state offers cash prizes to a few ticket holders. These prizes represent only a fraction of the total money raised, and the remainder can be used to pay for state government operation. New Hampshire initiated a state lottery in 1964, and more than eight states have done likewise since then. As long as lotteries can raise money for state governments without increasing taxes, they will remain popular.[9]

STEPS IN THE BUDGETARY PROCESS

The budgetary process is largely a policy-making procedure involving competing priorities in government programs. The budget itself represents a yearly summation of public expenses. At the federal level, it is a process flowing initially from the executive branch and subsequently acted on by Congress and a variety of special interest groups. It was not until passage of the Budget and Accounting Act in 1921 that the budget became largely controlled by the president.[10]

The purpose of a budget is to enable decision makers to gain a sharp picture of sources of revenue, cash flow, expenditures, and reserves. Insofar as it also serves as an outline for public policy, it is a continuous process. A budget is a report of the past and present fiscal years with an estimate for future years. There are essentially three types of budget authorities. In the executive type, the power to formulate economic policy rests with the chief administrative officer—the president, governor, mayor, or city manager. The second type allows budgeting to be done by a commission or board which may consist of administrative and legislative officers working either separately or together. In the third type, the budget may be the product of legislative appropriations or finance committees. This is an unusual arrangement, however; only the state of Arkansas has such a plan. The first type is most frequently used because of the advantages of executive flexibility in determining policy, the prestige of the office, and its relative isolation from special interests.

Preparation Although the procedure of preparing the typical executive budget is fairly structured by legal statutes, political and economic demands still influence the behavior of the participants. The first step is to obtain from operating agencies a detailed estimate of their needs for the coming fiscal year (FY). This estimate should be based on the current fiscal year, which is 1 July to 30 June of the following year. In the federal government, after a fiscal policy statement is delivered, usually in May, budget estimate request forms are distributed to department agencies. A definite schedule of dates is followed in handling fiscal matters. Agencies start their estimates in June because the budgetary process takes more than eighteen months to complete. Estimates for fiscal year 1978-79 must therefore be in the Office of Management and Budget, or the OMB (until 1970, the Bureau of the Budget) by 15 September 1976—nearly two years in advance.

Estimates returned to the OMB usually consist of two categories: personal services and supplies. Shrewd administrators base the amount of their requests on a number of variables, including political support, the personalities of such decision makers as congressmen and state assemblymen, and the type of agency. Wildavsky was told by one federal executive, "It's not what's in your estimates, but how good a politican you are that matters."[11] In an effort to get more funds, the Soil Conservation Service declared, for example, that money spent on soil erosion now would save costs in dredging channels and reservoirs later.[12]

During July and August OMB examiners review the estimates, which, by September, are returned to the agencies accompanied by statements justifying OMB action. The operating agency may be informed that its estimates must be reduced, and a process of reconciliation begins that may eventually require political authorization to end in a compromise. Budget analysts in the OMB know that a certain amount of padding is added by various departments. After the agencies review their estimates and resubmit them to the OMB, they are then submitted to the president. Finally, the bulky report is submitted to the legislature with a message from the president and drafted bills ready for approval. Budgets at the federal and state level may compose two volumes or more than 600 pages. The president exercises major policy leadership insofar as the budget is framed within the executive branch. Consequently, the legislature depends to a great extent on the executive branch and OMB for budgetary information.

The new OMB has substantially altered the former pattern of budget preparation. For more than fifty years the president appointed the director of the Bureau of the Budget, who, with some 350 experts, put together the federal budget regardless of who was president at the time. On 21 July 1970, however, it was announced that while the new OMB would continue to prepare the federal budget and oversee its execution, the President's Council of Domestic Advisers would be primarily responsible for advising the president on all domestic policy. President Nixon explained, "The Domestic Council will be primarily concerned with what we do; the OMB will be primarily concerned with how we do it; and how well we do it."[13] Thus the Domestic Council was to set domestic policy while the OMB would carry it out.

Approval Process

Congress must authorize all budgetary legislation before funds can be appropriated or distributed to agencies. The budget goes first to the House Appropriations Committee, as provided by article 1, section 7 of the U.S. Constitution, and is divided among subcommittees that specialize in the consideration of given agencies. Then hearings are held, at which time the departments have another opportunity to sell their proposals and estimates. When the subcommittees' work is complete, the appropriations committee submits the budget to the House, where it follows the same procedure as a regular bill.

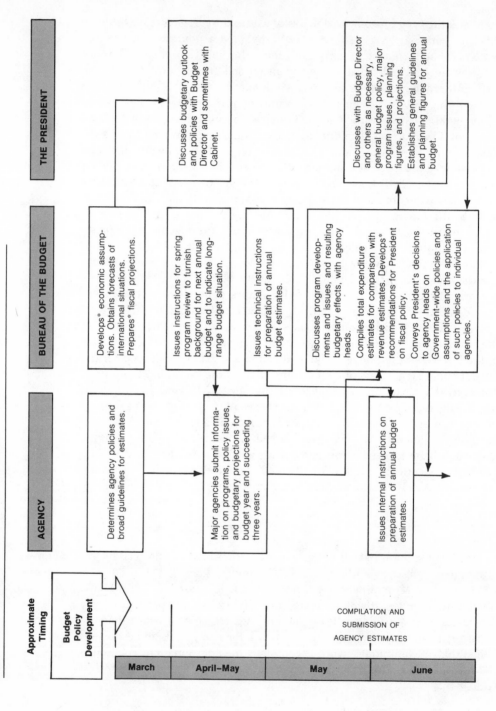

Table 2 FORMULATION OF EXECUTIVE BUDGET

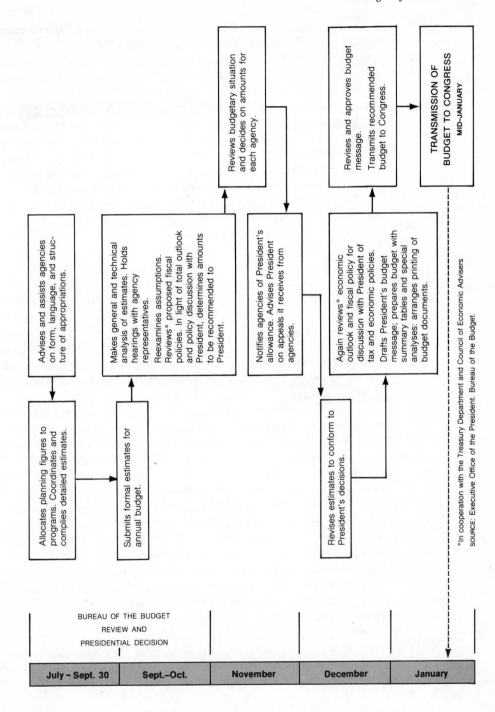

Reviews budgetary situation and decides on amounts for each agency.

Revises and approves budget message. Transmits recommended budget to Congress.

TRANSMISSION OF BUDGET TO CONGRESS MID-JANUARY

Advises and assists agencies on form, language, and structure of appropriations.

Makes general and technical analysis of estimates. Holds hearings with agency representatives. Reexamines assumptions. Reviews* proposed fiscal policies. In light of total outlook and policy discussion with President, determines amounts to be recommended to President.

Notifies agencies of President's allowance. Advises President on appeals it receives from agencies.

Again reviews* economic outlook and fiscal policy for discussion with President of tax and economic policies. Drafts President's budget message; prepares budget with summary tables and special analyses; arranges printing of budget documents.

Allocates planning figures to programs. Coordinates and compiles detailed estimates.

Submits formal estimates for annual budget.

Revises estimates to conform to President's decisions.

BUREAU OF THE BUDGET
REVIEW AND
PRESIDENTIAL DECISION

| July – Sept. 30 | Sept.–Oct. | November | December | January |

*In cooperation with the Treasury Department and Council of Economic Advisers

SOURCE: Executive Office of the President. Bureau of the Budget.

After House action, the appropriations bill is sent to the Senate where it goes through another appropriations committee. The procedure is the same, although the Senate has the reputation of restoring appropriations deleted from the House version. The House-Senate Conference Committee often meets to effect compromises between the two houses on this bill. Under the Constitution, the president must either accept or reject the entire bill because, unlike certain state governors, he does not have an item veto. Thus it is not unusual for Congress to attach a rider to an appropriations bill needed by the president in order to force him to approve a budgetary item or an amount of money to which he objects. It should be noted here that revenue measures follow the same route as the budget, except that they are first considered by the House Ways and Means Committee and then by the Senate Finance Committee. The consideration of expenditures and tax measures is not coordinated in Congress.

Legislative Review

The legislative or congressional approval process of the budget has several disadvantages. Studies of federal spending from 1948 to 1963 supported the view that the congressional record of holding down agency requests for more money was poor. These studies reveal a pattern in which agencies and bureaus ask for increasing percentages each year, which the OMB and Congress in turn both expect and proceed to cut, the amount depending on the agency or program.[14] Such a procedure has been called "creeping incrementalism in spending."

Poor expenditure control is not only to be found in the federal government but in nearly all state and local governments as well. Legislators do not have an adequate basis of information on which to make comprehensive decisions about the progress and needs of the agencies involved. Several examples of the information gaps that render congressmen less than effective have been provided by Professor Richard Fenno. "Senators view their performance in the hearing just about the way agency officials do. They admit that their attendance at hearings and their knowledge of the agencies is not praiseworthy, but they plead, as always, the lack of time."[15] One subcommittee clerk commented: "Sometimes we're holding subcommittee hearings in two adjacent rooms, and it's like a floating crap game. A Senator will tell the clerk to let him know when a certain item comes up in the next room, and the clerks will be giving [the congressmen] messages so they can float."[16] The role of the clerk can be even more significant, as Fenno indicates:

> The chairmen of these subcommittees are powerful—very powerful. And that's one reason—they have the clerks working for them. Haven't you ever wondered why the chairman asks most of the

questions at these hearings? They've got the clerks' questions, that's why. Old _____, God bless his soul, sits there and just reads off the clerk's questions. He asks seventy-five percent of the questions, and most of them he doesn't care about but five per cent of the questions, but he gets them in the record. People who read the hearings probably say, "Doesn't he know a lot." Well, he does. He's had the experience or he wouldn't be subcommittee chairman. But he isn't that much smarter than all the rest of us. It's the clerks, too.[17]

Nevertheless, inspection trips, telephone calls, and informal contacts partially compensate for the inadequacies of public hearings. The informal web is vital for communication and for the creation of stable relationships between congressional committees and executive agencies. Informal meetings with department budget directors, for example, may be an excellent source of information.

Occasionally members of Congress will publicly challenge the way money is being spent, one case involving the amount of funds allegedly used to improve security at former President Nixon's Western White House in San Clemente, California, and his residence in Florida. According to some charges, several hundred thousand dollars were spent on home improvement rather than on security. The president was particularly vulnerable on the home financing issue because of the previous campaign finance and Watergate scandal which resulted in his resignation.

Another case occurred in August 1973 when Senator William Proxmire (of Wisconsin) received a report from the General Accounting office that attacked an Air Force general for spending $670,000 in public funds to convert his four-engine C-135 jet tanker into a plush executive jet.[18] General Jack Catton, head of the Air Force Logistics Command, had installed in his plane a specially designed galley with a range, freezer, trash compactor, air force blue carpeting, two divans that converted into beds, and three bathrooms. Proxmire, a frequent critic of military expenditures, charged in this case that a sink and cabinet had cost $4,986 dollars.

A government employee takes great job risks in challenging the way in which money is spent. In 1968 A. Ernest Fitzgerald, a financial analyst in the air force, testified before a subcommittee headed by Proxmire that the C-5A jet transport, the world's largest aircraft, would cost $2 billion more than the original estimate of over $3 billion, blaming the increase on faulty estimating by the air force and inadequate controls and planning among other factors. Fitzgerald was later notified that he had been dismissed as one of about 850 military and civilian reductions ordered in the service. But Senator Proxmire believed the dismissal was largely a result of Fitzgerald's testimony before the subcommittee. Three years later the U.S. Civil Service

Commission ordered the air force to rehire Fitzgerald with back pay. Proxmire subsequently released another report telling of $26.3 billion cost overruns based on a General Accounting Office (GAO) report for the development of fifty-five new weapons systems. (Because the Department of Defense figures in some of the nation's most famous budget battles, the first case study at the end of this chapter was selected to illustrate the competition for funds between military and nonmilitary domestic programs.)

Many attempts have been made to improve congressional review of expenditures. Congress has used investigating committees and reorganized departments and bureaus such as the GAO; it has used citizens' groups and program budgeting for examining budgets. One proposal suggested making some program authorizations on a permanent basis or for periods of from three to five years rather than yearly.[19] Budget authorizations for longer than a year would reduce competition between legislative and appropriations committees, save time by reducing the amount of congressional review, give the legislature more time to deal with fewer appropriations per year, and improve long-range planning. With few exceptions to date, however, Congress remains reluctant to make authorizations for longer periods.

Another method of improving congressional review of administrative spending would be to control the amount of spending during the fiscal year by requiring that all financial transactions be completed at the end of the year and that unexpended monies be returned to the U.S. Treasury. The disadvantage of this requirement, however, is that it might induce last-minute spending to use up all remaining revenues. On the one hand, it is argued that because of large carry-overs, Congress has lost much of its control over expenditures. On the other hand, it is true that the House Appropriations Committee gets full reports on the unexpended monies and has the power to change the authority to spend that which was previously granted.

Professor Joseph P. Harris has described how Congress has attempted to control spending at the time authorizations are made.[20] Under section 138 of the Legislative Reorganization Act of 1946, both the House Ways and Means and Appropriations committees and the Senate Appropriations and Finance committees would have an annual joint meeting and by the middle of February make a report to Congress recommending suggested expenditures. But this process was tried only once and has not been repeated since 1949.[21] Still other proposals have been made but never approved. Congress's most significant point of control over both the president and administration lies in the appropriations process; but budget management is more than control of appropriations. Merely because Congress authorizes expenditures does not compel spending.

Ideally, the execution stage of the budget should permit a balance between legislative intent and administrative flexibility. But some government departments frequently ask Congress for a supplemental appropriation; other agencies are permitted to carry over unused portions of funds for future periods. This is a better policy than requiring all unused monies to be returned to the general fund, as is required under some city charters, because the latter often results in last-minute splurges or revenue shifts to other items for immediate spending.[22]

Both the president and the OMB, which is located in the executive branch, have from time to time impounded funds, which involves placing funds in reserve because of the president's belief that spending large appropriations would be inflationary or otherwise damaging to the economy at a particular time. Congress has at times overridden an executive veto by voting more funds for a project than the president believed was necessary.[23] Former President Nixon vetoed a congressional spending legislation that would have required him to spend an additional $300 million for rural water and sewer grants from 1973 to 1976, arguing that his action was a further attempt to control inflation and observing, "It should also come as no surprise that over the time the program has attained a distinct flavor of pork barrel." In April 1973 the House upheld one veto for a vocational rehabilitation authorization bill and another one on water aid.[24] However, Congress refused to give the president the unprecedented power to cut whichever government programs he chose in order to keep total federal spending within the proposed budget.[25]

When Nixon vetoed a Health, Education and Welfare bill because he felt an additional appropriation of $19 billion would be inflationary, Congress overrode his veto. Shortly before he resigned from office Nixon approved the Budget and Impoundment Act on the basis of which the House and Senate established their own budget committees.[26] These committees would be responsible for setting limits on the amount of money that could be appropriated and would review all bills to see that they did not exceed the ceiling set. The committees could also recommend to Congress that if the president impounded funds merely to defer spending, he could, by a congressional resolution of a simple majority, be forced to spend the money during the current fiscal year.

The battles over the budget illustrate that budgetary decision making is incremental. The most significant factor in determining the size and content of a current budget is last year's budget. Most of the budget is a product of earlier decisions. There are mandatory programs, such as veterans' pensions, whose expenses must be met; but those programs that are not mandatory arouse competition among different interests in shaping

Table 3 CONGRESSIONAL ACTION ON APPROPRIATIONS, JANUARY–JULY*

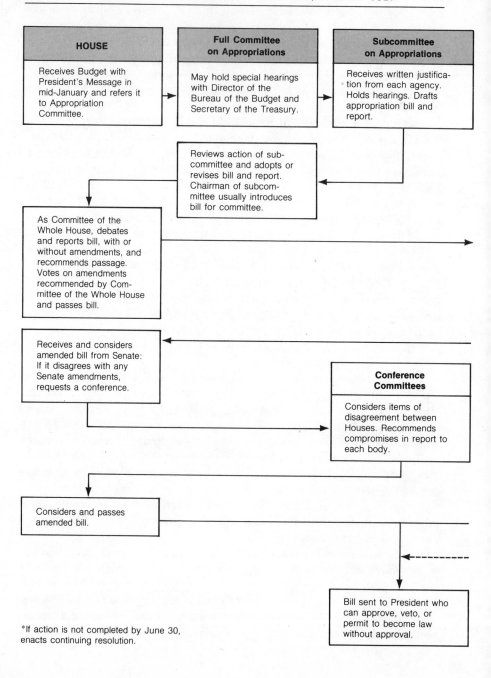

HOUSE	Full Committee on Appropriations	Subcommittee on Appropriations
Receives Budget with President's Message in mid-January and refers it to Appropriation Committee.	May hold special hearings with Director of the Bureau of the Budget and Secretary of the Treasury.	Receives written justification from each agency. Holds hearings. Drafts appropriation bill and report.

Reviews action of sub-committee and adopts or revises bill and report. Chairman of subcommittee usually introduces bill for committee.

As Committee of the Whole House, debates and reports bill, with or without amendments, and recommends passage. Votes on amendments recommended by Committee of the Whole House and passes bill.

Receives and considers amended bill from Senate: If it disagrees with any Senate amendments, requests a conference.

Conference Committees

Considers items of disagreement between Houses. Recommends compromises in report to each body.

Considers and passes amended bill.

Bill sent to President who can approve, veto, or permit to become law without approval.

*If action is not completed by June 30, enacts continuing resolution.

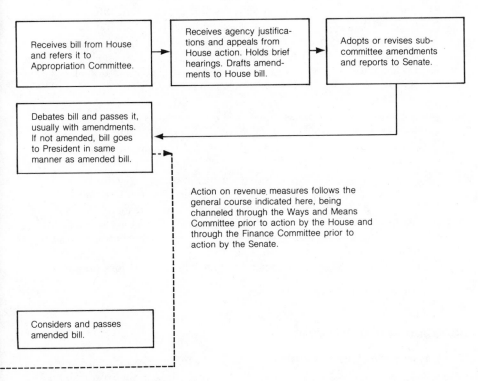

SENATE

Receives Budget with President's Message in mid-January and refers it to Appropriation Committee.

Subcommittee on Appropriations

Full Committee on Appropriations

Note: Senate hearings are sometimes held before House completes action.

Receives bill from House and refers it to Appropriation Committee.

Receives agency justifications and appeals from House action. Holds brief hearings. Drafts amendments to House bill.

Adopts or revises subcommittee amendments and reports to Senate.

Debates bill and passes it, usually with amendments. If not amended, bill goes to President in same manner as amended bill.

Action on revenue measures follows the general course indicated here, being channeled through the Ways and Means Committee prior to action by the House and through the Finance Committee prior to action by the Senate.

Considers and passes amended bill.

Bureau of the Budget prepares Midyear Review, a summary of Congressional determinations and revised budget outlook for new fiscal year.

SOURCE: Executive Office of the President. Bureau of the Budget.

national priorities.[27] Thus budgeting is incremental, not comprehensive. Those who make up a budget are working with the tip of an iceberg in the sense that they are concerned with a relatively small increment to a large existing base.[28] The incremental nature of budgeting generates some interesting informal strategies as well. Thomas Anton summarizes some of these rules:[29]

1. Spend all of your appropriation. A failure to use up an appropriation indicates that the full amount was unnecessary in the first place, which in turn implies that your budget should be cut next year.

2. Never request a sum less than your current appropriation. It is easier to find ways to spend up to current appropriation levels than it is to explain why you want a reduction. Besides, a reduction indicates your program is not growing and this is an embarrassing admission to most government administrators.

3. Put top priority programs into the basic budget, that is, that part of the budget which is within current appropriation levels. Budget offices, governors, and mayors, and legislative bodies will seldom challenge programs which appear to be part of existing operations.

4. Increases that are desired should be made to appear small and should appear to grow out of existing operations. The appearance of a fundamental change in a budget should be avoided.

5. Give the budget office, chief executive, and the legislature something to cut. Normally, it is desirable to submit requests for substantial increases in existing programs and many requests for new programs, in order to give higher political authorities something to cut. This enables them to "save" the public untold millions of dollars and justify something to cut and also diverts attention away from the basic budget with its vital programs.[30]

METHODS OF BUDGETING AND ACCOUNTING

One way to understand the various types of budgets is to examine them on a spectrum ranging from very restrictive to very flexible in their provisions for spending public money. We will look first at the line-item cash-based budget, which is highly restrictive, followed by more flexible program budgets generally termed planning-programming-budgeting systems (PPBS) or cost-benefit analysis budgets. There are several variations on these two types, such as some organizational budgets that have both line-item and program-budget provisions. In addition, we will examine the basic elements of accrual accounting, which has several advantages over line-item or cash-based accounting.

Line-item or Cash-based Budgeting

Line-item or cash-based budgeting operates on a pay-as-you-go basis. Generally, you can spend only the amount approved for each item, such as salaries and supplies; you cannot introduce other expenses unless the money is later appropriated, and you cannot transfer funds between items or programs in the organization. That is, you cannot increase salaries because the money for supplies is not spent or transfer more money into a program for street improvement if it is not used for salaries.

Cost-Benefit Analysis Budgeting (PPBS)

Program budgets offer substantial flexibility insofar as money may be made available that will allow any combination of expenditures. Money for salaries and supplies can be adjusted as necessary to achieve the goals of the program most effectively. The director of a department or program may spend either 80 percent of the budget on salaries and 20 percent on supplies or vice versa as long as the combination of expenditures will achieve the program's objective and yield the best possible benefit for the costs involved. The success of the program can thus be analyzed and measured in advance by determining whether the amount and way the money is spent meets the program's stated goals. This very elementary explanation does not take into account various complexities to be found in this type of budgeting, but these will become clearer in the course of this discussion.

PPBS originated in both industry and government. General Motors was examining its potential as early as 1924; it was studied again by the War Production Board's Controlled Material Plan during World War II.[31] It was not until the 1950s that it received greater use in weapons systems studies by the Department of Defense, but it was employed by President Lyndon Johnson's administration in 1965.[32] PPBS was advanced primarily by three postwar developments. First, economists and accountants began to demand longer-range estimates of government spending and classification of expenses according to program or function. Second, the development of computers with rapid calculation and recall abilities made PPBS a better alternative than the line-item budget. Third, performance budgeting began to be applied to management programs outside government use to assess administrative performance against a department's stated objectives.

Table 4 EXECUTION OF ENACTED BUDGET

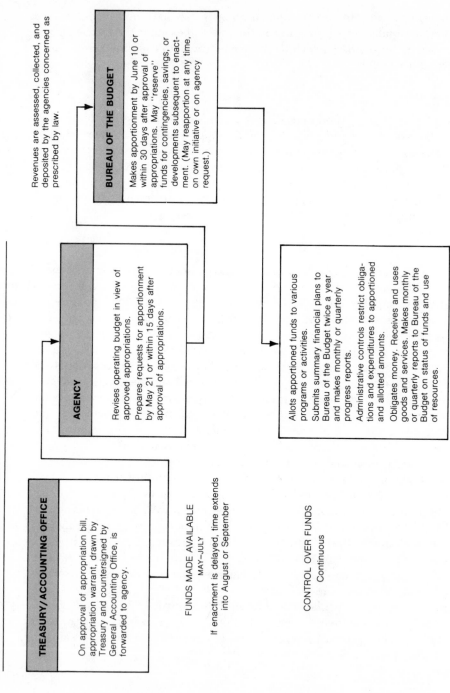

TREASURY/ACCOUNTING OFFICE

On approval of appropriation bill, appropriation warrant, drawn by Treasury and countersigned by General Accounting Office, is forwarded to agency.

FUNDS MADE AVAILABLE
MAY–JULY

If enactment is delayed, time extends into August or September

AGENCY

Revises operating budget in view of approved appropriations.

Prepares requests for apportionment by May 21 or within 15 days after approval of appropriations.

BUREAU OF THE BUDGET

Makes apportionment by June 10 or within 30 days after approval of appropriations. May "reserve" funds for contingencies, savings, or developments subsequent to enactment. (May reapportion at any time, on own initiative or on agency request.)

Revenues are assessed, collected, and deposited by the agencies concerned as prescribed by law.

CONTROL OVER FUNDS
Continuous

Allots apportioned funds to various programs or activities.

Submits summary financial plans to Bureau of the Budget twice a year and makes monthly or quarterly progress reports.

Administrative controls restrict obligations and expenditures to apportioned and allotted amounts.

Obligates money. Receives and uses goods and services. Makes monthly or quarterly reports to Bureau of the Budget on status of funds and use of resources.

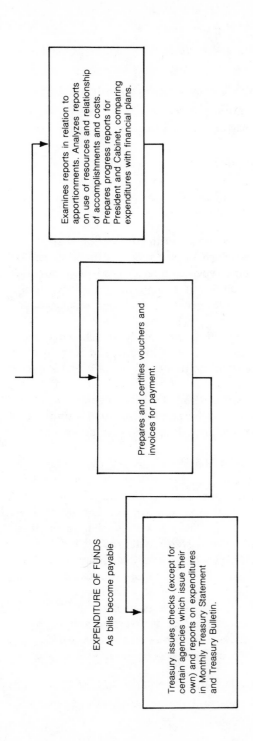

Examines reports in relation to apportionments. Analyzes reports on use of resources and relationship of accomplishments and costs. Prepares progress reports for President and Cabinet, comparing expenditures with financial plans.

Bureau of the Budget makes informal review of agency operations. Conducts, or guides agencies in, organization and management studies. Assists President in improving management and organization of the executive branch.

Prepares and certifies vouchers and invoices for payment.

EXPENDITURE OF FUNDS
As bills become payable

Treasury issues checks (except for certain agencies which issue their own) and reports on expenditures in Monthly Treasury Statement and Treasury Bulletin.

MANAGEMENT APPRAISAL AND INDEPENDENT AUDIT
Periodic

Agency reviews compliance with established policies, procedures, and requirements. Evaluates accomplishment of program plans and effectiveness of management and operations.

General Accounting Office performs independent audit of financial records, transactions, and financial management, generally. "Settles" accounts of certifying and disbursing officers. Makes reports to Congress.

SOURCE: Executive Office of the President. Bureau of the Budget.

PPBS has six basic objectives which, when combined, will maximize departmental outputs:

1. To identify and examine the goals of each area of governmental activity
2. To establish priorities among these goals
3. To compute the costs of existing and alternative programs over a period of years
4. To examine a program's output in terms of its goals
5. To measure the benefits of alternative programs over a period of time
6. To select those programs that achieve the desired goals at the lowest cost

In the process of implementing PPBS, the government developed six categories of programs on the basis of which to plan federal expenditures: (1) national security programs, (2) most types of international programs, (3) natural resource programs, (4) human resource programs, (5) science, technology, and economic programs, and (6) general government-management programs.

The objectives of PPBS—which aims principally at achieving budgetary flexibility, a new method of predetermining benefits and of evaluating them on the basis of money to be spent on programs, and a possible overall assessment of government agency policies for a period exceeding three years—represent a substantial departure from the incremental system of budgeting. Heavy emphasis is placed on human rationality and on the institutionalization of budgetary procedures designed to improve rational decision making.

The key to PPBS lies in its definition of outputs and evaluation for a particular program. The most difficult aspect of policy analysis is the impartial evaluation of outputs for the purpose of gathering information to improve existing programs or to seek alternative programs. Each individual agency must first define its goals and then find the most efficient methods of accomplishing them. Agencies like the Government Printing Office may find this an easy function. The Post Office Department, too, may have easily definable goals, such as determining the amount of first-class mail delivered. Alternative programs may then be analyzed for cost effectiveness, which may show that first-class mail arrives just as fast as air mail, and this may then bring about discussions of rate changes or of first-class and air-mail–category combinations. Because of resource limitations and constraints in the public and economic sector, it may be necessary to choose among alternative outputs.

Once these data are generated, however, the officers of OMB, the president, and the President's Council of Domestic Advisers can make decisions concerning the relative merits of alternative programs in relation to their estimated needs as they see them. Because of their size and purpose, of course, some agencies, such as Health, Education and Welfare, or more specifically the Office of Education, may have far more elusive goals than others. The vast variety of programs of the Office of Education, for example, makes it difficult for that agency to define exact goals for each, or even measurable goals for all, of its activities.

Role of cost-benefit analysis. Cost-benefit analysis is designed to provide government decision makers with a means of assessing the relative virtues of alternative government programs.[33] While an agency can also use this means to evaluate its own performance over a period of time, the technique is designed for interagency performance comparison. Cost-benefit analysis aims at providing data to the OMB, the president, and his advisers to guide their policy choices. Any student of accounting knows that figures can be manipulated to suggest that performance achieved is in a favorable relationship with costs spent. David Hyman explains cost-benefit analysis as "a statement of the 'pros and cons' of a particular activity over a period of time. It is a very systematic way of gathering information." There are essentially three steps involved in a cost-benefit analysis: (1) enumeration of all costs and benefits of the proposed project, (2) evaluation of all costs and benefits in dollar terms, and (3) discounting of future net benefits.[34] In practice, the process is more complicated than this because administrative expertise in several fields is necessary to evaluate costs and benefits properly.

The Defense Department provides a good example of cost-effectiveness in a comparison of two fighter aircraft which were identical except that one flew ten miles an hour faster than the other. The cost of the faster aircraft per unit was over $10,000 more than the slower aircraft. To have used one thousand more of the expensive planes would have resulted in the expenditure of another $10 million. Those determining policy had to decide whether a faster fighter would be worth the additional $10 million. If military planners examined only combat capability, they must then have determined whether that capability could be obtained at lower cost by purchasing more of the less-expensive aircraft. The type of cost-effectiveness being determined here is the crux of PPBS.[35] Essentially, is the greater speed worth the greater cost?

A practical example of total cost-effectiveness in military spending was provided by the TFX case (Tactical Fighter, Experimental—later named the F-111). The decision by Robert McNamara, then secretary of defense, initially to award the $439 million contract to develop the new fighter to General Dynamics Corporation involved more than a controversey over performance characteristics of the "swing-winged" jet. Robert Art's book, *The TFX Decision,* illustrates how the controversy produced a split between military decision makers and civilian officials of the Defense Department. Speaking for the Kennedy administration, McNamara argued that to pay more for a weapons system than was necessary to meet the military requirement would mean fewer resources available to spend on other weapons systems necessary to meet other military requirements. The military decision makers, representing the air force and navy, wanted two completely different aircraft, while McNamara argued for one plane, the F-111, modified to fit both services at less expense. McNamara concluded that this biservice aircraft made for better cost-effectiveness.[36]

PPBS is thus a circular process of collecting data, building models, weighing costs against effectiveness, testing for effectiveness, questioning assumptions, examining new alternatives, formulating new problems, selecting objectives, designing alternatives, and collecting new data again.[37] The purpose is to allow decision makers to determine the cost-benefit results of alternative programs in order to utilize their resources better. If meaningful alternatives are identified by cost-benefit analysis, those making policy should be able to maximize the returns of their competing programs.

Problems of PPBS. The fundamental flaw of PPBS is its inability to apply techniques consistently to all agencies within the public sector. Departments or agencies with more easily defined goals, such as the Post Office Department, may gain from its use. Departments with less easily defined goals, such as Health, Education and Welfare, will provide poor information for comparison.

PPBS can be better understood by a description of its use in the Defense Department, which, as a result of a presidential order, expanded the system on a government-wide basis.[38] Before August 1965, the major budget categories for the Department of Defense were: Military Personnel, Operation and Maintenance, Procurement, Military Construction, Research, Development, Test, and Evaluation. Professor David Novick's studies urged combinations of programs so that the role of each service command would be clarified and better coordinated. Under McNamara's supervision the department identified nine major programs: Strategic Forces, General Purpose Forces, Specialized Activities (Intelligence), Airlift and Sealift, Guard and Reserve Forces, Research and Development, Logistics, Personnel Support, and Administration (each program having several subcategories that contained program elements, such as Land Based Missile Forces). These elements were then given priorities in order to compete for revenues based on their effectiveness.

The application of PPBS by the Department of Defense was successful partly because of the department's strong management and military orientation. Other government departments have had far less success because of the diversified goals of PPBS and the difficulty for many personnel in understanding how it works. PPBS has been strongly criticized by employees who experience difficulty in understanding and implementing it. One of the most outspoken critics of program budgeting is Professor Wildavsky, who criticizes the system for failing to provide data on three types of political costs:

1. Exchange costs—the costs of calling in favors owed and the costs of making threats in order to get others to support a policy
2. Reputational costs—the loss of popularity with the electorate, the loss of esteem and effectiveness with other officials, and the subsequent loss of one's ability to secure programs other than those currently under consideration
3. The costs of undesirable redistributions of power—those disadvantages that accrue from the increase in the power of individuals, organizations, or social groups who may become antagonistic to one's own interests.[39]

In a subsequent article Wildavsky argues that PPBS will encounter serious future difficulties that will result in overwhelming failure.[40] He fears that the policy analysis itself will be rejected together with its particular manifestation in PPBS and contends that the Defense Department was a poor model on which to begin applying PPBS in the first place. It was more successful there than anywhere else in the government because a group of talented people were available who had spent years on strategy and logistics; they had used a common terminology to guide policy analysis; they had demonstrated leadership that understood policy analysis; and there existed a variety of planners who developed contingency reports, logistical plans, and the like.[41] The unusually favorable conditions that existed in the Department of Defense for the limited use of PPBS did not exist in most other domestic agencies, however.

The fall of PPBS began when the OMB submitted the following memorandum to all agencies on 21 June 1971: "Agencies are no longer required to submit their budget submissions, the multi-year program and financing plans, program memoranda and special analytical studies . . . or the schedules . . . that reconcile information classified according to their program and appropriation structures."[42] Without mentioning PPBS by name, the memo announced the termination of PPBS as part of "continuing OMB efforts to simplify budget submission requirements."[43]

PPBS failed in some government agencies because many government analysts were unable to understand the connection between their work and budgeting.[44] Modified versions of PPBS are still used at all levels of government and have spread among local governments, too, because of program and budget flexibility; but the modified versions are in many cases also simplified from the more structured form used by the Defense Department.

Other federal agencies, such as the State Department and the Bureau of the Budget, fought over the system's implementation. Although the State Department argued for its own modified system of PPBS, it was forced to accept instead an imposed system about whose design it had no say and little understanding. The reaction was one of complete departmental divorce from PPBS.[45] But more than departmental subversion was responsible for the demise of this system in some agencies. The Bureau of the Budget itself failed to convince the departments that it was genuinely committed to PPBS. Indeed the Bureau of the Budget never fully implemented the system within its own department. Peter C. Sarant has summed up the reasons for PPBS failures.

> PPBS died because of the manner in which it was introduced, across-the-board and without much preparation. PPBS died because new men of power were arrogantly insensitive to budgetary traditions, institutional loyalties, and personal relationships. PPBS died because of inadequate support and leadership with meager resources invested in its behalf. At its peak, the BOB [Bureau of the Budget] staff charged with monitoring and promoting the government-wide effort numbered fewer than a dozen professionals. PPBS died because good analysts and data were in short supply, and it takes a great deal of time to make up the deficit. The causes of PPBS's demise are as varied and numerous as the perspectives of those who have studied the debacle.[46]

Another problem was that PPBS was originally conceived almost exclusively from an executive perspective, as if Congress played no part in reviewing the budget. PPBS was designed in such a way as to ensure that the Bureau of the Budget would bypass Congress, but Congress continued to evaluate government appropriations in its accustomed ways.

PPBS is not dead in state and local governments because a few school districts, colleges and universities, city, county, and special districts, and state governments have undergone substantial budgetary renovation. California's Stull Bill, for instance, has compelled school districts to require teachers to outline objectives for their courses.[47] Some local governments have found that PPBS provides an opportunity to introduce performance standards into their budgetary process. Thomas Dye observes:

> A common example of performance budgeting is found in school systems, where pupils are designated as a basic unit of service and standards for numbers of teachers, supplies and materials, auxiliary personnel, building floor space, and many other cost items are calculated on the basis of number of pupils to be served. Thus, standards may allocate teachers on the basis of 1 to 25 students, or

a full-time principal for every 250 students, or a psychologist for every 1,000 students, or twenty dollars worth of supplies for every student, and so on. These formulas are used to determine the allocation of resources at budget time. One political consequence of the use of formulas in performance budgeting is the centralization of budgetary decision-making. Departments are merely asked to provide the number of pupils or patients or recipients or other units of service they expect to serve in the coming fiscal year. A central staff of budget analysts then determines allocations through the application of formulas to the service estimates provided by the departments.[48]

Because of their smaller size the use of PPBS in local governments may be a bit easier to implement. But even the formulas mentioned by Dye can remain inflexible. Also many teachers do not like central staff analysts making policy decisions that will affect their classroom situations, preferring less bureaucratic procedures that do not include formulas. PPBS remains difficult to implement at any level of government without specialized and experienced budgetary personnel.

Under line-item or cash-based accounting, no expenditures are recorded in the accounts until the money is actually paid out or received. Accrual accounting, a method of handling the timing of expenditures within the budget, permits government agencies to spend money, or to commit money to be spent, before it is received from the taxpayers. Expenditures are recorded immediately, not delayed until payments are made to those supplying goods and services. A task force of the first Hoover Commission (1949) recommended that the government adopt the accrual system, observing, "If several months' supply of coal is purchased and received during one fiscal year, but will not completely be consumed until the next fiscal year, it would be improper to charge all of the cost of the coal as an expense of the year in which it is purchased and received."[49] This method of accounting is significant, then, because it allows money appropriated for one year not to be really spent until two or three years later or to be committed before it was received.

In 1956 Congress changed the Budget and Accounting Act of 1950 to permit department heads to maintain their accounts on an accrual basis. By 1969 departments had begun to develop what is known as a "unified budget" distinguishing between new and existing authorizations of planned expenditures. The unified budget also contains a report that suggests how deficits or surplus funds are to be financed, which helps Congress to trade the flow of new monies and study the impact of federal debt policy on the

Accrual Accounting

levels of economic activity. One of the most important results of the unified budget is that it officially shifted the government to the accrual method of accounting.

The two major means of checking on the accuracy and honesty of those making and implementing budgets are auditing and the General Accounting Office.

Auditing. Auditing means reviewing proposed or past expenditures to determine their desirability and legality. Usually a preaudit is conducted in the executive branch to determine the control over the use of funds by subordinates. The postaudit takes place after payment. Auditors can be either elected and independent from both the legislature and executive or be located within the executive branch or GAO.[50] The postaudit is used because the budget is by no means a revealing document. Disguised or hidden funds, capital commitments, or intergovernmetal transfer of funds all create problems for an auditor. An item may be mentioned but without indicating details of how monies will be appropriated; budget headings may fail to indicate whether expenditures are for new or continuing activities. Complicated pension plans and social welfare reimbursement formulae are fixed expenses and not subject to budget controls. Moreover, it is difficult to identify exactly who makes up the budget because auditors or outsiders do not always know who makes the estimates or how they are determined.

Major political budget fights rarely occur on the floor of the legislature. Instead, they are fought out in the committee and subcommittee hearing rooms. One congressman has commented:

> . . . No human being regardless of his position and . . . capacity could possibly be completely familiar with all the items of appropriations contained in this defense bill. . . . There is a saying around the Pentagon that . . . there is only one person in the United States who can force a decision, and that is the Government Printer (when the budget must go to the press.)[51]

The lack of comprehensive information and the brevity of time promotes incremental budget decisions.

General Accounting Office. In addition to forming the Bureau of the Budget (now reorganized into the Office of Management and Budget), the Budget and Accounting Act of 1921 also created the General Accounting Office (GAO). The comptroller general, who is appointed by the president for a fifteen-year term with Senate approval, heads the GAO. The GAO can perform both preaudits and postaudits, as well as "prescribe the forms, systems and procedure for administrative appropriation and fund accounting in the several departments and establishments, and for the administrative examination of fiscal officers' accounts and claims against the United States."[52]

Thus, control of the audits and auditing systems is the responsibility of the GAO. Many attempts have been made to remove the control of accounting from the GAO and to transfer it to other departments such as the Treasury. One comptroller general stated, however, that "the General Accounting Office is an agency of the Congress."[53] Congress finds the GAO's role crucial to its control of appropriations and expenditures in the executive branch and in areas such as campaign spending.

The GAO has an Office of Federal Elections which prepares reports on campaign contributions that must be reported. In a 1972 four-volume report of nearly two thousand pages, GAO auditors made their first annual accounting of donations and spending on behalf of national political candidates as required by the 1971 Federal Election Campaign Act. This report helped the Watergate committee in discovering illegal campaign contributions, particularly from major corporations, to the 1972 Nixon campaign.

The GAO conducts most of its audits at agency locations and has attempted to provide program evaluations or some review of federal programs in its auditing reports.[54] For example, GAO audit findings that some defense contractors were charging unnecessarily high prices for defense materials were a major reason for Congress's passage of the 1962 Truth-in-Negotiations Act (Public Law 87–653), which requires suppliers to submit cost and pricing data with their estimates, as well as certification that the information given is accurate, complete, and current.[55] This is not to say that the GAO is always correct in its findings or recommendations. Its ability to perform is inhibited by budget restrictions as well as by congressional and executive limitations on its legal authority. Congress and agencies can determine the appropriateness of policy formulation and execution except where the GAO determines legal matters pertaining to government contracts.

Under the Budget and Accounting Act of 1950,[56] the GAO in 1968 was able to issue a statement of accounting principles and to review agency systems for conformance but was able to approve only half the accounting systems used. Only one of the eighteen agencies within the Defense Department, where PPBS was first introduced, has been approved. Congress next approved a bill that would prevent agencies from initiating PPBS until they had obtained the GAO's approval of their use of accrual accounting systems and had made comprehensive audits.[57] The delays were the result of complexities in the development of the cost data in such a large government, as well as of the resistance to both PPBS and accrual accounting systems.

REVENUE SHARING

As the 1970s began, it rapidly became clear that state and local levels of government had insufficient economic resources to meet demands for increased governmental services. Under the power of Congress to "tax and spend for the general welfare," federal agencies can provide grants-in-aid to state and local governments. Indeed, more than one-sixth of all state and community revenues come from federal grants and matching funds whose requirements for minimum standards and guidelines involve federal intervention in policy making. The federal government can approve or deny grants, set its own priorities, determine its own funding methods, set its own eligibility procedures, and create any number of separate programs. State and local officials cannot participate effectively in planning or setting their own priorities.

As a result of general dissatisfaction with federal programs and their "strings-attached" provisions, in 1972 Congress, with the strong recommendation of the Nixon administration, instituted the idea of revenue sharing—distributing federal tax revenues to state and local governments with few or no strings attached. Revenue sharing has been debated for years in Congress since it was first proposed by Walter Heller in the 1950s.[58] Throughout the struggle, proponents centered among state and local governments that would benefit from a new windfall. Opponents included congressmen who did not like to see the federal government becoming a tax collector for all levels of government. The leader of the opposition in the House, Representative Wilbur Mills of Arkansas, then chairman of the House Ways and Means Committee, argued that revenue sharing would not place federal funds where they are most needed, would cause inflation and require higher federal taxes to pay for unrestrained local and state expenditures, and would create a dependency relationship of subnational governments to the federal government, which would be difficult to stop.[59]

Nevertheless, Congress instituted revenue sharing in 1972 by incorporating it into the State and Local Fiscal Assistance Act. Any revenue sharing plan must have four basic elements: (1) a formula for determining the total amount of federal revenues to be distributed to subnational governments per year; (2) a formula determining allocation of revenues distributed according to need; (3) a formula specifying the percentage of funds that should go to local governments in each state and which levels of local government that should be included, and (4) a clarification of any restrictions on the spending of federal revenues by local governments.[60]

Under former President Nixon's proposal, revenue sharing would last five years, from 1 January 1972 to 31 December 1976, at which time Congress would consider a renewal. The first formula, or the total amount of funds for revenue sharing, was about 2 percent of all state and local government revenue. Under the provisions of the act, this would amount to more than $30 billion over five years. Next, the Nixon plan established a formula for state-by-state distribution of revenues. Funds would be distributed among states and communities according to size of population with an adjustment for "tax effort." That is, each state and community would receive a percentage of total monies equal to its proportion of total national population adjusted by the extent to which the state tapped its tax base. The effect of this formula is to reward poorer states that heavily tax their populations; it is also an incentive for higher tax rates. Furthermore, urbanized states would receive the most funds because they depend on "social service" funds from Washington to finance 75 percent of the cost of programs in juvenile services, mental retardation, and aid to the blind, deaf, aged, alcoholics, and drug addicts.

The formula specifying the percentage of funds to be distributed between states and communities resulted in the states getting one-third of the money and the nation's 37,800 counties, cities, towns, and townships getting two-thirds. The payments will come to all recipients directly from the U.S. Treasury.[61] Finally, the bills imposed only a few restrictions on the usage of monies. The act denied the use of these funds for education and welfare because of heavy federal assistance already being provided. Although the provisions for grants-in-aid for these social programs would not be reduced because of revenue sharing, some states have noticed gradual reductions in non-revenue-sharing funds from the federal government. Furthermore, state and community governments are not permitted to use revenue sharing to match, directly or indirectly, federal categorical aids, although this restriction may be very hard to enforce, particularly for projects spanning several fiscal years.

It is too soon to evaluate revenue sharing, but some initial observations can be made. This type of federal aid to state and local governments could be used as a weapon against subnational governments that fail to use the revenues wisely. Some of the possible pitfalls of revenue sharing include: the refusal of Congress to renew the program and to allocate money only with "strings attached"; an attempt by recipients to use revenue sharing to match federal categorical aid funds, which was not Congress's intent; pressure from citizens to lower taxes using revenue sharing funds, which would be counterproductive because the more taxes paid, the greater the federal revenues returned; and in some communities, the hiring of new employees or initiation of long-term programs that would result in serious budget deficiencies should revenue sharing be terminated.

This chapter has attempted to present an overview of the field of public finance and to show that, at any level of government, the budgetary process is both complex and incremental. It is complex because of the competition for limited public activity of interest groups, detailed procedures, the introduction of new methods like PPBS, the political, social, and economic repercussions of budgetary decisions, lack of precise standards for allocating resources, the length of time involved in preparation and approval, and a variety of other fluid factors. Budgeting is incremental because it is based on last year's budget, with particular attention given to only a narrow range of increases or decreases. Those who work with budgets are concerned with a relatively small increment to an already existing base. Their attention is concentrated on a relatively small number of items over which the finance battle is fought.

Nevertheless, budgets must be prepared and finances managed or government machinery will grind to a halt. There is nothing automatic about managing the public's revenues. A great many decisions and judgments must constantly be made, often with great difficulty, especially in view of increasing concern over the priorities of government spending because of inflation, poverty, pollution, and other domestic problems. There has also been long-standing debate among citizens groups over the expenditures of the military establishment and their impact on domestic priorities. It is in the acquisition and expenditure of the public's money that the essence of government stands revealed.

CASE STUDY 1

Weapons Costs: Congress Shares Responsibility for Cost Overruns

As the result of a change in attitude toward military preparedness following Pearl Harbor and World War II, the Department of Defense, with more than 160,000 employees in 1972, has become one of the largest administrative organizations in the U.S. government; and defense, one of the major continuing factors in the current high cost of government. Congress shares the responsibility for approving or disapproving the Defense Department's new programs and proposed new weapons systems; but decisions relating to these matters, whose costs frequently run into the billions of dollars, are both politically sensitive and technically complex.

"Congress Shares Responsibility for Cost Overruns," from *The Power of the Pentagon*, Congressional Quarterly, Washington, D.C., 1972, pp. 84–86.

Whether the committee involved is a major one, such as the Senate Armed Services or House Appropriations committees, or one of any number of subcommittees, public hearings are crucial to the budgetary process insofar as they serve to educate both the congressmen on the committee and the public at large in the intricacies of financial policy determination in government. The appearance before the committee of representatives of numerous interest groups, various government agencies, and the public provides a valuable opportunity for the exercise of budgetary strategy, defense of the continuing existence of already established programs, justification of cost overruns, other significant exchange of information, and, above all, for the exercise of administrative accountability. As you read this selection, ask yourself the following questions:

1. *What problems does Congress encounter in evaluating defense programs?*
2. *What considerations confront defense contractors in having their proposals approved by Congress?*
3. *In what ways do defense contractors generate higher costs of weapons systems?*
4. *Judging from the testimony in this case, in what ways is the weapon systems acquisition process inadequate?*
5. *What techniques of budgeting, if any, might help congressmen evaluate defense proposals?*

In five days of poorly attended hearings late in 1971, the Senate Armed Services Committee tried to find answers to the nagging questions of increasing weapons costs.

The unusual hearings, held in the final crush of legislative activity before the 92nd Congress adjourned at the end of its first session, were aimed at educating the committee and the public to the problems involved in the weapons acquisition process.

Sen. John C. Stennis (D Miss.), chairman of the committee, said the hearings were to explore the methods used in contracting for research and development of weapons and the methods employed in purchasing a tested weapon system.

The testimony showed that Congress was as much to blame for rising cost of weapons as either the Defense Department or defense contractors.

"The budgetary process has become a ritual with no content," said Dr. William B. McLean, technical director of the Naval Underseas Center, San Diego, Calif. "It occupies more than 50 percent of the productive time of our best technical people at the laboratory and the full time of large numbers of technical people in Washington."

Between McLean and an earlier witness—Gilbert W. Fitzhugh, chairman of the President's Blue Ribbon Defense Panel—the testimony showed that Congress:

> Caused costly delays in programs because the House and Senate were so slow in providing funds—often failing to appropriate defense money until the fiscal year was half over.

> Required people responsible for developing the weapons to spend too much time on Capitol Hill and not enough time in their workshops.

> Interfered too much during the research and design phase, then failed to challenge defense witnesses with sufficient vigor once they said a weapon was ready for production.

"One feels that life would be much more enjoyable if the amount of funding to be spent were known at the beginning of the year, whatever its amount," McLean told the committee.

Stennis regularly complimented his witnesses for their frankness. "It certainly is refreshing to hear your views," Stennis told two Rand Corporation witnesses. "Most of the witnesses we get in here are asking for money."

Pentagon problems. While many witnesses implicated Congress as partially responsible for rising costs of weapons systems, they also indicated that the Pentagon:

> Had ignored the need to develop a weapon prototype (working model) before writing specifications on weapons which might be technically impossible.

> Allowed the services—Army, Navy and Air Force—to demand a weapon system that ignored cost implications and existing technology.

> Rewarded complex and expensive systems and penalized designers and manufacturers for developing simpler and less expensive weapons.

Dr. Pierre M. Sprey, a former Pentagon weapons designer, said that under the existing system at the Defense Department, "interesting techno-logical possibilities become user requirements without any need for the user to concern himself with future cost."

Defense contractors. The leading critic of the manufacturers who make weapons systems was Dr. F. M. Scherer, a University of Michigan economics professor and author. "The weapons industry is in its worst disarray since the late 1940s,'' he said. According to Scherer and other witnesses, defense contractors:

> Have devoted their primary resources to winning defense contracts, not to producing weapons.
>
> Were blindly optimistic on cost estimates when bidding for weapons contracts when they knew full well their estimates would be exceeded.

"One simply cannot expect weapons suppliers to devote their top resources to anything but winning new orders when their very survival depends upon such orders,'' Scherer told the committee.

Excerpts from the five days of hearings:

Testimony Dec. 3

John C. Stennis, chairman of the Senate Armed Services Committee, explained why he was holding the hearings: "If the weapons we develop are so costly that we cannot afford enough of them and if they are so technically complex that they are unreliable and difficult to maintain, we have done the nation a disservice by developing and procuring them. . . . I am a lawyer by training and, quite frankly, the discussion of weapon systems in the Congress has seemed to me to be sadly deficient in its understanding of process and procedures. . . .

"I hope that in these brief initial hearings we will be able to begin to understand some of the underlying problems of the weapon systems acquisition process: how the system functions, why individuals and institutions within it behave as they do, what their real incentives are, what sort of reforms in the process will give us a better product.

"We're getting into something I've been wanting to get into for a long time . . . down to the fundamentals, get the problem described . . . get it on the record for staff analysis as well as the press."

Gilbert W. Fitzhugh, chairman of the President's Blue Ribbon Defense Panel (1969–1970) and chairman of the board of directors, Metropolitan Life Insurance Company: "One of the most urgent needs for improvement for the entire weapons systems acquisition process is more effective operational test and evaluation. . . . Operational testing is done to determine, to the extent possible, whether such systems and materiel can meet operational requirements. It must provide advance knowledge as to what their capabilities and limitations will be when they are subjected to the stresses of the environment for which they were designed (usually combat). . . . Funding throughout the Department of Defense has been and continues to be inadequate to support most necessary operational testing. . . . In fact, there is no agency that can even identify the funds that are being spent on operational testing.

"Evaluation type functions, including test and evaluation, should not be within the control of either those charged with the responsibility for acquiring weapons systems nor of those charged with the responsibility for using the weapon system as an end product. Dominance of the evaluation function by either the producer or the user has a strong tendency to weight any evaluation."

The services spend so much time "building up a file to defend the program (a weapon system) that they don't build the plane." Too many people in Congress are looking into the Pentagon's business. Committee inquiry, which is valuable in itself, should be limited to perhaps two or four committees. A completely new set of procurement regulations is needed. "They're so bogged down in paper work over there (Pentagon) they can't do the job they're supposed to do." Merely improving procedures has not and will not work as a solution to the problem. Rather, a systematic change in the acquisition process is called for.

Dr. John S. Foster Jr., director of defense research and engineering for the Department of Defense: "From the outset, this Administration has been concerned about cost growth of weapon systems, the lack of authority and stature of program managers and shortfalls in performance or delay in some important systems. Since taking office, Secretaries Laird and Packard have placed heavy emphasis on improving procedures in these areas."

The "most important single element for ensuring the proper execution of programs is the selection of qualified program managers." Six months ago, only 12 flag officers were assigned as program managers; now, 20 of the 82 managers are of flag rank. A school—the Defense Systems Management School, Fort Belvoir, Virginia—is handling an increasing number of officers to participate in the weapons acquisition process.

The new position of Deputy Director of Defense (test and evaluation) was created to provide "over-all supervision of test and evaluation that heretofore had been lacking.

"The services have changed their organizations to ensure that a command independent of the developer participates in all operational testing and evaluation. This command renders a separate report, through a strong service focal point, to the chief of the service to assist him with his later decisions."

Dec. 6

J. A. Stockfish, member of the Rand Corporation, specializing in weapons acquisition: "Since it is the military user who must assume the ultimate responsibility for commanding military operations in the field and in conducting war, it is their preferences that should dominate the decision-making process. . . . Since World War II the technicians have been making the decisions. . . . High technical precision has been equated with good weaponry. This is not true."

Stuart Symington (D Mo.), a member of the committee: "Why is the United States not getting more for the billions it spent on research and development?"

Stockfish: "A large part is all too frequently caused by overspecifying the system. The user is often as much at fault because he also insists on these specifications."

The [Senate Armed Services] committee should give the military an incentive to do more testing by placing greater budget restraints on the Pentagon. "Whenever you encounter assertions that this is the most cost-effective system . . . find out whether the model or theory was based on sufficient or valid testing. . . . Has the model been validated by some independent testing?

"I would not be too disturbed at a three-fold cost overrun if the system was good," but all too frequently the system overruns do not result in solid weapon systems.

Dr. F. M. Scherer, professor of economics at the University of Michigan, defense consultant and author: The insecurity of defense contractors has been "a major source of incentive breakdowns and disfunctional behavior. Today, with the weapons industry in its worst state of disarray since the late 1940s, the problem is even more critical. One simply cannot expect weapons suppliers to devote their top resources to anything but winning new orders when their very survival depends upon such orders. One cannot expect them to estimate costs and technical risks accurately when optimistic estimates enhance the prospect of capturing a new program assignment. One cannot expect them to refrain from hoarding personnel under whatever contractual blanket they can find when long-run organizational viability demands that they keep the team together. . . .

"Contractors must somehow be induced to maximize output given their limited resources, not to maximize the quantity of resources they can spread over a restricted array of programs.

"It must be made crystal clear through word and deed that organizations which consistently do a good job will be allowed to grow while those which repeatedly fail will find their support progressively withdrawn. This is admittedly a radical proposal. But I am convinced that unless we move in that direction, channeling the insecurity of national security contractors in constructive rather than counter-productive directions, we are not likely to eliminate the intolerable inefficiency and waste presently pervading the weapons acquisition process."

Dec. 7

Robert Perry, director of system acquisition studies and specialist on European aircraft acquisition, Rand Corporation: "An analysis of programs of the 1950s and the 1960s has disclosed that in terms of schedules, cost and weapons performance which vary from those specified at program inception, the prediction and control of system acquisition programs in general did not significantly improve. . . . In the 1960s typical major programs in all three services continued to exhibit an average cost growth of about 40 percent (after corrections for inflation and changes in quantity of items purchased); schedule slippages of about 15 percent; and weapon system performance that characteristically deviated by 30 or 40 percent from original specifications.

"It appears that changes to system specifications imposed after programs had begun accounted for about half of cost growth. . . . Engineering difficulties encountered in the course of development accounted for at least an additional one third; and native (inherent) imprecision of cost estimating processes was responsible for the residual 15 to 20 percent."

"Separate the development phase of weapon system acquisition from the subsequent production phase, both sequentially and contractually . . . conduct the initial research and development for a new weapon in a highly austere manner, concentrating first on demonstrating system performance and deferring more expensive tasks of detailed production design and reliability demonstration until both the technical and the requirement uncertainties have been very substantially reduced."

Arthur J. Alexander, specialist on Soviet aircraft acquisition, Rand Corporation, described the Soviet Union's process: "The competitive system of design and the importance attached to production have promoted a philosophy based on simplicity, commonality and inheritance. Simplicity implies an unadorned product which performs only what is required; commonality means the use of standardized parts and assemblies as well as the sharing of design features among different aircraft; design inheritance is an intergenerational concept which favors modification rather than introduction of entirely new products.

"Ironically, Soviet aircraft production is similar to the way the American industry operated before the government began to participate heavily in project management. . . ."

Dec. 8

Dr. William B. McLean, technical director of the Naval Undersea Center (projects designer), San Diego, Calif: "Based on some 30 years experience with military procurement, I believe the weapon systems acquisition process is now dangerously inadequate because . . . the need for development prototypes to demonstrate technical feasibility before the writing of military requirements has been ignored; the total acquisition process rewards the design of complex and expensive systems and penalizes work of simpler and, therefore, less expensive ones; the budgetary process has become a ritual with no content, which is occupying more than 50 percent of the productive time of our best technical people at the laboratory level and the full time of large numbers of technical people in Washington.''

The development and testing of prototype weapons prior to procurement and prior to the writing of detailed specifications for performance is essential to lowering the cost of weapons development. ''Requirements (for what a weapon should be able to do) written before the demonstration of a developmental prototype are worse than useless, because they have the effect of interfering with and even excluding technically possible means of approach.''

Dr. Pierre M. Sprey, systems manager of Enviro Control Inc. (water pollution devices); former systems analyst at the Pentagon, developing paper studies of light-weight fighters; consultant to Dr. Wayne Smith of Henry Kissinger's White House foreign policy staff: ''The weapons cost explosion has reached the stage where national defense is being severely impaired. Furthermore, I believe that the issues involved are so pervasive and fundamental that we cannot continue to treat this problem on a technical case-by-case basis; instead the issue must be raised to the level of national policy.''

The military is requesting such complex weaponry that the development stages are taking years longer, the final product is produced in smaller numbers to cover cost overruns, the weapon produced is more likely to suffer mechanical breakdown than more austere versions of the same weapon. The military would get more weapons, better service at less money if the services were forced to write specifications which took into account existing technology and severe cost restraints.

Procurement Policy. In a related inquiry, the Subcommittee on Priorities and Economy in Government of the Joint Economic Committee held one day of hearings April 28, 1971, on defense contract procurement policies.

Vice Admiral H. G. Rickover, director, division of Navy reactors, Atomic Energy Commission; and deputy commander for nuclear propulsion of the Naval ships system command: ''Today, the businessman who demonstrates acuity in business acquisitions, cash flow and financial manipulation gets more recognition in the business world than his counterpart who spends his time trying to manufacture high quality products efficiently. Consequently, many large companies today are virtually unmanaged while their officers are busy acquiring new businesses, lobbying for more favorable laws and regulations or devising new ways to make their actual profits look higher or lower depending on whether they are talking to stockholders, to the customer or to the Internal Revenue Service.

"Large defense contractors can let costs come out where they will and count on getting relief from the Defense Department through changes and claims, relaxation of procurement regulations and laws, government loans, follow-on sole source contracts or other escape mechanisms. Wasteful subcontracting practices, inadequate controls, shop loafing, and production errors mean little to these contractors since they will make their money whether their product is good or bad, whether the price is fair or higher than it should be, whether delivery is on time or late.

"The Atomic Energy Commission and the General Services Administration report that the computer industry as a whole refuses to provide the cost and pricing data required by the law, even though the government buys about $3-billion worth of computer equipment each year. I am told the same is true

---

Combat Readiness

The General Accounting Office (GAO) May 8, 1972, issued a report on the readiness capabilities of the Strategic Army Forces—general purpose forces relied upon for military actions short of nuclear war.

"It would be difficult for STRAF (Strategic Army Forces) units to deploy quickly at full strength because many units are not combat ready," the GAO report stated. More than one-third of the essential equipment for combat and combat-support operations was not functional.

The GAO report also found that:

"About 83 percent of the M-60 tanks available to units of two divisions had deficiencies which seriously impaired their ability to perform effectively."

Fifty-five percent of the tracked vehicles inspected were unable to perform their primary mission.

In three of the divisions studied no stock was available for about 25 percent of the repair parts authorized for stockage.

"No follow up actions were being taken on unfilled requisitions."

The GAO report concluded: "The high turnover of personnel, lack of qualified personnel and funding restrictions which were beyond the direct control of the divisions, prevented them from achieving and maintaining a high state of readiness. The two divisions were being manned almost entirely with Vietnam returnees who had only a few months of service remaining. . . ."

The only portion of the GAO report which was released to the public was a four-page summary of their classified report.

in the tire, ball bearing and communications industries. I am plagued by this problem in my work.

"This disregard for the law exists because the Defense Department does not enforce the Act. The Defense Department has been unwilling to require compliance from large defense contractors. Computer manufacturers, steel manufacturers, nickel producers, forging suppliers, divisions of some of the nation's largest defense contractors—whole segments of the defense industry—refuse to comply with the Truth-in-Negotiations Act."

CASE STUDY 2

High Finance or the Point of Vanishing Interest
C. NORTHCOTE PARKINSON

Parkinson's Law, which asserts that work expands to fill the time available for its completion, has application to many aspects of administration and not least to the unfolding of committee hearings. The complexities of budget making can cause an unprepared congressman or any other inept legislator to become dependent upon staff for answers (and sometimes for questions as well), which clearly defeats the purpose of administrative accountability. Lack of a fundamental working knowledge of the subjects on the agenda prevents the asking of the right questions or an intelligent examination of viable alternatives. When "groupthink" sets in, the questioning and examination of budgetary items is often reduced to nothing more than a discussion of thousand-dollar rather than million-dollar items. As you read this selection, ask yourself the following questions:

1. *In what way does this example demonstrate Parkinson's Law?*
2. *Can Parkinson's Law be applied to defense spending?*

People who understand high finance are of two kinds: those who have vast fortunes of their own and those who have nothing at all. To the actual millionaire a million dollars is something real and comprehensible. To the applied mathematician and the lecturer in economics (assuming both to be practically starving) a million dollars is at least as real as a thousand, they having never possessed either sum. But the world is full of people who fall between these two categories, knowing nothing of millions but well accustomed to think in thousands, and it is of these that finance committees are mostly comprised. The result is a phenomenon that has often been observed but never yet investigated. It might be termed the Law of Triviality. Briefly stated, it means that the time spent on any item of the agenda will be in inverse proportion to the sum involved.

On second thoughts, the statement that this law has never been investigated is not entirely accurate. Some work has actually been done in this field, but the investigators pursued a line of inquiry that led them nowhere. They assumed that the greatest significance should attach to the order in which items of the agenda are taken. They assumed, further, that most of the available time will be spent on items one to seven and that the later items will be allowed automatically to pass. The result is well known. The derision with which Dr. Guggenheim's lecture was received at the Muttworth Conference may have been thought excessive at the time, but all further discussions on this topic have tended to show that his critics were right. Years had been wasted in a research of which the basic assumptions were wrong. We realize now that position on the agenda is a minor consideration, so far, at least, as this problem is concerned. We consider also that Dr. Guggenheim was lucky to escape as he did, in his underwear. Had he dared to put his lame conclusions before the later conference in September, he would have faced something more than derision. The view would have been taken that he was deliberately wasting time.

If we are to make further progress in this investigation we must ignore all that has so far been done. We must start at the beginning and understand fully the way in which a finance committee actually works. For the sake of the general reader this can be put in dramatic form thus:

Chairman We come now to Item Nine. Our Treasurer, Mr. McPhail, will report.

Mr. McPhail The estimate for the Atomic Reactor is before you, sir, set forth in Appendix H of the subcommittee's report. You will see that the general design and layout has been approved by Professor McFission. The total cost will amount to $10,000,000. The contractors, Messrs. McNab and McHash consider that the work should be complete by April, 1959. Mr. McFee, the consulting engineer, warns us that we should not count on completion before October, at the earliest. In this view he is supported by Dr. McHeap, the well-known geophysicist, who refers to the probable need for piling at the lower end of the site. The plan of the main building is before you—see Appendix IX—and the blueprint is laid on the table. I shall be glad to give any further information that members of this committee may require.

Chairman   Thank you, Mr. McPhail, for your very lucid explanation of the plan as proposed. I will now invite the members present to give us their views.

It is necessary to pause at this point and consider what views the members are likely to have. Let us suppose that they number eleven, including the Chairman but excluding the Secretary. Of these eleven members, four—including the Chairman—do not know what a reactor is. Of the remainder, three do not know what it is for. Of those who know its purpose, only two have the least idea of what it should cost. One of these is Mr. Isaacson, the other is Mr. Brickworth. Either is in a position to say something. We may suppose that Mr. Isaacson is the first to speak.

Mr. Isaacson   Well, Mr. Chairman, I could wish that I felt more confidence in our contractors and consultant. Had we gone to Professor Levi in the first instance, and had the contract been given to Messrs. David and Goliath, I should have been happier about the whole scheme. Mr. Lyon-Daniels would not have wasted our time with wild guesses about the possible delay in completion, and Dr. Moses Bullrush would have told us definitely whether piling would be wanted or not.

Chairman   I am sure we all appreciate Mr. Isaacson's anxiety to complete this work in the best possible way. I feel, however, that it is rather late in the day to call in new technical advisers. I admit that the main contract has still to be signed, but we have already spent very large sums. If we reject the advice for which we have paid, we shall have to pay as much again. (*Other members murmur agreement.*)

Mr. Isaacson   I should like my observation to be minuted.

Chairman   Certainly. Perhaps Mr. Brickworth also has something to say on this matter?

Now Mr. Brickworth is almost the only man there who knows what he is talking about. There is a great deal he could say. He distrusts that round figure of $10,000,000. Why should it come out to exactly that? Why need they demolish the old building to make room for the new approach? Why is so large a sum set aside for "contingencies"? And who is McHeap, anyway? Is he the man who was sued last year by the Trickle and Driedup Oil Corporation? But Brickworth does not know where to begin. The other members could not read the blueprint if he referred to it. He would have to begin by explaining what a reactor is and no one there would admit that he did not already know. Better to say nothing.

Mr. Brickworth   I have no comment to make.

Chairman   Does any other member wish to speak? Very well. I may take it then that the plans and estimates are approved? Thank you. May I now sign the main contract on your behalf? (*Murmur of agreement*) Thank you. We can now move on to Item Ten.''

Allowing a few seconds for rustling papers and unrolling diagrams, the time spent on Item Nine will have been just two minutes and a half. The meeting is going well. But some members feel uneasy about Item Nine. They wonder inwardly whether they have really been pulling their weight. It is too late to query that reactor scheme, but they would like to demonstrate, before the meeting ends, that they are alive to all that is going on.

Chairman   Item Ten. Bicycle shed for the use of the clerical staff. An estimate has been received from Messrs. Bodger and Woodworm, who undertake to complete the work for the sum of $2350. Plans and specifications are before you, gentlemen.

Mr. Softleigh   Surely, Mr. Chairman, this sum is excessive. I note that the roof is to be of aluminum. Would not asbestos be cheaper?

Mr. Holdfast   I agree with Mr. Softleigh about the cost, but the roof should, in my opinion, be of galvanized iron. I incline to think that the shed could be built for $2000, or even less.

Mr. Daring   I would go further, Mr. Chairman. I question whether this shed is really necessary. We do too much for our staff as it is. They are never satisfied, that is the trouble. They will be wanting garages next.

Mr. Holdfast   No, I can't support Mr. Daring on this occasion. I think that the shed is needed. It is a question of material and cost. . . .''

The debate is fairly launched. A sum of $2350 is well within everybody's comprehension. Everyone can visualize a bicycle shed. Discussion goes on, therefore, for forty-five minutes, with the possible result of saving some $300. Members at length sit back with a feeling of achievement.

Chairman   Item Eleven. Refreshments supplied at meetings of the Joint Welfare Committee. Monthly, $4.75.

Mr. Softleigh   What type of refreshment is supplied on these occasions?

Chairman   Coffee, I understand.

Mr. Holdfast   And this means an annual charge of—let me see—$57?

Chairman   That is so.

Mr. Daring   Well, really, Mr. Chairman. I question whether this is justified. How long do these meetings last?

Now begins an even more acrimonious debate. There may be members of the committee who might fail to distinguish between asbestos and galvanized iron, but every man there knows about coffee—what it is, how it should be made, where it should be bought—and whether indeed it should be bought at all. This item on the agenda will occupy the members for an hour and a quarter, and they will end by asking the Secretary to procure further information, leaving the matter to be decided at the next meeting.

It would be natural to ask at this point whether a still smaller sum—$20, perhaps, or $10—would occupy the Finance Committee for a proportionately longer time. On this point, it must be admitted, we are still ignorant. Our tentative conclusion must be that there is a point at which the whole tendency is reversed, the committee members concluding that the sum is beneath their notice. Research has still to establish the point at which this reversal occurs. The transition from the $50 debate (an hour and a quarter) to the $20 debate (two and a half minutes) is indeed an abrupt one. It would be the more interesting to establish the exact point at which it occurs. More than that, it would be of practical value. Supposing, for example, that the point of vanishing interest is represented by the sum of $35, the Treasurer with an item of $62.80 on the agenda might will decide to present it as two items, one of $30.00 and the other of $32.80, with an evident saving in time and effort.

Conclusions at this juncture can be merely tentative, but there is some reason to suppose that the point of vanishing interest represents the sum the individual committee member is willing to lose on a bet or subscribe to a charity. An inquiry on these lines conducted on race courses and in Methodist chapels, might go far toward solving the problem. Far greater difficulty may be encountered in attempting to discover the exact point at which the sum involved becomes too large to discuss at all. One thing apparent, however, is that the time spent on $10,000,000 and on $10 may well prove to be the same. The present estimated time of two and a half minutes is by no means exact, but there is clearly a space of time—something between two and four and a half minutes—which suffices equally for the largest and the smallest sums.

Much further investigation remains to be done, but the final results, when published, cannot fail to be of absorbing interest and of immediate value to mankind.

NOTES

1. "$375,000 to Study the Frisbee," *U.S. News & World Report,* 24 June 1974, p. 3.

2. This act also established the Council of Economic Advisers, whose job it is to advise the president, analyze the national economy, and recommend changes in the interests of maintaining economic stability. The council consists of three members appointed by the president and approved by the Senate.

3. The strength of the Federal Reserve System lies in its ability to control the government's desire to raise interest rates and tighten money, by: requiring increased money reserves by member banks, raising the discount or interest rate on acceptance of loans, expanding the margin requirements for buying stocks on credit in order to limit installment buying in the stock market, and its influence over the selling of securities and federal reserve notes.

4. U.S., Congress, Hearing before Joint Economic Committee, 1971 Midyear Review of the Economy, 92d Cong., 1st sess., 20 July 1971, pp. 72–88.

5. Gerald E. Caiden, *The Dynamics of Public Administration*, p. 178.

6. Aaron Wildavsky, *The Politics of the Budgetary Process*, p. 113.

7. The new tax came about by Senate Bill 325 which extended the sales tax to include gasoline. In return for this, the state allocates to the counties one-quarter of 1 percent of the total sales tax with the stipulation that the money be placed into a special mass transportation fund. Priority is given to improving existing transit systems and planning for future transit needs. The funds may also be used for road projects. While the constitutionality of this measure is questionable, the governor refused to veto it (*Los Angeles Times*, 17 August 1972).

8. *Facts and Figures on Government Finance* (New York: Tax Foundation, Inc., 1970), p. 64.

9. California has been trying to get a state lottery through the legislature that would bring in a possible $200 million yearly for the state treasury. Proponents argue that it would drive illegal bookmaking out of business. Opponents charge that it would open the door to illegal gambling, which preys on the weaknesses of the poor and uneducated (*Los Angeles Times*, 28 August 1973).

10. For details, see U.S., Congress, Senate, *Financial Management in the Federal Government*, 87th Cong., 1st sess., Senate Document no. 11 (Washington, D.C.: Government Printing Office, 1961), pp. 275–369.

11. Wildavsky, *Politics of the Budgetary Process*, p. 19.

12. Ibid., p. 118.

13. Reorganization Plan no. 2, 12 March 1970. President Nixon's 1972 budget, which went to Congress in January 1971, was the first product of the new OMB. Former Secretary of the Treasury George Shultz, later replaced by his former deputy, Caspar W. Wienberger, set out to use the OMB to break up carefully nurtured relationships among career budget professionals in the federal agencies and in the budget bureau. Also, the OMB helped to place more control of the budget process in the hands of presidential appointees. The frustrations of drafting the budget, according to former Commerce Secretary Maurice Stans, himself a former budget director (1958–61), involve "the uniform distribution of dissatisfaction." This proved especially true when the new budget called for revenue sharing, increases in social security benefits, welfare reform, and the formation of an all-volunteer army.

14. Otto A. Davis, M. A. H. Dempster, and Aaron Wildavsky, "A Theory of the Budgetary Process," *American Political Science Review* 60 (September 1966): 529–47.

15. Richard F. Fenno, Jr., *The Power of the Purse*, pp. 570–71.

16. Ibid.

17. Ibid.

18. "Proxmire Told General Spent $670,000 on Jet," *Los Angeles Times*, 24 August 1973.

19. *Budgeting for National Objectives* (New York: Committee for Economic Development, 1966), pp. 60–65.

20. Joseph P. Harris, *Congressional Control of Administration*, pp. 125–27.

21. Ibid.

22. The president can control the budget by apportioning the rate at which funds are expended and by requiring departments to withhold unneeded funds as reserves. The president assumed this power under the Budget and Accounting Act of 1921 and the General Appropriations Act of 1950.

23. One author notes that the Senate is today more liberal than the House in appropriating monies. In the area of natural resources, for example, the interests wanting increased appropriations are better represented in the Senate. Furthermore, the House, knowing that the Senate will increase revenues, lowers its amount for the purposes of bargaining, while the Senate, in turn, increases its amount in expectation of House action (see Lewis A. Froman, Jr., *Congressmen and Their Constituencies*, pp. 69–85).

24. "Nixon Vetoes Bill to Force Him to Spend Millions in Water Aid," *Los Angeles Times,* 6 April 1973.

25. "Nixon Presses for Control of Budget: Says Power over Spending Would Insure against Any Tax Increases," *Los Angeles Times,* 8 October 1972.

26. U.S., Congress, House, Public Law 93-344, *Budget and Impoundment Act,* H.R. 7130, 93d Cong., 2d sess., 12 July 1974.

27. See Charles L. Schultze et al., *Setting National Priorities,* pp. 449–68.

28. See Aaron Wildavsky, "The Annual Expenditure Increment" (Berkeley: University of California, 1973), U.S. Congress, House, Working Papers on House Committee Organization and Operation, 93d Cong., 1st sess. (Washington, D.C.: Government Printing Office, 1973). Incrementalism is becoming institutionalized in rich countries. Of four countries for which information is available, three—Great Britain, France, and Japan—not only practice incrementalism but have built it into their formal machineries for making the annual budget.

29. For an excellent description of state budgetary politics, see Thomas J. Anton, *The Politics of State Expenditures in Illinois,* p. 49.

30. Ibid., pp. 49–53.

31. David Novick, "Origin and History of Program Budgeting," in *Planning-Programming-Budgeting,* prepared for the Subcommittee on National Security and International Operations of Senate Committee on Governmental Operations, 90th Cong., 1st sess., 1967, pp. 28–31.

32. PPBS is most closely associated with Robert McNamara, secretary of defense from 1961 to 1968.

33. Cost-benefit analysis was first used by the Army Corps of Engineers in 1900 in various water resource projects.

34. David N. Hyman, *The Economics of Governmental Activity,* pp. 136–37.

35. Gene H. Gisher, "The Role of Cost-Utility Analysis in Program Budgeting," in *Program Budgeting,* ed. David Novick, pp. 61–78.

36. Robert J. Art, *The TFX Decision,* pp. 157–66.

37. See E. S. Quade, "Systems Analysis Techniques for Planning-Programming-Budgeting," in *Planning-Programming-Budgeting,* ed. Fremond J. Lyden and Ernest G. Miller, p. 295.

38. U.S., Congress, Senate, Committee on Governmental Operations, Subcommittee on National Security and International Operations, *Planning, Programming, Budgeting,* 90th Cong., 1st sess. (Washington, D.C.: Government Printing Office, 1967), pp. 1–3.

39. Aaron Wildavsky, "The Political Economy of Efficiency: Cost-Benefit Analysis, Systems Analysis, and Program Budgeting," *Public Administration Review* 29 (December 1966): 292–310.

40. Aaron Wildavsky, "Rescuing Policy Analysis from PPBS," *Public Administration Review* 29 (March–April 1969): 189–202.

41. Ibid., p. 191. Wildavsky argues that the problem with PPBS is that "no one knows how to do program budgeting"—that is, no one can apply it to his own particular case.

42. Office of Management and Budget Transmittal Memorandum, no. 38, 21 June 1971.

43. Ibid.

44. See Allen Schick, "A Death in the Bureaucracy," *Public Administration Review* 33 (March–April 1973): 146–56.

45. An excellent study of this can be found in Frederick C. Mosher and John E. Harr, *Programming System and Foreign Affairs Leadership.*

46. See Peter C. Sarant, *Is PPBS Dead?,* U.S. Civil Service Commission, December 1971, mimeographed. The problems of implementing PPBS as it pertains to federal recreation programs are reported in some detail in Jeanne Nienaber and Aaron Wildavsky, *The Budgeting and Evaluation of Federal Recreation* Programs; see also Adrian Gilbert, "PPBS and the Forest Service Pest Control Programs," paper read at Forest Pest Control Work Conference, 30 April 1969, in Washington, D.C., xeroxed. Gilbert is director of the Division of Programs and Special Projects, Forest Service, U.S. Department of Agriculture.

47. For an excellent description of the budgetary process in big city school systems, see H. Thomas James, *Determinants of Educational Expenditures in Large Cities of the United States.* On the costs and benefits study for public higher education in California, see W. Lee Hansen and Burton H. Weisbrod, *Benefits, Costs, and Finance of Public Higher Education.*

48. Thomas R. Dye, *Politics in States and Communities,* p. 543.

49. See Felix A. Nigro, ed., *Public Administration,* p. 368.

50. U.S., Congress, Senate, Committee on Governmental Operations, Subcommittee on National Policy Machinery, *The Budget and the Policy Process,* 87th Cong., 1st sess., vol. 107, 1961, p. 1061; see also Wildavsky, *Politics of the Budgetary Process,* p. 10, whose work attempts to show what really goes on behind the scenes.

51. See U.S., Congress, House, *Financial Management in the Federal Government,* 87th Cong., 1st sess., Document no. 11 (Washington, D.C.: Government Printing Office, 1961), pp. 275–89 for the text of this act.

52. Elmer B. Staats, "Protecting the Taxpayer's Dollar" (Address by the Comptroller General of the United States to the 80th Annual Meeting of the American Institute of Accountants, Portland, Oregon, 26 September 1967), p. 2.

53. The GAO also noted that wealthy contributors took advantage of an Internal Revenue Service ruling permitting them to escape federal gift taxes by dividing their donations into amounts of $3,000 or less and spreading them among several fund-raising committees. The GAO report listed in alphabetical order all contributors who had given $100 or more between 7 April and 31 December 1972 in gifts, ticket purchases, loans, and other transactions. Also listed were about 2,570 political committees that had registered with the GAO as raising money for the national candidates (*Los Angeles Times,* 24 August 1973).

54. Staats, "Protecting the Taxpayer's Dollar," p. 8.

55. Comptroller General of the United States, *Annual Report, 1967* (Washington, D.C.: Government Printing Office, 1967), pp. 106–108.

56. This act was broadened and renamed the Joint Financial Management Improvement Program in 1965. A steering committee consisting of representatives from GAO, OMB, and the Department of the Treasury helps in handling personnel matters, including recruitment and training.

57. U.S., Congress, House, H.R. 12998, 90th Cong., 1st sess., 1967.

58. For details, see Walter W. Heller and Ronald Ruggles, *Revenue Sharing and the City,* ed. Harvey S. Perloff and Richard P. Nathan (Baltimore: Johns Hopkins Press, 1968); also Henry S. Reuss, *Revenue Sharing.*

59. For some of the problems of implementation and fears about revenue sharing, see Charles J. Goetz, *What Is Revenue Sharing?;* also *U.S. News & World Report,* 8 February 1971, p. 40.

60. See Murray L. Weidenbaum and Robert L. Joss, "Alternative Approaches to Revenue Sharing," *National Tax Journal,* March 1970, p. 11.

61. Payments were made beginning October 1972, retroactive to January.

SELECTED BIBLIOGRAPHY

Anthony, Robert. "Closing the Loop between Planning and Performance." *Public Administration Review* 31 (1971): 388–89.

Anton, Thomas J. *The Politics of State Expenditures in Illinois.* Urbana: University of Illinois Press, 1966.

Art, Robert J. *The TFX Decision: McNamara and the Military.* Boston: Little, Brown & Co., 1968.

Black, Guy. "Externalities and Structure in PPB." *Public Administration Review* 31 (1971): 637–43.

Brundage, P. F. *The Bureau of the Budget.* New York: Praeger Publishers, 1970.

Caiden, Gerald E. *The Dynamics of Public Administration: Guidelines to Current Transformations in Theory and Practice.* New York: Holt, Rinehart & Winston, 1971.

Carlson, William A. "PPB Systems and Agricultural Programs." Paper read at PPBS Workshop for the Institute of Food and Agricultural Sciences, 7 July 1969, at the University of Florida, Gainesville, Fla. Xeroxed.

Chaikin, Harris. "Evaluation Research and the Planning-Programming-Budgeting System." In *Planning-Programming-Budgeting Systems and Social Welfare,* edited by Edward E. Schwartz, pp. 27–34. Chicago: University of Chicago, School of Social Science Administration, 1970.

Crecine, John P. *Governmental Problem-Solving: A Computer Simulation of Municipal Budgeting.* Chicago: Rand McNally & Co., 1969.

———. "A Simulation of Municipal Budgeting: The Impact of Problem Environment." In *Policy Analysis in Political Science,* edited by Ira Sharkansky, pp. 270–303. Chicago: Markham Publishing Co., 1970.

Davie, Bruce F., and Duncombe, Bruce F. *Modern Political Arithmetic: The Federal Budget and the Public Sector in National Economic Accounts.* New York: Holt, Rinehart & Winston, 1970.

Davis, James W., Jr., ed. *Politics, Programs and Budgets: A Reader in Government Budgeting.* Englewood Cliffs, N.J.: Prentice-Hall, 1969.

Davis, Otto A. "The Potential Application of the Planning-Programming-Budgeting System and Congressional Control of Federal Appropriations." In *Analysis and Evaluation of Public Expenditures: The PPB System,* prepared for the Subcommittee on Economy in Government of the Joint Economic Committee, 91st Cong., 1st sess., vol. 1, pp. 67–86. Washington, D.C.: Government Printing Office, 1972.

Davis, Otto A.; Dempster, M. A. H.; and Wildavsky, Aaron. "A Theory of the Budgetary Process." *American Political Science Review* 60 (1966): 529–47.

Dye, Thomas R. *Politics in States and Communities.* 2d ed. Englewood Cliffs, N.J.: Prentice-Hall, 1973.

Fagin, Henry. "The Relation of Planning to Programming and Budgeting in a Comprehensive State Administrative System." Paper read at Institute of Governmental Affairs Research Conference, 22 May 1969, at University of California, Davis, Calif. Xeroxed.

Fenno, Richard F., Jr. *The Power of the Purse: Appropriations Politics in Congress.* Boston: Little, Brown & Co., 1966.

Fisher, Gene H. "The Role of Cost Utility Analysis in Program Budgeting." In *Program Budgeting: Program Analysis and the Federal Budget,* edited by David Novick, pp. 61–78. Cambridge, Mass.: Harvard University Press, 1967.

Froman, Lewis A., Jr. *Congressmen and Their Constituencies.* Chicago: Rand McNally & Co., 1963.

Gettings, Robert M. "Mental Retardation and the Planning-Programming-Budgeting System." *Mental Retardation,* New York, December 1968. Xeroxed.

Gilbert, Adrian. "PPBS and the Forest Service Pest Control Programs." Paper read at Forest Pest Control Work Conference, 30 April 1969, in Washington, D.C. Xeroxed.

————. "Program Budgeting to Coordinate Resource Use." Paper read at Institute for Budgeting for State Natural Resource Programs, 22 May 1968, at University of Kentucky, Lexington, Ky. Xeroxed.

Goetz, Charles J. *What Is Revenue Sharing?* Washington, D.C.: Urban Institute, 1972.

Hansen, W. Lee, and Weisbrod, Burton H. *Benefits, Costs, and Finance of Public Education.* Chicago: Markham Publishing Co., 1969.

Harris, Joseph P. *Congressional Control of Administration.* New York: Doubleday & Co., 1964.

Haveman, Robert H., and Margolis, Julius, eds. *Public Expenditures and Policy Analysis.* Chicago: Markham Publishing Co., 1970.

Hinrichs, Harley H., and Taylor, Graeme M. *Program Budgeting and Benefit-Cost Analysis: Cases, Text and Readings.* Pacific Palisades, Calif.: Goodyear Publishing Co., 1969.

Hovey, Harold A. *The Planning-Programming-Budgeting Approach to Government Decision-Making.* New York: Praeger Publishers, 1968.

Hyman, David N. *The Economics of Governmental Activity.* New York: Holt, Rinehart & Winston, 1973.

Jacqmotte, J. P. "Tentative Comparative Study of RCB in France and PPBS in Belgium." *International Review of Administrative Sciences* 36 (1970): 47–55.

James, H. Thomas. *Determinants of Educational Expenditures in Large Cities in the United States.* Stanford, Calif.: Stanford University School of Education, 1966.

Kimmel, Lewis H. *Federal Budget and Fiscal Policy 1789–1958.* Washington, D.C.: Brookings Institution, 1959.

Lyden, Fremont J., and Miller, Ernest G., eds. *Planning-Programming-Budgeting: A Systems Approach to Management.* 2d ed. Chicago: Markham Publishing Co., 1968.

Manley, John F. *The Politics of Finance: The House Committee on Ways and Means.* Boston: Little, Brown & Co., 1970.

Meltsner, Arnold J. *The Politics of City Revenue.* Berkeley and Los Angeles: University of California Press, 1971.

Mosher, Frederick C., and Harr, John E. *Programming System and Foreign Affairs Leadership.* New York: Oxford University Press, 1970.

Mushkin, Slema J.; Hatry, Harry P.; Cotton, John F.; Richards, Robert T.; Surmeier, John J.; and Trinkl, Frank H. *Implementing PPB in State, City, and County.* Washington, D.C.: George Washington University, State-Local Finances Project, 1969.

Nienaber, Jeanne, and Wildavsky, Aaron. *The Budgeting and Evaluation of Federal Recreation Programs: or Money Doesn't Grow on Trees.* New York: Basic Books. 1973.

Nigro, Felix A. *Modern Public Administration.* 3d ed. New York: Harper & Row, 1973.

_____, ed. *Public Administration: Readings and Documents.* New York: Holt, Rinehart & Winston, 1951.

Novick, David. "Origin and History of Program Budgeting." In *Planning-Programming-Budgeting: Selected Comments,* prepared for the Subcommittee on National Security and International Operations of Senate Committee on Governmental Operations, 90th Cong., 1st sess., 1967.

_____, ed. *Program Budgeting: Program Analysis and the Federal Budget.* Cambridge, Mass.: Harvard University Press, 1967.

Padgett, E. R. "Programming-Planning-Budgeting: Some Reflections upon the American Experience with PPBS." *International Review of Administrative Sciences* 27 (1971): 353–62.

Pfiffner, John M., and Presthus, Robert. *Public Administration.* 5th ed. New York: Ronald Press Co., 1967.

Pierce, Lawrence C. *The Politics of Fiscal Policy Formation.* Pacific Palisades, Calif.: Goodyear Publishing Co., 1971.

Quade, E. S. "Systems Analysis Techniques for Planning-Programming-Budgeting." In *Planning-Programming-Budgeting: A Systems Approach to Management,* edited by Fremont J. Lyden and Ernest G. Miller, p. 295. Chicago: Markham Publishing Co., 1968.

Reagan, Michael D. *The New Federalism.* New York: Oxford University Press, 1972.

Rehfuss, John. *Public Administration as a Political Process.* New York: Charles Scribner's Sons, 1973.

Reuss, Henry S. *Revenue-Sharing: Crutch or Catalyst for State and Local Governments?* New York: Praeger Publishers, 1970.

Rourke, Francis E. *Bureaucratic Power in National Politics.* 2d ed. Boston: Little, Brown & Co., 1972.

Schick, Allen. "A Death in the Bureaucracy: The Demise of Federal PPB." *Public Administration Review* 33 (1973): 146–56.

Schultze, Charles L., Fried, Edward R., Rivlin, Alice M., and Teeters, Nancy H. *Setting National Priorities: The 1973 Budget.* Washington, D.C.: Brookings Institution, 1972.

Segsworth, R. V. "PPBS and Policy Analysis: The Canadian Experience." *International Review of Administrative Sciences* 38 (1972): 419–25.

U.S. Congress. Senate. Committee on Governmental Operations. Subcommittee on National Policy Machinery. *The Budget and the Policy Process,* 87th Cong., 1st sess., vol. 107, p. 1061, 1961.

_____. Senate. Committee on Governmental Operations. Subcommittee on National Security and International Operations. *Planning, Programming, Budgeting,* 90th Cong., 1st sess. Washington, D.C.: Government Printing Office, 1967.

_____. Senate. Joint Economic Committee. Subcommittee on Economy in Government. *The Analysis and Evaluation of Public Expenditures: The PPB System.* Washington, D.C.: Government Printing office, 1969.

Weidenbaum, Murray L., and Saloma, John S., III. *Congress and the Federal Budget.* Washington, D.C.: American Enterprise Institute for Public Policy Research, 1965.

Wildavsky, Aaron. "Does Planning Work?" Reprinted from *Public Interest,* no. 24 (1971), pp. 95–104.

_____. *The Politics of the Budgetary Process.* Boston: Little, Brown & Co., 1964.

Wildavsky, Aaron, and Hammon, Arthur. "Comprehensive versus Incremental Budgeting in the Department of Agriculture." *Administrative Science Quarterly* 10 (1965): 321–46.

PUBLIC PERSONNEL ADMINISTRATION

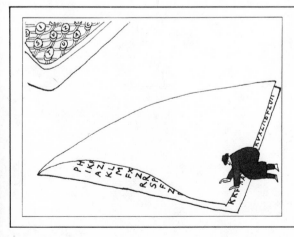

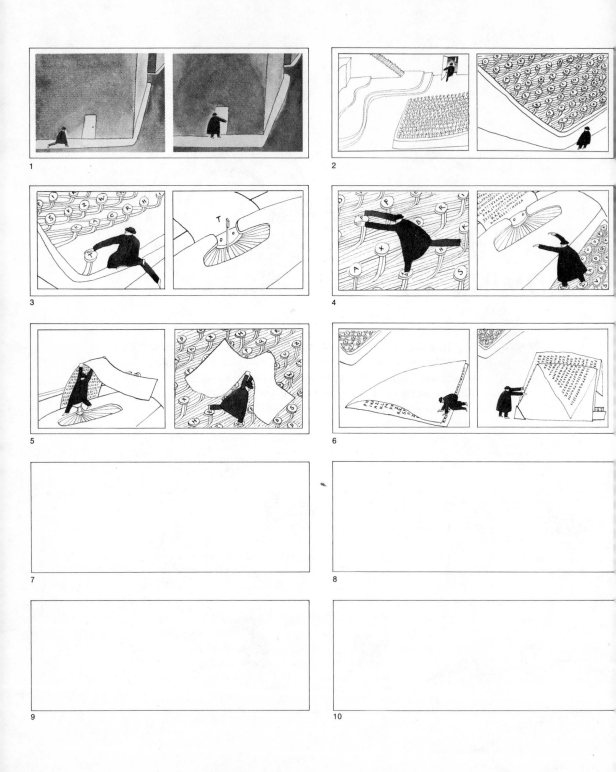

It was a strike.

It was illegal.

It had an immense impact on the nation—an impact equalled only by the enormity of the grievance which provoked it.

It's our guess that the postal service will never be the same again—and that goes for the federal services generally.

Union Postal Clerk
April 1970

6 Because it is vital to an organization's effectiveness and survival, personnel administration—the management of people in an organization—is one of the most crucial aspects of public administration. A highly complex process arising from regulations and procedures designed to ensure objective, professional handling of people, its functions include position classification, employee testing, evaluation procedures, in-service training, promotion practices, and disciplinary policies.

The character of personnel administration will often depend on the size of the organization. In a small organization a supervisor may have little or no personnel training but nevertheless be responsible for employee management. In large departments of government that have central or separate personnel units, the supervisor will be more impersonal and governed by more prescribed procedures.

Policy making in personnel matters is often complex and frustrating. What will be the effect on fellow employees if an employee is forced to retire early because he cannot be transferred to another job within the government, as a result is now subject to reduced retirement benefits, and is unemployable elsewhere because of age? What policies can be developed to avoid this type of event? How would you react if an employee in the Paris office of your department were offered a job in California and, having received a letter confirming the job, had moved to California only to find that the president of the organization had canceled the appointment, asserting that neither the department head nor anyone else had the authority to make this appointment without his approval. Perhaps the president has stated that "he is not the kind of person we want in this job." Such events pose major challenges to those managing personnel policy.

This chapter will examine the history, functions, and current problems of public personnel administration, a product of long evolution and now, with public employee unionization and cost of personnel, in one of its most critical periods. The three case studies at the end of the chapter deal with issues in recruitment ("A Supervisor for Unit II"), personnel evaluation ("Managerial Prerogative or Social Objective?"), and the public employee strike against the Post Office in 1970—all selected to illustrate some of the practical problems involved in personnel administration.

EVOLUTION OF PERSONNEL ADMINISTRATION

Competency and the Spoils System

A variety of authors have characterized the growth of personnel administration in terms of time periods or phases.[1] In the first period (1776–1829), job fitness or competency was the criterion for filling positions in government. This was followed by the spoils system (1829–83) and the civil service reform movement.

During the administrations of the first six presidents of the United States, primary emphasis was placed on job fitness in filling positions in the administrative branch of government. Competence was theoretically associated with merit, but in reality merit also included one's family background, social status, education, and loyalty to the administration currently in office. Indeed, a man's personal philosophy and who he knew in government may have been more important than his education or expertise. During this period, too, employees in top policy positions changed with newly elected presidents, while those below the top enjoyed longer periods of service.

With Andrew Jackson, the seventh president, came the motto "to the victor belong the spoils," which at this time were primarily government jobs. As the political party system became better organized, the party held a virtual monopoly on access to government jobs. This is not to say that Jackson did not rely on capable educated people in making government appointments. Intelligent men exercising common sense could operate governmental departments because the departments were still relatively uncomplicated. The era of professionalism had not yet arrived.

The spoils system developed in local and state governments around 1800, and by 1830 it was firmly entrenched. The party machinery provided access to government as well as to rapid upward mobility. An increasing number of jobs were being filled by friends of politicians in return for past favors, and the government was being weakened at all levels because of the frequent turnover of personnel. The competence of these people, who often had had no experience in the jobs they held, was at least questionable. Even though President Grant and Congress had authorized a merit and civil service system by 1871, Congress and the political parties gave the system little support. The reform mood did not gain great momentum until President Garfield was assassinated in 1881 by a disappointed job seeker.

The Pendleton Act of 1883, which marked the beginning of regularized civil service in the United States, challenged the spoils system of political patronage by ensuring that capable people selected on a nonpartisan basis would hold the higher offices of government. This act required that a merit system, such as that then in use in Great Britain, be set up to operate under a civil service commission modeled on the British civil service system but revised to fit our form of government.

The United States Civil Service (1883–1975)

The commission's activities would include testing for job qualification, establishment of job criteria, employment, and promotion, among other aspects of personnel management. A merit system designed to professionalize public employees is a process used for recruitment in almost every public service position. In theory, it is based on competitive entrance examinations, security from partisan removal, political neutrality, and nonpartisanship in public office.[2] A merit system had already been used for certain positions in the departments of the Interior and Treasury before passage of the Pendleton Act. As a result of the act, however, about 10.5 percent of all federal jobs came under competitive service.

The Pendleton Act required that a nonpolitical civil service commission be set up with three commissioners, of whom no more than two could hold the same party affiliation, to be appointed by the president with the approval of Congress. Each commissioner's term would last six years, with one new commissioner coming in every two years. That is, the terms were spaced in such a way that a new president was enabled to select a new commissioner and, at the same time, select a chairman (or chief executive officer) for his term. The commission meets monthly, or more often if need be, behind closed doors. Only those who are on the agenda may attend.

The organization of the federal civil service is relatively simple. In addition to the three commissioners at the top who are responsible to the president, the commission has an executive assistant, executive director, general counsel, and board of appeals and review. Under the supervision of the executive director, who acts as chairman, is the Interagency Advisory Group, which is composed of top-personnel federal agency officials. This group was developed so that the department and agencies could work out solutions to personnel problems and initiate ideas and proposals for personnel policies.[3] A final major division includes six bureaus: Programs and Standards, Recruiting and Examining, Personnel Investigation, Inspections, Management Services, and Retirement and Insurance. At the bottom of the organizational structure are ten regional offices spread throughout the country.

The commission, created to carry out the Pendleton Act by using the merit system, has been considered the "personnel arm" of the president.[4] Commissioners exercise five basic functions:

1. They are policy makers, issuing and approving civil service regulations and policy directions under presidential rule, and they recommend changes to the president.
2. They act as judge for final appeals regarding unfair practices of hiring, firing, and promoting.
3. They are spokesmen for the merit system and are often in the position of having to defend the system.
4. They are responsible for preventing political activity from occurring within the civil service.
5. They help the president solve personnel problems.

As the commission's power grew, Congress enacted various legislation that had the effect of increasing its responsibility as well. The Retirement Act of 1920 established the age limit at which an employee may retire with annuity. The Classification Act of 1923 ensured equal pay for equal work and established a system of pay schedules. The Veterans Preference Act of 1944 assured veterans of initial preference in employment and guaranteed job stability once employed. The Training Act of 1958 was created to improve efficiency by keeping employees informed of latest techniques and developments.

The U.S. Civil Service Commission originally depended on the secretary of interior for accommodations and supplies. But by 1890 it had grown dissatisfied with having to share resources with the Department of Interior, with the inadequate amounts of money being allocated for departmental use, and with a number of departments that still had not adopted the merit system. Under the Pendleton Act, not all agencies were required to use the merit system, but as new jobs were created, these were placed under this process. That more agencies came under this system toward the end of a presidential term was called "blanketing-in." It placed positions under the competitive service so that incumbents could retain their positions.[5] The civil service system can operate under the patronage or merit system or a combination of both. In fact, the Federal Bureau of Investigation, the Atomic Energy Commission, the Tennessee Valley Authority, and the Foreign Service are exempt from the merit system by act of Congress.

By 1932 the merit system had been incorporated into almost 80 percent of government offices, although the Civil Service Commission, the central personnel agency, still lacked control over agencies exempt from the system. President Franklin Roosevelt was encouraged to increase the number of positions outside the merit system. With his reelection and a lessening of pressures for patronage, Roosevelt issued a series of executive orders placing under civil service more than 200,000 positions which had previously been exempt.

After World War II the commission demonstrated its efficiency in finding personnel and expanding its coverage to about 90 percent of the government offices as a result of executive orders. President Lyndon Johnson made the commission his assistant in personnel management, and, as a result, the commission became accountable for all personnel appeals in the federal government. Although few would argue any longer for patronage positions, particularly since Watergate, President Nixon could still appoint certain patronage positions, such as federal district attorneys, and there remain over six thousand top policy-making positions filled through political appointments.[6]

Particularly since 1938, civil service reforms at the federal level have evoked similar efforts in state and local government. Federal laws encouraged reform by requiring certain state and community employees to come under the merit system for programs funded partly with federal monies. There is no such thing as a full civil service system in state and local government, however. Substantial variation exists, among cities particularly. Most states do not yet have comprehensive civil service systems. While some thirty-five states have merit systems covering particular positions, only about twenty have comprehensive coverage for nearly all personnel. With the passage of the Intergovernmental Personnel Act of 1970, however, the federal Civil Service Commission was permitted to provide grants to state and local governments to improve or to initiate civil service programs.[7]

Local governments have more employees under civil service. In 1970, over 80 percent of the municipalities, with more than 500 employees, not counting employees in education, had merit systems.[8] This included more than half of all state and local workers. But some smaller cities and counties have no civil service or merit systems, or coverage for only specific groups of employees.[9]

Because of variation in local government, the spoils system is alive and well among smaller jurisdictions.[10] In Chicago, for example, Mayor Richard Daley, while supporting civil service development, has also circumvented it by using temporary employees. "Temporaries" make up nearly 40 percent of Chicago's public employees; theoretically they hold jobs no longer than 180 days, but in fact some have remained politically active for more than twenty years. In some states, patronage also flourishes. Pennsylvania, New York, and Illinois state governors are permitted to control thousands of jobs, while the governor of Oregon controls only about a dozen.[11]

As a result of political patronage, bureaucracy, specialization, and numerous employee-management problems, the modern civil service system and personnel office perform a variety of functions for federal, state, and local government. The following is a list of the most important elements in a personnel system.[12]

1. Job classification
2. Staffing positions
3. Fixing pay
4. Training
5. Incentive awards
6. Conduct and discipline
7. Performance evaluation and testing
8. Appeal of administrative actions
9. Employee-management relations
10. Sick leave and vacations
11. Health and life insurance
12. Retirement system–fringe benefits
13. Reduction-in-force
14. Excepted services (exclusion from civil service).

Using these elements, the Civil Service Commission today attempts to provide for nonpartisan employment and to guarantee fair hiring, firing, promotions, and competitive entrance examinations.

Challenges for Modern Personnel Administration   The terms "civil service" and "merit system" have thus far been used interchangeably because for all practical purposes they mean the same thing. The personnel system performs the fourteen operational functions just listed. But the principles of merit to which the civil service system is presumably dedicated need reform in order to meet the changing needs of employees, to assure that merit systems are not discriminatory, particularly against minorities, and to meet the challenges of increasingly powerful and influential unions. Before examining these challenges, consider the merit principles that civil service systems need to use as guides for reform. These are set out in the Intergovernmental Personnel Act of 1970 and consist of six rather deceptively simple statements:

1. Hiring and promoting employees on the basis of ability, with open competition in initial appointment
2. Providing fair compensation
3. Retaining employees on the basis of performance, correcting inadequate performance and dismissing those whose inadequate performance cannot be corrected
4. Training employees as needed for high-quality performance
5. Assuring fair treatment of applicants and employees in all aspects of personnel administration, without regard to political affiliation, race, color, national origin, sex, or religious creed, and with proper regard for their privacy and constitutional rights as citizens
6. Protecting employees against political coercion, and prohibiting use of official position to affect an election or nomination for office.[13]

Some minority groups and poor charge that they have been filtered out of jobs by most employers using the standard merit system. The simple requirement of a high-school degree eliminates a large percentage of minority and poor. But the Civil Rights Act of 1964, the Equal Employment Opportunity Act of 1972, executive orders from presidents and governors, new civil service policies, and court decisions—all combine in various ways to ban discrimination in employment, in both the public and private sectors. The Equal Employment Opportunity Act brought state and local governments under the provisions of the Civil Rights Act of 1964.

The concept of affirmative action grew out of title 7 of the Civil Rights Act of 1964. The major proponents of the act soon realized that merely to remove discriminatory practices was not enough—that injuries worked by illegal practices had, in effect, established a psychological barrier that few minority-group members could overcome. There was a need to mitigate those injuries and compensate for lost opportunities.

Affirmative action has come into practice by several methods: first, by searching for minority group members and encouraging desirable applicants for a specific position; second, by establishing training programs and special services, such as testing programs that have no built-in cultural bias designed to exclude minorities, to compensate for earlier low-quality education and techniques used to stifle initiative. The case study at the end of the chapter entitled "Managerial Prerogative or Social Objective?" illustrates some of the problems encountered in implementing affirmative action programs.

It must be demonstrated to minority group members that once they are hired by a business, university, or government agency, they have an equal opportunity to advancement and promotion. A government agency that has a work force of over 95 percent blacks but none in supervisorial or administrative positions, for example, is probably guilty of discriminatory practices. But these may involve very subtle forms of discrimination, and there is a very fine line between compensatory and preferential treatment.

Many people object to those aspects of affirmative action policies calling for compensatory or preferential treatment in the hiring and training of people as a threat to quality. Applicants are today expected to have education and job performance abilities without extensive further training by employers. Furthermore, employers who hold government contracts must use affirmative action to eliminate either intentional or unintentional discriminatory action. About one-third of the American labor force is employed by companies that hold government contracts, with the result that government affirmative action requirements can have a massive impact on American industrial employment practices.[14]

The role of the courts in enforcing antidiscriminatory legislation is to be seen in a number of decisions. One of the most notable U.S. Supreme Court decisions was the case of *Griggs* v. *Duke Power Company*, in which the court ruled that title 7 of the 1964 Civil Rights Act makes it unlawful for employers to require

> . . . a high school education or passing of a standardized general intelligence test as a condition of employment in or transfer of jobs when (a) neither standard is shown to be significantly related to successful job performance, (b) both requirements operate to disqualify Negroes at a substantially higher rate than white applicants, and (c) the jobs in question had been filled only by white employees as part of a long-standing practice of giving preference to whites.[15]

Chief Justice Warren Burger, who considered this decision among the most important of 1971, also noted that "if an employment practice which operates to exclude Negroes cannot be shown to be related to job performance, the practice is prohibited."[16] This far-reaching statement did not "command that any person be hired simply because he was formerly the subject of discrimination, or because he is a member of a minority group," nor did court action eliminate use of tests as measurement instruments, but these methods can be overruled if they are not reasonable measurements of job performance.[17] An employer continues to have the right to insist that all applicants, black or white, meet job qualifications. Title 7 is designed to ensure that hiring is on the basis of job qualification rather than on the basis of race or color.[18]

In March 1974 the U.S. Supreme Court heard still another case with haunting implications. *DeFunis* v. *Odegaard* raised the problem of discrimination in reverse.[19] Marco DeFunis applied for admission to the University of

Washington Law School in 1971. Notified of his rejection, he filed a suit claiming that the admission procedure had admitted minority applicants with test scores and grades lower than his. The trial court ordered that he be admitted, which was done in the fall of 1971. When the law school appealed to the courts and had the decision overturned, DeFunis appealed to the Supreme Court.

The Supreme Court ruled that because DeFunis was in his last year in law school when the case reached the high court, he was no longer affected by the school's admission procedures. The case was adjudged moot on its merits, and the Court would not challenge the procedure. Even though the majority of court members acknowledged that the issues raised in the case will not "in the future evade review," Justice William O. Douglas urged the Court to challenge the law school's unfair admissions procedure, observing that "to eliminate all . . . sources of invidious discrimination" was the central purpose of the Fourteenth Amendment.[20] Nevertheless, how to redress discrimination is likely to be debated for some time. Should one type of discrimination be permitted to be redressed by another type? Should quotas be a basis for the hiring and promoting of minorities (including women) for every white male promoted or hired? Will this practice be upheld by the courts?[21]

Some government agencies have overreacted to the issue of minority hiring policy, thereby creating their own problem of reverse discrimination. In 1971, for example, after consultation with the U.S. Civil Service Commission, the Federal Aviation Administration changed its hiring policies by dropping the statement: "If a minority group person cannot be appointed in each succeeding fifth vacant position, then neither that position nor any further positions should be filled until a minority group person is appointed."[22] As a result of pressure from the academic world, the Department of Health, Education and Welfare (HEW) in undertaking a revision of affirmative action guidelines to end reverse discrimination. One HEW report concluded in part that federal insistence on hiring more women and blacks is lowering faculty quality and standards.[23] A qualified white male employee could be denied due process as a result of such a policy.

Collective bargaining and public employee strikes are developing problems at all levels of government but particularly at the local level. Civil service and union leaders clash on the question of the benefits conferred by each group handling employee affairs. Unions, which often regard civil service as management oriented, see collective bargaining and the threat of strike as the only effective measures to correct inequalities in pay and to ensure greater job protection. At present, however, unions are themselves experiencing problems with corruption, racial discrimination, and questions of seniority versus merit. The challenge to civil service systems of unionization will be discussed later in this chapter.

POSITION CLASSIFICATION, RECRUITMENT, AND SELECTION

Personnel administration involves a continual process of position classification, recruitment, selection, training, examination, evaluation, promotion, discipline, and retirement procedures. While these functions may be shared or controlled by other departments or individual supervisors, they are generally performed in accordance with guidelines developed by the personnel office and administrative policy makers.

Labor Force Government is the largest single employer in the United States. "More than one out of every six Americans works for a government—federal, state, or local."[24] In the United States, nearly 13 million people were employed by government in 1970.[25] State and local governments employ about 75 percent, or approximately 10 million people, and the expansion of government jobs is occurring primarily in state and local governments. From 1959 to 1971 the number of jobs at state and local levels increased by over 4 million, while federal jobs increased by about 500,000 during the same period.[26] Government employees, particularly in state and local government, have become a major factor in our economy and a significant element in our labor force. In addition, many thousands of people not directly employed by government are retained by government for consulting, management, and research work and are located throughout the United States, not just in Washington, D.C.

Public demands for more government services stimulate the need for more government employees, and there is no sign that this cycle is slowing down. Further, government competes with industry and the professions for bright young college graduates because business and the professions, such as law and medicine, offer graduates opportunities for more pay and greater personal prestige.

Position Classification Position classification is the nucleus around which a personnel program is built. The methods of classifying positions, which help to determine salary levels, are very similar in business and government. The personnel office examines each position in terms of duties and responsibilities but not in terms of the person filling the position. As a result of this examination, the office issues a position classification for each "class" of job, such as Administrative Assistant I, Clerk Typist II, Policeman IV, or Fireman III, and assigns a salary or "grade" or "step" range for each. The classes or steps are grouped into a series of positions for the same type of job, though differing in responsibility, tenure, and presumably difficulty.

Non–civil service jobs also use position classification systems. Professors, for example, are generally ranked according to four classes: lecturer, assistant professor, associate professor, and full professor, with each rank containing five steps. The applicant who is hired is placed in a rank commensurate with his experience and education. Assistant Professor, step V, usually means that the person has a Ph.D. degree and five years of teaching experience. In some personnel systems, tenure would come with obtaining the position of Associate Professor, step I, or to a person with six years of experience and a Ph.D. Similarly, a city government may have five steps each in the positions of police officer, sergeant, lieutenant, captain, and chief of its law enforcement department.

In state and local government, most positions, classes, series, or steps are placed under a General Schedule (GS). This might include, for example, Urban Planner GS 5, GS 7, GS 9, and up to GS 15 or GS 18. While most state and local agencies stop at the level of GS 15 or GS 18, the federal government employs a dual classification system for employees; GS 18 at $36,000 a year is the maximum for all career employees regardless of duties. Above the General Schedule is the Executive Schedule, ranging from $36,000 to $60,000 for political appointees to cover classifications created by a variety of statutes developed by agencies such as the Central Intelligence Agency, Postal Service, and Foreign Service. Like the General Schedule, the Executive Schedule classifies employees according to their duties.[27] Table 5 illustrates the range of the GS federal salary schedule, the entry level depending on education and experience.

Modern position classification techniques were not developed until early in this century. In 1912 Chicago placed its employees under a classification program, the federal government following with a partial classification program in 1923. The classification system was designed to solve conditions of

> utter confusion, great waste, and excessive political and personal
> favoritism in determining the duties and pay of public employees.
> There were no standard job titles or descriptions. Scores of
> different jobs were given the same title. The same job might have
> ten or twenty different titles and pay rates. Pay had only sketchy
> relations to work actually performed.[28]

The results of position classification, then, were to clarify job description to aid in recruitment, to establish career ladders or promotional possibilities, and to standardize pay.

Clarification of job descriptions is essential in recruitment for jobs ranging from clerical assistant to director of a large agency. Descriptions of job functions, qualifications, and testing scores for eligibility lists must be

Table 5 FEDERAL SALARY SCHEDULE, EFFECTIVE OCTOBER 12, 1975

Grade	Minimum	Maximum	*Recommended Academic Preparation Entry Level*
GS 5	$ 8,925	$11,607	
GS 6	$ 9,946	$12,934	B.A. Degree
GS 7	$11,046	$14,358	
GS 8	$12,222	$15,885	Masters or Law Degree
GS 9	$13,482	$17,523	
GS 11	$16,255	$21,133	Ph.D.
GS 12	$19,386	$25,200	
GS 14	$26,861	$34,916	
GS 16	$36,338	$37,800	
GS 18	$37,800	$37,800	

NOTE: For all classifications shown, one generally must have a B.A. degree; and depending upon type of job and experience, academic degrees may place a prospective employee at a higher entry level of GS grade. Present law establishes $37,800 as pay ceiling.

SOURCE: Campus Courier Insert, San Francisco Region, U.S. Civil Service Commission, Nov.–Dec., 1975.

available during the recruiting of a large group of people. Once a person is hired, the job classification will help to clarify the degree of authority for that job. It is therefore not surprising that an enormous amount of time and energy is expended in the writing of job descriptions.

An understanding of promotion eligibility and rate of mobility up the career ladder is important for all employees. An employee's awareness of future prospects can help motivate him to greater productivity. Certainly, if there are no promotion possibilities to better paying and more prestigious positions in government, the employee will in all likelihood look for another job.

Pay standardization is intended to assure equal pay for equal work by the use of pay scales or grades. A General Schedule pay grade, such as a GS 11 for a state accountant with three years experience and a college degree, will be the same salary regardless of location in the state. A GS 11 may be the same for a federal accountant with the same background regardless of geographic location.

Classification of positions can also have a negative effect by setting limits on employee communication, as, for example, when an employee informally by-passes his immediate supervisor to complain about a personnel or policy matter decided by that supervisor. While this action may anger the immediate supervisor, the informal rule of going through channels may avoid conflict between line and staff but can have a negative effect on employee ability to communicate with others about grievances. Classifying positions is an integral part of formal bureaucratic structure but coexists with an informal organizational structure that compensates for deficiencies in the formal organization.

Another common complaint about classifying positions is that it emphasizes position rather than the qualifications and abilities of the individual holding the job.[29] In this respect, classification systems have been described as "more of a muddle than a model" for ambitious and progressive employees.[30] Moreover, if a job classification is improperly made, the corresponding salary will often not be in accord with the principle of equal pay for equal work. One Civil Service Commission survey showed that sixteen states had used their job evaluation and classification systems to solve pay problems.[31]

Classification of positions with uncompromising minimum education and experience requirements frequently decreases employee retention rates, complicates matters of promotion, and makes recruiting more difficult by requiring a higher level of skill and education than the job may actually require.[32] As a practical matter, the more applications an employer has, the more selective he can afford to be. Finally, position classification can be misused to push an employee into early retirement, or as a disciplinary action by reclassifying his job downward in organizational importance and pay. Thus public personnel activities have often been criticized as having a negative function in the organization.

> Personnel officers in public personnel administration do not have the same discretion as their private counterparts. Instead, they are glorified technicians in work study and salary administration, or training, recruitment and classification specialists. Rarely are they rounded personnel administrators capable of instigating new programs, heading off labor troubles, or developing creative relationships. Too often, they are not organized for positive action, only for routine administration of set laws and procedures. Positive personnel administration goes by default.[33]

Wage and Salary Administration

Federal, state, and local governments also utilize a standard pay scale, usually assigning given salaries to given positions. Government agencies may also have their own classification system with respective pay scales set by law. Or, according to the Coordinated Federal Wage System, a "prevailing rate" may be paid so that the wages of government employees are comparable to those of private employers in a particular geographic area.

Salary administration consists of two main parts: devising a salary structure to reflect the salary market and administering the salaries of individuals in respect to their job performance. Government salaries have often been out of line with the pay patterns of private industry. Government pay-setting procedures have been inflexible for several reasons. First, there may be a scarcity of private industry jobs to compare with those in government. Second, legislative ceilings may be imposed by certain top political appointees and elected officials. The government pays more to lower and middle-level positions, while top positions may have salaries below what private industry pays for jobs involving comparable responsibility.[34] In fact, it is possible for an elected official, such as a local district attorney, to receive less pay than his assistant if, because of union action, a 5 percent wage increase was granted but not applicable to anyone in an elected position until the end of his term. Third, congress, state legislatures, and city councils may be reluctant to grant increases in pay if a tax increase will result. In California, however, the governor can fix salary scales for white-collar employees and make adjustments in them without approval of the legislature. The legislature need only pass the necessary appropriations to finance any increases.

For the federal government, it was not until passage of the Federal Salary Act of 1962 that the pay comparability principle became a requirement.[35] This act permitted federal pay scales to be comparable with private industry salary scales, but the power to accomplish this was not delegated to the president until the Pay Comparability Act of 1970.[36] Still, the new federal legislation did not cover postal employees under the Postal Reorganization Act of 1970 because postal pay was covered through postal union collective bargaining and management. As a result of a postal strike and call for higher wages, the U.S. Postal Service has had to raise its rates for postage.

Job performance and administering the salaries of individuals are directly related. In the days of scientific management, it was generally assumed that pay was the major reason why men worked and that organizations needed employees mainly for their ability to be productive performers. But research has indicated that salary increases do not necessarily motivate better work performance and that "there is no reason to suspect that pay influences satisfaction in the same manner that it influences motivation.[37]

> Most salary increases, bonus, and profit-sharing plans and many commission and incentive pay plans do not provide an increment that is large enough to motivate any action other than the purely passive action of staying in the organization. They are not usually large enough to motivate extra effort, extra creativity, or any kind of nonroutine performance.[38]

However, another study has argued that the pay systems such as those used by the federal government are full of "demotivators." That is, employee performance is not necessarily related to improved pay insofar as "almost all the managers in the federal system are unwilling to discriminate in salary administration between the outstanding, average, and poor performer. Except for promotion, all tend to be treated alike."[39] When the hard worker and the deadwood are treated alike, the motivation to excel suffers.

Table 6   DETERMINANTS OF PAY SATISFACTION

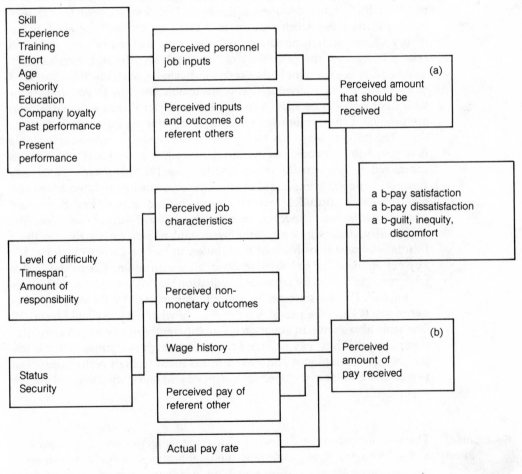

SOURCE: Edward E. Lawler, III, *Pay and Organizational Effectiveness: A Psychological View* (New York: McGraw-Hill, 1971), p. 215.

Salaries are considered by many researchers to be organizational maintenance factors rather than motivating factors. If, however, pay is geared to achievement that receives definite recognition, such as promotion, and is perceived as such by the employee, then the achievement factor can also act as a motivating factor. It has been shown that "those managers who saw their pay as dependent upon their job performance were the most effective and highly motivated managers."[40] Of course, government and business both have mechanisms to reward outstanding employees, although there are fewer constraints on business to offer a major promotion or salary bonus to an outstanding employee. Also, if there is an expanding job market, employees who feel they deserve and can make higher salaries will tend to seek better-paying jobs, which may mean leaving government for a job in industry. A substantial increase in pay that will change one's life style will take priority over the possibility of better job security in government. In any event, if government loses experts to business, such positions will tend to be occupied by individuals who are unable to grow in government or with it, or possibly by those who reflect the "Peter Principle"—that is, who are promoted to positions for which they are not competent.[41]

The importance of pay to the worker in either government or business is very significant in other ways as well. According to the Hawthorne studies conducted at Western Electric during the late 1920s and early 1930s, pay was not particularly important to employees. According to Elton Mayo and his colleagues, attitudes toward coworkers and supervisors dominated worker motivation. However, research by Edward Lawler has identified almost fifty studies in which employees ranked pay among the top three factors in almost two-thirds of the studies. In table 6 Lawler illustrates the key determinants of pay satisfaction in an organization. The model in this table represents the pay satisfaction equation that each employee completes for himself. Pay satisfaction "is basically determined by the difference between pay (b) and the person's conception of what his pay should be (a)."[42] The table also shows an equation for an inherently rigid position classification program. Thus, pay will tend to motivate high performance if it is important to the employee and linked in his mind to high performance. But pay cannot eliminate the need for adequate employee selection, training, or supervision.

Recruitment Effort   The recruitment process consists of making people aware of job openings and encouraging those who meet the qualifications to apply. It may have negative aspects, such as examination deadlines, requirements of local residency, and reliance on printed announcements appearing in professional journals, newspapers, or contact with university placement offices.

Government is currently dealing with these problems by offering continuous open examinations such as the Professional and Administrative Career Examination (PACE) and California's State Service Entrance Examination (SSEE). In addition, recruiting teams may visit placement offices, have candidates complete simplified job applications, conduct examinations and interviews, and make job offers all in one visit. To improve job prospects for college graduates, state governments and several universities have initiated programs to allow students to "try out" different occupations before making long-term commitments. Legislation passed in 1970 gave California one of the most far-reaching internship programs of any state in the nation.[43] In competing for college graduates, government is often restricted compared to industry because it is not able to authorize payment of travel expenses for interviews and examinations.

The recruitment of minorities requires special effort and techniques. As an example of the extra attention given to minority groups, the U.S. Civil Service Commission has ordered federal agencies no longer to certify job openings based on one sex, except for such special positions as jet fighter pilot. As a result of affirmative action programs, there has been a surge of activity to employ minority groups, including the physically handicapped. But the hiring procedures facing affirmative action programs are compounded because of the limited number of qualified minorities.

Selection and Examination

The selection process screens applicants to evaluate and rank those who meet job qualifications. Having studied the job announcement or description to determine whether he meets the minimum qualifications, the candidate files a job application. Many jobs call for experience or education which the applicant does not have. If he has had extensive education, he may be overqualified but at the same time lacking in experience. Once the application has been accepted, an examination process usually begins which may include written, oral, or performance tests or a combination of these. In addition, there are reference checks and an evaluation of the applicant's experience and relevant educational background.

Written tests, such as the PACE exams, are usually standardized for most jobs except higher specialized positions. Only a few states, including California, use state service entrance examinations similar to those of the federal government. Many state and local governments still have no systematic selection or examination process or programs based on merit.[44] Usually tests based on a multiple-choice format are used because they can be graded conveniently by machines. There are two types of written tests: aptitude tests to determine the applicant's ability to learn or his potential to do the job, and achievement tests to determine the accumulated knowledge the

PACE (Professional T Administrative Career Examination)

applicant has for a specific job. For career recruitment, the aptitude test is most important.

Minorities have charged that some written tests are culturally biased. In addition, minorities deprived of equal educational opportunity may not score well on the language sections of aptitude tests. The case of *Griggs* v. *Duke Power Company* prohibits testing of aptitude if it is not related to job performance and operates to disqualify minorities. Examinations often fail to test inherent intelligence or actual achievement; but once a person is hired, there are performance tests to ascertain how well he is learning his job.

The oral interview is often an important part of the examination process. Interviews may be used together with written examinations to evaluate those characteristics not revealed by college records, such as appearance, attitudes, ability to relate to others, and mental alertness. The oral examination may also involve a person-to-person interview with the prospective employer or a group interview involving several candidates being interviewed at once by an employer. While most entry-level job interviews involve one person being interviewed for a specific period of time by an employer or panel, group interviews usually involve middle-management positions.

State and local governments use oral exams far more than the federal government does. The technique is challenging to the applicant; questions are asked that are "up for grabs," or a situation question may be asked— "what do you think of this situation?" or "what do you think of that answer?"—first to an individual and then to other candidates. For example, you are an applicant for the position of assistant chief of police. The oral interview board consists of the personnel director, the district attorney, the city attorney, a police commissioner, and the police chief. A member of the panel poses the following hypothetical situation: "You are the assistant police chief. The mayor comes to you and states: 'We want to fire the police chief. If you will help by supplying the assistant city manager and me with some damaging information on his activities, I will make you the police chief.' What would your response be?" The purpose of such questions is to observe individual behavioral reactions or applicant interaction in the case of a group interview. But oral interviews are ultimately subjective because the evaluator reacts to the applicant on the basis of his own experience and value system.

Reference checks may consist of a telephone call, a mailed evaluation form, or a personal interview by an investigator in cases of FBI security clearance. In practice, the network of friendships among personnel managers, police chiefs, and heads of government agencies can often be a very important source of information about a candidate. Among state and local governments, especially, the number of these informal communications is amazing.

Once the applicants complete this screening process they are ranked in order of their test scores on all examinations and placed on an eligibility list. Most governments follow the "rule-of-three" in selecting candidates. That is, the top three names from the eligibility list are certified by the personnel office when calls come from agencies seeking eligible names for a job opening. Eligibility lists may remain active indefinitely or be canceled after a period of time.

In practice, those eligible are often separated by only one or two points. If there are many applicants for a single job, the test score or oral-interview ranking can be crucial. If only one applicant applies for a job, however, testing and interview may be used only to meet civil service requirements. The department hiring the applicant, particularly for a specialized job, may be unconcerned with details of testing since it may be otherwise obvious that this is the best person for the job. Civil service systems are becoming more flexible and relying more on oral interviews, application evaluation, and reference checks. But when several candidates for a job possess similar qualifications, the decision becomes difficult.

Appointment and Probation

The personnel office does not make an appointment, although it does conduct all the processes mentioned above. At the federal level and in many states following the "rule-of-three," the personnel agency provides a certified list to the department that needs someone with particular qualifications. After the department interviews those certified, it will select whom it wishes to hire with no legal obligation to appoint the one with the highest score. The names of those not selected will be returned to the eligibility list.

The final phase of the selection process is the probationary period when an employee's attitudes and performance are observed and evaluated. While the length of probationary periods varies from usually six months to a year, the mortality rate among probationary employees is low. Although the initial appointment is regarded as permanent, probationary employees are not afforded the same job protections as permanent employees until this period is over. Only then may the employee begin to look forward to such rights as promotion possibilities, improved job mobility, and retirement benefits. At this stage, dismissal usually occurs only on the basis of cause and is accompanied by the right to grievance hearings.

ON-THE-JOB PERSONNEL MANAGEMENT

The difficult task of managing people in the organization is compounded by the need for organizational incentives to encourage new employees to remain in the public service. These incentives will be determined largely by the outcome of such management functions as training, evaluation of performance, promotion, and discipline. All the effort and costs of recruitment will be lost if programs such as these do not meet employees' needs at various stages of their tenure.

Training An in-service training program, either at a special institute or on the job, is essential to modern personnel management. Opportunity must be provided for employees to improve their competence. Training programs can include orientation sessions for new employees as well as advanced education refresher courses for top management. An employees' supervisor can take the lead in acquainting new employees with their jobs and the objectives of the organization.

Before World War II the federal government provided little external training of this type and was hampered by monetary restrictions imposed by the General Accounting Office. The Government Employees Training Act of 1958 added a new dimension to this aspect of management by requiring heads of federal agencies to provide employee training using both internal and external government facilities. The Civil Service Commission helped by providing interagency in-service training, or training in agencies specializing in specific types of programs open to employees from other agencies.

In 1967, by Executive Order 11348, President Lyndon Johnson enlisted the Civil Service Commission to enforce agency requirements of at least yearly review of training needs and evaluation of their effectiveness.[45] When Johnson's task force on career advancement concluded that interagency training was still inadequate, the U.S. Bureau of Training was created along with regional training centers around the country. To meet the needs of senior career employees (those in GS grades 16 through 18), the federal government created the Federal Executive Institute in Charlottesville, Virginia, in 1968. Here intensive eight-week training sessions are conducted by academic staffs on leave from their educational institutions.

Training centers for supervisorial personnel are equally essential. When an employee is promoted to a first-line supervisor, his function changes from that of an accountant, planner, and administrative assistant to that of a personnel coordinator in achieving organizational goals. This process is continual. As a person moves up the promotion ladder he becomes less a specialist and more an administrator responsible for policymaking, coordination, and leading the agency or organization. To accommodate identification and training of those approaching this stage, middle-management training facilities covering GS grades of 12 to 15 were established by the government at Kings Point, New York, Berkeley, California, and Oak Ridge, Tennessee.

Training centers can also help high-level administrators to inform themselves about new theories and techniques in administration. Government therefore meets the training needs of career executives in two ways. First, it enables employees to move up the organization ladder to a policy-making position. Second, it provides intensive training at special institutes at which executives can update their management skills.

As a result of the Intergovernmental Personnel Act of 1970, state and local governments have also profited from federal training programs. Under this act, any federal agency can open its training programs to state and local governments and allow for temporary assignments between federal and local governments or educational facilities.[46]

Job Performance and Employee Evaluation

Most employees want to know how well they are doing and how they can improve their performance. Management, too, is interested in obtaining the highest quality of work from employees, but the process of employee evaluation is among the most difficult problems that management has. Employees are constantly being evaluated, particularly during their probationary period. Over the years the ratings accumulate and become a permanent case history which follows the employee throughout his career.

There are essentially two kinds of rating plans. One is "trait ratings," which has many variations but basically includes the rating of desirable personal traits such as dependability, intelligence, cooperation, and initiative. The drawback of this method is that it is subjective. There is no agreement on what the various traits mean or to what extent an employee may possess a particular trait. This method often involves supervisors giving employees such adjective ratings as "excellent," "good," "fair," or "unacceptable." The first Hoover Commission of 1949 suggested that Congress discard this type of system. Employees consider performance ratings of less than good as threats to promotion and pay, with the result that supervisors tend to overrate unless there is some obvious problem.[47]

In the second plan, the supervisor evaluates the employee's work performance and production but not his personal traits. By emphasizing production, a supervisor can establish work goals for the employee to achieve and in this way have more of a positive effect on personnel. Each agency indicates which factors are important and develops the appropriate form or plan for evaluation. But the type of form used is immaterial because the evaluation constitutes a written memorandum or other documentation describing performance and production. One study has noted that "bright, energetic individuals are readily identified and become well known to the chain of authority through the normal course of daily communication and association," regardless of the particular appraisal form used.[48]

Experts in the field have studied the objectives of job evaluation and list the following as among the most fundamental:[49]

1. To provide a functional internal wage structure to simplify chaotic wage structures due to chance, custom or favoritism

2. To provide an agreed upon method for setting rates for new or changed positions

3. To provide a means for realistic comparisons between wage and salary rates of employing organizations

4. To provide a basis upon which individual performance can be measured

5. To reduce grievances over wage and salary rates

6. To provide incentive values to employees to strive for higher level jobs

7. To provide documentation for wage negotiations

8. To provide data on job relationships for use in selection, training, transfers and promotions.[50]

Evaluation forms often combine trait performance with written summary evaluation of work production. California, for example, uses the format illustrated in table 7. No matter how careful supervisors are about evaluation, however, not everyone is going to be pleased with his own, and problems often arise. When employees are clearly outstanding or clearly unable to perform, the evaluation process is relatively easy, but borderline cases are difficult to rate without solid evidence to substantiate the rating, and, as already noted, the evaluation is complicated by the fact that the process is subjective.

Employee expectations cannot be disregarded either. Employees resent average or low ratings because they think of them in terms of money, promotion, and survival.[51] For this reason, ratings for permanent employees tend to be higher. If the evaluation will result in loss of a pay increase, supervisors may be apprehensive about having to justify a grievance to a higher authority. Employees generally do not regard evaluation as a counseling process to help improve their performance.

A well-documented, unbiased appraisal during an interview is essential to the evaluation process. One study has listed six items to guide a supervisor in an evaluation interview:

1. Understanding the problems involved in human communication. Encourage frequent talks about progress in performance

2. Empathy—a genuine attempt at understanding another's feelings in a given situation

Table 7 Report of Performance for Probationary Employee, State of California

<table>
<tr><td>STATE OF
CALIFORNIA</td><td colspan="2" align="center">REPORT OF PERFORMANCE
FOR PROBATIONARY EMPLOYEE</td><td>☐ FIRST
☐ SECOND
☐ FINAL</td></tr>
</table>

| Last Name | First Name | Initial | Social Security Account Number | Date of Report |

| Civil Service Title | | Position Number | Date Probation Ends |

| State Department | Subdivision of Department | Headquarters of Employee |

Your work performance will determine whether you attain permanent civil service status.

RATINGS ARE INDICATED BY "X" MARKS

QUALIFICATION FACTORS:

		UNACCEPTABLE	IMPROVEMENT NEEDED	STANDARD	OUTSTANDING
1. **SKILL**—Expertness in doing specific tasks; accuracy; precision; completeness; neatness; quantity.	1				
2. **KNOWLEDGE**—Extent of knowledge of methods, materials, tools, equipment, technical expressions and other fundamental subject matter.	2				
3. **WORK HABITS**—Organization of work; care of equipment; punctuality and dependability; industry; follows good practices of vehicle and personal safety.	3				
4. **RELATIONSHIPS WITH PEOPLE**—Ability to get along with others; effectiveness in dealing with the public, other employees, patients or inmates.	4				
5. **LEARNING ABILITY**—Speed and thoroughness in learning procedures, laws, rules and other details; alertness; perseverance.	5				
6. **ATTITUDE**—Enthusiasm for the work; willingness to conform to job requirements and to accept suggestions for work improvement; adaptability.	6				
7. **PERSONAL FITNESS**—Integrity; sobriety; emotional stability; physical condition; appearance and habits.	7				
8. **ABILITY AS SUPERVISOR**—Proficiency in training employees and in planning, organizing, laying out and getting out work; leadership.	8				
9. **ADMINISTRATIVE ABILITY**—Promptness of action; soundness of decision; application of good management principles.	9				
10. **FACTORS NOT LISTED ABOVE** (Use additional sheets if more space is needed).	10				
OVER-ALL RATING: (The over-all rating must be consistent with the factor ratings and comments, but there is no prescribed formula for computing the over-all rating.)					

COMMENTS TO EMPLOYEE: (Supervisor should include factual examples on work especially well or poorly done and give suggestions as to how performance can be improved. Factor and over-all ratings of Unacceptable and over-all ratings of Outstanding must be substantiated. Use additional sheets if more space is needed.)

Rater Discussed Report with Employee. ☐ Yes ☐ No

I recommend that you be granted permanent civil service status. ☐ Yes (To be checked only on final report. If the probationer is rejected, ☐ No notification must be given as prescribed by Government Code Section 19173.)

Signature
of **RATER**_____Title_____Date_____

In signing this report I do not necessarily agree with the conclusions of the rater.

Signature
of **EMPLOYEE**_____Date_____

☐ I would like to discuss this report with the Reviewing Officer.

I concur in the ratings given by the rater. I have made no change in the report.

Signature of
REVIEWING OFFICER_____Date_____

As requested, Reviewing Officer discussed report with employee on_____ (DATE) (INITIALS)

STD. 636 (REVISED 1-71)

25253-750 6-74 180M QUAD W OSP

3. Focusing on *performance* rather than the personality of the worker
4. Getting the worker to participate—even take the lead—in the evaluation
5. Acting as a guide or coach in the process
6. Emphasizing what's ahead rather than what has happened.[52]

Supervisors generally do not enjoy "playing God" and thus find evaluation an unpleasant task. But with or without a formal evaluation program, employees will nevertheless have to be evaluated for promotion.

Promotion   Promotion is often determined on the basis of seniority, merit, or a combination of the two. Seniority is the most objective basis for determining promotion but not necessarily the best. It assumes that an employee becomes more competent and valuable to the organization as a result of his length of service, but this may not, in fact, be the case. An employee may be repeating his first year of experiences in his subsequent years by merely fulfilling the functions expected of him and not rocking the boat. After years with the organization he may move up the organizational ladder when vacancies occur for which he is qualified but not necessarily the best qualified.

A major problem with seniority is that after several years an individual becomes organizationally oriented—that is, he becomes a conservative protector of organization values and goals, no longer an innovator seeking different and better ways to do his job but preferring to compromise and get along with others at almost any cost. Thus, senior employees concerned with organizational survival may feel threatened by young, sharp, innovative employees who, for their part, may not understand the informal methods of compromise and agreement or why senior members are reluctant to enact procedural changes and who also see their own promotional paths obstructed by a seniority system.

A merit system is the most frequently discussed alternative to the seniority system, but merit is very subjective and there is no easy way to measure it in exact terms that will satisfy everyone. We have seen that comprehensive examinations have been used to rate the top three people as candidates certified to be selected for a particular job, but tests have their limitations as well. A combination of merit and seniority might be attempted as a compromise solution. That is, after a given number of years, a qualified person becomes eligible for promotion to the next highest rank. But even here it is difficult to make promotions free from the influence of such irrelevancies as age, sex, and race.

In 1969 a revised Federal Merit Promotion program was begun by the Civil Service Commission to ensure that agency promotions were made equitably, on the basis of merit and from a broad spectrum of candidates. Ranking procedures based on job-related criteria and length of service were also factors. This program superseded a federal service requirement of ten years earlier that agency promotion plans would be required by the Civil Service Commission. Today the employee must meet more than minimum qualifications for a particular job in the opinion of a supervisory officer. Where necessary, the new procedures require written or oral promotional tests.

State and local merit systems have used similar competitive methods for promotions, including written tests, oral interviews, and certification usually by the "rule-of-three." But on state and local levels, promotion opportunities are often limited to employees in one particular agency, which again makes seniority a crucial factor. National or state-wide searches for those best qualified for promotion increase the importance of merit because they mean that the senior members of an agency will have to compete for promotion with others outside the organization. On the other hand, promotion directed to those outside the organization may damage the morale of those within the organization who were qualified for the jobs but passed over. Perhaps a mixture of internal and external promotion would best serve the purposes of the organization, but the question of who has the best qualifications will always be a matter of controversy.

Discipline

Any organization has the right to discipline employees for unproductive or improper services, while, at the same time, the right to grievance hearings and job security is an important consideration for any employee. Regulations are necessary to protect both the employee and the organization with regard to formal actions of discipline, demotion, or dismissal. Civil service regulations, statutory regulations, and union contracts can stipulate the types of actions permitted an organization.

In some state and local jurisdictions the civil service commission reviews various types of formal actions, such as suspension and dismissal, taken against employees. The commission can order a hearing and require the employee's supervisor to reinstate him if there are sufficient grounds for reinstatement. At the federal level, the U.S. Civil Service Commission has discretionary power to reverse disciplinary actions taken against federal employees. At all levels of government, reversals are most likely to occur if sufficient evidence is available that the employee did not receive procedural due process or that actions were taken against him primarily for reasons of political, religious, or racial bias.

But an employee may be disciplined or removed without an appeal to a civil service commission because of inefficient service or for not meeting departmental standards during his probationary period. In the event of dismissal, the commission can determine that the procedure used or facts of the case did not warrant such action; but this time the supervisor is not obligated to comply with commission findings. The commission can order reinstatement only where there is proof of racial, religious, or political discrimination. In some cases a supervisor avoids the whole problem by transferring the employee to another position in the organization where his chances of improved performance are better.

Unless disciplinary actions are explained in writing during the period of employee evaluation, the employee can argue that there is insufficient evidence of improper or poor performance. Thus the importance of well-documented employee evaluation should never be underestimated. In any event, if an employee is not satisfactory to a supervisor and the civil service commission rules that he must be reinstated, both organization and supervisor must deal with him for an indeterminate future period.

COLLECTIVE BARGAINING AND STRIKES

Since 1960, employees at all levels of public service have participated in a substantial increase in unionization. Between 1960 and 1970 the number of federal employees joining the American Federation of Government Employees (AFGE), a federal employees' union, increased by a phenomenal 362 percent. Similar unions developed rapidly among state and local government employees. The American Federation of State, County, and Municipal Employees (AFSCME) had an increase in membership of nearly 112 percent between 1960 and 1970.[53] Between 1966 and 1972 union membership among state and local employees nearly doubled, as illustrated by figure 1. Public-school teachers joined organizations such as the American Federation of Teachers (AFT), which grew by more than 260 percent during the same ten-year period. The larger national teacher organization, the National Education Association, was forced to become demanding on such issues as cost-of-living increases when its membership began to flow to the more aggressive AFT and the United Teachers of Los Angeles (UTLA). At the beginning of the sixties, more than half of all federal employees belonged to unions. While the proportion of unionized state and local employees was smaller, with no more than one-third in any state, there is nevertheless clear evidence of considerable expansion.[54]

Figure 1   THE GROWTH OF UNIONISM IN STATE-LOCAL GOVERNMENT, 1964–1972

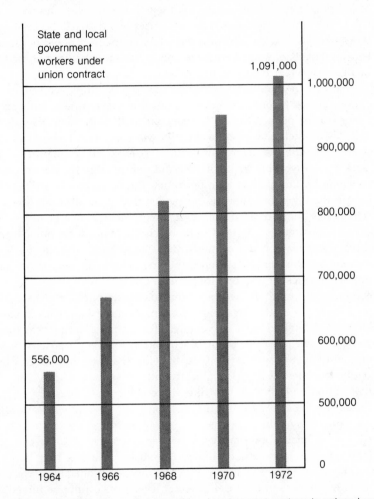

In less than eight years, the number of state and local government workers in unions has almost doubled. Three-fourths of those workers in 1972—or 821,000—are employees of local governments.

An additional 944,000 government workers belonged in 1972 to associations that, though not considered unions, bargain on behalf of employees—bringing to a total of 2,035,000 the number of state and local government workers in unions or bargaining associations. That is, one-fifth of all the people who work for states, cities, or counties.

SOURCE: U.S. Dept. of Labor

Reprinted from *U.S. News & World Report.* Copyright 1974, U.S. News & World Report, Inc., 8 July 1974, pp. 70–71.

Public Employee Unions

The growth of public employee unions has necessitated a major change in attitude on the part of legislators, the bureaucracy, and the public alike. Many public employees argue that they, like employees in private industry, have the right to join employee organizations that will represent their interests before boards of supervisors, city councils, school boards, and state legislatures. The right to organize and to have unions has not made government subservient to union organizations, however.

It has frequently been argued that public employee unions will gain enough power through strikes to compromise government authority and the wishes of the people. But no factual confirmation of this is readily available, and it is unlikely that a political entity will yield its authority without investigating whether its sovereignty could be destroyed in the process. The New York transit workers strike of 1968 did not result in the destruction of state sovereignty. Europe has long permitted public employee strikes regardless of specific laws, but there is no evidence that legalization of unions and strikes has compromised public or governmental sovereignty.[55]

Governments are not weak when challenged by unions and strike threats. Legislators and administrators may be unable to meet union or striking worker demands even if they wish to do so. Legislators, taxpayers, political parties, other pressure groups, and legal restrictions can block easy solutions to union and worker demands at the public expense. As long as legislators are elected by the people, they cannot be forced to bargain collectively. Members of a city council, for example, argue that they cannot delegate their power to binding arbitration for the purpose of establishing new employee wages and fringe benefits that will be reflected in higher public tax rates. Many local officials still refuse to deal with labor relations. In addition, in the event of strike, there is increased pressure on strikers in the form of lost wages and the possibility of government canceling union agreements by subcontracting.

As a matter of practice, however, legislative bodies can no longer ignore public labor organizations. If a strike occurs, it may best serve the public interest to resolve the conflict by means of collective bargaining, even if old ordinances or laws indicate that legislators cannot be forced into such negotiation. The courts have generally upheld the use of compulsory arbitration between unions and legislative bodies.[56] In addition, in 1971, the United States District Court in Washington, D.C. held in *Postal Clerks* v. *Blount* that there was no constitutional right for striking on the basis of freedom from the First Amendment but that state legislatures could pass laws to allow public workers to strike. The U.S. Supreme Court refused to reverse the lower court decision.

Labor unions have been growing for several decades in the private sector, and it was only a matter of time before public workers, would become organized as well. Unions have essentially undergone three stages of development.[57] First, skilled tradesmen were unionized. Then from 1930 to 1955 unions expanded to cover a larger segment of semiskilled tradesmen in the mass-production industries. The third stage centered on "service-producing industries," or those that cater to the public, particularly since government had become one of the largest industries in the country whose employees were "numerous, needed, and neglected."[58]

Unions began to fill a definite need for public employees. By organizing into large numbers, employees could collectively press unified demands for changes in work hours, pay, promotions, and job security. Unions such as the AFL-CIO, competed with one another for membership, particularly when membership was declining in the private sector. Dedication to public service was not enough; employees wanted, for example, to be on a par in terms of salary and benefits with similar workers in private industry. As companies were raising the quality of employee benefits, public employees began to examine what labor unions were offering.

States became involved in collective bargaining at about the same time as the federal government. Wisconsin, in 1959, was the first state to pass a law allowing collective bargaining to occur. By 1971 twenty-one states had required public employers to use either collective bargaining or the "meet and confer" process with representatives.[59] Collective bargaining is a process in which employee representatives and the employer negotiate and agree on such employee matters as wages and fringe benefits. Most definitions include at least four elements, or related but distinguishable processes, in collective bargaining: (1) negotiations over wages, hours, and other terms of employment, (2) the execution of a written contract, (3) negotiation concerning interpretation of the contract, and (4) negotiation over the terms of a new agreement or of proposed modifications of an agreement.[60]

"Meet and confer" is basically the same thing as collective bargaining but means that management makes the final decision on all matters. Because not all states have legislation on collective bargaining, many cities and counties have passed ordinances establishing these rights. Unfortunately, the variety of rules and procedures are confusing and less efficient than those of the federal government.

The Advisory Commission on Intergovernmental Relations (ACIR) has urged states to pass laws supporting either "meet and confer" or collective negotiations, generally favoring the former because it is likely to be more acceptable to state and local government. The ACIR is also aware of the potential threat of the federal government passing legislation to mandate standardized labor practice policies which may be detrimental for state and local governments.

The first major federal policy for public employee organizations was the Lloyd-LaFollette Act of 1912. This act allowed federal employees individually or collectively to petition Congress to organize and make demands, rights which many employers refused to recognize. President Kennedy's Executive Order 10988 permitted employee organizations and top management to carry on cooperative relationships on labor matters as long as agreements did not conflict with existing laws.[61] This means that salaries, hours, and fringe benefits could not be bargained nor could an agency's budget, mission, or organization be negotiated.[62] Other important items covered included health services, vacation periods, and training and recreation programs.

By 1940 the Civil Service Commission had required "grievance machinery" to be established in all federal agencies. But in 1955 it was still illegal for federal employees to strike or belong to any organization that would support strikes. As unions grew larger and more militant, the U.S. Civil Service Commission set up an Office of Labor-Management Relations in 1966.

The next major change was President Nixon's Executive Order 11491 in October 1969.[63] This allowed for the recognition of only one union in order to eliminate fragmentation of competitive unions, and it created a "third-party machinery." The assistant secretary of labor rather than the department head or agency heads issues cease-and-desist orders to labor organizations violating the executive order.[64] Since then strikes have occurred, and the executive orders have undergone their first tests.[65]

The Right to Strike

In the last ten years the public has witnessed a number of major strikes—by the postal workers in 1970, the New York City schoolteachers in 1967, Los Angeles teachers in 1971, Baltimore police in 1974, the San Francisco transit workers in 1974, as well as other strikes by hospital workers, nurses, policemen, and firemen. One researcher has reported:

> The difference between 1958 and 1968 starkly illuminates the [strike] trend pattern. The number of work stoppages went from 15 near the end of the 1950s to 254 a decade later; the number of workers involved went from 1,700 to 202,000; the number of idle days exploded from 7,500 to 2.5 million. All of these figures represent rates of expansion far in excess of developments in private industry in the same period. The situation has been notoriously more serious in New York City: between 1964 and 1968 alone almost 2 million man-hours were lost due to strikes.[66]

There has been no leveling off in the number of strikes since the 1960s. The Federal Mediation Service reported 588 strikes involving more than 230,000 workers for the week ending 15 July 1974 as compared with 259 walkouts idling 70,000 workers for the same week in 1973. These figures were the highest since the service began keeping weekly strike records in

Figure 2   THE BIG JUMP IN WAGES, 1971–1974

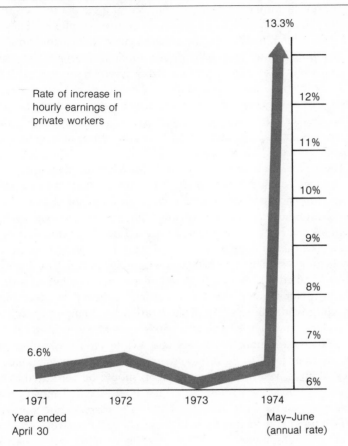

Reprinted from *U.S. News & World Report*. Copyright 1974, U.S. News & World Report, Inc., 22 July 1974, pp. 86–87.

1959. The labor dispute wave of 1974 was one of the most sweeping in the United States since World War II.[67] But, with the double-digit inflation and high interest rates beginning in 1974, that there will be more strikes involving more people is inevitable. With the ending of economic controls on wages and prices from 1971 to 1974, labor unions are scrambling to make up lost wages while employees are more militant to get pay increases and more willing to strike.

There is continuing disagreement over the right of public employees to strike. Academic literature on the subject was at one time nearly unanimously hostile toward public worker strikes, although it has recently begun to support strikes by public employees under certain circumstances.[68] As a matter of practice, if a union majority vote calls for a strike, little can be done to prevent public employees from walking off the job. Court injunctions and other laws may in some instances force employees back to work after a period of time, but public services cease during the stoppage.

How much interference to public services, for how long, and with what services, is tolerable? Strikes involving essential services, such as police and fire protection, may jeopardize public health, safety, and welfare. If strikes are to be legalized, essential services must be protected. If strikes in essential services do occur as a result of explosive and ugly grievances, however, the courts, legislators, and people may not be able to contain or end them.

There are additional problems in developing standards to protect those services considered essential. For example, who is to decide on the necessity for ending a strike that enters the realm of essentiality? Three methods can be used. First, an executive officer at the various levels of government should have the authority to use a Taft-Hartleylike law to prevent a legal strike that endangers an essential public service. Second, an independent commission of some type could have this power. Third, the decision could be handled by the courts. Another question is whether a distinction should be made among the various levels of government employees in determining who should strike. That is, are federal employees more essential than local employees? The affirmative view is weak. Many federal employees, such as Pentagon janitors and White House plumbers, are less important than local policemen and firemen. Finally, what kinds of employees, at any given level of government, should be permitted to strike? It is virtually impossible to determine just how essential most government services are, and how can they be ranked to satisfy public workers?

Two other considerations: will strikes have a disastrous effect on relations between employees and their supervisors, and what impact do they have on the civil service commission merit system? First, strikes are likely to have a detrimental effect on employee-supervisor relations, harming the mutual sense of trust and possibly causing a decline in work performance. Teacher strikes, for example, can result in greatly deteriorated relations that may continue for long after the strike has ended. San Francisco school officials who tried to keep classes going in 1974 were frustrated when school bus drivers honored the teachers' picket lines. Students reacted toward the strike in a variety of ways, including failure to attend classes. Parents may object to the teachers' demands, knowing that the strike will probably mean a tax rate increase.

Other examples, which also damage relationships between government employees and the community as well as relationships within government, are the transit strike that snarls travel for hundreds of thousands of commuters or a case of sewage-treatment plant employees opening the valves that allow raw sewage to flow into lakes, bays, or oceans because of insufficient personnel to operate the plant. Strikes by nurses in intensive-care units of public hospitals are not likely to be forgotten soon by patients.

Second, are strikes incompatible with merit systems? Civil service proponents fear that unions armed with the threat of strikes may replace the system of open competition for jobs and promotion based on merit.[69] One study has shown that collective bargaining is replacing the civil service as the protector of the public employee. The threat of union strike action on merit systems is ever present, and the significance of the threat to the civil service system and merit systems in general will become clearer in the years ahead.[70]

Finally, it has been argued that, as a way of controlling and directing them, strikes could be legalized; in this way illegal strikers and unions would lose credibility and legitimacy. As one researcher has observed:

> One of the problems with illegal government worker strikes is that they often occur sporadically in different bureaucracies, often without coordination, and they sometimes involve small and particularistic groups. Legalizing strikes might make possible the setting of conditions under which strikes could take place, including provision for large-unit strikes only. This might bring some order to the confusion of myriad public employee walkouts. Heavy penalties for striking will not work as a substitute; they have demonstrably failed. More and more strikes can be expected, since public unions contend that being militant and generating strikes is effective. Perhaps the best strategy is to legalize the strikes, so that one may endeavor to guide them.[71]

Laws prohibiting strikes were essentially ineffective at the federal level after the postal and air traffic controllers' strikes of 1970. Even though it was a felony, carrying a fine and possible imprisonment, for federal employees to strike, the postal workers were neither convicted nor punished.[72] Under the Taft-Hartley Act of 1955, strikes by federal public servants were prohibited if they "endangered the health, safety, or welfare of the public." This was also stated in a 1967 law in Vermont and held true for most state and local governments.[73]

Antistrike legislation was not much better among the states. In the state of New York, for example, it was illegal for employees to participate in strikes under the Condon-Wadlin Act of 1947, which stipulated that all employees who did so would be fired; if rehired, their pay would be frozen for three years, and they were required to serve a new five-year probationary period. The act proved unworkable, particularly after the 1966 transportation and subway strike in New York City. Employees were needed to run

Copyright © 1974 The Chicago Sun-Times. Reproduced by courtesy of Wil-Jo Associates, Inc. and Bill Mauldin.

the subway and therefore could not be fired. New legislation entitled the Taylor Law was enacted which stipulated that unions would be held responsible for any strikes that occurred. The Taylor Law required unions to pay heavy fines for each day a strike continued, but this did not deter New York schoolteachers from striking for fourteen days in 1967. The president of the union played the martyr and went to jail. Because the Condon-Wadlin Act and Taylor Law were not effective, the New York legislature in 1969 increased the fines, but this, too, proved ineffective in deterring public work stoppages.

Regardless of the laws and moral issues involved, what techniques are available for settling grievances, especially deadlocks? The procedures used in government are essentially the same as those used in private business: clarifying the list of demands and determination of the facts, mediation and conciliation, and arbitration.

Collective Bargaining

First, each side assembles a list of preliminary demands, indicating their cost and providing supporting evidence. These demands are often padded, and both sides realize that not all will be accepted. There may be "bridgehead demands" in which the union would like to see some new area, such as guaranteed employment, become effective in the future.[74] To ensure that collective bargaining is successful, both sides must observe "fair labor practices" or common rules. A government entity, such as a county or city, that refused to meet and bargain with employee organization representatives would be guilty of unfair labor practices.

Industry uses the National Labor Relations Board (NLRB) to handle complaints of improper labor practices. If either a union or business violates a procedure, appeals can be made to the NLRB, and cease-and-desist orders can result which are enforceable in federal courts. In government negotiations, unfair labor practices follow similar procedures of enforcement. However, the policies are primarily statements of intent and are not necessarily legally binding, although they generally represent a written pledge.

After demands are prepared by both sides, serious bargaining begins which both sides hope will result in a compromise rather than an impasse. Before contracts are signed, either mediation or arbitration may need to be used. Mediation is when an independent third party comes in to help resolve the dispute by recommending a solution that may or may not be accepted. Conciliation is the same as mediation except that no solution is suggested by the conciliator to either side. Individuals who fill mediation positions may come from state or federal government agencies such as the Federal Mediation and Conciliation Service. In a dispute, mediation is preferred because it is voluntary aid to help solve a labor deadlock.

Arbitration is a formal process, similar to a court procedure, of holding hearings and evaluating facts. Arbitration may be either voluntary or compulsory. Under voluntary arbitration, both sides agree in advance to accept as binding whatever the arbitrator decides. This is not as popular a technique as mediation but may be appropriately used when an impasse results in work stoppage involving an essential service.

Perhaps the least desirable method of solving disputes is compulsory arbitration because this results in the law binding both groups to accept the arbitrator's decision. More and more state and local governments may prefer this method for strikes that affect essential services, but unions can also take advantage of it by holding out for a longer period, hoping to get a better deal from the arbitrators. What happens if an arbitrator grants a pay increase to schoolteachers when voters have made clear to the school board that no more tax-increase bonds will be passed?

Collective bargaining will require increasingly experienced negotiators to avoid such pitfalls as demands that cannot reasonably be met. Because future strikes by public workers are inevitable, government representatives must be able to compromise and to determine the extent to which demands go beyond the public interest. While no amount of discussion or analysis will satisfy the strongest proponents or opponents of the legality of public worker strikes, some compromises must be sought while government is still in the saddle. The straps are already growing loose.

CASE STUDY 1

A Supervisor for Unit II

ROBERT T. GOLEMBIEWSKI and MICHAEL WHITE, eds.

The following case study, which illustrates a problem in personnel selection, appears deceptively simple because the situation is so commonplace. Of two positions to be filled, the first lends itself to easy solution because the candidate has all the necessary qualifications. The second position is problematic, however, because the division chief must select one candidate out of four, all of whom have desirable qualities. A hasty or ill-advised decision made in this circumstance may lead to employee unrest and discipline problems that can have a cumulative damaging effect on the organization and its per-

Robert T. Golembiewski and Michael White, "A Supervisor for Unit II" in Robert T. Golembiewski and Michael White (Eds.), CASES IN PUBLIC MANAGEMENT, © 1973 by Rand McNally College Publishing Company, Chicago, pp. 12–14.

sonnel, especially those who are repeatedly passed over for promotion. As you read, ask yourself these questions:

1. *Would the knowledge that your decision is being watched with considerable interest by all parties make any difference in your decision-making process?*
2. *In what ways is this problem of selecting new people typical for heads of agencies and departments?*
3. *Would the fact that all employees belonged to unions make any difference in your decision making?*
4. *How would you decide?*
5. *What would be the basis of your decision, and how would you justify it to your superior?*

A substantial increase in the volume of work in the division you head, Administrative/Technical, results in a management survey designed to provide better utilization of personnel. One recommendation calls for the creation of two new units to be made up of personnel specialized in the handling of certain kinds of cases.

This recommendation is approved by your bosses and you, as chief of the division, are told to go ahead and fill the two positions. The two units are to be made up of GS-14s and GS-13s, with a GS-15 in charge. One unit poses no problems: the person selected is clearly well qualified for the job and, in addition, is one of the most experienced people in the organization. He is well thought of by both supervisors and subordinates.

In Unit II, however, the case is not as clear-cut. The leading candidates are:

George Wilson, a man who has been with Admin/Tech for sixteen years, who has both a legal and an accounting background and is the most senior person available. He is regarded as a good technical man, with a reputation for thoroughness. But he is also known as a stickler for detail. It pains Wilson to let a case leave him unless it reflects the best possible thinking he can give it. This means, of course, that he is limited in the number of cases he can handle, although he puts in a fair amount of overtime.

His superiors know that when they get a recommendation from Wilson, however, they can depend on it.

Wilson also has the respect of his associates, but they do not find it easy to work with him. When they have been members of task forces of which he has been in charge, they have felt that he required too much of them, took too great an interest in the detail of the job, and was likely to tell them precisely how to go about doing it.

Wendell Rogers is ten years younger than Wilson and has had his GS-14 rating only six months. He is a goal-setter who believes in getting the job done. Twice in the past two years, however, he has pushed ahead faster than the information he had would warrant. Consequently, major errors were made. One of these errors was caught before it left Admin/Tech, so no harm was done. But the other error resulted in considerable controversy in which the agency's chief executive himself became involved. In fairness to Rogers, it should be noted that both these errors were work done by subordinates which he had not examined carefully.

Rogers is well-liked by his associates and would be a popular choice for unit head.

Marbury Madison had been in Admin/Tech earlier in his career, but he is now in the San Francisco region where he has been on special assignment for the past two years. He has been a GS-14 for three years, and is regarded by those at agency headquarters as well-qualified for the position.

Madison also has the respect of those who have worked with him, although he is not regarded as GS-16 talent.

Madison and his wife both like living in San Francisco, where they recently bought a house. They do not really want to return to Washington, but they might be persuaded to do so if they felt they were badly needed.

Hannibal Hyde, the fourth possibility for the position, has spent most of his career in another area of Admin/Tech, but he has handled some of the same kinds of cases that would be given to the new unit he might head. However, the general feeling is that it would take him at least six months to get on top of the job.

There is some reason to believe that his promotion would cause some resentment by division members because an "outsider" was brought in.

Hyde also believes that he has a good chance for promotion within a few months where he is now.

Several added factors which may bear on the selection should be noted. The Deputy Administrator of your agency knows Wilson personally and has a high respect for his ability on technical matters, although he is aware of the fact that Wilson is likely to be tough on his subordinates. As for Rogers, there is some fear in the front office that he may not be careful enough with detail, although they admit that this opinion is based largely on only two cases in which errors were made.

The Personnel Office, on the other hand, prefers a good supervisor who can bring his subordinates along; they are inclined toward Rogers. Whatever is done, Personnel urges that no appointment be made on an "acting" basis.

The Training Division points out that Madison has not been through its management-training programs. Training does not want to see anyone given a job of this nature who has not participated in its programs, although Training does not denigrate Madison's abilities. All other possible promotees have been through these programs.

CASE STUDY 2

Managerial Prerogative or Social Objective?

ROBERT T. GOLEMBIEWSKI and MICHAEL WHITE, eds.

With the passage in 1972 of the Equal Employment Opportunity Act and because of several court decisions prohibiting job discrimination on the basis of race, sex, age, religion, national origin, or physical handicap, it has become essential for responsible supervisors to know and understand the requirements of new affirmative action programs. Some employees may object to the enforcement of these requirements if they believe that the candidates selected for a particular job are not the best qualified. Non-minority applicants may resent what they regard as reverse discrimination.

The problem in this case involves the enforcement of affirmative action requirements, personnel attitudes toward such programs, and the legal and morale problems that may arise if the situation is mishandled. As you read, ask yourself:

1. *What kind of report would you write?*
2. *Is it wise to overlook one agency that is not complying with the enforcement program and emphasize the outstanding job that another agency, such as Pleasantville, is doing?*
3. *What alternatives are available to you?*

You are in the headquarters of the Personnel unit of Agency Z, and are mulling over the form and substance of a report you are going to write. That report poses some knotty issues, particularly because you only recently joined Agency Z.

Robert T. Golembiewski and Michael White, "Managerial Prerogative or Social Objective?" in Robert T. Golembiewski and Michael White (Eds.), CASES IN PUBLIC MANAGEMENT, © 1973 by Rand McNally College Publishing Company, pp. 96–100.

The basic details are direct. As a representative from the Personnel Department at national headquarters in Washington, D.C., you call on the field office at Pleasantville, Md., to ascertain its state of compliance with the agency's Affirmative Action (AA) program. AA seeks to strongly encourage the hiring of black, female, and minority employees. Your agency is deeply committed at the highest administrative and political levels. Your own Department of Personnel has taken a leading role in sponsoring and selling AA and similar programs, often at the expense of being criticized as social reformers who seem to forget there is a job to be done.

Although you find yourself in clear personal agreement with your agency's AA objective, you sense that old organizational irony again. The Personnel Department is supposed to provide advice, counsel, and help; it is outside the lines of command, and does not issue orders. But in this case, as in many others, the "staff" is put in the position of checking up on the lower "line." Often, the "staff" is even accused of spying for top management, of being informants for the executive "line" officials who want to control operations at the lower "line" levels.

Specifically, the report you eventually write will go up through the several levels of Personnel, and thence to upper-line management. From there, Pleasantville will variously learn about the tone and impact of your report—whether it is good, bad, or indifferent, but especially if it is bad. You are going to Pleasantville, then, as a kind of policeman, who may be helpful and can blow whistles, but who has no authority to make arrests.

As such visits go, the one to Pleasantville goes very well. Not only are you pleasantly surprised at being given such a nice assignment so soon; and not only do you enjoy being out of the office; but paramountly, things go well because the local office has done a really great job in implementing AA. Very early, it becomes clear that the Pleasantville office has a strong commitment to AA. And you come to conclude, after two days of probing, that there probably is no other local office in your agency which can boast of a stronger record over the past twenty-four months in hiring blacks, women, and minority group members. Moreover, Pleasantville managers clearly have not been going for numbers alone. They seek and attract qualified personnel, and have specialized training programs to help their new employees smoothly move into the organization. Problems with AA at Pleasantville are minor ones.

But one unit of the Pleasantville office stands out prominently. The unit has some twenty-five employees, which is about 8 percent of the total Pleasantville work force. However, the unit has no black employees in 1972. In fact, it had more black employees two years ago. No women have ever worked in this unit, moreover, except as clerks and stenographers. You also notice the entry "1" under the column "Other Minority Employees" on the AA Report of this deviant unit. That employee, as you learn on checking, turns out to be a highly skilled and elderly employee of Spanish birth, from a wealthy family, who fled to this country as an adult in 1934 to avoid the revolution. He has been employed by the Pleasantville office for sixteen years. Hardly an AA recruit, he!

You check further, and find that the supervisor of the unit—uniformly referred to as Mr. Johnson—is both extremely competent and extremely prejudiced. He has been with the agency for twenty-three years, almost all of it in his present position. He is sixty-one, almost sixty-two.

Johnson's competence is almost legendary. The head of the Pleasantville office honestly believes that Johnson is the best in his specialty he has ever seen, a man who could have been promoted many times but who has decided simply to become better and better at what he is doing. Moreover, his external clients swear by the supervisor. They consider him both fair and extremely competent in subtle and demanding work.

Mr. Johnson's prejudices are also strong and open, but he does such an outstanding job that almost all his employees quickly develop strong loyalties to him. A small minority of his employees do learn that they and Johnson are on different wave lengths, and they quickly transfer or leave the agency. Those who remain refuse even to discuss the supervisor's "one unfortunate blind spot." Their loyalty has many sources, no doubt. Note only that the supervisor is successful to an unprecedented degree at getting "his people" promoted. A number of them have already reached positions in the lower levels of senior management in your agency. They are even known as Johnson's Boys, you learn.

About three years before, in 1969, the head of the Pleasantville office did attempt to broaden Mr. Johnson's perspectives by insisting on his adherence to AA. Several eligibles were hired, in fact, but their experience was uniformly bad. Most left the agency quickly, or requested reassignment. They complained of harassment, constant criticism, and lack of training opportunities. The supervisor explained he was too concerned with efficiency to give much time to "sociological experiments." Management investigated, and found no blatant misuse of supervisory power. But Mr. Johnson's lack of enthusiasm, at least, is patent.

Pleasantville management takes the easy route, after a year of the unit being a revolving door for AA recruits. Management transfers all remaining AA recruits into other units; and the local Personnel office is instructed by local management not to send any future lists of AA eligibles to Mr. Johnson.

The result is one lily-white unit, save for the elderly Spanish-American, in a local office with an otherwise-splendid AA record. . . .

Your decision will not be easy. Consider only these issues:

From at least one point of view, Pleasantville's management has exercised a reasonable managerial prerogative in a sensible way. Where does headquarters staff draw the line on such issues to avoid being accused by field management of constantly intruding into operating matters, of unnecessary meddling?

What is the extent of your staff job? Certainly, you have the responsibility of making certain that Pleasantville management knows of the situation. Beyond that, given Pleasantville's outstanding AA record, does your responsibility extend so far as to risk relationships by raising the issue at headquarters?

What of the Personnel unit at Pleasantville? For whom do they work? What are the implications of their agreeing not to forward lists of AA eligibles to Johnson? Will Personnel at headquarters discipline their field representatives if the accommodation is revealed? Will Pleasantville management try to protect the local Personnel representatives?

Since Johnson is almost sixty-two, would not the prudent course be to wait on his retirement? . . .

CASE STUDY 3

The Post Office Strike of 1970

J. JOSEPH LOEWENBERG

Before the nationwide postal strike of 1970, the most active public employee groups, including the police, schoolteachers, fire fighters, and sanitation workers, were to be found at the level of local government. But as public employee unions grow more militant, the potential for strikes is increasing at all levels of government today. Collective bargaining is where the action is these days, and the threat of strikes is a serious problem for government entities that may be unwilling or unable to meet strikers' demands. The following case study traces the union background, reform proposals, and negotiations accompanying one of the first major strikes against the federal government. As you read, consider these questions:

1. *What factors were responsible for this strike?*
2. *Why were most unions opposed to government reform proposals for the Post Office?*

J. Joseph Loewenberg, "The Post Office Strike of 1970," in J. Joseph Loewenberg and Michael H. Moskow, COLLECTIVE BARGAINING IN GOVERNMENT: Readings and Cases, © 1972, pp. 192–202. Reprinted by permission of Prentice-Hall, Inc., Englewood Cliffs, New Jersey.

3. In your opinion, was this strike justified and legal?

4. Should government's response to a no-strike policy be compulsory arbitration?

Until the postal strike, the most sacrosanct, inviolate rule of federal employment relations was that employees could not strike against the federal government. The introduction and development of collective bargaining between the government and its employees in the 1960s in no way diminished the standing of this rule.

The rash of strikes and strike threats that plagued public employee labor relations at the local level in the 1960s had no counterpart at the federal level. The federal government had experienced several work stoppages, but these involved relatively few people and brief time periods, and they were dealt with promptly. In one case, for example, eighty-five sheet-metal workers who struck the Tennessee Valley Authority in 1962 were fired.

BACKGROUND

The Post Office Department

The Post Office Department of the United States traces its history back to 1775. In 1970 it was, next to the Department of Defense, the largest department in the federal government, employing a total of approximately seven hundred fifty thousand workers who were located in almost every community of the United States.

The Post Office Department, as one of the executive departments of the federal government, received its funds from Congress. Any revenue collected by the department was turned over to the General Fund of the United States. By 1970 congressional appropriations to operate the department amounted to over $8 billion annually. The deficit between these appropriations and revenues was about $1¼ billion annually.

Congress also determined the wages, hours, and benefits of Post Office employees. Postal workers were on a separate wage classification system from other federal employees, but wage rates were traditionally linked among the various systems. Vacations, pensions, insurance, and other forms of supplementary compensation were identical for all federal employees.

When collective bargaining was introduced into the federal government on a large scale in 1962, only matters that were determined by the separate agencies or by lower levels within the agency were potential subjects of bargaining. Unions representing post office employees were quick to set up negotiations at the local level and at the national level of the post office. But they found it necessary to continue lobbying with Congress over economic matters, just as they had done long before the advent of collective bargaining.

The unions
Postal employees had a long history of organization; many of the pronouncements of government officials on unions in the first decade of this century were specifically directed toward postal unions. By 1970 almost 90 percent of all postal workers were represented by unions that bargained in their behalf.

Seven major postal unions represented workers on a craft basis and were members of the AFL-CIO. The largest of these were the United Federation of Postal Clerks (UFPC) and the National Association of Letter Carriers of the U.S.A. (NALC); together the two unions represented over five hundred thousand workers. The seven unions held exclusive recognition at the national level, which meant that they could bargain with the department for all workers in their craft. To facilitate bargaining, these unions dealt jointly on matters of common interest with the department.

Two other unions that represented nonsupervisory employees were organized on an industrial basis. The larger of these, the National Postal Union, had considerable strength in some major cities. Neither was recognized at the national level and therefore could not take part in bargaining with the agency at that level.

Despite the unions' bargaining activity and their continuing lobbying efforts with Congress, union members showed signs of unrest. In 1968 the United Federation of Postal Clerks and the National Postal Union eliminated the no-strike provisions from their constitutions. A similar move failed in the convention of the National Association of Letter Carriers, but the convention subsequently directed its officers to seek ways that would grant federal employees the right to strike. The union introduced legal suits to test the constitutionality of the federal statutes forbidding strikes by federal employees and the affidavit not to assert the right to strike required of every employee. The affidavit was declared unconstitutional by a federal court in December 1969; the government appealed the decision. Meanwhile, in the summer of 1969, eighty-eight clerks stayed away from work in a Bronx (N.Y.) post office; it was officially declared a two-week leave without pay rather than a strike.

By early 1970 many postal workers were becoming increasingly restive with their working conditions, the government's proposals for reform of the Post Office Department, and the leaders of their unions. The pay scale for the vast majority of postal employees, including carriers and clerks, ranged from $6,176 to $8,442; the range was paid in twelve steps over twenty-one years. A pay raise contemplated for late 1969 was stalled in Congress and was tied to a postal reform. In addition, post office employees complained about outdated and dilapidated facilities and equipment, the hazards of delivering the mail in an increasingly violent society, and post office policies discriminating against regular employees. For instance, workers charged that the department had reduced overtime for regular employees and had given this work to part-timers in order to save money. The result of deteriorating conditions was that the post office has a high turnover and some unfilled jobs in large cities.

The conditions prevalent throughout the country were aggravated in New York City by the high cost of living, the relative success of municipal employees in collective bargaining, and the relative militancy of the postal unions in New York. Although inflation was a national concern, the Bureau of Labor Statistics' cost-of-living index showed that prices had increased faster in New York City than the national average; in actual dollar terms, the overall cost had always been higher in New York. The federal government's figures showed that a family of four needed $11,236 for a moderate standard of living in New York City. Meanwhile, New York City employees had managed to outstrip federal employees in economic improvements. Postal workers claimed that municipal employees such as police or sanitation workers were receiving substantially higher pay than they were receiving, thereby completely reversing the relative financial standing of the occupations of two decades earlier. Within three years of starting, sanitation workers received $1,500 more than a postal worker could expect to receive after twenty-one years. Other benefits gained in collective bargaining gave further advantages to the municipal employees. Suggestions by New York letter carriers that the union support area wage differentials in the postal service was not accepted by the national leadership. Some members planned to depose the incumbent president at the convention in August 1970. The New York City local, Branch 36, had always been considered progressive; it had led the unsuccessful attempt to change the union's no-strike provision in the 1968 convention.

Pay raise proposals

In the fall of 1969 the House of Representatives and the Senate considered legislation to provide pay raises for all federal employees. The House bill, passed in October, provided postal workers with a 5.4 percent increase effective October 1, 1969, and an additional 5.7 percent increase as of July 1970; it lowered the number of years required to make the top salary of a grade from twenty-one to eight years. In addition, the House bill provided for a Federal Employee Salary Commission and Board of Arbitration to determine yearly salary changes for federal employees. In December 1969 the Senate approved a different bill providing for a 4 percent increase for federal workers earning under $10,000, with relatively smaller increases going to employees in the higher grades; these increases would be effective January 1, 1970. No joint conference was held on these two bills because of the pending debate on post office reform.

In the federal fiscal 1971 budget presented in January 1970, President Nixon proposed a 5.75 percent pay increase for federal employees to bring their wages in line with those paid in comparable jobs in private industry. He postponed the effective date of the increase from July 1970 to January 1971 to give evidence to the country of the administration's anti-inflationary position and to help keep the budget balanced. White House spokesmen continued to press for tying a pay raise for postal workers to passage of the administration's proposals for post office reform.

Post Office reform proposal

The concept of a public corporation to take over the operation of the Post Office Department had been initiated by the Johnson administration. Nevertheless, the pressures for reform were stronger in 1969 and 1970 than ever before.

The administration proposed that the Post Office Department be removed from the President's cabinet and be converted into a public corporation. The corporation would be governed by nine members, two appointed by the President. The corporation would be responsible for its own financing, including the sale of bonds to raise funds, and for setting postal rates. Employees of the postal corporation would no longer be covered by Civil Service regulations and would bargain collectively for their wages and working conditions. The no-strike provision, however, would remain.

Most unions representing postal employees were opposed to the reform proposal, presumably because they would no longer have access to Congress and they doubted the effectiveness of collective bargaining without a right to strike. One exception was the president of the letter carriers, who supported the reform proposal if Congress also approved the 5.4 percent pay increase. Congressional leaders of the post office committees were also dubious about the reorganization proposal which would remove considerable power and prestige from Congress. On March 12, 1970, however, the House Post Office and Civil Service Committee approved the President's proposal for a public corporation for the postal service.

THE STRIKE

On the same day that the House Post Office and Civil Service Committee recommended the reorganization of the postal system, NALC leaders were preparing for a regular monthly membership meeting of Branch 36 in New York City to discuss the progress of wage legislation. Much to the surprise of the leadership, the members at the meeting decided to take a strike vote on March 17 to enforce a demand for a 40 percent increase in pay and a reduced-step pay scale.

Of the 6,700 members enrolled in Branch 36, 2,614 participated in the strike vote; the final tally showed the strike was approved, 1,555–1,055. As other postal unions, NALC had no strike fund. Nonetheless, the walkout started the next morning. The letter carriers in Manhattan and the Bronx were quickly joined by the letter carriers in Brooklyn. The twenty-six thousand member Manhattan-Bronx Postal Union, which represented clerks and mail handlers, respected the letter carriers' picket lines. The result was an immediate and complete disruption of mail service in New York City. The first major strike in the 195-year history of the U.S. postal service was on.

The strike caught everyone unprepared. Business, heavily dependent on mail service to transmit bills and collect receipts as well as to supply a regular stream of communications, was severely hampered. Organizations using the mails to deliver services, whether financial advice or relief checks found they could no longer do business. A Harris poll taken after the strike showed that 61 percent of the public sympathized more with the demands of the postal employees than with the federal government, while 25 percent favored the government. The average citizen found the discomfort of not receiving personal mail mitigated by the absence of bills and ''junk'' mail and the unexpected extension of payment deadlines. The public press, while critical of the postal workers' tactics, generally was sympathetic to their demands.

The government followed the rhetorical and legal precedents used in previous work-stoppage situations, but the monumentality of the postal situation soon showed the traditional methods to be ineffective. Postmaster General Blount announced, ''We simply cannot tolerate a mail strike in this country.'' At the same time he placed an embargo on all mail in New York City and adjacent areas, thereby affecting the mail service of 10 million persons. All employees absent without permission were put on nonpay status.

On the first day of the strike the government obtained from a federal district court a civil injunction ordering an end to the strike. The strike was considered a violation of the Federal Code which makes such action a criminal offense and the offender subject to a fine up to $1,000 and/or up to a year and a day in prison. Leaders of Branch 36 announced the injunction to their members and withdrew pickets to avoid charges of violating the injunction. However, the work stoppage in New York City continued and soon spread to other areas.

Other unions representing postal employees were also quick to disavow complicity and official sanction of the work stoppage. The presidents of the seven unions holding exclusive national recognition from the post office telegraphed their respective local units as follows:

> Because of the provisions of Executive Order 11491, the labor agreement existing between our organization and the Post Office Department, and the existing statutes, we cannot support or condone the service interruption which has occurred and we collectively instruct all affected postal employees to return to work immediately.
>
> We further request an immediate, full and objective congressional investigation of all the conditions and circumstances which brought this situation about.

Nevertheless, more letter carriers were going off the job, and other postal workers refused to work if the letter carriers were not.

The spread of the walkout at first represented the ripple effect of a pebble thrown into a pool. The strike spread from New York City to its suburbs, then into New Jersey and Philadelphia. But then it jumped quickly to the Midwest and West Coast. Within three days half of the country was hit by the mail strike, with major metropolitan areas from Boston to Los Angeles affected. Only the South and Southwest continued to enjoy normal mail service. At the height of the strike, four days after it had started, over two hundred thousand or 28 percent of all postal workers were off the job.

By then congressional leaders were becoming increasingly concerned with the economic impact of the strike and the futility of legal action and public appeals to end the strike. They declared that Congress would consider pay legislation only after the strike had ended. This attitude, endorsed by the administration, was also supported by the leaders of the national postal unions who felt threatened by their members' continuing refusal to follow direction. In an effort to provide a satisfactory way out of the impasse, a meeting was held on March 20 between the leaders of the postal unions with exclusive national recognition and Secretary of Labor George P. Shultz, which resulted in an agreement to discuss "the full range of issues being raised . . . as soon as we are assured that the work stoppages are ended." This agreement became the administration's position throughout the remainder of the strike.

The agreement could not be implemented. Letter carriers in one city after another rejected the agreement and voted to continue the strike. President Rademacher of the NALC was hanged in effigy. Continuing communications between Secretary Shultz and his staff and the unions for the purpose of getting striking employees back to work failed. Pressure was mounting on the administration to take more drastic action.

On Monday, March 23, President Nixon declared a national emergency:

> What is at issue then is the survival of a government based upon law. Essential services must be maintained and, as president, I shall meet my constitutional responsibility to see that those services are maintained.

The president ordered twenty-five hundred active-duty troops to help move essential mail in New York City and called up sixteen thousand members of the National Guard to stand by. It marked the first time that troops had been used to replace workers of the federal government.

The reaction to the President's move by organized labor was predictable; George Meany, president of the AFL-CIO, declared:

> We deplore the use of military personnel to perform work of civilian employees of the post office. . . . This action will not restore mail services nor contribute to an early resolution of the problems and circumstances which caused the stoppage of those services.

At the same time he urged postal employees to return to work.

Congressional attitudes also indicated a shift. In its eagerness to see the strike end, it was reported that Congress was willing to consider an increase in wages for postal employees before the complete end of the strike.

Postal employees began to return to work. On Monday about 20 percent of those who had stayed away from work returned, principally in Pittsburgh, Milwaukee, and cities in Connecticut. On Tuesday even more returned in Boston, Buffalo, Philadelphia, Cleveland, Detroit, Chicago, and San Francisco. Although over one hundred thousand postal employees were still off the job, fifty-seven thousand in New York City, it was becoming clear that the strike was waning.

On Wednesday, March 25, the strike ended in New York City. The 10,600 troops who had been used to handle the mail had accomplished little more than indicate the administration's interest in restoring mail service. Yet local postal union leaders in New York recommended a return to work so that the promised negotiations could commence in Washington. Their action was prompted by a federal court order finding Branch 36 in contempt of court, ordering the letter carriers back to work, and levying fines against Branch 36 if the strike continued after March 25, with the fines escalating from $10,000 for the first day to $20,000 on the second day, and so on. The leaders talked of a package including a 12 percent pay increase retroactive to October 1969, a reduced longevity scale, full payment by the government of health benefits, binding arbitration of disputes, and amnesty for strikers. Moreover, if the negotiations failed to produce results in five days, they promised to recommend resumption of the strike. The membership heartily endorsed the recommendations.

THE NEGOTIATIONS

When it became obvious to the administration that the strike was crumbling, negotiations between the government and the postal unions were set to begin on March 25. The government team was composed of officials of the Post Office Department under the leadership of the deputy postmaster general. The spokesman for the seven unions was an aide of President Meany of the AFL-CIO.

The week of collective bargaining covered a range of subjects, but talks centered principally on pay, the postal authority, and amnesty for strikers. Everyone was aware of the significance of bargaining on each of these subjects. Congress, which had been impatient to settle the outstanding issues involved in the strike, was now content to await the result of negotiations before acting.

On April 2 the parties reached agreement and signed a memorandum with the following provisions:

1. A 6 percent wage increase for all postal employees retroactive to December 27, 1969.
2. A jointly bargained and sponsored reorganization of the Post Office Department to provide for:
   a. collective bargaining procedures under a statutory framework establishing methods for conducting elections, providing one or more methods for resolving negotiating impasses, and requiring collective bargaining over all aspects of wages, hours, and working conditions including grievance procedures, final and binding arbitration of disputes, and in general all matters that are subject to collective bargaining in the private sector.
   b. an additional 8 percent wage increase for postal workers effective as of the date the enabling legislation becomes law.
   c. negotiations with the unions, to be immediately undertaken to establish a new wage schedule whereby an employee reaches the maximum step for his labor grade after no more than eight years in that grade.
   d. a structure for the department so that it can operate on a self-contained basis and endow it with authority commensurate with its responsibilities to improve, manage, and maintain efficient and adequate postal services.
3. A promise of no disciplinary action "against any postal employee with respect to the events of March 1970, until discussions have taken place between the Department and such employee's union on the policy to be followed by the Department."

The government had assured the leaders of other federal unions that the results of any retroactive wage increases negotiated by the seven postal unions would be extended to cover all federal employees. The 6 percent agreed to in bargaining increased the federal budget by almost $3 billion.

Despite concern about the effects of such an added expenditure on the precariously balanced budget and the economy, there was no resistance to the basic proposal. Both houses of Congress quickly held hearings and voted on the legislation to effect the increase. On April 15 President Nixon signed the implementing legislation.

The details of the independent postal service and of labor-management relations in that service were negotiated and agreed to by the parties. On April 16 President Nixon sent a message to Congress endorsing the results of that agreement:

1. An independent United States Postal Service under the direction of a nine-member bipartisan commission. The postal service would set its own rates, subject to congressional veto, and would be empowered to borrow funds.

2. Collective bargaining between the postal service and employee representatives "over wages, hours, and, in general, all working conditions that are subject to collective bargaining in the private sector." The National Labor Relations Board would be given jurisdiction over unit determinations, representation issues, and unfair labor practices involving postal service employees. The ban on strikes would continue. The final step for negotiation impasses would be binding arbitration.

3. A pay raise of 8 percent when the reorganization law would be enacted, and prompt bargaining to compress pay steps to not more than eight years. The President also proposed new postal rates to reduce the amount of subsidy required by the Post Office Department. The proposal was for a 33 percent increase in first class mail, a 50 percent increase in second class mail, and a 33 percent increase in third class mail. At the same time the President proposed that the federal subsidy would decline annually until 1978 when the postal service should be self-supporting.

The heart of the reorganization proposal was similar to what President Nixon had proposed in 1969 and what the House Post Office and Civil Service Committee had approved in March 1970. The labor-management sections were more elaborate than they had originally been, but fundamentally no different. The President had been forced by political pressure to reduce his request for an increase in first class postal rates from 67 percent to 33 percent. The tie-in of an 8 percent wage increase to passage of the reorganization was undoubtedly an inducement for the postal unions to agree to the reorganization. In fact, it was the endorsement of the postal unions which marked the biggest change between the reorganization proposal of April 1970 and earlier versions.

In a joint press conference with Postmaster General Blount, George Meany commented on the reason for the changed position by the labor unions:

This is one of the most significant events in the history of collective bargaining. This legislation which the Administration will introduce and which we will support in Congress is proof positive that collective bargaining is viable and effective.

We in the AFL-CIO, quite candidly, see these negotiations as setting the stage for the future. We believe that collective bargaining can be and should be extended to all workers in the Federal Government.

OBSERVATIONS

In retrospect, it is perhaps not so surprising that the first major strike against the federal government occurred in March 1970 as that it occurred at all and that the result was not catastrophic. Contrary to the doomsayers, the nation survived and federal employee-management relations were altered to adjust to the new circumstances.

Certainly the postal workers, long well organized and closely identified with blue-collar trades because of their pay and working conditions, felt they were caught in a political squeeze by the administration's insistence that pay increases and postal reform be considered as a single package. Traditional lobbying methods with Congress were ineffective in breaking the log jam. The New York letter carriers, who were already disenchanted with national union leadership and had particular financial problems, had only to look around them to understand the role and effect of pressure activity:

Everybody else strikes and gets a big pay increase. The teachers, sanitation men and transit workers all struck in violation of the law and got big increases. Why shouldn't we? We've been nice guys too long.

But the basic issues confronting New York postal employees were common throughout the postal service. Once it became apparent that the Post Office Department could not or would not act decisively to end the walkout, strike fever spread rapidly. The spell—and the law—of not striking against the government had been broken.

While the strike had an immediate effect on business and the economy, it was apparent that a short strike did not really disturb the public. Even those who believed a strike was wrong supported the postal employees in the issues they were striking for. The government therefore could not expect public pressure to end the strike.

One of the main problems confronting the parties was how to end the strike once it had begun. Since national leaders of the postal unions immediately disavowed support of the strike, they had little control over the actions of striking employees. Moreover, the government showed that it really could not handle a major postal crisis without regular employees. The use of troops in New York City was symbolic but limited in application and ineffective in moving the mails. Perhaps major contributing factors to the end of the strike were the small size of union treasuries, the lack of personal resources by strikers, and the realization that some of the major objects of the strike had been gained. The federal court order levying fines against Branch 36 provided a timely rationale for defining the end of the walkout.

The role of George Meany, president of the AFL-CIO, was critical in the postal strike of 1970. He welded the position of the seven postal unions, became the communications link between the postal unions and the administration, provided the spokesman for labor in negotiations, and in general assumed the leadership position. In so doing, he added to his stature within the labor movement, in government circles, and with the public. His actions demonstrated the AFL-CIO's new interest in and commitment to public sector bargaining.

The repercussions of the strike were likely to continue for some time. The strike served to highlight the division between members and leaders of some of the unions; challenges to incumbent leaders and established policies were quickly forthcoming in NALC, for instance. The issue of postal reorganization was resolved, but the implementation would undoubtedly bring new problems. The most significant impact of the postal strike would concern neither the postal unions nor the postal service. The strike raised the question of the future of collective bargaining in the federal service in a new light. The existing framework and practices seemed suddenly anachronistic. . . . Perhaps the significance of the impact of the strike was best summarized in an editorial of the postal clerks:

> It was a strike.
> It was illegal.
> It had an immense impact on the nation—an impact equalled only by the enormity of the grievance which provoked it.
> It's our guess that the postal service will never be the same again—and that goes for the federal services generally.

NOTES

1. For a thoughtful discussion of the system, see Paul P. Van Riper, *History of the United States Civil Service*. Frederick Mosher has noted, "Clearly each [period] began before the beginning date assigned, and the influence of none of them has yet ended" (F. C. Mosher, *Democracy and the Public Service*, p. 54).

2. Van Riper, *United States Civil Service*, p. 100.

3. Robert T. Golembiewski and Michael Cohen, *People in Public Service*, p. 128.

4. O. Glenn Stahl, *Public Personnel Administration*, p. 355.

5. Donald R. Harvey, *The Civil Service Commission*, p. 9.

6. For an excellent discussion of the patronage problems of presidents, see Martin Tolchin and Susan Tolchin, *To the Victor*, especially chap. 6; also see G. William Domhoff, *The Higher Circles*, chaps. 5–7.

7. U.S., Congress, Public Law 91–648, *Intergovernmental Personnel Act of 1970*, 91st Cong., 1st sess., 5 January 1971.

8. "Survey of Current Personnel Systems in State and Local Governments," *Good Government* 88, no. 1 (spring 1971): 1–3.

9. Albert H. Aronson, "Personnel Administration," *Civil Service Journal* 13, no. 3 (January–March 1973): 37–41.

10. Tolchin and Tolchin, *To the Victor*, pp. 40–41. However, according to a survey conducted in 1970 by the National Civil Service League, 84 percent of the nation's cities and 83 percent of the counties have merit systems (Jacob J. Rutstein, "Survey of Current Personnel Systems in State and Local Governments," *Good Government* 87, no. 2 [spring 1971]: 2 ff.).

11. Tolchin and Tolchin, *To the Victor*, p. 96.

12. Louis Fougere, ed., *Civil Service Systems*, pp. 20–32.

13. Robert E. Hampton, "Rededicating Ourselves to Merit Principles," *Personnel Administrations Public Personnel Review*, July–August 1972, p. 59.

14. For application of EEOC guidelines to employment tests, see *George Washington Law Review* 41, no. 3 (March 1973): 505–37. For suggestions for meeting requirements for the EEOC testing validity standards, see Lee R. Hess, "Synthetic Validity," *Training and Development Journal* 27, no. 2 (February 1973): 48–50; also see William F. Glueck, *Personnel: A Diagnostic Approach* (Dallas, Tex.: Business Publications, 1974), especially chap. 17. For details regarding some of the requirements that businesses holding government contracts may need to implement to ensure affirmative action, see David W. Pearson, "Federal Guidelines Force Affirmative Action Programs," *Personnel Administrator*, September–October 1971, pp. 26–28.

15. *Supreme Court Reporter* 91 (1971): 849; impact of case discussed in *Villanova Law Review* 17, no. 1 (November 1971): 147–58.

16. *Supreme Court Reporter* 91 (1971): 853.

17. Ibid.

18. Title 7, sec. 713(a) of the Civil Rights Act of 1964 as amended by the Equal Employment Opportunity Act of 1972.

19. *Supreme Court Reporter* 94 (1974): 1704.

20. Ibid., p. 1718.

21. See "Reverse Discrimination Means—Scram, White Man," *National Observer*, 13 July 1974, pp. 1, 14.

22. Don Mace, Jr., "FAA Modified Minority Hiring Program," *Federal Times*, 2 April 1971, p. 1.

23. Richard A. Lester, "Antibias Regulation of Universities"; also *U.S. News & World Report*, 22 July 1974, pp. 53–54.

24. Mosher, *Democracy and the Public Service*, p. 134.

25. Figures taken from *Occupational Outlook Handbook: 1972–1973*, p. 808.

26. See Thomas F. Fleming, Jr., "Manpower Impact of Purchases by State and Local Government," *Monthly Labor Review* 96, no. 6 (June 1973): 35.

27. A detailed position classification description at the federal level has been published by the U.S. Civil Service Commission, Bureau of Policies and Procedures (Washington, D.C.: Government Printing Office, 1971).

28. Leonard D. White, *Introduction to the Study of Public Administration*, pp. 352–53.

29. Congressional committee staff in 1969 found this to be a major problem (U.S., Congress, House, Committee on Post Office and Civil Service, Subcommittee on Position Classification, *Report on Job Evaluation and Ranking in the Federal Government*, 91st Cong., 1st sess., H.R. 91–28, 27 February 1969, pp. 21–53).

30. Harold Suskin, "Strengthening Position Classification in the Federal Government," *Public Personnel Review* 14, April 1958, p. 124.

31. Jay M. Shafritz, *Position Classification*, p. 28; see also U.S., Civil Service Commission, *Report on Survey of Job Evaluation and Pay for State Merit and Civil Service Systems Developed by Job Evaluation and Pay Review Task Force*, p. 9.

32. Bertram M. Gross, *The Managing of Organizations*, p. 408.

33. Gerald E. Caiden, *The Dynamics of Public Administration*, p. 213.

34. Arch Patton, "To Reform the Federal Pay System," *Business Week*, 9 March 1974, p. 34.

35. U.S., Congress, Public Law 87–973, *Federal Salary Reform Act of 1962*, H.R. 7927, 87th Cong., 2d sess., October 1962.

36. U.S., Congress, House, Public Law 91–656, *Federal Pay Comparability Act of 1970*, H.R. 13000, 91st Cong., 1st sess., 8 January 1971.

37. See Donald Schwab and Herbert Heneman, III, "Pay," *Personnel Administrator*, January–February 1974, pp. 19–21; also Shafritz, *Position Classification*, pp. 28–29.

38. Saul W. Gellerman, *Management by Motivation*, p. 189, maintains that only exceedingly large raises—the kind that can be granted by industry for outstanding service or that can change one's lifestyle—can motivate an employee to a higher level of performance; see Gellerman's condensed work in "Motivating Men with Money," *Fortune*, March 1968, p. 144.

39. Patton, "Federal Pay System," p. 34.

40. Schwab and Heneman, "Pay," pp. 19–20.

41. Fred K. Foulkes, *Creating More Meaningful Work*, p. 19; also David W. Belcher, "Ominous Trends in Wage and Salary Administration," *Personnel* 41, September–October 1964, p. 44. For a discussion of the Peter Principle, see Laurence J. Peter and Raymond Hull, *The Peter Principle*.

42. Edward E. Lawler, III, *Pay and Organizational Effectiveness*, pp. 214–15.

43. U.S., Congress, Senate, Senate Bill no. 385, chap. 815, signed 2 September 1970.

44. Municipal Manpower Commission, *Governmental Manpower for Tomorrow's Cities*, p. 116.

45. U.S., President, Executive Order 11348, *Providing for the Further Training of Government Employees*, 20 April 1967.

46. Robert E. Hampton, "Intergovernmental Personnel Act," *Good Government* 88, no. 4 (winter 1971): 13–17.

47. Commission on Organization of the Executive Branch of the Government, *Task Force Report on Federal Personnel*, pp. 60–62, 70–72.

48. Donald E. Britton, "A Critical Look," *Personnel Administrator*, January–February 1974, p. 27.

49. See Arthur H. Dick, "Job Evaluation's Role in Employee Relations," *Personnel Journal*, March 1974, pp. 176–79; Anthony M. Pasquale, *A New Dimension in Job Evaluation*, p. 3; John A. Patton et al., *Job Evaluation*, pp. 7–10; Robert G. Pajer, "A Systems Approach to Results Oriented Performance Evaluation," *Personnel Administration/Public Personnel Review*, November–December 1972, pp. 42–47.

50. Dick, "Job Evaluation in Employee Relations," p. 177.

51. Schwab and Heneman, "Pay," pp. 19–21.

52. Pajer, "A Systems Approach," pp. 45–46. Another study has observed that "evaluators should worry less about giving negative evaluations and more about giving each employee a well documented, unbiased appraisal" (see Thomas H. Stone, "An Examination of Six Prevalent Assumptions Concerning Performance Appraisal," *Public Personnel Management,* [November–December 1973], p. 414); see also Richard Schmuck et al., *Handbook of Organizational Development in Schools,* pp. 334–409.

53. *LMRS Newsletter* 3, no. 1 (January 1972): 5.

54. H. Conany and L. Dewey, "Union Membership among Government Employees," *Monthly Labor Review* 93, no. 7 (July 1970): 15–20; Robert E. Walsh, *Sorry—No Government Today,* chap. 4; and Carl W. Stenberg, "Labor-Management Relations in State and Local Government," *Public Administration Review* 32 (March–April 1972): 102–107.

55. R. Kelley, "Some Sensational Strikes in the Public Sector," in *Crisis in Public Employee Relations in the Seventies,* ed. Richard Murphy and Morris Sackman, chap. 7.

56. See Karl A. Van Asselt, "Impasse Resolution," in "A Symposium: Collective Bargaining in the Public Service," ed. Felix A. Nigro, *Public Administration Review* 32 (March–April 1972): 114–19.

57. Gus Tyler, "Why They Organize," in ibid., pp. 97–101.

58. Ibid., p. 99.

59. See Stenberg, "Labor-Management Relations," p. 104.

60. See the comprehensive work of Kenneth O. Warner, ed., *Management Relations with Organized Public Employees,* p. 104.

61. For full text of executive order, see Kenneth O. Warner and Mary L. Hennessey, *Public Management at the Bargaining Table,* pp. 349–58.

62. Ibid., p. 73.

63. See full text in U.S., Advisory Commission on Intergovernmental Relations, *Labor-Management Policies for State and Local Governments* (Washington, D.C.: Government Printing Office, 1969), pp. 220–30.

64. The secretary can be bypassed by the Federal Labor Relations Council (FLRC), which is made up of the chairman of the Civil Service Commission, the secretary of labor, a presidential representative, and other officials whom the president may need to designate.

65. 1971 Nixon issued Executive Order 11616 which added other provisions, such as permitting grievance procedures in all new agreements and limited negotiation by union representatives on government time.

66. Robert B. Fowler, "Normative Aspects of Public Employee Strikes," *Public Personnel Management,* March–April 1974, p. 130.

67. *Los Angeles Times,* 17 June 1974.

68. Anne M. Ross, "Public Employee Unions and the Right to Strike," *Monthly Labor Review* 92, no. 3 (March 1969): 14–18; J. Finkelman, "When Bargaining Fails," in *Collective Bargaining in the Public Service,* ed. Kenneth O. Warner, pp. 116–39; H. Wellington and R. Winter, Jr., "More on Strikes by Public Employees," *Yale Law Journal,* January 1970, pp. 418–43; R. Doherty and W. Oberer, *Teachers, School Boards, and Collective Bargaining,* pp. 102–5; Gordon T. Nesvig, "The New Dimensions of the Strike Question," *Public Administration Review* 28 (March–April 1968): 126–32; David Ziskind, *One Thousand Strikes of Government Employees,* pp. 232–40; and J. Joseph Loewenberg and Michael Moskow, *Collective Bargaining in Government,* pp. 192–202.

69. Charles Feigenbaum, "Civil Service and Collective Bargaining," *Public Personnel Management,* May–June 1974, pp. 244–52.

70. Mosher, *Democracy and the Public Service,* chaps. 6 and 7.

71. Fowler, "Public Employee Strikes," p. 136; also E. W. Bakke, "Reflections on the Future of Bargaining in the Public Sector," *Monthly Labor Review* 93, no. 7 (July 1970): 21–25.

72. See U.S., Congress, Public Law 84–330, H.R. 6122, 84th Cong., 1st sess., August 1955.

73. 1967 Executive Committee, National Governors' Conference, *Report of Task Force on State and Local Government Labor Relations*, p. 89.

74. Herbert J. Chruden and Arthur W. Sherman, Jr., *Personnel Management*, p. 469.

SELECTED BIBLIOGRAPHY

Aronson, Albert H. "Personnel Administration: The State and Local Picture." *Civil Service Journal* 13 (1973): 37–41.

Belcher, David W. "Ominous Trends in Wage and Salary Administration." *Personnel* 41 (1964): 44.

Britton, Donald E. "A Critical Look: Common Practice in Wage and Salary Administration." *Personnel Administrator*, January–February 1974, pp. 25–29.

Caiden, Gerald E. *The Dynamics of Public Administration: Guidelines to Current Transformations in Theory and Practice.* New York: Holt, Rinehart & Winston, 1971.

"Campus Courier Insert," San Francisco Region, U.S. Civil Service Commission, June–July 1972.

Chruden, Herbert J., and Sherman, Arthur W., Jr. *Personnel Management.* Cincinnati: South-Western Publishing Co., 1972.

Commission on Organization of the Executive Branch of the Government. *Task Force Report on Federal Personnel.* Washington, D.C.: Government Printing Office, 1949.

Conany, H., and Dewey, L. "Union Membership among Government Employees." *Monthly Labor Review* 93 (1970): 15–20.

Delap, Donald J. *Civil Service Manual.* Fond Du Lac, Wis.: North Central Press, 1964.

Dick, Arthur H. "Job Evaluation's Role in Employee Relations." *Personnel Journal*, March 1974, pp. 176–79.

Doherty, R., and Oberer, W. *Teachers, School Boards, and Collective Bargaining: A Changing of the Guard.* Ithaca, N.Y.: New York State School of Industrial and Labor Relations, 1967.

Domhoff, G. William. *The Higher Circles: The Governing Class in America.* New York: Random House, 1970.

EEOC Guidelines to Employment Tests. *George Washington Law Review* 41 (1973): 505–37.

Feigenbaum, Charles. "Civil Service and Collective Bargaining: Conflict or Compatibility?" *Public Personnel Management*, May–June 1974, pp. 244–52.

Finkelman, J. "When Bargaining Fails." In *Collective Bargaining in the Public Service: Theory and Practice*, edited by Kenneth O. Warner, pp. 116–39. Chicago: Public Personnel Association, 1967.

Fleming, Thomas F., Jr. "Manpower Impact of Purchases by State and Local Government." *Monthly Labor Review* 96 (1973): 35.

Fougere, Louis, ed. *Civil Service Systems.* Brussels: La Fonction Publique, International Institute of Administrative Services, 1967.

Foulkes, Fred K. *Creating More Meaningful Work.* New York: American Management Association, 1969.

Fowler, Robert B. "Normative Aspects of Public Employee Strikes." *Public Personnel Management,* March–April 1974, p. 130.

Gellerman, Saul W. *Management by Motivation.* New York: American Management Association, 1968.

Golembiewski, Robert T., and Cohen, Michael. *People in Public Service.* Itasca, Ill.: F. E. Peacock Publishers, 1970.

Gross, Bertram M. *The Managing of Organizations.* New York: Free Press, 1964.

Hampton, Robert E. "Intergovernmental Personnel Act: New Resources for Improving Public Service." *Good Government* 88 (1971): 13–17.

———. "Rededicating Ourselves to Merit Principles." *Personnel Administration/Public Personnel Review,* July–August 1972, p. 59.

Harvey, Donald R. *The Civil Service Commission.* New York: Praeger Publishers, 1970.

Kelley, R. "Some Sensational Strikes in the Public Sector." In *Crisis in Public Employee Relations in the Seventies,* edited by Richard Murphy and Morris Sackman, chap. 7. Washington, D.C.: Bureau of National Affairs, 1970.

Lawler, Edward E., III. *Pay and Organizational Effectiveness: A Psychological View.* New York: McGraw-Hill, 1971.

Lester, Richard A. *Antibias Regulation of Universities: Faculty Problems and Their Solution.* New York: McGraw-Hill, 1974.

LMRS [Labor-Management Relations Service] *Newsletter* 3 (1972): 5.

Loewenberg, J. Joseph, and Moskow, Michael. *Collective Bargaining in Government: Readings and Cases.* Englewood Cliffs, N.J.: Prentice-Hall, 1972.

Mace, Don, Jr. "FAA Modified Minority Hiring Program." *Federal Times,* 2 April 1971, p. 1.

Mosher, F. C. *Democracy and the Public Service.* New York: Oxford University Press, 1968.

Municipal Manpower Commission. *Governmental Manpower for Tomorrow's Cities.* New York: McGraw-Hill, 1962.

Nesvig, Gordon T. "The New Dimensions of the Strike Question." *Public Administration Review* 28 (1968): 126–32.

1967 Executive Committee. National Governors' Conference. *Report of Task Force on State and Local Government Labor Relations.* Chicago: Public Personnel Association, 1967.

Occupational Outlook Handbook: 1972–1973. Washington, D.C.: Bureau of Labor Statistics, p. 808.

Pajer, Robert G. "A Systems Approach to Results Oriented Performance Evaluation." *Personnel Administration/Public Performance Review,* November–December 1972, pp. 42–47.

Pasquale, Anthony M. *A New Dimension in Job Evaluation.* New York: American Management Association, 1969.

Patton, Arch. "To Reform the Federal Pay System." *Business Week,* 9 March 1974, p. 34.

Patton, John A.; Smith, Reynold S.; Littlefield, C. L.; and Self, Stanley A. *Job Evaluation.* Chicago: Richard D. Irwin, 1964.

Pearson, David W. "Federal Guidelines Force Affirmative Action Programs." *Personnel Administrator,* September–October 1971, pp. 26–28.

Peter, Laurence J., and Hull, Raymond. *The Peter Principle: Why Things Always Go Wrong.* New York: William Morrow & Co., 1969.

Rosenbloom, David H. *Federal Service and the Constitution.* Ithaca, N.Y.: Cornell University Press, 1971.

Ross, Anne M. "Public Employee Unions and the Right to Strike." *Monthly Labor Review* 92 (1969): 14–18.

Rutstein, Jacob J. "Survey of Current Personnel Systems in State and Local Governments." *Good Government* 87 (1971): 2.

Schmuck, Richard; Runkel, Philip J.; Saturen, Steven L.; Martell, Ronald T.; and Derr, C. Brooklyn. *Handbook of Organizational Development in Schools*. Palo Alto, Calif.: Mayfield Publishing Company, 1972.

Schwab, Donald, and Heneman, Herbert, III. "Pay: A Road to Motivation and Satisfaction?" *Personnel Administrator,* January–February 1974, pp. 19–21.

Shafritz, Jay M. *Position Classification: A Behavioral Analysis for the Public Service.* New York: Praeger Publishers, 1973.

Stahl, O. Glenn. *Public Personnel Administration.* 6th ed. New York: Harper & Row, 1971.

Stenberg, Carl W. "Labor-Management Relations in State and Local Government: Progress and Prospects." *Public Administration Review* 32 (1972): 102–107.

Stone, Thomas H. "An Examination of Six Prevalent Assumptions Concerning Performance Appraisal." *Public Personnel Management,* November–December 1973, p. 414.

"Survey of Current Personnel Systems in State and Local Governments." *Good Government* 88 (1971): 1–3.

Suskin, Harold. "Strengthening Position Classification in the Federal Government." *Public Personnel Review* 14, April 1958, p. 124.

Title 7, sec. 713(a) of the Civil Rights Act of 1964 as amended by the Equal Employment Opportunity Act of 1972.

Tolchin, Martin, and Tolchin, Susan. *To the Victor: Political Patronage from the Clubhouse to the White House.* New York: Random House, 1971.

Tyler, Gus. "Why They Organize." In "A Symposium: Collective Bargaining in the Public Service. A Reappraisal," edited by Felix A. Nigro. *Public Administration Review* 32 (1972): 97–101.

U.S. Civil Service Commission. *Report on Survey of Job Evaluation and Pay for State Merit and Civil Service Systems Developed by Job Evaluation and Pay Review Task Force.* Washington, D.C.: Government Printing Office, 1971.

U.S. Congress. Public Law 84–330. H.R. 6122, 84th Cong., 1st sess., August 1955.

――――. Public Law 87–973. *Federal Salary Reform Act of 1962.* H.R. 7927, 87th Cong., 2d sess., October 1962.

――――. House. Public Law 91–656. *Federal Pay Comparability Act of 1970.* H.R. 13000, 91st Cong., 1st sess., 8 January 1971.

――――. Public Law 91–648. *Intergovernmental Personnel Act of 1970.* 91st Cong., 1st sess., 5 January 1971.

U.S. President. Executive Order 11348. *Providing for the Further Training of Government Employees,* 20 April 1967.

Van Asselt, Karl A. "Impasse Resolution." In "A Symposium: Collective Bargaining in the Public Service. A Reappraisal," edited by Felix A. Nigro. *Public Administration Review* 32 (1972): 114–19.

Van Riper, Paul P. *History of the United States Civil Service.* Evanston, Ill.: Row, Peterson, 1958.

Walsh, Robert E. *Sorry—No Government Today; Unions vs. City Hall.* Boston: Beacon Press, 1969.

Warner, Kenneth O., ed. *Management Relations with Organized Public Employees: Theory, Policies, Programs.* Chicago: Public Personnel Association, 1963.

———— and Hennessey, Mary L. *Public Management at the Bargaining Table.* Chicago: Public Personnel Association, 1967.

Wellington, H., and Winter, R., Jr. "More Strikes by Public Employees." *Yale Law Journal,* January 1970, pp. 418–43.

White, Leonard D. *Introduction to the Study of Public Administration,* 4th ed. New York: Macmillan Co., 1958.

Ziskind, David. *One Thousand Strikes of Government Employees.* New York: Arno Press, 1971.

SOURCES OF BUREAUCRATIC POWER

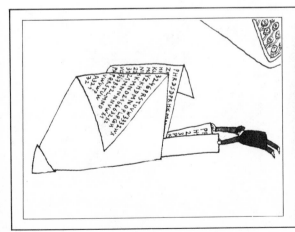

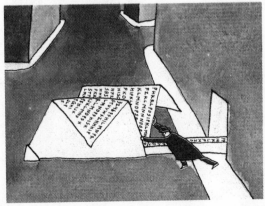

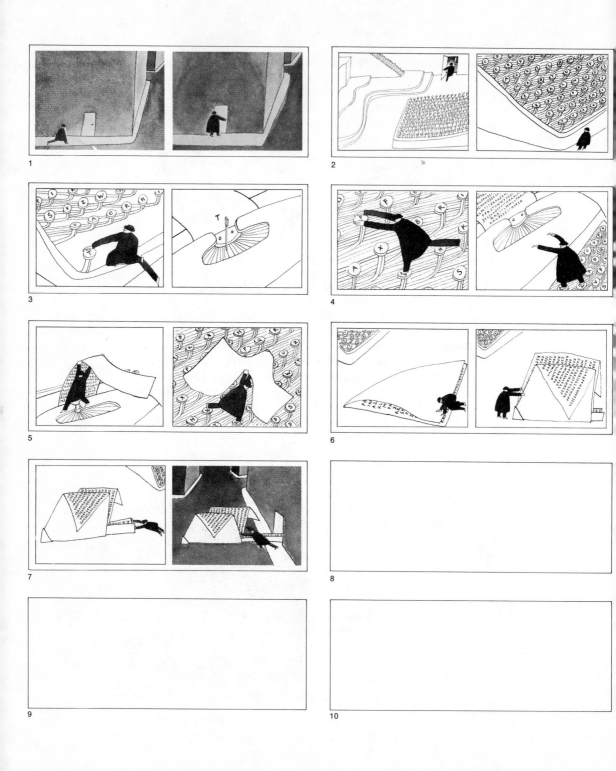

Sometimes I feel I'm pushing my shoulder against a mountain. . . . My feet are churning away and the mountain won't budge. But I'm determined to blast things through. Every week, I tell the commissioners at the cabinet meeting to get out of their offices into the streets and find out what their departments are doing with people. I'm always on them to act, and to follow through on the action.

JOHN V. LINDSAY

ADMINISTRATIVE POWER

7 American bureaucracy has acquired considerable authority and power in the formulation and implementation of public policy since World War II.* Although an administrative staff can be regarded as primarily advisory in character and not generally having direct public policy-making authority, the size, training, and experience of staff members in recent years has enabled them to acquire unofficial power far beyond the authority suggested by their formal job descriptions. The staff personnel who make up the bureaucracy frequently play key roles in the clarification and implementation of vague legislative and executive decisions. Thus bureaucracy represents a potentially dangerous instrument of power insofar as it may influence decision makers or even be instrumental in making policy in the course of translating public policy into practice.[1]

The first two parts of this chapter examine how bureaucracy acquires and uses power. The second part focuses on two regulatory agencies, the

---

*The term *authority* refers to the official power of the decision maker or officeholder, regardless of his actual power to force compliance. The term *power* refers to the ability to compel informal or formal compliance to accomplish a goal.

243

Interstate Commerce Commission (ICC) and the Federal Trade Commission (FTC), quasi-judicial commissions designed to regulate policy and personnel in both public and private agencies and corporations. The first two case studies at the end of the chapter illustrate the impact on government programs and personnel of special interest groups and local interests. The third case study demonstrates abuses of state and local bureaucratic power in New York City.

How Bureaucracy Mobilizes Power

Bureaucracy derives its support from five main sources: (1) its public constituents and interest groups, (2) the legislative branch of government, (3) the executive branch of government, (4) the expertise, or technical and administrative training and experience, of its personnel, and (5) a massive, multilevel civil service system. Some authors suggest other sources of influence, such as the strategic position of public bureaucracy and its discretionary powers in carrying out policy.[2] These are not mutually exclusive categories; an administrative agency can use any combination of them to further its growth and goals. In addition, sources of power vary from agency to agency and at different levels of government.

The relationship of public opinion to sources of administrative power must be taken into account as well. The public can be a major source of support or opposition to nearly any administrative organization or program. But its attitude toward individual government agencies is generally vague and apathetic, with the result that special interest groups frequently have a far greater effect on policy formulations and decisions than the public. Interest groups are issue oriented and will react in a selective way to government policy. While enthusiastic public support can override the influence of pressure groups, it is very difficult to sustain public enthusiasm, which tends to diminish over the course of time as negative reactions develop and interest-group support declines. The Johnson administration's War on Poverty, for example, which advocated expanding services to the poor and creating the Office of Economic Opportunity (OEO), fell on hard times under President Nixon, partly because of its diminished organized support from the poor and partly because of criticism of its service-rendering effectiveness.

Public constituents. A government agency must have the support, or at least the acquiescence, of some constituency to become established and to survive. The constituency may consist of the general public or of several interest groups or both. The regulatory agencies, for example, can regulate a particular industry and protect the public's interest at the same time. Agencies such as the Food and Drug Administration (FDA) may receive instant public support for revealing that a product is dangerous. The discovery that use of the drug thalidomide by pregnant women can cause fetal deformities generated an immediate and tremendous public outcry for the FDA to protect the public from the dangers of improperly tested drugs. This event justified the existence of the FDA and helped it to obtain an important budget to test a greater number of drugs on the market. This, however, is among the rare instances in which regulatory activity aroused popular attention.

The Food and Drug Administration has a larger public constituency and visibility than is normal for a federal agency. Others have far smaller constituencies but may nevertheless have the same degree of power as the FDA. State agencies, such as public utility commissions, experience considerable pressure from local utility companies to set favorable rates. Independent agencies, such as the Small Business Administration and Farm Credit Administration, perform services that benefit other governmental bureaus and special interest groups alike. Government corporations, such as the Tennessee Valley Authority (TVA) and the Federal Home Loan Bank Board, perform specific tasks that arouse support or opposition from an issue-oriented segment of the business community. Philip Selznick's study of the TVA illustrates the high priorities that agencies set in seeking support from their constituencies.

Huge agencies such as the departments of State and Defense create their own interest-group support. The State Department has maintained a close liaison on foreign policy matters with more than three-hundred groups.[3] During the Johnson administration a committee of distinguished citizens, with the illustrious title of Citizens Committee for Peace and Freedom in Vietnam, was organized by the State Department to support Vietnam policies. Support-group activities are often initiated by the agency rather than by external means. The American Farm Bureau Federation, the largest agricultural interest group in the United States, was formed with the help of the Department of Agriculture and has also organized its own interest-group support.[4] The Department of Labor receives considerable support from trade unions and independent wage earners. These relationships can mutually benefit agency and groups alike.

A public constituency provides bureaucracy with power at any level of government as long as citizens demand an increasing number of services from government agencies. Bureaucracy in turn can represent a large segment of society. The greatest hazard for any agency is a loss of constituent support or a turning against the agency by its constituency. The loss of labor support by Nixon's Council on Wage and Price Stability during phase one of the wage and price freeze in 1971 jeopardized the administration's attempt to control inflation. In early 1973 Nixon announced that the controls of phase two would be modified to voluntary regulation of prices and profits by industry. The policy failed, resulting in increased inflation and a loss of confidence by Wall Street and the public alike. The stock market dropped by more than 150 points, the American dollar came under attack abroad, and the public was angered by rapidly rising prices. The loss of labor and other organized support, followed by public dissatisfaction with wage and price controls, helped to bring about the demise of the commission.

Being controlled by constituent groups can be as dangerous to an agency as losing their support. Samuel P. Huntington's "The Marasmus of ICC" illustrates how the railroads became so powerful that they began eventually to control the agency designed to regulate them. Formal or informal cooptation, or the control of a larger agency by the demands of a group vital to the agency's operations, is well demonstrated in Philip Selznick's analysis of the TVA case. In order to gain support from the residents of the Tennessee Valley, the TVA had to modify those objectives of its agricultural program that were opposed by the local community.[5] Without community help, the program would have been delayed or diminished in effectiveness.

Legislative branch. A number of authors have discussed how legislative supports and controls of bureaucracy have been obtained.[6] In general, the legislature has supported administrative agencies both financially and legally. Money is a major asset to all administrative agencies, and congressional appropriations committees are therefore crucial to their survival and growth. If an agency is highly regarded by Congress, it may receive the necessary allocation of monies. The FBI constantly obtains renewed support, because crime reports indicate a need for increased law enforcement and because the FBI's competence inspires some congressmen to give it strong support. Organizations need not be highly visible either politically or economically to enjoy considerable respect among legislators. The Bureau of Customs and the Bureau of Public Debt are Treasury Department agencies that enjoy strong congressional support.[7]

While an agency's ratio of success in gaining a desired budget allocation is one measure of legislative support, its rate of growth is a less-revealing yardstick. An agency may experience considerable growth but still undergo a number of budget cuts. At the same time, agencies that have the fewest budget cuts may show the least amount of growth. Richard Fenno explains: "High growth rates can be accounted for primarily by factors external to the Appropriations Committee, whereas the ability to keep budget cuts to a minimum can be accounted for primarily by factors internal to the Committee-agency relationship."[8] An agency that enjoys good relations with congressional representatives may be most effective in minimizing budget cuts while maximizing growth. Strong external support can be used, however, to pressure lawmakers for greater appropriations. A department's reduction in services to its constituents may result in pressures and protests from the clientele to the appropriations committee for either a restoration of budget cuts or supplemental appropriations.

Aaron Wildavsky has outlined similar tactics that agencies have used to force or pressure legislators for greater funding.[9] Wildavsky notes accurately that budgetary decision making is incremental in character because it is basically a pluralistic process. It may be stated, for example, that if the budget is cut, the entire program will have to be scrapped. "Reducing the fund to $50,000 would reduce it too much for us to carry forward the work. We have to request the restoration. . . ."[10] A crisis may give agencies like the TVA or Defense Department the opportunity to solve an urgent problem. The TVA can meet a crisis by supplying large amounts of power to atomic energy installations. On one occasion the air force used advertising as a tactic to save an aircraft appropriation.

> The B-70 bomber became the RS-70 (reconnaissance strike) overnight as soon as the Air Force discovered that it could not get funds by attempting to justify the plane as useful for its original mission and had to find a new one with more appeal. What some call "Peter Rabbit" presentations—fancy brochures, stirring pictures, simple graphs—are used to advertise the program in Congress and the public media of information. Congressmen are taken on grand guided tours and constituency response is encouraged. An astronaut is paraded before a committee to make a pitch. Releases are distributed to the press. Attempts are made to tie the program to heartfelt needs—a cure for cancer, protection against old age, the joys of outdoor living. [RS-70 has been carried on in the development of the B-1 bomber.][11]

Senator J. William Fulbright has also reviewed the many ways in which bureaucracy sells itself.[12] In 1969, for example, the Pentagon sent a number of public speakers, including a variety of generals, admirals, and other commissioned officers, on a tour of the country to advocate the importance of Pentagon programs. Although there are service regulations on these speakers to restrict their talks to their own areas of competence, it is hard to stop a four-star general from making statements about policy. In November 1969 the Washington, D.C., *Evening Star* noted:

> While President Nixon has been seeking support for his efforts to win the Vietnam war, high-ranking Pentagon officers have been out giving the word to the "silent majority."
> In an almost steady stream, they have been speaking to Rotary Clubs, Reserve Officers meetings, at ship launchings, and almost anywhere a responsive audience might be expected to

gather. Frequently they have taken a tough line—using language more forceful than the President and even outdoing Vice President Spiro T. Agnew on occasion, according to a spot check of speeches delivered over the last two months.

Speaking to the Association of the U.S. Army here on October 15, for example, General Earle G. Wheeler, chairman of the Joint Chiefs of Staff, referred caustically to "groups of interminably vocal youngsters, strangers alike to soap and reason. . . . For my part, I must confess to be a bit fatigued on this score when new words are produced, most often by the 'academic-journalistic' complex, which describe vacillation as being flexible and nervousness as being compassionate."

Controversial examples of Pentagon promotional activities were revealed in the 1971 television documentary "Selling of the Pentagon." The Defense Department, which objected to the way the network had depicted defense promotional efforts, failed in its attempt to force CBS to hand over some of the unaired film to determine whether there had been a security leak. Agencies frequently cultivate good relationships with legislators at all levels of government. In some cases it has been helpful to the armed services that several legislators are in military reserve units. In the Eighty-eighth Congress (1963–64), for example, more than sixty-eight congressmen, fifteen senators, and over 200 staff assistants were in reserve units.[13]

Some evidence of legislative support for administration is to be found in the enabling law, or legislative grant of power, that agencies have. The enabling legislation can be a major controlling device at the same time that it provides organizational structure, specific power, and so forth. Agencies are aware that the legislature can not only withdraw legal and monetary support but can initiate potentially embarrassing investigations of agency corruption. Delays in funds and nomination approvals can also create havoc. But strong support from appropriations committees help to ensure an agency's survival in the face of opposition from other agencies, loss of constituency support, or loss of support from other branches of the government, such as the executive branch.

Executive branch. The executive branch provides considerable support and autonomy for a variety of agencies. Indeed, the degree of autonomy and protection enjoyed by certain agencies under the presidential wing has aggravated relations between the chief executive and Congress. The Bureau of Reclamation, supported by the president, and the Army Corps of Engineers, supported by Congress, have occasionally experienced conflict when the two branches of government disagree over which agency will control certain projects.[14] Agencies with closely related goals often experience greater conflict than those with widely different goals. Conflict could be resolved if the Office of Management and Budget (OMB) or Congress required that agencies have different types of goals, or if the agencies were forced to work together on a single program, but these proposals work against organizational autonomy and survival. Competition among agencies is a significant factor in determining and controlling bureaucratic power.

Agencies within the executive branch, concerned with the control of resources, generally possess considerable power. The Civil Service Commission, which controls personnel regulations, and the General Services Administration, which builds and operates the majority of government buildings, are influential because they control this resource allocation. The Office of Management and Budget not only controls a major segment of resources but also has considerable power because of the size and expertise of its staff. Even after it was reorganized from the Bureau of the Budget in 1970, the OMB continued to be one of Washington's most feared and powerful agencies. As guardian of the federal budget and aide to the president in budget preparation, the OMB's public administration specialists, lawyers, economists, and political scientists (even a microbiologist) act as the shock troops of the president's office to modify and eliminate federal programs. President Nixon's vow to minimize federal spending in 1972 caused the OMB to cut or eliminate many existing programs. This compensates for built-in cost increases in other ongoing programs such as military pay increases and expanded Social Security benefits. The OMB can use other government agencies as its constituency because other executive agencies must clear their communications with Congress through the OMB to ensure consistency of these messages with the president's policy goals.

Expertise. Administrative agencies have concentrated vast talent within the government and used it to provide technical advice on policy decisions that legislators or the president may not be willing or able to handle. How do experts acquire power? How can it be controlled?

Experts acquire power in six ways: (1) by making the results of long- and short-term decisions more predictable, (2) by their ready access to centers of power and control, (3) by using specialized information as a political tool, (4) by their monopoly of position and knowledge, (5) by means of outside intervention to influence policy, and (6) by their ability to form coalitions both within and outside government.[15]

(1) As long as government officials rely on experts to reduce uncertainty in policy outcomes, the technician or staff expert will occupy an advantageous position. The expert may lead an official to make a decision that will be convincing to others. Using experts' advice, for example, city planning commissioners can recommend land-use policies that take account of future limitations on development and not be forced to make decisions that will prove embarrassing or need to be reversed later.

(2) Experts have ready access to powerful decision makers from the city councilman to the president. Although access is not guaranteed, those responsible for making final decisions generally wish to know what experts recommend.

(3) Access to information is an asset because knowledge can be used as a political tool to exert pressure. There is therefore no assurance that an administration will always provide it freely on request. An individual legislator cannot readily acquire technical information for making important decisions, and the expert provides this politically valuable information.

(4) Monopolistic power can be the expert's greatest tool or weapon. Persons holding important positions in government, whether appointed or elected, know that experts often offer conflicting advice. Experts, for their part, are aware that disagreement among themselves and division within major departments of government can constitute a major weakness to their power. As a result, experts seek to monopolize their position by acquiring professional consensus on policy from those outside government and from large research staffs whose fact-finding abilities cannot be disregarded.

As the Watergate revelations demonstrate, however, experts can be preempted by advisers who may not be expert in anything but still have almost total control over access to policy makers. H. R. Haldeman and John Ehrlichman, respectively chief of staff and chief assistant to the president during the Nixon administration, held the greatest concentration of administrative and political power within the White House in modern times—enough power to force professional consensus because experts depended on them for assignments in conducting research and carrying out policy.

An incumbent president has the power to mobilize forces behind him during an election, but he can easily lose control of staffs operating his nationwide campaign. The Nixon staff was powerful enough to isolate the president, who did not object to some isolation because he preferred to reach decisions on the basis of staff papers rather than on the basis of direct confrontation. According to R. W. Apple, Jr.: "One associate remarked that when Haldeman sensed something wrong, he would sometimes delay implementing a Presidential order. After waiting an hour or even a day, he would go back to the oval office, the associate said, and ask, 'Do you really want to do that?' More than once the President changed his mind."[16] Another observer has commented:

> According to Federal investigators, Haldeman was one of five persons authorized to approve disbursements from the secret—and probably illegal—campaign fund that financed the Watergate bugging and sundry other acts of political espionage during the campaign of 1972. Much of the money went to Jeb Stuart Magruder, whom Haldeman had installed as the number two man

at the Committee to Re-elect the President, and from him to G. Gordon Liddy, who ran the Watergate operation. Magruder is only one of the Haldeman proteges (the group came to be known in the White House as "the beaver patrol" because of its eagerness) who has been caught up in the scandal. . . . It is conceivable, of course, that Haldeman intended to set in motion only an espionage campaign, probably legal, if doubtfully ethical, and that his underlings, in their zeal to insure "four more years," exceeded their mandate.[17]

(5) Another source of power is the expert's ability to initiate programs and ongoing policies that are difficult for the outsider to break into or to change. The informal but solid network of information exchange among small groups of experts shows up the outside expert's isolated position as one of considerable financial disadvantage and little impact. Key Nixon staff members, such as Ehrlichman and Haldeman, presidential counsel John Dean, and Attorney General John Mitchell, constituted such a close-knit group that investigation of government expenses by external experts or groups, such as the General Accounting Office, would have been extremely difficult and costly.

(6) Experts also acquire power through the combined expertise resulting from coalitions with experts in other government departments. Coalitions formed to implement certain policies, because they are issue oriented, may not be permanent. Coalitions may also cause one department to become dependent on another. Nevertheless, a group of experts such as the Council of Economic Advisers finds the president depending increasingly on its advice. While there has been no noticeable problem arising from the council's influence on the president, the latter should not permit one adviser or group of advisers to exercise monopolistic influence over his decisions. The reliance on a committee of expert advisers, such as the Council of Economic Advisers, the Joint Chiefs of Staff, or the National Security Council, gives the president greater alternatives as well as greater sources of advice and information. While the key decision maker needs the advice of experts, he must always keep them under control.

Civil service system. In the view of the early pioneers of public administration, the administrator carried out policy but exercised no discretion to act or judge on his own.[18] With the increase of governmental autonomy, expertise, and constituency support, however, the discretion of bureaucracies has extended not only to the means of carrying out policy but also to which goals and new policies should be formulated. The civil service system has resulted in better employee training for job qualification and promotion, and this in turn has affected employee attitudes and discretion. Herbert Kaufman has shown that an administrative agency can influence policy goals as a result of its own training program for employees; his study of the Forest Service indicates that subordinate employees are so thoroughly trained regarding policies that little discretion is left.[19] Agency goals are carried out against a uniform internal background of manuals and in-service training, which guarantees that agency policies will not be modified.

Other agencies permit considerable employee discretion. The Army Corps of Engineers and the Central Intelligence Agency, for example, have histories of administrators exercising their own discretion on important policy matters. Congress can intervene in this freedom of discretion where policy outcomes could affect public reaction to congressional policies. Since 1964, Congress must receive from the secretary of defense a thirty-day notice on the phasing out of any military installation.[20]

The civil service system provides a major source of power for administrative agencies by protecting bureaucracy from radical changes and allowing large segments of administrators to become entrenched. During the Eisenhower administration, many highly placed Republicans were recruited for the federal bureaucracy to curb the influence of administrators remaining from the Roosevelt and Truman administrations but protected by civil service.[21] Because most civil service decisions are influenced by appointed rather than elected officials, newly elected officials must be able to override entrenched elements.[22] Too often the new official becomes dependent on the old, experienced civil servant.

The civil service system can protect the administrator very effectively, as Sayre and Kaufman's study of New York City illustrates.

> Extending the merit system of employment for city employees has had . . . a history of steady and eventually almost complete acceptance in the city's government. . . . The consequences have included not merely the anticipated increase in competence and conventional rationality in the conduct of the city government, but also, and equally significant, the rise of a new form of political power in the city: the career bureaucracies, and especially the organized bureaucracies (e.g., unions). Once closely allied to, and greatly dependent upon, the party leaders, the bureaucracies now have the status and the capacity of autonomous participants in the city's political process.[23]

Because of its size and pluralistic character, however, New York City is not the most representative example of bureaucratic influence.

An entrenched administration can be a powerful force when labor disputes arise. Like many other large American cities, New York has problems when its bureaucracy organizes and participates in union activity and strikes. During the 1968 sanitation strike, for example, Mayor John Lindsay refused to challenge the unions, and sanitation employees worked only half-days. Although the New York Office of Collective Bargaining (OCB) attempted to prevent strikes, it did not explicitly prohibit them.[24] As the city sank into an ocean of garbage in 1968, Lindsay and a good part of the citizenry became fed up with the public employees' behavior. Other employee unions threatened sympathy strikes if Lindsay did not accede to the demands of the Uniformed Sanitationmen's Association. The garbage strike was followed by the 1968 teachers' strike, the police strike of 1971, and a variety of other work stoppages and pension disputes. Although in 1971 the New York State Legislature put a lid on skyrocketing civil service labor costs and on union power as a force determining basic public policy, there is no adequate way of preventing administrative dissatisfaction or work stoppages.

Other studies, such as those on power structure by Robert Dahl and M. Kent Jennings, show that bureaucracies do not have the same degree of policy-making power in all cities.[25] Although administrators are always present, their direct influence is usually felt on issue-oriented problems and in instances where policymakers, such as elected officials, depend on their expertise. As cities grow in size and complexity, the need for administrative experts and civil servants also grows.

Why, with all these sources of power, are bureaucracies not more powerful? The reason most frequently cited is that bureaucracies are divided into many competitive groups at the various levels of government. Competition between federal agencies, coupled with the number and types of agencies at different levels of state and local government, makes it nearly impossible for the personnel of these organizations to exercise their full power. Specialized expertise, different constituencies and territories have resulted in a patchwork of agencies devoted to many different specialized interests.

Checks on Bureaucratic Power

Entrenched bureaucracies can develop their power by collective bargaining and threat of strike as well as by representing certain constituents. John Lindsay's term as mayor of New York City was marked by stormy labor problems with city employees. The number of strikes and threatened work stoppages consumed much of his time.

The ability of bureaucracy to obtain and retain power is directly related to personnel attitudes and problems. There is a continuing demand for reclassification of jobs, new job security, promotion, and retention. For an organization that has a questionable future, retaining good people and avoiding personnel problems will not be easy. There is also the problem of how administrative leaders can handle agency personnel problems as well as demands from constituents whom the organization serves. If there is a salary dispute, for example, a city may face the problem of a "right to strike by employees" including the danger to public health and safety of striking police and fire employees. Local groups and organizations have been successful in coopting government problems to meet the demands of local constituents, as will be seen in the TVA and ICC cases at the end of this chapter. However, a city with a strong administrative leader who has the support of a political machine may have enough power to control administrative subordinates. As the case study of New York illustrates, however, the mayor may expend considerable energy getting the bureaucracy to do his bidding.

The methods administrators use to gain power are similar to those favored in maintaining power. As the RS-70 example shows, an agency's goals are often redefined for this specific purpose. Other methods include: providing the government with experts and consultants otherwise not available in government; contracting out to other organizations jobs that help to increase the size of a constituency; performing jobs that government personnel is not equipped to perform; and having a staff of trained public relations men to communicate with congressional committees, particularly those of appropriations and general accounting. Finally, all agencies like to advertise how successful their program is and how vital it has become.

With these sources of administrative power in mind, it is worthwhile to see how quasi-judicial administrative bodies are influenced by the bureaucracy. Regulatory agencies, such as the Federal Trade Commission, the Food and Drug Administration, and the like, provide a significant point of departure for examining the power of bureaucracy because these agencies should be the most impervious to outside administrative influence. Although the quality of these commissions is determined by the men appointed to serve on them, their subsequent effectiveness may change rapidly as bureaucratic and constituent pressures grow. How these commissions are influenced by bureaucracy will be examined before the issues of administrative controls and responsibility and the public interest are discussed.

BUREAUCRATIC NEUTRALITY

Western ideologues have embraced the ideal "that politicians should take a self-denying ordinance, put aside their personal and party ambitions and ensure that their decisions are executed in a rational, universal, equalitarian and impersonal manner through a neutral or depoliticized bureaucracy.[26] In other words, the personal political opinions of public officials should neither obtrude on their jobs nor be voiced in public.

The view that bureaucracy should be a neutral instrument was expressed by Max Weber, was an article of faith for civil service reformers, and has been central to much public administration literature. The Hatch Act of 1939 and financial disclosure laws in many states preclude most overt political activities and conflicts of interest by civil service employees. This concept of a disinterested civil service is an extension of the Anglo-Saxon notion of the equality of law, which holds that the state will judge an individual, regardless of his station in life, solely on the basis of whether he is congruent with the law. This suggests that if you and the mayor were exceeding the speed limit, you would both be apprehended by the police. Unfortunately, this is not always the case. President Gerald Ford's pardon of Richard Nixon prevented the latter's prosecution and caused many to wonder whether presidents are above the law. America's bureaucracy showed a remarkable continuity, however, and, on the whole, has maintained its neutrality.

At the height of the Watergate malaise in August 1974, one week before Nixon's resignation, millions of federal, state, and local public officials carried out their duties with neither dissension nor rancor. The military remained in their barracks. The Federal Trade Commission acted to stop advertisements claiming that eggs were not connected with heart disease, citing evidence to the contrary.[27] The General Accounting Office moved to plug a loophole that permitted the Pentagon to give away millions of dollars worth of arms without congressional consent or supervision.[28]

On 5 August 1974 political columnist David Broder pointed out that despite the Watergate trauma, our states and cities were doing remarkably innovative things to meet the needs of their people. Missouri was trying to identify and aid all of its handicapped children; Oklahoma was experimenting with prison education; and South Carolina was using hortitherapy, or gardening, as a treatment for the mentally retarded, alcoholics, and criminal offenders.[29] It should not go unnoticed, Broder added, that

> . . . San Diego has developed a model conflict of interest
> ordinance or that the Minneapolis–St. Paul metropolitan council
> is steadily proving the feasibility of regional government, or that
> cities from Pawtucket to Glendale have found ways to make
> schools true centers of community life for people of all ages or
> that four states have tired of waiting for Congress and the
> Administration to resolve their differences and have provided
> insurance against catastrophic illness for all their citizens
> themselves.[30]

The public bureaucracy works, then. But can a public servant realistically be expected to be neutral, and is neutrality always a good thing? In reply to the first question, Gerald Caiden argues that any public agency is a mixture or organization of laws and activities drawing resources from

society and transforming them into public services.[31] The public bureaucracy is subject to a variety of pressures which political leaders will want to
turn to their own advantage in order to enlarge their reputations. Social
classes want and expect special, favorable treatment. Public officials want
higher status and greater rewards for their service. Special interests want
to preserve their autonomy while extracting special consideration from
various public agencies. Unorganized interests expect the public bureaucracy to be open to all.

In addition, people are not neutral. They are loyal to party, unions,
clients, class, religion, profession, and family, and they are subject to cross-
pressures as well. The bureaucracy must try to balance all these competing
demands, and the end result is frequently to compromise ideals and service.
To expect a neutral bureaucracy or bureaucrat may be to expect too much.

The question of whether neutrality is always a good thing is more
difficult to answer. Watergate was an attempt, in part, to politicize government agencies. Frederick Malek's job during Nixon's 1972 re-election campaign was to conduct a "responsiveness" program whose purpose was to
politicize the executive branch by assuring that the day-to-day operations
of the government departments and agencies were conducted as much as
possible to support Nixon's re-election. Critics agreed that this policy resulted in lucrative federal grants and contracts being directed toward Nixon
supporters and away from nonsupporters.[32]

Bureaucrats are often forced to pay the price for having their own
ideas. In 1974 Alvin J. Arnett was appointed to liquidate the Office of
Economic Opportunity (OEO), a beseiged outpost for the remnants of the
War on Poverty. Instead, Arnett lobbied Congress for a bill that would
preserve the OEO as an independent agency, admitting that he was guilty
of trying to preserve its programs. His resignation was demanded and received.[33]

A few months before Nixon's resignation, Paul Nitze, chief negotiator
of the Strategic Arms Limitation Talks (SALT II), resigned citing Watergate
as his reason. If other leading bureaucrats had followed Nitze's example and
done so even sooner, would the Watergate impasse have lasted as long as
it did? Deputy Attorney General Henry Petersen, charged with prosecuting
the government's case during Watergate, had a close and friendly relationship with Nixon and was described by a Nixon aide as being a "soldier."
Clearly, overemphasis on continuity and neutrality on the part of bureaucrats is not a good thing.

Government agencies, too, often do not act in a neutral way. Agencies
develop their own political cultures and clients and have a great deal of
discretion and power. The FBI often takes right-of-center positions on issues relating to law enforcement. The Department of Health, Education and

Welfare often takes a left-of-center position toward providing welfare services to the nation's population.

Moreover, agencies are often coopted by various client groups. An economic anlayst has noted that Americans so desperately want lower airline fares that they are willing to take flights in the early hours of the morning to take advantage of reduced rates at those hours. Despite the fact that the nation's largest airlines are awash in red ink, however, they chose to increase the cost of flights, disregarding the fact that traffic would expand if rates were reduced. When the Civil Aeronautics Board supported the airlines, the economic analyst observed that this gave credence to the charge that the CAB and other regulatory agencies do not regulate in the interest of the public but for the benefit of the industry they are supposed to regulate.[34]

Congress and the legislature give the bureaucracy considerable leeway in enforcing their mandate. This is essential in view of the bureaucracy's expertise and the complexity of much contemporary legislation, but it also means that agencies can favor certain groups. For example, the Atomic Energy Commission (now the Energy Research Development Administration and the Nuclear Regulatory Commission) bears the responsibility of assuring the safety of the nation's atomic power facilities. But a *New York Times* report stated that although the AEC found violations in almost 1 out of 3 atomic power installations, it rarely imposed the penalty prescribed by law.[35] From 1969 to 1974 the commission conducted 10,320 inspections and found 3,704 installations with one or more violations; yet civil penalties were imposed only twenty-two times. A report by L. V. Gossick and M. L. Enst, released by Ralph Nader, said:

> The large number of reactor incidents, coupled with the fact that many of them had real safety significance, were generic in nature and were not identified during the normal design fabrication, erection, and preoperational testing phases, raises a serious question regarding the current review and inspection practices on the part of the nuclear industry and the AEC.[36]

Anthony Mazocchi, legislative director of the Oil, Chemical, and Atomic Workers Union, charged that "these numbers are proof positive that the commission is more interested in the health of the corporation rather than the health of the worker."[37]

Discretion is not the only source of power that has accrued to the public bureaucracy. A study of public education by the University of California reported that public school educators have proliferated and organized to the point where their enterprise is beyond the control of those who pay for it. School districts have become so large that school board members have been forced to turn the running of the schools over to a new class of professionals who form a barrier between the public and the schools. Although Americans spend as much on schools as on all other local services combined, the public is increasingly being denied a say in how the schools are run. In addition, unions have in effect given teachers a veto over most educational policy. The group omitted from this picture, the report said, was the public.[38]

The bureaucracy has grown immensely powerful, as Watergate and other events have shown. But do we deserve what we get? Senator Lowell Weicker, Jr. of Connecticut has observed:

> Several years ago many Americans were willing to silently tolerate illegal government activity against militants, terrorists or other subversives as expeditious ways to circumvent the precise process of our justice system, though quick [sic], it also proved to be only a short step to using such illegal tactics against any dissenting Americans.
>
> The result was we almost lost America. Not to subversives, terrorists or extremists of the streets but to subversives and extremists of the White House.[39]

That America's bureaucracy reflects America's culture cannot be overemphasized. Corruption can flourish in our society. Millions of us pride ourselves that we succeed in cheating on our income taxes. It is estimated that amateur and professional agents steal approximately $6 billion a year in ideas, information, and materials from U.S. business and industry, and the practice is becoming more widespread. The figure quoted is conservative because so many cases go unreported. One firm of private investigators has reported that it receives two or three calls a day from businessmen or industrialists who want to engage in industrial espionage, which they regard as merely another form of market research.[40]

THE REGULATORY AGENCIES

In order to soften some of the deleterious effect of industrialization, most advanced nations have brought major industrial enterprises under public control (nationalization). Public ownership sought to achieve political control, better economic distribution, and greater efficiency—some famous examples include the BBC, Air France, and SAAB. But the United States, in its desire to curb industrial abuses and to assure a reasonable distribution of the benefits of technology, has taken a different path—the regulatory agencies. According to one study:

> The growth of regulation in the United States has not been the product of any farsighted plan or design, inspired by general philosophy or

governmental control. Step by step, whether in state or nation it has been a series of empirical adjustments to field abuses to deal with specific problems as they arose.[41]

The appropriateness of this response in serving the public interest remains a matter of debate.

In the late eighteenth century and during most of the nineteenth century, American ideology was dominated by the doctrine of laissez faire, which emphasized minimal governmental intervention in economic affairs. Governmental activity, in accord with Jeffersonian-Jacksonian beliefs, was centered in the states rather than in Washington. That attitudes began to change during the post–Civil War period was perhaps best symbolized by the views that Americans adopted toward the railroads.

The Rise of Regulation

Especially during the period of western expansion, the railroads were viewed enthusiastically because they enabled farmers, merchants, and others to get their goods and services to market rapidly and inexpensively. But the harbingers of civilization soon became tools of exploitation. Farmers and merchants began to complain of gross discrimination among individuals and localities, of exorbitant rates, collusion among corrupt state officials, watered stocks, and fraudulent practices designed to eliminate competition. In response to these abuses, the Grange agricultural reform movement was formed and succeeded in obtaining state railroad regulatory agencies in Iowa, Minnesota, and Wisconsin. But railroad interests soon severely weakened the powers of the agencies in Minnesota and Wisconsin, and in 1886 the Supreme Court ruled that railroad regulation was a proper concern of the federal government, not of the states. This decision forced those aggrieved by the railroads to shift their focus to Washington.

Between 1867 and 1887 more than 150 bills were introduced into Congress to provide for some regulation over the railroads.[42] The result of these efforts was the creation in 1887 of the Interstate Commerce Commission (ICC), which would serve as the model for all subsequent regulatory agencies, especially the so-called independent regulatory commissions.

The ICC was granted quasi-legislative, quasi-executive, and quasi-judicial powers by which it was enabled to make regulations that were as binding as laws (legislative), to enforce these regulations (executive), and to adjudicate appeals (judicial). All subsequent independent commissions would have these powers, though in varying degrees. The creators of the ICC envisioned a bipartisan agency staffed by independent men of high professional caliber. To this end they granted commissioners salaries exceeding those of Supreme Court justices and terms of office exceeding that of the president. Originally, ICC members served for six years. These terms now range from five to fourteen years. The only grounds for removal are neglect of duty, malfeasance, or gross inefficiency.

The ICC was originally under the Department of the Interior, but, according to the Brownlow Committee, it achieved independent status because of a Texas senator's hatred of President Benjamin Harrison, who was elected in 1889.[43]

> . . . Mr. [John Henninger] Reagan of Texas, author of the interstate commerce bill, said that since a railroad lawyer named Ben Harrison had been elected President, he did not trust the President any more in this matter, so he invented the . . . independent commission. Thereafter, any bill or regulatory matter that came to the Interstate and Foreign Commerce Committee resulted in the appointment of a commission.[44]

The commission form had a number of advantages. Its emphasis on independence and bipartisanship was congruent with progressive notions of "good government." It was also hoped that this form of organization would provide flexible and expert regulation. Because it would be a permanent and expert body, the ICC could formulate plans and make legislative recommendations to Congress. It was hoped, too, that the commission would be able to defend the public and those who might otherwise be defenseless. Cutthroat competition would be eliminated because the commission would adjudicate differences, alleviating the burdens of adjudication on the courts, although the courts would hold the power of decision. Many of ICC's objectives for improved government regulation of business would be eroded in practice, however, as Huntington's case study, "The Marasmus of the ICC," demonstrates.

The creation of other major regulatory agencies was induced by a public sense of social injustice, by adverse economic conditions, and by problematic technological innovations. Following progressive impulses, President Woodrow Wilson created the Federal Reserve System to determine monetary and credit policy for the system and to regulate member commercial banks. In 1914 the Federal Trade Commission was created to administer certain antitrust, advertising, and labeling regulations.

The next burst of regulatory activity was due in major part to the upheavals of the Great Depression. The Federal Power Commission (FPC) was created in 1930 to regulate the sale and transportation of natural gas and electrical energy. The Federal Deposit Insurance Corporation was established in 1933 to prevent the bank failures that had traumatized millions in the early 1930s. The Securities and Exchange Commission, established in 1934, was intended to police the "villain" of the depression, the securities industry. The Federal Communications Commission was created in the

1930s to regulate radio, later television and cable and wire service. The National Labor Relations Board (1935) was empowered to conduct labor union elections and investigate unfair labor practices. Aircraft and shipping regulation and subsidization became the responsibilities of the Civil Aeronautics Board (1938) and the Maritime Commission (1936). The Atomic Energy Commission was created in 1946 to promote and regulate the uses of atomic energy. The Equal Opportunity Commission was established in 1964 to investigate charges of discrimination in hiring practices by employers and labor unions.

In addition to these independent commissions, more than one hundred governmental agencies regulate private enterprises, obligations, and practices. They employ over 100,000 people, and their activities, which affect the daily lives of most Americans, range from decisions regarding the safety of the food and drink we consume, the fares we pay on planes and trains, and the cost of our utility bills to the availability of credit at department stores.[45] Their importance can perhaps best be illustrated by two case studies involving the FTC and the FDA.

The FTC and Rapid Shave. In order to increase its sales, the Colgate-Palmolive Company in 1960 sponsored a television commercial which sought to demonstrate by means of a mock-up that Rapid Shave was effective enough to shave dry sandpaper.[46] The announcer asserted that all that was required was to apply Rapid Shave, soak, and the sand was off in a stroke—the implication being that if Rapid Shave could shave sandpaper, it would work wonders on a mere human beard. The FTC issued a cease-and-desist order against Colgate-Palmolive, charging that the commercial was misleading and deceptive because sandpaper had not been used but rather a plexiglass model to which sand particles had been glued. Thus the commercial proved nothing of the product's alleged moistening capacity. Consumers had been misled, and other companies had faced unfair competition.

The company decided to fight the cease-and-desist order but was unable to convince the FTC. Undeterred, Colgate-Palmolive took its case to the U.S. Court of Appeals, which upheld the FTC's order but refused to uphold its corollary edict that all similar mock-ups could not be used in future television commercials. The FTC narrowed its ruling, but the court was not satisfied. The FTC then took the case to the Supreme Court, which, in a decision written by Chief Justice Earl Warren, reversed the Appeals Court ruling and held that all similar advertising on television would be banned. The consumer would be protected even though it had taken five years to accomplish. Colgate-Palmolive had had its day in court, and both the letter and spirit of the law had been observed.

The FDA and thalidomide. The Food and Drug Administration arose in response to the abuses of an unregulated economy so vividly depicted in

Upton Sinclair's *The Jungle* (1906). The agency was first located in the Department of Agriculture but was moved to the Federal Security Administration in partial response to its overpermissiveness in the tolerance of pesticides in fresh fruit. Among its many tasks, the FDA must determine whether food and drugs are safe to consume. The problem for medical doctors was summarized by Dr. Leona Baumgarten, health commissioner for the city of New York: ". . . The physician is bombarded by selective advertising which fails to tell the truth, whole truth, and nothing but the truth. This often misleads him into prescribing a new drug without adequate warning about its possible side effects."[47]

Thalidomide, a sedative to relieve the nausea accompanying pregnancy, was a new "wonder drug" in 1960 when the William S. Merrell Company sought FDA approval to market it. The application came to Dr. Frances Kelsey, who, in spite of fifty direct appeals to the FDA, including some to her superiors, insisted on delaying permission until further testing could assure the drug's safety. During this period it was learned that some five thousand deformed babies had been born to mothers who had ingested thalidomide. As a result of this case, in 1962 Congress passed a strong bill regulating the sale, patenting, and manufacture of drugs. Dr. Kelsey was awarded the Distinguished Federal Service Medal.[48]

Some Problems of Regulation

The American people support the regulatory agencies because they perform essential and sometimes dramatically important public services. But the public is often apathetic in its support, and the probusiness attitude on the part of the public is far from dead. The regulatory agencies must often turn to the president, to Congress, and even to the industries they are supposed to regulate for organizational survival and funds.

Presidential power over the regulatory agencies is strong. All budget and legislative proposals must be cleared through the president's Office of Management and Budget. The president makes both initial nominations and renominations, although in *Humphrey's Executor* v. *United States* (1935), a case involving FTC Commissioner G. F. Humphrey, President Franklin Roosevelt learned that he could not remove a commissioner until the latter's term of office had expired. (Roosevelt lost that battle but won the war. Despite the fact that the other regulatory commissioners had been appointed by Roosevelt's predecessors, they offered no resistance to his New Deal programs after the Humphrey episode.) Moreover, the president has sole discretion in appointing the heads of scores of nonindependent regulatory agencies, such as the FDA and the Environmental Protection Agency.

Congress, too, plays a major role in the regulatory process. The Senate must give its assent to presidential nominees, and Congress must approve the budgets of the various agencies. Although it does not always choose to do so, Congress also has the power to investigate the various agencies. These investigations can be most embarrassing—for example, the 1958 investigations that exposed scandals involving the FCC's awarding of television stations and the FTC's dubious relations with President Eisenhower's Chief Counsel, Sherman Adams. Most significantly, there is a very thin line between a legislator's inquiry on behalf of his constituents and an inquiry pressed on his own behalf.

The relationship between regulatory agencies and the industries they are supposed to regulate has raised serious questions about whose side the agencies are on: the public's or industry's? Marver Bernstein argues that regulatory agencies pass through four stages: gestation, youth, maturity, and old age.[48] In old age the agency's primary mission is to maintain the status quo in the regulated industry and its own position as recognized protector of the industry. As Samuel Huntington's masterful study of the relationship of ICC and the railroads concludes, the commission has become the defender of the status quo.[49] Economist Walton Hamilton has observed that "so firmly entrenched is the scheme of controls that, in fluid milk and liquor, the most radical and tormenting measure which might be taken would be to return the commodities to the free and open market."[50] Ralph Nader's study of the FDA and ICC has added grist to this mill.[51]

Unique among the industrialized nations of the world, the United States has attempted to regulate rather than to nationalize its major industries. Although this solution is congruent with American values, it has nevertheless yielded mixed results. Whether the regulatory agencies in particular and bureaucracy in general can serve the public at large and not merely segments of the public will be the subject of the next chapter.

CASE STUDY 1

TVA and the Grass Roots
PHILIP SELZNICK

New Deal planners hoped that the Tennessee Valley Authority, one of the most promising economic and social schemes of this century, would demonstrate both the feasibility and great potential of regional planning and that the project would serve as a prototype for similar future endeavors.

Originally published by the University of California Press; reprinted by permission of The Regents of the University of California.

According to article 23 of the project's 1933 enabling act, the objectives of TVA were:

> For the especial purpose of bringing about in said Tennessee drainage basin and adjoining territory . . . (1) the maximum amount of flood control; (2) the maximum development . . . for navigation purposes: (3) the maximum generation of electric power consistent with flood control and navigation; (4) the proper use of marginal lands; (5) the proper method of reforestation . . . and (6) the economic and social well-being of the people living in said river basin.[52]

But many of these early hopes were unfulfilled. TVA was eventually coopted by the region's established, white middle and upper classes who stood to benefit most from the infusion of federal billions into the area. The economic and social condition of blacks and poor whites in the valley remains pitiful to this day. Sharecropping and tenant farming continue to be widespread, with tens of thousands of people subsisting below the poverty level. Moreover, there have been no new TVAs.

At the same time, however, TVA's achievements have been considerable. Once unnavigable, the Tennessee River and its tributaries have become a major 650-mile commercial artery. Disastrous floods, once a problem costing millions of dollars, ceased to occur after completion of the TVA's numerous dams. TVA has provided for the reforestation of more than one million acres of land, has pioneered the development and use of scores of new agricultural fertilizers and conservation methods, and has brought cheap electrical power to a region that desperately needs it.

Since World War II, TVA has been a major supplier of the energy needs of the Atomic Energy Commission (now the Energy Research Development Administration and the Nuclear Regulatory Commission). Its efforts have helped to eradicate malaria, once endemic in the Tennessee Valley. It has also stimulated a sizable recreation industry by such efforts as the development of the Great Lakes of the south. Every year thousands of foreign visitors come to the United States to study the TVA's methods, which have served as a model for India's Damodar Valley project and Colombia's Cauca River project.[53]

Philip Selznick's study shows how an organization must alter its original idea and methods of operation in order to survive. As you read this selection, consider the following questions:

1. *Explain the concept of cooptation as it relates to the TVA.*

2. *How would you, as an administrator in the TVA, guard against cooptation?*

3. *What are TVA's goals according to its planners and to President Franklin Roosevelt?*

4. Why, despite its success and popularity abroad, have there been no additional TVAs in the United States?

The Tennessee Valley Authority was created by Congress in May, 1933, as a response to a long period of pressure for the disposition of government-owned properties at Muscle Shoals, Alabama. During the First World War, two [government-owned and operated] nitrate plants and what was later known as Wilson Dam were constructed, at a cost of over $100,000,000. For the next fifteen years, final decision as to the future of these installations hung fire. The focal points of contention related to the production and distribution of fertilizer and electric power, and to the principle of government versus private ownership. Two presidential commissions and protracted congressional inquiries recorded the long debate. At last, with the advent of the Roosevelt administration in 1933, the government assumed responsibility for a general resolution of the major issues.

The TVA Act as finally approved was a major victory for those who favored the principle of government operation. The Muscle Shoals investment was to remain in public ownership, and this initial project was to be provided with new goals and to be vastly extended. A great public power project was envisioned, mobilizing the "by-product" of dams built for the purpose of flood control and navigation improvement on the Tennessee River and its tributaries. [Public] control and operation of the nitrate properties, to be used for fertilizer production, was also authorized, although this aspect was subordinated in importance to electricity. These major powers—authority to construct dams, deepen the river channel, produce and distribute electricity and fertilizer—were delegated by Congress to a [public] corporation administered by a three-man board of directors.

If this had been all, the project would still have represented an important extension of government activity and responsibility. But what began as, and what was generally understood to be, primarily the solution of a problem of fertilizer and power emerged as an institution of a far broader meaning. A new regional concept—the river basin as an integral unit—was given effect, so that a government agency was created which had a special responsibility neither national nor state-wide in scope. This offered a new dimension for the consideration of the role of government in the evolving federal system. At the same time, the very form of the agency established under the Act was a new departure. There was created a relatively autonomous public corporation free in important aspects from the normal financial and administrative controls exercised over federal organs. Further, and in one sense most important, a broad vision of regional resource development—in a word, planning—informed the conception, if not the actual powers, of the new organization.

The Message of the President requesting the TVA legislation did much to outline that perception: "It is clear," wrote Mr. Roosevelt, "that the Muscle Shoals development is but a small part of the potential public usefulness of the entire Tennessee River. Such use, if envisioned in its entirety, transcends mere power development: it enters the wide fields of flood control, soil erosion, afforestation, elimination from agricultural use of marginal lands, and distribution and diversification of industry. In short, this power development of war days leads logically to national planning for a complete river watershed involving many States and the future lives and welfare of millions. It touches and gives life to all forms of human concerns." To carry out this conception, the President recommended "legislation to create a Tennessee Valley Authority—a corporation clothed with the power of government but possessed of the flexibility and initiative of private enterprise. It should be charged with the broadest duty of planning for the proper use, conservation, and development of the natural resources of the Tennessee River drainage basin and its adjoining territory for the general social and economic welfare of the Nation.". . .

The partnership of TVA and the people's institutions
After some difficulties and initial disagreements, but still very early in its history, the Authority defined its approach to cooperation with the agencies and institutions already existing in the Valley. The alternatives seemed to be two: either to take a line which assumed that the TVA itself could and should carry out its programs by direct action; or to accept as legitimate and efficient a method which would seek out and even establish local institutions to mediate between the TVA and the people of the area. It was felt that an imposed federal program would be alien and unwanted, and ultimately accomplish little, unless it brought together at the grass roots all the region's resources: the local communities, voluntary private organizations, state agencies, and cooperating federal agencies. The vision of such a working partnership seemed to define "grass-roots democracy at work."

In the Authority's view, the fundamental rationale of the partnership approach is found in its implications for democracy. If the TVA can be "shaped by intimate association with long-established institutions," that will mean its vitality is drawn from below. By working through state and local agencies, the Authority will provide the people of the Valley with more effective means by which to direct their own destinies. The TVA may then become more integrally a part of the region, committed to its interests and cognizant of its needs, and thus removed in thought and action from the remote impersonal bureaucracy of centralized government.

The moral dimension of the grass-roots approach has been emphasized many times. The methods of TVA are proffered as more than technical means for the achievement of administrative objectives. They include and underline the responsibility of leadership in a democracy to offer the people alternatives for free choice rather than ready-made prescriptions elaborated in the fastnesses of planning agencies. . . .

The orientation toward local agencies is also a product of the conception that the resources of a region include its institutions, in particular its governmental agencies. The Authority deems it part of its obligation in connection with resource development that these local governmental institutions be strengthened rather than weakened, that they be supplemented rather than supplanted. In doing so, the Authority directs its effort toward developing a sense of responsibility on the part of the local organs and, what is equally important, toward providing them with a knowledge of the tools available to put that responsibility into action. . . .

A list of agencies with which the TVA has maintained some form of cooperative relationship includes nearly all of the governmental institutions in the area: municipal power boards, rural electric cooperatives, school and library boards; state departments of health, conservation, and parks; state and local planning commissions, agricultural and engineering experiment stations, state extension services, and others. In developing these relationships TVA has applied the rule that "wherever possible, the Authority shall work toward achieving its objectives by utilizing or stimulating the developing of state and local organizations, agencies and institutions, rather than conducting direct action programs." In addition, a number of federal agencies, notably technical bureaus of the U.S. Departments of Agriculture and the Interior, the Army Engineers, and the Coast Guard, have cooperative arrangements with the TVA. Notable also are the *ad hoc* organizations and conferences which have been established as vehicles for cooperation among the administrative agencies within the Valley. These include, among others, a semiannual conference of directors of extension services and of agricultural experiment stations of the seven Valley states, the U.S. Department of Agriculture, and the TVA; the Tennessee Valley Trades and Labor Council, bringing together fifteen international unions of the American Federation of Labor Building and Metal Trades; an annual conference of contractors and distributors of TVA power; and the Tennessee Valley Library Council. Such gatherings help to lay a sound foundation for regional unity, focusing the efforts of many agencies on the region as a central problem.

The form of cooperation with state and local agencies varies, but the pattern of intergovernmental contract has been most fully developed. Such contracts often include reimbursement by the Authority for personnel and other facilities used by the state in carrying on the cooperative program. In many cases, the ideal outcome is viewed as the tapering off of TVA contributions until, as TVA's responsibilities recede in importance, the local agency carries on by itself. Thus the states have in some cases begun planning work through their own commissions with the material help of TVA; later, state funds have been secured with a view to continuing the work then TVA's responsibilities for the readjustment of reservoir-affected urban communities would terminate. In cooperating with the local governments, TVA attempts to establish a pattern which may be continued after TVA aid has ceased.

The objective of stimulating local responsibility among governments and associations within the area is basic to the grass-roots approach. But there are other reasons which support it as sound administrative policy. The existing facilities of the states, even though they may be inadequate, are used to capacity, thus avoiding the establishment of duplicate services and personnel with parallel functions. The TVA is not anxious to have its own men in the field and is willing to forego the prestige that comes from identification as "TVA men" of agents performing services paid for out of TVA funds. The staff is educated to feel most satisfied when it can show evidence that a local organization has carried on TVA work and been permanently strengthened by the experience and in the eyes of its public. In addition, utilization of existing agencies permits TVA to shape its program in conformity with the intimate knowledge of local conditions which such agencies are likely to have; at the same time it is possible to restrict the size of the Authority's direct working force.

The attempt to create a working partnership between the TVA and the people in carrying out a common program for regional development goes beyond the strengthening of existing governmental agencies, though this objective is vital. The meaning of the partnership is contained as well in the use of the voluntary association as a means of inviting the participation of the people most immediately concerned in the administration of the program. In this way, the farmer or the businessman finds a means of participating in the activities of government supplemental to his role on election day. If there is fertilizer to be distributed, farmers are invited, on a county and community basis, to participate in locally controlled organizations which will make decisions as to the most effective means of using that fertilizer in the local area. If government land is to be rented, a local land-use association is organized so that the conditions of rental can be determined with maximum benefit for the community. If power is to be sold in a rural area, a cooperative provides a consumer ownership which retains profits in the community and makes possible a management guided by community problems and local needs. If the business area of a city must be modified because of newly flooded lands, let a locally organized planning commission work out the best possible adjustment of special interests and long-range planning goals. Thus, at the end-point of operation, the specific consequences of a federal program may be shaped and directed by local citizens so that its impact at the grass roots will be determined in local terms. This procedure is not only democratic and just, but undoubtedly adds measurably to the effectiveness of the programs, which will be conjoined to the special desires of those affected and thus have the benefit of their support and aid.

The policy of consciously working with and through local institutions is, in the Authority's view, integrally related to its relatively autonomous position within the federal system. It is precisely the flexibility accorded to the TVA management which has enabled it to keep in mind its broad concept of regional development and at the same time to seize upon whatever opportunities might arise to implement the concept concretely. Nationally directed restrictions as to employment of personnel, a host of regulations framed in national terms, would doubtless greatly restrict the ability of TVA to establish procedures attuned both to its substantive objectives and to the grass-roots methods by which they are carried out. It would surely inhibit the freedom to search out techniques uniquely adapted to the special situations of some particular state government or community if TVA did not have the power to make its own decisions and to take the initiative in fostering cooperative relationships. Moreover, the absence of discretion might well be psychologically decisive in hobbling the TVA staff by binding it to the customs and traditional modes of action laid down by the broader hierarchy into which it might be absorbed. . . .

Inherent dilemmas

Tension and dilemma are normal and anticipated corollaries of the attempt to control human institutions in the light of an abstract doctrine. . . . Practical leadership cannot long ignore the resistance of social structure, and is often moved thereby to abandon concern for abstract goals or ideas—for which it is often criticized out of hand by the moralists and idealists who lack experience with the vicissitudes of practical action. But a leadership which, for whatever reason, elects to be identified with a doctrine and professes to use it in action, is continuously faced with tensions between the idea and the act. Ideological symbols may fulfill useful functions of communication and defense and may be long sustained as meaningful even when effective criteria of judgment remain lacking; but an act entails responsibility, establishing alliances and commitments which demand attention and deference. . . .

The TVA, in relation to its policy of grass-roots administration, is not immune to such difficulties. Though seldom made explicit, sources of tension are recognized by members of the staff, and have already entered into the process of administrative decision. Among these may be noted: . . .

Emphasis on existing institutions as democratic instruments may wed the agency to the status quo. A procedure which channels the administration of a program through established local institutions, governmental or private, tends to reinforce the legitimacy of the existing leadership. This is especially true when a settled pattern claims the exclusive attention of the agency, so that other groups striving for leadership may find their position relatively weakened after the new relationships have been defined. In strengthening the land-grant colleges in its area, the TVA has bolstered the position of the existing farm leadership. There is some evidence that in the process of establishing its pattern of cooperation, TVA refrained from strengthening independent colleges in the area not associated with the land-grant college system. Again, the relatively dominant role of the American Federation of Labor unions in TVA labor relations, especially as constituting the Tennessee Valley Trades and Labor Council, is objectively a hindrance to the development of labor groups having other affiliations. In general, to the extent that the agency selects one set of institutions within a given field as the group through which it will work, the possibility of freezing existing social relationships is enhanced. At least in its agricultural program, TVA has chosen to limit its cooperative relationships to a special group, so that the potential or inherent dilemma has been made explicit. . . .

Commitment to existing agencies may shape and inhibit policy in unanticipated ways. When the channels of action are restricted, programs may be elaborated only within the limits established by the nature of the cooperating organizations. The traditions and outlook of an established institution will resist goals which appear to be alien, and the initiating agency will tend to avoid difficulties by restricting its own proposals to those which can be feasibly carried out by the grass-roots organization. Where the grass-roots method is ignored, new institutions may be built, shaped *ab initio* in terms of the desired program. An attempt to carry forward a policy of nondiscrimination (as against Negroes) will not proceed very far when the instrument for carrying out this policy—usually as an adjunct of some broader program—has traditions of its own of a contrary bent. Moreover, the grass-roots policy voluntarily creates nucleuses of power which may be used for the furtherance of interests outside the system of cooperation originally established. Thus the TVA distributes electric power through electric power boards which are creatures of municipalities, with the contractual reservation that surplus income shall be used only for improvements in the system or for the reduction of rates. But the question has been raised: what if pressure arises to use surpluses for general purposes, that is, to finance nonpower functions of the municipal governments? And what if the state governments undertake to tax these surpluses, because of a restricted tax base and unwillingness to institute a state income tax? The logic of the grass-roots policy might force the Authority to agree. However, it is perhaps more likely that the Authority's commitment to function as a successful power project would take precedence over the grass-roots method.

Existing agencies inhibit a direct approach to the local citizenry. The participation of local people always takes place through some organizational mechanism, notably voluntary associations established to involve a public in some measure of decision at the end-point of operation. But such associations are commonly adjuncts of an administrative agency which jealously guards all approaches to its clientele. If, therefore, a federal agency establishes cooperative relations with such an agency, it will be committed as well to the system of voluntary associations which has been established. Hence the channels of participation of local people in the federal program will be shaped by the intermediary agency. In respect to its closeness to the people, the status of the federal government may not, in such circumstances, be materially altered. Viewed from this perspective, the grass-roots method becomes an effective means whereby an intrenched bureaucracy protects its clientele, and also itself, from the encroachments of the federal government. . . .

An administrative constituency

. . . The relationship between the TVA and the farm leadership in the Valley may be summarized in the concept of the administrative constituency. . . . A constituency is a group, formally outside a given organization, to which the latter (or an element within it) has a special commitment. A relation of mutual dependence develops, so that the agent organization must defend its constituency and conversely. This relation gains strength and definition as precedents are established in behavior and in doctrine, and especially as the constituency itself attains organized form. A group which finds its coherence in common interest, but remains unorganized, may enforce its demands in subtle ways, but a leadership and a machinery serve to mobilize its resources. At the same time, however, this machinery may become separated from its popular base and itself become the effective constituency.

The idea of an administrative constituency, however it may be phrased, is familiar to students of public administration, and in general may be thought of as a normal mechanism of social control whereby formal organizations are made responsive to relevent publics. Or, put in other terms, the creation of the constituency relationship is a form of cooptation, the informal involvement of local elements in the process of policy determination. One TVA staff member felt that the TVA's agricultural constituency operated as "one element in the general trend in the Authority toward conservatism and adjustment to Valley institutions.'' It is this adjustment which is one of the significant implications of the process of cooptation in administration.

The constituency relation varies widely in source, in intensity, and in meaning. One form may arise simply out of the need felt by an organization, public or private, to defend its continuing working relations with an outside group or agency. Interest may focus only accidentally upon the particular outside group involved, for it is the smooth avenue of operation which is being defended, and will not be readily jeopardized in the interests of the program in which the organization may have no great stake. It is often inconvenient and difficult to alter established procedures, so that a given form of cooperation may be defended in order to preserve the integrity and equilibrium of operations. This situation is analytically quite different from that in which the outside organization is defended for its own sake, as occurs in the relation between the TVA Agricultural Relations Department and the land-grant colleges. There is also a distinction to be drawn between short-run pressures upon an agency and the long-run strategy by which a measure of continuing control is achieved. In connection with the administrative relations analyzed above, the land-grant colleges have sought and gained a significant measure of influence upon the TVA; moreover, the TVA agriculturists do defend the colleges as valuable, and even indispensable, in themselves. That a constituency relation in this advanced form exists is well known in the higher circles of TVA, and is the subject of much comment.

The significance of a constituency relation depends in part upon the fact that the character of the constituency will tend to define and shape the character of the agency. This may involve the recruitment of personnel from the ranks of the constituency and, in an extreme form, the assumption by elements within the agency of a leadership status with respect to the constituency. The representatives of the constituency within the agency then come to define their role as one of leading a broad struggle for the furtherance of the interests of the constituency, and sometimes may be more conscious of those interests than members of the outside group themselves. Where the outside group is not the formal source of public policy, the constituency relation may remain more or less covert, and its representatives may find it necessary to devise and rely upon some doctrine or ideology to cover and defend the real relationships. An adequate comprehension of the full meaning of the grass-roots policy does not appear to be possible apart from some such principle as this.

In the relation of TVA to the land-grant colleges, the mechanics of representation include attempts by the Agricultural Relations Department of TVA to (1) channel all activities which may possibly be interpreted as within their subject-matter field through the land-grant colleges; (2) make itself the sole point of contact by the Authority with the institutions; (3) actively oppose all encroachments on the prerogatives of the colleges; and (4) further the policies of the colleges within the Authority, as opportunity may arise. . . .

The construction of an administrative constituency, whereby the dominant agricultural leadership in the Tennessee Valley area was afforded a place within the policy-determining structure of the TVA, is an example of the process of *informal* cooptation. . . . The unacknowledged absorption of nucleuses of power into the administrative structure of an organization makes possible the elimination or appeasement of potential sources of opposition. At the same time, as the price of accommodation, the organization commits itself to avenues of activity and lines of policy enforced by the character of the coopted elements. Moreover, though cooptation may occur with respect to only a fraction of the organization, there will be pressure for the organization as a whole to adapt itself to the needs of the informal relationship. Viewed thus broadly, the process of informal cooptation represents a mechanism of comprehensive adjustment, permitting a formal organization to enhance its chances for survival by accommodating itself to existing centers of interest and power within its area of operation. . . .

CASE STUDY 2

The Marasmus of the ICC

SAMUEL P. HUNTINGTON

Formed in 1887, the Interstate Commerce Commission was the model for subsequent U.S. regulatory agencies as well as for the nation's regulatory policy itself. Despite its early preeminence, however, the ICC no longer holds a leading position in either the regulatory or the transportation policy process. Indeed, its position in both fields has diminished steadily during the almost two decades since the following article first appeared in print.

The Department of Transportation (DOT), established over some industry opposition in 1966, was initially an amalgam of some thirty existing agencies, including the Bureau of Public Roads, the St. Lawrence Seaway Development Corporation, the U.S. Coast Guard, and the Alaska Railroad. Since its establishment, the DOT has replaced the ICC as the dominant governmental actor in the field of transportation, while its National Transportation and Safety Board has absorbed the safety functions once exercised by the ICC.

Reprinted by permission of The Yale Law Journal Company and Fred B. Rothman & Company from *The Yale Law Journal*, Vol. 61, pp. 467–508.

The decline of the ICC was further accelerated when it lost most of its jurisdiction over the nation's railroads. On 1 May 1971, AMTRAK, a quasi-public corporation, was given the responsibility of revitalizing the country's rapidly deteriorating railroad passenger service. Hence the ICC's struggles for organizational survival and viability have been even more difficult than Huntington had known in 1952. While reading this study, consider the following questions:

1. *Why was the ICC created?*
2. *How does Huntington's study of the ICC compare with Bernstein's concept of stages of regulatory policy?*
3. *What fundamental problems of organizational behavior are illustrated by Huntington's and Selznick's studies?*
4. *What factors have contributed to the "marasmus" of the ICC?*
5. *Is it inevitable that regulatory agencies will be dominated by those who are supposed to be regulated? If so, are there any alternatives by which the public interest can be protected?*

Among the myriad federal agencies concerned with transportation, the Interstate Commerce Commission has long been preeminent. It is the oldest transportation regulatory commission, and with exception of the Corps of Engineers it is the oldest federal agency of any type with major transportation responsibilities. It is the only federal agency immediately concerned with more than one type of carrier: its activities directly affect four of the five major forms of commercial transportation. It is one of the few significant transportation bodies which have not been absorbed by the Department of Commerce, and it is the only important transportation agency completely independent of the executive branch. It is the sole administrative agency to which Congress has delegated the responsibility for enforcing the National Transportation Policy. During its sixty-five years of existence the Commission developed an enviable reputation for honesty, impartiality, and expertness. Its age, prestige, and scope combined to make it the premier federal agency in the transportation field.

Despite this impressive past, however, there are many indications that the ICC is now losing its position of leadership. New developments threaten to bring about the end of the agency or to reduce it to a secondary position. The level of its appropriations and the number of its employees have been either stationary or declining. Its decisions are more frequently reversed in the courts than previously. Its leadership and staff have manifestly deteriorated in quality. The general praise which it once received has been replaced by sharp criticism. And, most importantly, it is now challenged by the rise of a new agency, the Office of the Undersecretary of Commerce for Transportation, which appears to be assuming federal transportation leadership. It is the purpose of this Article to analyze the causes of the decline of the ICC and the probable and desirable future position of this agency.

Successful adaptation to changing environmental circumstances is the secret of health and longevity for administrative as well as biological organisms. Every government agency must reflect to some degree the "felt needs" of its time. In the realm of government, felt needs are expressed through political demands and political pressures. These demands and pressures may come from the president, other administrative agencies and officials, congressmen, political interest groups, and the general public. If an agency is to be viable it must adapt itself to the pressures from these sources so as to maintain a net preponderance of political support over political opposition. It must have sufficient support to maintain and, if necessary, expand its statutory authority, to protect it against attempts to abolish it or subordinate it to other agencies, and to secure for it necessary appropriations. Consequently, to remain viable over a period of time, an agency must adjust its sources of support so as to correspond with changes in the strength of their political pressures. If the agency fails to make this adjustment, its political support decreases relative to its political opposition, and it may be said to suffer from administrative marasmus [i.e., wasting away without apparent cause]. The decline of the ICC may be attributed to its susceptibility to this malady.

Historical background

The history of the ICC in terms of its political support divides naturally into two fairly distinct periods. The Commission was created in 1887 after the Supreme Court invalidated state attempts to regulate the railroads' abuse of their monopoly power. The driving forces behind these early state regulatory laws and commissions were the farmers, who had suffered severely from exorbitant rates and discriminatory practices. This group plus equally dissatisfied commercial shippers were the political force responsible for the Act to Regulate Commerce. In addition, general public indignation and disgust at railroad financial and business practices provided a favorable climate of opinion for the creation of the Commission. President [Grover] Cleveland endorsed the legislation and enhanced the Commission's reputation by appointing Judge [Thomas M.] Cooley and other prominent figures as its first members.

From 1887 down to the First World War the support of the Commission came primarily from the groups responsible for its creation. Opposition came principally from the railroads and the courts. In its first two decades the Commission was severely hampered by the combined action of these two groups. Subsequently farmer and shipper interests with the vigorous support of President [Theodore] Roosevelt secured the passage of the Hepburn Act of 1906. This enlarged the Commission, extended its jurisdiction, gave it the power to prescribe future maximum rates, and prohibited railroads from owning the products they transported. The decade which followed the passage of this Act was the peak of the Commission's power and prestige while still dependent upon consumer, public and presidential support.

The end of the First World War marked a definite change in the nature of the transportation problem and in the attitudes of the various interests towards railroad regulation. The vigorous actions of the ICC in the period immediately prior to the war had eliminated the worst discriminatory practices and had convinced the railroads that the path of wisdom was to accept regulation and to learn to live with the Commission. This domestication of the carriers consequently reduced the interest and political activity of shipper groups. And increased urbanization reduced the power of farm groups which had been such a significant source of support to the Commission. Finally, "normalcy" had supplanted progressivism and Harding and Coolidge were significantly different from T. Roosevelt and Wilson. Consequently there was little likelihood that restrictive regulation would find much support from either the public or the White House.

All these factors dictated not only the shift in public policy which was made in the Transportation Act of 1920 but also a shift by the Commission in the sources to which it looked for support. Continued reliance upon the old sources of support would have resulted in decreasing viability. Therefore the Commission turned more and more to the railroad industry itself, particularly the railroad management group. This development was aided by the expansion of the Commission's activities and the resulting increased dependence of the Commission upon the cooperation of regulated groups for the successful administration of its program. The support which the Commission received from the railroads sustained it down to World War II and enabled it both to expand its authority over other carrier groups and to defend itself against attempts to subject it to executive control.

The present marasmus of the ICC is due to continued dependence upon railroad support. The transportation industry is not only large, it is also dynamic. Technological changes and economic development are basically altering the nation's transportation pattern. The tremendous expansion of air and motor transport, the resulting increase in competition, the economic development of the South and West, the rise of private carriage, and the

increased significance of defense considerations all make today's
transportation system fundamentally different from that of twenty-five years
ago. These technological and economic developments have given rise to new
political demands and pressures, and have drastically altered the old balance
of political force in the transportation arena. A quarter of a century ago,
commercial transportation was railroad transportation. Today, railroads are a
declining, although still major, segment of the transportation industry. Their
economic decline has been matched by a decrease in political influence. The
ICC, however, remains primarily a "railroad" agency. It has not responded
to the demands of the new forces in transportation. It has not duplicated the
successful adjustment of its sources of political support that it carried out after
World War I. Consequently, it is losing its leadership to those agencies which
are more responsive to the needs of the times.

Railroad support of the ICC

Railroad Praise of the ICC. The attitude of the railroads towards the
Commission since 1935 can only be described as one of satisfaction,
approbation, and confidence. At times the railroads have been almost effusive
in their praise of the Commission. The ICC, one subcommittee of the
Association of American Railroads has declared, "is eminently qualified by
nearly sixty years of experience to handle transportation matters with a
maximum of satisfaction to management, labor and the public." Another
representative of the same association has similarly stated that "[w]hat is
needed for the solution of the tremendously important problems of transport
regulation is the impartiality, deliberation, expertness, and continuity of policy
that have marked the history of the Interstate Commerce Commission."
Railroad officials and lawyers have commended the Commission as a "con-
spicuous success," a "constructive force," and as a "veteran and generally
respected tribunal." The American Short Line Railroad Association has
commented upon the "fair, intelligent treatment" its members have been
accorded by the Commission, and the Pennsylvania Railroad has been lavish
in its praise of the latter's policies. The ICC is probably the only regulatory
body in the federal government which can boast that a book has been
written about it by counsel for a regulated interest in order to demonstrate
"how well" the Commission has "performed its duty."

The railroads and the Commission have both praised their harmonious
relations. "The railroad industry," it has been said, "in wide contrast to other
industry, has learned to live under government regulation." The editors of
Railway Age have similarly spoken highly of the "collaboration" which exists
between the Commission and its regulated enterprises and have remarked
that this "stands out in strong contrast to the animosity and distrust which
now separates many regulatory bodies from the areas of industry which they

supervise.'' The Commission itself has noted with pride the lack of criticism which its administration of the Interstate Commerce Act has received from the carriers and has pointed out that while some interests have urged the abandonment of regulation the ''railroads have never joined in that suggestion.''

Railroad Defense of Commission Independence. The railroads have vigorously defended the independence of the ICC from control by other governmental units and have opposed all attempts to subordinate it to other agencies or to transfer from the Commission any of its function. This support for the Commission has taken three principal forms.

Opposition to ICC reorganization. The railroads have successfully opposed all reorganization proposals to subordinate the ICC or transfer any of its functions to the executive branch. In 1937 the President's Committee on Administrative Management recommended that the ICC along with all other regulatory commissions be divided into administrative and judicial sections and be placed in an executive department. The administrative section would be a regular bureau within the department; the judicial section would be in the department for ''housekeeping'' purposes only. These proposals raised a storm of protest from the ICC-railroad bloc and legislation to effect them was defeated in Congress. Over a decade later similar opposition was expressed by the railroads to legislation designed to create a Department of Transportation which would absorb the ''executive'' functions of the ICC. The Hoover Commission recommendations that the equipment inspection, safety, and car service functions of the Commission be transferred to the Department of Commerce were likewise opposed by the rail carriers. In general, the railroads have repeatedly emphasized the desirability of maintaining the independence of the Commission against all forms of executive encroachment.

The significance of railroad support for the Commission in this connection was perhaps best demonstrated by the fate of the presidential reorganization plan designed to centralize administrative authority within the Commission in a chairman appointed by the president. This plan was one of six, all submitted by the president at the same time, and devised to effectuate similar reforms in five other commissions as well as the ICC. Resolutions of disapproval of four of these plans were introduced in the Senate and referred to the Committee on Expenditures in Executive Departments. This committee reported three of the resolutions unfavorably; the fourth, that disapproving of the ICC reorganization, was reported favorably. The explanation of this obviously inconsistent action (since all four plans were virtually identical) can, in the words of the minority report, ''easily be found by reading the roster of the regulated interests (and their lawyers) which appeared in opposition.'' The hearings on the plans had been largely monopolized by railroad and associated witnesses appearing to defend the "independence" of the ICC. In the debate on the floor of the Senate the railroads were given primary credit for the committee's peculiar action, and in the end the ICC resolution was approved by a substantial majority. Railroad support saved the ICC from a reorganized fate to which five other commissions succumbed.

Opposition to the creation of new agencies which might rival the ICC. Within the last decade the railroads have generally opposed the establishment of new agencies which might in any way infringe upon or limit the powers of the ICC. In 1938 the railroad Committee of Six did recommend the creation of a new transportation authority which would take over the Commission's powers in regard to finance, entry, and abandonment, and the establishment of a special court to handle railroad reorganizations. Both recommendations, however, were opposed by numerous rail carriers and officials. Typical of the usual railroad attitude was the rejection in 1946 by one Association of American Railroads group of the proposal for a new transportation planning body because apparently this "would provide another agency duplicating the work of the Interstate Commerce Commission, and further complicate a situation now made difficult by the intervening of various government departments." Representatives of the AAR also opposed the creation of the new office of Undersecretary of Commerce for Transportation on the grounds that the ICC was the leading federal agency concerned with transportation and that this new official could only duplicate its functions and challenge its authority. Similarly, railroad opposition to the creation of a Department of Transportation has in large part been based upon the fear that even if this body did not initially absorb the ICC it would eventually encroach upon the Commission's functions. Railroads have frequently urged the creation of a single regulatory commission for all forms of transportation; the implicit or explicit assumption in all such proposals, however, is that this commission would be an enlarged and reorganized ICC.

Opposition to the interference of existing agencies with the Commission. Attempts by existing agencies to influence or dictate ICC policy through intervention in proceedings before the Commission, informal pressure upon commissioners, or by other means, have been severely attacked by the railroads. The argument is that the ICC has the responsibility to act in the public interest, and other agencies, if they interfere, must be doing so on behalf of some parochial interest. Appearances of the Secretary of Agriculture before the Commission have frequently been objected to, and the intervention of price control agencies in the general rate cases has likewise been attacked. The heaviest criticism along this line has been directed at the Department of Justice for its frequent interventions before the ICC and attempts to influence Commission policy in cases raising antitrust issues. On a much broader level, the railroads and associated groups have been staunch defenders of the independence of the Commission from presidential and congressional interference. . . .

Rail-Motor Competition. The affiliation of the ICC with the railroads has resulted in an ambiguous relationship between the Commission and the principal railroad-competitive group, the motor carriers. On the one hand, there is a close affiliation between the motor carrier industry and the ICC's Bureau of Motor Carriers, with the two cooperating in the enforcement of the Motor Carrier Act of 1935. The Bureau has consequently been praised by the motor carriers and criticized by the railroads. On the other hand, the relationship between the motor carrier industry and the Commission apart from the BMC has been cool and frequently antagonistic. The reason for this is Commission partiality towards the railroads in conflicts of interest between the two carrier groups. The price of railroad affiliation has been motor carrier alienation.

Because a large portion of railroad traffic is noncompetitive and must move by rail, the Commission has been able to aid the railroads by permitting selective rate-cutting during periods of intense rail-motor competition such as that from 1935 through 1941. For three years from 1937 to 1940 the Commission required motor carriers to bear the burden of proof in making competitive rate cuts while at the same time not requiring the railroads to do so. This policy was continued after Congress in 1938 amended the Motor Carrier Act to make its provisions concerning burden of proof identical with those applicable to the railroads. During this same period the Commission put further barriers in the way of motor carrier competition by prescribing comprehensive minimum rate level for motor carriers in the northeast and middle west. Although initially requested by the motor carriers, the subsequent effect of these orders was, as Commissioner Eastman pointed out in one dissent, to substitute a much more difficult procedure for motor carriers wishing to lower rates than for railroads. The Commission rejected, however, motor carrier petitions to remedy the situation. Throughout this period the Commission in a number of cases encouraged the railroads to exercise their managerial discretion by meeting motor carrier competition through various devices. The injurious effects of proposed railroad competitive rates upon motor carriers were not sufficient cause to invalidate the rates. Railroads were usually permitted to meet motor carrier competition by rate reductions, and to regain by this means traffic which had been lost to the truckers. Relief from the provisions of Section 4 of the Act prohibiting the charging of a higher rate for a short haul than for a longer one was frequently granted the railroads in this connection. Rate reductions on competitive traffic not accomplished by reductions upon similar noncompetitive traffic were held not to be prejudicial or discriminatory. On the other hand, attempts by the motor carriers to meet railroad competition or to undercut railroads were usually disapproved by the Commission.

Rail-Water Competition. Its affiliation with the railroads has dominated Commission action concerning water carriers and rail-water competition since the middle twenties when the Commission became dependent upon railroad support. Previous to this time the Commission had, with the exception of its administration of the Panama Canal Act, adequately balanced the interests of the two types of carriers. Beginning in this period, however, the railroads instituted a concerted competitive drive against the water carriers. In this they had the virtually complete cooperation of the ICC. The twenty per cent differential which had been established by the Director General of the railroads during World War I for water-rail competitive rates was reduced to ten or fifteen per cent in a number of cases. The persistent refusal of the railroads to enter into joint rates and through routes with the water carriers was acquiesced in by the Commission despite congressional pressure to the contrary. Where joint rates were established, the participating water carrier was made to bear the full burden of the differential, and the Commission on occasion even permitted the railroad division of the joint rate to be considerably higher than the local rate to the point of interchange, thus virtually penalizing the water carrier for entering into such a relationship. Reversing a previous policy adopted when it was dependent upon farmer and shipper support, the Commission began to permit railroads to charge discriminatory rates on traffic which had a prior or subsequent haul by water. Liberal use was made of the provisions of the Fourth Section of the Interstate Commerce Act allowing the ICC to permit railroads to charge a higher rate for a shorter haul than for a longer one, and the Commission frequently granted "flexible" relief permitting the railroads to meet automatically any competitive reductions by the water carriers. In many cases, the Commission cooperated with the railroads to evade the statutory requirement that railroads not be allowed to raise depressed rates solely because of the elimination of water competition. In approving general rate increases during this period the Commission frequently acquiesced to railroad requests for the exemption from such increases of heavily water-competitive traffic. The Commission also showed a marked tendency to permit the railroads to lower rates on highly competitive items, at times such reductions going below the fully compensatory level. In a series of cases concerning the important citrus fruit movement from Florida the Commission engaged in an administrative duel with the Maritime Commission: each agency successfully reducing the rates of the carriers subject to its regulation. In the one significant instance during this period in which the ICC was called upon to express its views on federal development of the inland waterways, the Commission delivered a report on a proposed Lake Erie–Ohio River canal which was hostile to waterways interests and favorable to the railroads.

As a result of these policies the water carriers, during the thirties, struggled against the extension over them of the power of the "railroad-minded'' ICC. Unlike the motor carriers, they never acquiesced to Commission regulation. In 1940, however, the railroads and the Commission triumphed and the water carrier industry was brought under a comprehensive system of control. This did not ameliorate the antagonism between the water carriers and the Commission, and, again unlike the motor carriers, the water carrier industry never developed affiliations with any significant segment of the ICC. The Commission does not have a separate water carrier division, and, whereas the Bureau of Motor Carriers is the Commission's largest bureau, the Bureau of Water Carriers and Freight Forwarders is one of its smallest. In 1950 this bureau had only twenty-one employees, and in addition to its water carrier duties it also supervised the regulation of freight forwarders and rate bureaus. The water carriers have consequently frequently complained that their interests are neglected, but these complaints have not produced any remedies. The Commission has remained closely affiliated with the railroads. . . .

Railroad affiliation and commission viability

The pattern of affiliation of the Commission with the railroads described in the preceding pages is the basic reason for the decreasing viability of the Commission. This decline has four significant aspects:

(1) The alienation of non–railroad interest groups. This process has been described in regard to the water carriers and motor carriers. The fourth major type of transportation, the air carriers, also recognize the Commission's railroad affiliations and have blocked the extension of Commission power into their field. Among shippers the Commission can only command qualified support from the large industrial shippers of the National Industrial Traffic League, which has always been closely associated with the railroads. Other shippers, and agricultural groups in particular, are generally hostile towards the Commission.

(2) The alienation of other government agencies. With some agencies, such as the Department of Agriculture and the Maritime Commission, estrangement has developed because these bodies are closely affiliated with interest groups alienated from the Commission. In a larger number of instances, however, it has been because the Commission's espousal of the relatively narrow interests of the railroads has conflicted with the responsibility felt by these other agencies to some broader interest and their dependence upon some broader basis of political support. This is particularly true of such agencies as the Departments of Commerce, Interior, and Defense, the Antitrust Division, and the price stabilization agencies.

(3) Subversion of congressional intent. In interpreting the Interstate Commerce Act in the interests of the railroads it is quite obvious that the Commission is applying the law in a manner not intended by the Congress. In 1940 Congress declared the national transportation policy to include ''fair and impartial regulation of all modes of transportation.'' Congress also wrote

into the acts of 1935 and 1940 various provisions designed to insure that this policy would be carried out. The failure of the Commission to do this has resulted in increased criticism of the Commission in Congress.

(4) Passivity and loss of leadership. The general purpose of the railroads during the past quarter century has been first the preservation, and then subsequently, after it had been lost, the restoration of their transportation monopoly. Because of its affiliation with the railroads the Commission has, like them, become a defender of the status quo. To this end it has maintained an outdated, formalistic type of procedure. It has been slow to introduce the most simple and accepted new techniques of modern management. It has failed to develop effective devices for representing the public interest. It has neglected administrative planning, and has failed to develop a coherent transportation policy aside from that of giving the railroads what they want. As a result, it has been slow to recognize and deal with obvious evils, such as the freight classification problem or the question of state limitations on truck sizes and weights. It has also been unable to adjust its thinking and actions to the new demands of an era in which defense considerations are paramount. These failures of the Commission have inevitably led to the formation within the executive branch of a responsible office which can take the lead in national transportation policy and planning.

CASE STUDY 3

A Mayor Speaks on the Bureaucracy
NAT HENTOFF

From 1966 to 1973 John Lindsay was the mayor and chief administrator of an almost flamboyantly troubled metropolis that is normally characterized in complacent superlatives—as the nation's largest, most colorfully pluralistic city, containing the nation's wealthiest and most powerful corporations as well as the richest cultural resources in the United States. But New York City is also the site of the Harlem-Bedford-Stuyvesant district, one of the most appalling urban slums in the nation. The city is administered by a vast, powerful, entrenched bureaucracy and, like many another large American city, has immense problems when its public employees organize and participate in union activism and strikes.

John Lindsay's term as mayor of New York City was marked by stormy labor problems with city employees. The sanitation workers' strike

of 1968, the teachers' strike of 1968, the police strike of 1971, and a variety
of work stoppages, threatened work stoppages, and labor and pension disputes preoccupied much of the mayor's time. The problem of preventing
administrative dissatisfaction and harmful public work stoppages has not
been satisfactorily resolved to the present day. The following case study
shows how the bureaucracy of New York City responded to the problem
of urban deterioration, one of the major crises of the 1960s, and discusses
Mayor Lindsay's problems in attempting to make the city's powerful bureaucracy do his bidding. As you read this selection, ask yourself:

1. *What were the sources of power of New York City's bureaucracy?*
2. *What methods did Lindsay use to force the bureaucracy to cooperate?*
3. *Did the mayor really govern the city?*

". . . For the first time, I think there's an awakening among some of the
labor leaders to *their* responsibility to be more flexible. That's a big step—very
big step. We've still got problems with the municipal unions, though,
particularly with regard to our right to move men around, which is an essential
right. Take the Fire Department. I was struck with luck in appointing Bob
Lowery as Fire Commissioner, incidentally. He turned out to be a brilliant
administrator. Furthermore, he knows when to roll with a punch and when
not to. And he's very sensitive to what the pros call the high-hazard areas
for fires. However, over the years fire companies have put down deep roots
in certain neighborhoods. For a long time, the men were given limited
privileges to moonlight in neighborhoods where they were stationed, and
those part-time jobs have made for even deeper roots. Until Bob, no Fire
Commissioner had moved them, even when more men were needed in the
high-hazard areas. Since he *is* doing that, he's anathema to the heads of their
unions. When Bob took men who weren't needed after dark in lower
Manhattan and put them in Bedford-Stuyvesant, where there are twelve fires
a night, Gerald Ryan, the president of the Uniformed Firemen's Association,
was appalled. I said to him, 'Gerry, isn't it logical we do this shifting around?'
'Well, no, not exactly,' he said. 'These people are part of that neighborhood.
They have their cars there. They have to get those cars washed at a certain
hour—that kind of thing.' It hasn't been easy, and Lowery, while skillful, *is* a
Negro dealing with a largely white organization. So sometimes he needs
reassurance, and that's why I spend a good deal of time with him. I told him,

'If it gets to that point, crack Ryan over the head publicly, and I'll support you.' "

With some relish, as if at the prospect of more head-cracking to come, the Mayor continued, "This business of trying to get the separate parts of the administration working at maximum efficiency leads to all kinds of resistance. For example, in the Human Resources Administration, under our reorganization plan, there'll be a major division advising me on public-education policy. The Board of Education resisted the idea, but we told them it wouldn't kill them. I've finally got the Police Department responsive to the Mayor, and now the Board of Education and its empire cannot continue to travel in *its* own orbit. Education has to be made an integral part of community development, and therefore it has to be subject to a good deal of guidance from City Hall. No matter how many asbestos walls are put between me and the Board of Education, at the end I get the blame if there's trouble, and so I bloody well ought to have something to say about what's going on.

"God, they're slow in that empire! You remember when Freeport, on Long Island, refused a federal program on teaching machines? The government was going to supply not only the money but the bodies to go with it. You couldn't get a better package. We read about it in the paper, and I asked the Board for an immediate decision on whether we should take it over. No, they said, they needed a month to decide. Bernard Donovan, the Superintendent of Schools, was in Europe, and someone else was away. I told them they had twelve hours. You never saw such a crisis and so many telephone calls. But they came to a decision within those twelve hours, and we got the program.

"Then, there was the time the people filming 'Up the Down Staircase' wanted the use of a school building. The Board said it would take months to come to a decision, and that, besides, the picture might present a poor image of our school system. The filming had to take place during the summer, mind you. The schools were empty. So what if they showed a brick going through a window? At least, that would indicate a little activity. Anyway, I called Moe Iushewitz, a labor official who's on the Board. 'Do you realize that you're losing a million dollars in jobs by taking this stuffy attitude?' I asked him. 'How would you like to see *that* in the paper, Moe?' I signed him up, and he delivered the rest of the Board."

Lindsay broke into laughter. "I've got a new slogan—'Wasp Power!' Thought of it the other day. Someone was teasing me about the number of Jews in the administration, and I said, 'We Wasps may have only eleven percent of the vote in this city, but one day we're going to rise.'"

A phone call was put through. The Mayor, striking his desk with a pencil, listened for a while, and then he said, "Well, do what you have to do.

I'll back you up.'' He hung up and turned back to me. "The things you have
to deal with!'' he said. "We had a very interesting one a few weeks ago.
We got word that the Ku Klux Klan in Baltimore planned to march through
Harlem. Howard Leary, the Police Commissioner, sent a couple of smart
guys to talk to them—to tell them they were damn fools and they'd get their
skulls split open. I thought they'd been convinced, but two weeks later Leary
got a telegram signed by the big Grand Wizard saying they were coming
by way of the George Washington Bridge in full regalia, and since it was to be
a peaceful march, they demanded police protection. Leary called me. 'Well,
chief, what do I do now?' he said. 'What are the rights and liberties on this
one?' Lee Rankin, the Corporation Counsel, was in transit somewhere and
couldn't be reached. But I happened to be talking to Bruce Bromley. He's a
former Court of Appeals judge who's now a partner in Cravath, Swaine &
Moore. He volunteered to research this one himself. The next day, he called
me up in triumph. He'd found an old statute that goes back about a thousand
years. 'Does Rankin know?' he said, 'that it's illegal to walk through New York
City with something on your head other than a hat?' Well, we didn't actually
use that statute. Leary sent the Wizard a telegram that said, 'You are coming
to New York only to incite racial disturbance. Don't come. If you do, we'll
lock you up.' That settled it. And here I'd had visions of a great scene on the
George Washington Bridge. Before we were sure they wouldn't come, by the
way, Leary asked me what to do if they did come. 'Surround them with
Negro cops,' I told him, 'and you and I will go up to the roof of a tenement
and throw bottles at them.' '' Lindsay roared with laughter. . . .

I had been in the Mayor's office for nearly an hour, and, as in February
[an earlier visit], I had been feeling the pressure rise—on him, and on me
as an obstacle to the furthering of city affairs. The lights on the Mayor's
phone had been flashing almost continually, and frequently the door would
open and a head would pop in, look at me—reprovingly, I thought—and pop
out. But I did want to find out in the time I had left how much progress, if any,
there had been in making certain that new policies, once adopted by the
Mayor, were actually being carried through on the lower levels of the
administration.

When I asked about this, the Mayor sighed. "Sometimes I feel I'm
pushing my shoulder against a mountain," he said. "My feet are churning
away and the mountain won't budge. But I'm determined to blast things
through. Every week, I tell the commissioners at the cabinet meeting to get
out of their offices into the streets and find out what their departments are
doing with *people*. I'm always on them to *act*, and to follow through on the
action. I'd rather they made three errors out of ten decisions, as long as they
made the decisions and got them into operation. I know it's tough, and
sometimes the bottlenecks have nothing to do with the people in the lower

echelons. I've walked by those rattrap buildings in East New York—the ones
with rubble and beer cans inside, and, at night, a few guys mainlining it.
They've been abandoned by owners we can't find. All the city can do is
board them up. Three days later, the boards are down. The logical thing
to do would be to tear down those buildings, blacktop the area, and put a
basketball or handball court there. Or a place to get cars off the street. But
by law you can't pull the mess down without going to court over the damn
thing. But I did see one terrible block in East New York and I told the
Buildings Commissioner to just pull down the buildings. Sometimes that's the
way you have to operate. I learned that in the Navy during the war. Before
I became gunnery officer on my destroyer, I was in charge of damage control.
I was the housekeeper. My job was to get the necessary repairs done, get the
guns we needed, get the ship painted, and get out to sea. You stole from
the next guy, you borrowed from somebody else, but you got it done.
Cumshawing, we called it. If you'd waited for the paperwork to get to you
from this agency and that agency in Washington, you would never have got
out to sea again." Lindsay suddenly looked glum. "Of course, you had a great
advantage in the Navy. You could shove off. Nobody could do anything to you
once you were in the middle of the Pacific." His spirits seemed to rise again.
"But the thing is to keep moving and to keep others moving," he said. "We'll
break through. And that's one of the reasons I go out into the streets as
often as I can—to show movement, to show concern."

"What if you're just raising hopes in the ghettos when you're out in the
streets—hopes that will turn into even deeper frustration if movement doesn't
lead to visible change?" I asked.

The Mayor frowned. "I've done a lot of thinking about that, but I honestly
believe people are reasonable. They don't expect miracles. They do expect
some understanding and knowledge of their troubles. And when I'm around
they do see some signs of visible change on some level. I was in a Bronx
neighborhood where a kid got killed because there was no traffic light. When
I left there, I called Henry Barnes, the Traffic Commissioner, and made sure
it wouldn't take the usual four months to get a light where the people wanted
it. I will *not* walk out of a situation like that without being able to assure the
people in the neighborhood that there'll be immediate action." Lindsay
grinned. "Sometimes there's even action before I get there. The Sanitation
Department, for instance, has a real information system. If they find out I'm
going to be in a certain neighborhood, they'll clean it up before I come.
That's what they've always done with Mayors. But I don't always tell them
where I'll be. Sometimes I don't tell *anyone* where I'm going. And then, when
I get there and see they haven't been moving their butts, I yell and scream
to get the trucks into that neighborhood. And I go back, or I send someone
back, to see if they've followed through. Also, going out on those streets

is of immense value to *me*. It's the one way I can really find out what people are sweating about, what they care about. I wouldn't have had those houses in East New York torn down if seeing them hadn't hit me in the guts. You see so much grief on those streets.''

NOTES

1. For a look at the functional aspects of bureaucracies in national and cross-national political systems, see Fred Riggs, *Administration in Developing Countries* (Boston: Houghton Mifflin, 1964); and Joseph La Palombara, *Bureaucracy and Political Development* (Princeton: Princeton University Press, 1963).

2. Gerald E. Caiden, *The Dynamics of Public Administration*, pp. 103–104; and Guy Beneviste, *The Politics of Expertise*, pp. 119–36.

3. W. W. Chittick, "The Domestic Information Activities of the Department of State," p. 158; for further discussion, see J. William Fulbright, *The Pentagon Propaganda Machine*, pp. 147–50.

4. See David B. Truman, *The Governmental Process*, pp. 90–92.

5. Philip Selznick, *TVA and the Grass Roots*, pp. 225–26.

6. Francis E. Rourke, *Bureaucracy, Politics, and Public Policy*, pp. 5–38. Joseph P. Harris, *Congressional Control of Administration*; and Aaron Wildavsky, *The Politics of the Budgetary Process*.

7. Rourke, *Bureaucracy, Politics, and Public Policy*, p. 25.

8. Richard F. Fenno, *The Power of the Purse*, p. 404.

9. Wildavsky, *Politics of the Budgetary Process*, pp. 64–123.

10. Ibid., p. 104.

11. Ibid., p. 121.

12. Fulbright, *Pentagon Propaganda Machine*, pp. 128–29.

13. *Congressional Quarterly Weekly Report* 18 (December 1963): 2815–16; see also Samuel P. Huntington, "Interservice Competition and the Political Roles of the Armed Services," *American Political Science Review* 55 (March 1961): 40–52.

14. Arthur Mass, *Muddy Waters*, pp. 24–214.

15. For a detailed discussion of expertise and sources of power, see Beneviste, *Politics of Expertise*, pp. 30–38, 119–70.

16. R. W. Apple, Jr., "Haldeman the Fierce, Haldeman the Faithful, Haldeman the Fallen," *New York Times*, 6 May 1973, pp. 38–39, 104.

17. Ibid.

18. "The broad plans of governmental action are not administrative, the detailed execution of such plans is administrative" (Woodrow Wilson, "The Study of Administration," *Political Science Quarterly* 2 [June 1887]: 212).

19. Herbert Kaufman, *The Forest Ranger*.

20. Harris, *Congressional Control of Administration*, pp. 226–27.

21. J. Leiper Freeman, "The Bureaucracy in Pressure Politics," *Annals of the Academy of Political and Social Sciences* 319 (1952): 10–19.

22. Frederick C. Mosher, *Democracy and the Public Service*, pp. 1–2.

23. Wallace S. Sayre and Herbert Kaufman, *Governing New York City*, p. 732.

24. A. H. Raskin, "Politics Up-ends the Bargaining Table," in *Public Workers and Public Unions,* ed. Sam Zagoria, pp. 122–46.

25. Robert A. Dahl, *Who Governs?,* pp. 89–163; and M. Kent Jennings, *Community Influentials,* pp. 1–10.

26. Caiden, *Dynamics of Public Administration,* pp. 82–83.

27. "FTC Acts against Egg Ads," *San Francisco Chronicle,* 2 August 1974.

28. "GAO Spots Legal Arms Giveaway," *San Francisco Chronicle,* 4 August 1974.

29. David Broder, "The Other News," *Newsweek,* 5 August 1974, p. 13.

30. Ibid.

31. Caiden, *Dynamics of Public Administration,* p. 91.

32. "Top Nixon Aide Leaves," *San Francisco Chronicle,* 13 August 1974.

33. "OEO Chief Forced Out," *San Francisco Chronicle,* 16 July 1974.

34. Milton Moskowitz, "Hard Way to Save on Plane Fares," *San Francisco Chronicle,* 6 July 1974.

35. David Burnham, "AEC Penalizes Few Nuclear Facilities despite Thousands of Safety Violations," *New York Times,* 25 August 1974, p. 1.

36. Ibid.

37. Ibid.

38. "The Powerful Public School Bureaucracy," *San Francisco Chronicle,* 27 June 1974.

39. "Weicker Says Nixon Trod on Us," *San Francisco Chronicle,* 30 June 1974.

40. Al Martinez, "Growing Industrial Spying and One Industry Counterspy," *San Francisco Chronicle & Examiner Sunday Punch,* 1 September 1974.

41. Merle Fainsod, Lincoln Gordon, and Joseph Palamountain, *Government and the American Economy,* p. 243.

42. Marver H. Bernstein, *Regulation of Business by Independent Commissions,* p. 22.

43. Ibid., p. 27.

44. Ibid., p. 23.

45. John M. Pfiffner and Robert Presthus, *Public Administration,* pp. 478–79.

46. Ibid., p. 132 ff.

47. Ibid., pp. 131–33.

48. Bernstein, *Regulation of Business,* p. 92.

49. Samuel P. Huntington, "The Marasmus of the ICC," in *Bureaucratic Power in National Politics,* ed. Francis E. Rourke, p. 85.

50. Walter Hamilton, *The Politics of Industry,* p. 54.

51. James S. Turner, *The Chemical Feast;* and Robert Fellmeth, *Interstate Commerce Ommission.*

52. Cited in Gordon Clapp, *The TVA,* p. 9.

53. John Moore, *The Economic Importance of TVA* (Knoxville: University of Tennessee Press, 1967), p. 157.

SELECTED BIBLIOGRAPHY

Apple, R. W., Jr. "Haldeman the Fierce, Haldeman the Faithful, Haldeman the Fallen." *New York Times Magazine,* 6 May 1973, pp. 38–39.

Beneviste, Guy. *The Politics of Expertise.* Berkeley, Calif.: Glendessary Press, 1972.

Bernstein, Marver H. *Regulation of Business by Independent Commissions.* Princeton: Princeton University Press, 1955.

Caiden, Gerald E. *The Dynamics of Public Administration: Guidelines to Current Transformations in Theory and Practice.* New York: Holt, Rinehart & Winston, 1971.

Chittick, W. W. "The Domestic Information Activities of the Department of State." Ph.D. dissertation, Johns Hopkins University, 1964.

Clapp. Gordon. *The TVA.* Chicago: University of Chicago Press, 1955.

Dahl, Robert. *Who Governs?* New Haven, Conn.: Yale University Press, 1961.

Fainsod, Merle; Gordon, Lincoln; and Palamountain, Joseph. *Government and the American Economy.* 3d ed. New York: W. W. Norton & Co., 1959.

Fellmeth, Robert. *Interstate Commerce Omission: The Report on the Interstate Commerce Commission and Transportation.* New York: Grossman Publishers, 1970.

Fenno, Richard F. *The Power of the Purse:* Appropriations Politics in Congress. Boston: Little, Brown & Co., 1966.

Freeman, J. Leiper. "The Bureaucracy in Pressure Politics." *Annals of the American Academy of Political and Social Sciences* 319 (1952): 10–19.

Fullbright, J. William. *The Pentagon Propaganda Machine.* New York: Liveright, 1970.

Hamilton, Walter. *The Politics of Industry.* New York: Alfred A. Knopf, 1965.

Harris, Joseph P. *Congressional Control of Administration.* New York: Doubleday & Co., 1964.

Hentoff, Nat. "The Mayor." *New Yorker,* 14 October 1967, 61–64.

Hinckle, Warren, and Welsh, David. "The Five Battles of Selma." *Ramparts,* June 1965, pp. 19–52.

Huntington, Samuel P. "The Marasmus of the ICC." In *Bureaucratic Power in National Politics,* edited by Francis E. Rourke, pp. 73–86. Boston: Little, Brown & Co., 1965.

Jennings, M. Kent. *Community Influentials.* New York: Free Press of Glencoe, 1964.

Kaufman, Herbert. *The Forest Ranger: A Study in Administrative Behavior.* Baltimore: Johns Hopkins Press, 1960.

Mass, Arthur. *Muddy Waters.* Cambridge, Mass.: Harvard University Press, 1951.

Mosher, Frederick C. *Democracy and the Public Service.* New York: Oxford University Press, 1968.

Pfiffner, John M., and Presthus, Robert. *Public Administration.* 5th ed. New York: Ronald Press Co., 1967.

Raskin, A. H. "Politics Up-ends the Bargaining Table." In *Public Workers and Public Unions,* edited by Sam Zagoria, pp. 122–46. Englewood Cliffs, N.J.: Prentice-Hall, 1972.

Rourke, Francis E. *Bureaucracy, Politics, and Public Policy.* Boston: Little, Brown & Co., 1969.

Sayre, Wallace S., and Kaufman, Herbert. *Governing New York City: Politics in the Metropolis.* New York: Russell Sage Foundation, 1960.

Selznick, Philip. *TVA and the Grass Roots.* Berkeley and Los Angeles: University of California Press, 1949.

Truman, David B. *The Governmental Process.* New York: Alfred A. Knopf, 1951.

Turner, James S. *The Chemical Feast.* New York: Grossman Publishers, 1970.

Wildavsky, Aaron. *The Politics of the Budgetary Process.* Boston: Little, Brown & Co., 1964.

DILEMMAS OF
BUREAUCRATIC
RESPONSIBILITY

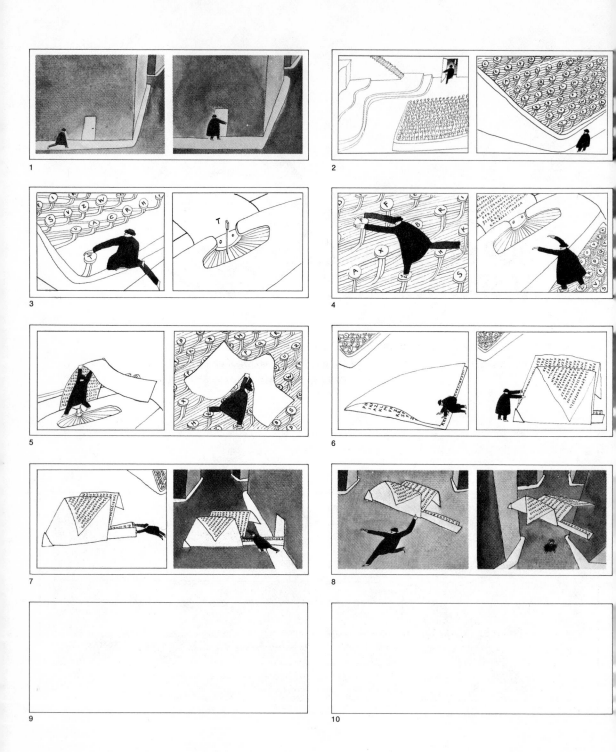

1

2

3

4

5

6

7

8

9

10

Why do so many bureaucrats, deans, preachers, college presidents, try to smile when the mau-mauing starts? It's fatal, this smiling.

Mau-Mauing the Flak Catchers
TOM WOLFE

8 One of the most serious questions facing American democracy today is whether the power that the bureaucracy has arrogated to itself can be restrained and held accountable to the American people and their representatives. This chapter will explore the responsiveness of our public bureaucracy, abuses of bureaucratic power, and the professional caliber of those who man the public service. The two case studies at the end of the chapter, concerning the War on Poverty in San Francisco and the issue of bureaucratic lies and leaks, illustrate some of these problems.

WHO OWNS AMERICA'S PUBLIC BUREAUCRACY?

In the words of William E. Connolly:

The Legacy of Pluralism

> Pluralism has long provided the dominant description and ideal of American politics. As description it portrays the system as a balance of power among overlapping economies, religions, ethnic, and geographic groups. Each "group" has some voice in shaping socially-binding decisions; each constrains and is constrained through processes of mutual group adjustments; and all major groups share a broad system of beliefs and values which encourage conflict to proceed within established channels and allows initial disagreements to dissolve into compromise solutions.

As an ideal, the system is celebrated not because it performs any single function perfectly, but because it is said to promote, more effectively than any known alternative, a plurality of laudable and public ends. Pluralistic politics claims the best features from the individualistic liberalism of John Locke, the social conservatism of an Edmund Burke, and the participatory democracy of a Jean-Jacques Rousseau.[1]

The pluralist system is believed to benefit the individual in a number of ways. By actively participating in group life, he develops skills and a sense of purpose that advance his personality development. Through his access to a multiplicity of groups, he broadens his personal experience. In addition, his affiliation with one group may counter the activities of another group that is attempting to constrain him.

Society is also believed to benefit from pluralism. Because of the multiplicity of groups in American society, it is assumed that all major issues will be channeled through government for consideration and redress and that governmental outcomes will reflect the balance of power of groups in society. Stability is also believed to be enhanced by citizen involvement in public affairs, which, by deepening the individual's stake in society, encourages a polity requiring little coercion. Because new groups reflecting new problems can readily be formed, change and innovation are encouraged. "Thus," Connolly continues, "pluralism reflects a society which permits individual self-actualization, civil rights, the identification of societal problems, encourages incremental change while maintaining a stable society based on mutual consent."[2] As Theodore Lowi points out, however, there has been a moratorium on the examination of pluralism and other accepted doctrines of political science for some thirty years.[3]

During the 1960s the ideal world of the pluralists seemed to fall apart at the seams. Poverty, urban blight, racial discrimination, environmental pollution, and an archaic educational system appeared all the more odious as the nation frittered away billions on such dubious projects and priorities as the moon race and "defending freedom" in South Vietnam. Many were outraged to learn that some people whose income exceeded hundreds of thousands of dollars annually paid little or no taxes. Some questioned whether America's pluralistic political system could respond to the legitimate needs of its citizens. In *The End of Liberalism,* Theodore Lowi extensively documents his thesis that big governments, big business, big labor, and other dominant groups in America have formed unresponsive, undemocratic oligarchies that disregard the needs of minorities, the poor, and the public in general.[4] American Agriculture provides a good example.

In 1963 President Lyndon Johnson asked the leaders of major agricultural interests and interest groups to formulate programs which they and their organizations could administer and benefit from as well. The result of this activity, Lowi suggests, was to surrender governmental sovereignty to private interests. In effect, the nation's largest, most prosperous farmers make and administer our agricultural policies. Agricultural Extension Service, for a classic example, is administered by the prosperous and privately run American Farm Bureau Federation but is supported by the Association of Land Grant Colleges and Universities and its tributary, the National Association of County Agricultural Agents. Agricultural self-government is also to be found in the Farm Home Administration, the Farm Credit Administration, and a host of other agencies dealing with forestry, conservation, and electrification.

In addition, agricultural interests dominate congressional and state legislative agricultural committees. In the post–World War II period studied by Lowi, for example, only one member of the House Agriculture Committee, Victor Anfuso of Brooklyn, was from a nonfarm state.[5] The effect of agricultural policy was to exclude the consumer from this nexus. In July 1973 the General Accounting Office criticized the Department of Agriculture for acquiescing to the 1972 Soviet grain deal, in which one-quarter of our crop was sold to the Soviet Union at a considerable profit to U.S. wheat dealers, mostly large corporate interests, but at considerable expense to the average consumer in the increased cost of bread and meat.

Lowi asserts that labor, business, and industry enjoy similar agreements. In August 1971 consumer advocate Ralph Nader criticized Secretary of Commerce Maurice Stans (1968–72) for representing a narrow business point of view and for opposing the Clean Air Act of 1970, the relaxation of oil import controls, the regulation of phosphates and detergents, the regulation of auto mechanics, no-fault insurance, FTC-stiffened regulation of false advertising, class action suits, the banning of federal contracts to firms that pollute the environment, and mandatory state inspection of cars for pollution. On the other hand, Stans had favored the Supersonic Transport, the environmentally questionable Alaska pipeline, relief programs for corporations, and dismantling of the Flammable Fabrics Act. Nader argued that Stans was better qualified to be a Washington lobbyist for business than a public official.[6] Clearly, many major governmental agencies serve dominant interest groups better than they serve the public interest, especially those agencies and departments that are supposed to regulate segments of the American economy.

"I'm not being disloyal," said Secor Browne with a smile. Pictured on the side of his morning coffee mug was not the jumbo jet one might expect from the Chairman of the Civil Aeronautics Board (CAB), but an old fashioned railroad caboose: "A gift from my wife. . . ."[7]

The Regulatory Agencies Revisited

Disloyalty to government-regulated industries has not always been a sin. The independent regulatory commissions were intended to be nonpartisan expert organizations designed to protect the public. There is much to indicate that they are partisan, however; not expert, and more interested in protecting the industries they are supposed to regulate than in pursuing the interests of the consumer public.

Secrecy. The regulatory process has been greatly criticized for its secrecy. The major regulatory agencies make some 100,000 decisions annually, of which 90 percent are informal—that is, without formal public hearings, sworn testimony, or other usual judicial procedures. The FCC renews thousands of licenses annually; the CAB permits airlines at the Chatanooga airport to pool their baggage facilities; the FTC allows hundreds of garment makers to "promise" that they will not discriminate against customers.[8] Such activities permit the regulatory agencies to avoid bureaucratic red tape while omitting the public from the process and making a mockery of the concept of checks and balances.

Nor, as the Nader reports complain, have the regulatory agencies been cooperative in granting access to interested citizens and scholars. Their 1969 study of the Interstate Commerce Commission was hampered by the commission's refusal to provide legitimate information, citing clauses of the Freedom of Information Act for the exclusion of investigatory files, internal rule and procedure, and interoffice memoranda. Four commissioners sought support from Senator Warren Magnuson of Washington, chairman of the Senate Commerce Committee, and his staff in their decision to deny the Nader study group's request for documents as required by the Freedom of Information Act. Interviewees required the presence of stenographers to make memos of the interviews for agency files. That such procedures accompany visits from industry representatives is doubtful. Some employees believed that their cooperation would mean denied promotions, unpleasant work assignments, harrassment, and possible dismissal. It took twenty-nine hours and a full commission vote for the Nader Group to gain permission to photograph a routine ICC travel voucher.[9]

The Nader study of the Federal Trade Commission expressed similar complaints. Transcripts of public hearings were made available in one copy at a Washington, D. C., office. An interested, affluent citizen could purchase a copy, numbering hundreds of pages at fifty cents a page.[10] Under the pressure of intense public interest in the tire safety issue, the commission made available one additional copy of the hearing that had been held in its Chicago offices, but it refused to print the hearing records, citing an FTC contract with Warde Paul, Stenographers,[11] to the effect that advisory opinions are never printed in full; only digests, without identifying details or background, are made public—a practice that precludes effective public criticism of commission decisions. Requests for advisory opinions, freely given to trade associations, were also denied the study group. Communications involving voluntary business compliance with FTC rules are not made public, and citizens are denied knowledge of thousands of business transgressions.[12]

Kenneth C. Davis, a professor at the University of Chicago and author of a four-volume treatise on administrative law, was interested in studying premerger clearances issued by the FTC. In August 1966 he visited Chairman Paul Rand Dixon to request to see commission files on merger clearances, but Dixon refused on the grounds that the request must be made in writing. Davis wrote out his request in November. In December he revised it, stating that he wished to see only the three latest cases in which approval for merger had been granted. On 13 January 1967 Dixon agreed to make available the digests of the cases. Davis protested that digests were inadequate for his purposes, which were purely scholarly in intent. When this letter was ignored, Davis sent follow-up letters in October and November 1967. On 27 November the commissioner again refused. On 29 November Davis cited the relevant provisions of the Freedom of Information Act, but the commission refused to be threatened.

In January 1968 Davis further narrowed his request, emphasizing that he desired only nonconfidential information. On 18 January 1968 the commissioner again refused. Davis wrote his seventh letter of the seventeen-month period, again citing the Freedom of Information Act, and the commission, on 30 April 1968, again denied his request. At this point Professor Davis abandoned his efforts, but he had by then learned a good deal about the administrative process.[13]

Presidential and congressional influence. Despite the legal mandate that the agencies should be independent, presidential and congressional influence on them has been profound. The extent of this influence is illustrated by the cases of Miami's Channel 10 and the Texas Broadcasting Corporation.

The FCC was established in 1934 to regulate communications in the radio and wireless industries and to encourage competition and diversity of ownership. In 1955 President Dwight Eisenhower appointed Richard A. Mack commissioner of the FCC. A Floridian who had been recommended by that state's senators George Smathers and Spessard Holland, Mack was sworn in on 7 July 1955, just as the commission was considering awarding the franchise for Miami's Channel 10, a plum estimated to be worth some $10 million.

There were four applications for the new station: (1) WKAK, owned by Frank Katzentine (who had helped Mack get into a fraternity when they had been students at the University of Florida); (2) L. B. Wilson, Inc.; (3) North Dade Video, Inc.; and (4) Public Service Television, Inc., owned by National Airlines. The first commission vote was inconclusive, and in the ensuing year Katzentine asked senators Smathers, Holland, and Estes

Kefauver of Tennessee to urge Mack to vote for him. National Airlines, aware of the outside pressure on the commissioner, sought the aid of Thurman Whiteside, a long-time friend of Mack. Not to be outdone, North Dade Video hired a Washington, D. C., lawyer, Robert F. Jones, a former congressman and one-time FCC commissioner, to help them.

On the final vote, National Airlines won. Learning that Mack had sold his vote to Whiteside for $2,600, Katzentine brought the case before Senator Kefauver's standing committee for the investigation of this type of matter. Although Whiteside was acquitted and Mack's trial resulted in a hung jury, both men committed suicide. L. B. Wilson, Inc. was awarded Channel 10 because its hands were the cleanest.[14]

The Texas Broadcasting Corporation case also demonstrated the weight of congressional and presidential influence on a regulatory agency. Lyndon B. Johnson's career in broadcasting began when he returned from a brief tour in the navy in 1942. Johnson had already spent five years in the House of Representatives when he heard that radio station KTBC, serving his Austin constituency, was for sale. At the same time, another group, including E. G. Kingsberry, a wealthy businessman, was interested in purchasing the station. Reminding Kingsberry that he, Johnson, had secured his son's appointment to the Naval Academy, Kingsberry stepped aside.

Mrs. Johnson then bought the station for $17,500. KTBC soon won FCC permission for unlimited broadcast time and the right to quadruple its power. In 1952 Austin was one of the largest cities to be authorized only a single VHF station. There were 716 applications, but the one bearing the name of Claudia T. Johnson was hurried through "in deference," as one FCC staffer put it, "to the Senator from Texas and the number two Democrat in the Senate." Although KTBC was placed in trust during Johnson's presidency, it continued to prosper, obtaining license renewals and cable television franchises. As one Democratic member of the commission said, "the Commission was aware of the family's interests."[15]

Newton Minow, FCC chairman under President Kennedy, eluded an attempt by the Kennedy administration to influence the news media through the FCC. After watching a certain Huntley-Brinkly news broadcast, the president telephoned Minow to ask whether he had seen the "damn program" and to demand that Minow do something about it. Some FCC chairmen would have phoned NBC; instead, Minow phoned a Kennedy aide and told him to inform the president that he was fortunate to have as FCC chairman a man who did not do everything he was told to do. Minow said that this was his only such episode with the president but that he received similar calls from members of Congress all the time.[16]

The Nixon administration's influence on the regulatory process was profound. A *New York Times* study released shortly after Nixon's first term claimed that the independent regulatory agencies had been turned into bastions of Nixonian Republicanism.[17] The study argued that the commissions had fewer liberals, academics, and consumer-oriented people than they had had formerly and that they now reflected Nixon's philosophy of less interference by government in business and industry.

Nixon's nomination of Lee R. West to the Civil Aeronautics Board provides a typical reflection of his attitude. West's name was submitted by Republican Senator Henry R. Bellmon of Oklahoma and had the support of fellow Oklahoman, Speaker of the House Carl Albert. West was to replace the consumer-oriented, antimerger, pro-competition-minded Robert T. Murphy. The Oklahoma representatives were supportive of their constituent, American Airlines, which had been disappointed by a CAB refusal to permit a merger with Western Airlines.

Professor Kenneth C. Davis maintains that the difference between the independent agencies and the departments that are directly administered by the president is much smaller than most people suspect.[18] Moreover, there is a very strong tradition of Senate accession to presidential nominations. By May 1973 Nixon had named chairmen to twenty-eight of thirty-eight commissions in the major regulatory agencies, and by the end of his second term there were no individuals remaining from previous administrations.

The president can exercise a considerable influence over the regulatory agencies because he recommends the budget. Thus, under President Nixon, a relatively vigorous and consumer-oriented FTC found its budget reduced by $620,000 and its staff trimmed of seventy-two employees. Ultimately the budget reduction resulted in the loss of 208 positions.[19]

The personnel problem. Ideally, those who manage the regulatory agencies are nonpartisan, consumer-oriented experts supported by able staffs. In actuality, however, this ideal is more farce than fact. In 1973, for example, the Federal Power Commission reflected the influence of both partisan politics and the power industry. Chairman John N. Nassikas had been general counsel for the Manchester (New Hampshire) Gas Company. Other members included Albert D. Brook, a former newspaperman and friend of former Senator Thurston Morton of Kentucky; Pinckney Walker, former consultant to Missouri River Transmission and Missouri Power and Light; and Rush Moody, Jr., a lawyer whose former clients included representatives of the oil and gas industry.[20]

The Nader study of the Interstate Commerce Commission was especially critical of its lack of experts in transportation. In examining the backgrounds of the last eleven ICC commissioners as of 1972, the study found that only three had backgrounds in transportation, that all had major political supporters in Congress, and that their appointments had the consent of major industrial groups, such as the American Transportation Association. The study concluded that political connections and industrial acceptability were the dominant factors in determining ICC appointments.[21]

Even more disappointing was the personnel of the Federal Trade Commission. The Nader study emphasized that the FTC was hampered by congressional influence, laziness, and a staff chosen for reasons other than merit alone. Chairman Paul Rand Dixon had been appointed under strong pressure from Senator Estes Kefauver. The next-ranking official, A. Everett MacIntyre, had been sponsored by Representative Wright Patman of Texas. A lawyer in the Bureau of Deceptive Practices confessed that everyone in the FTC who intended to be successful could name his political benefactor. Not surprisingly, the Nadar study expressed the view that party politics and congressional ties had the effect of defusing the FTC's work.

Even more harmful to the FTC's effectiveness was the "small southern town" syndrome, which, according to the Nader study, was so pervasive as to render the FTC incapable of understanding the complex problems confronting urban society. The commission's five bureau chiefs had all come from towns in Arkansas, Tennessee, Texas, and South Carolina with populations numbering fewer than ten-thousand people. Of the fifteen assistant bureau chiefs whose records were available, nine had small-town southern backgrounds. Bright young lawyers, especially graduates of northern schools, encountered regional discrimination.

Young southern lawyers were frequently recruited by interviewers because of old school ties, or regional and local backgrounds, or through political endorsement. The FTC accepted only three of eleven Harvard Law School graduates, three of nine from the University of Pennsylvania, and three of thirty-four applicants from New York University; but it accepted nine of eleven applicants from the University of Kentucky and six of sixteen from the University of Tennessee.

Given the ascriptive orientation of FTC hiring practices, it is not surprising that its employees were unfamiliar with modern corporation record-keeping procedures or that they did not appreciate the value of computers, a point on which Chairman Dixon was criticized by the Civil Service Commission.[22] Nor did those hired by the FTC work overly hard. "Leisurely morning and afternoon coffee breaks, long lunches to permit shopping, extended reading in the afternoons and early departure . . . were routine."[23]

A high rate of turnover was another serious personnel problem in the regulatory agencies. Chairman Dixon hired 750 lawyers over a five-year period to maintain a staff of 400. The Securities and Exchange Commission annually lost 75 of 390 people to private practice; the Federal Power Commission lost 10 of 70; the Federal Communications Commission lost 35 out of 200; and the Civil Aeronautics Board lost 20 of 80.[24] Partisan politics helps to account for some of this. When Dixon took over the FTC in 1951, he assumed that the best men were Democrats. Republicans in high positions were therefore confronted with the choice of becoming trial lawyers, a position low in the organizational hierarchy, or of resigning. So many resigned in the late 1960s that only 40 of 500 Republican attorneys remained with the FTC.[25] As Engler and others have noted, many of those who left joined firms or industries prosecuted by the regulatory agencies.[26]

Clearly, then, the regulatory agencies are not manned by people who are nonpartisan consumer-oriented experts. Instead, partisan politics and congressional ties are the chief factors determining appointments, practices that severely inhibit the regulatory agencies' effectiveness.

Industrial influence. Joseph Goulden has termed the regulatory agencies of the federal government "one of the most miserable failures of American government."[27] The picture at the state level is not bright either. In a masterful study, Robert Engler documents how the oil industry was able to dominate all segments of government, national and state alike, that presumed to regulate it.[28] In the postwar years, Lyndon Johnson of Texas, Robert Kerr of Oklahoma, Carl Albert of Oklahoma, and Wilbur Mills of Arkansas helped to remake the Federal Power Commission and other agencies exercising power over the oil industry. Kerr, himself a millionaire oil man, partner in Kerr-McKee (a giant oil corporation), and close associate of Phillips Petroleum, was especially important. Kerr got his campaign manager, Herrington Wimberly, appointed to the FPC in 1945, and Wimberly declared that he was Kerr's friend above all else. To remake the commission, the industry replaced certain consumer-oriented men such as Leland Olds, William R. Connole, and Thomas C. Buchanan.[29]

The case involving Olds was especially grievous. Olds had spent a lifetime developing knowledge about natural resources and utility rate regulation, had gained a reputation as an honest and able advocate of consumer interests, and was regarded as one of the few public servants whose technical expertise equaled that found in the private sector. The effect of these assets was to make him a hated man by the oil and gas industry. A liberal, he was denounced by Representative John E. Lyle, who implied that Olds was a Communist (Lyle represented an oil- and gas-producing region of Texas). His renomination was defeated in the Senate.[30]

Other FPC members who favored the consumer were systematically ignored for reappointment. Buchanan, who dissented when the FPC chose to move away from its regulatory responsibilities, was replaced in 1953 by Jerome K. Kuykendall, a lawyer who had represented utility companies. Also named to the commission in 1953 was Seaborn Digby, a lawyer for oil interests who had been hailed by the *Oil and Gas Journal* as "one of the foremost advocates of nonregulation."[31] Under Kuykendall's chairmanship, four of the five commissioners actively pushed the industry's position even though the Supreme Court ruled that the FPC should regulate it. The commission's majority echoed the industry's view in asserting, "We have heard no demand that the oil industry should be regulated as a public utility and do not understand why natural gas production should be so regulated, and oil production should remain unregulated."[32]

The pipelines that transport much of the nation's oil and gas are regulated by the ICC. Yet a 1959 investigation by the House of Representatives concluded that ". . . in practice the industry decides what the ICC will do,"[33] that the public interest was subordinated to private interests, and that the ICC served as an instrument to protect the industry.[34]

The relationship between the regulators and the regulated is too cozy to ensure that the public interest is served. Regulators regularly attend the national and regional conventions of the industries they are supposed to regulate. The chairman of the Securities and Exchange Commission traditionally attends the annual convention of the Investment Banker's Association; the FCC chairman speaks to the annual National Association of Broadcasters, and it is not unusual for several commissioners to attend this event. The regulator's door is normally open to industrial representatives for private chats. The Nader study of the ICC observed: "Industry regularly pays for luncheons, hotel rooms, even a hairdresser for Madame Chairman. Commissioners and upper staff are commonly transported around at their convenience by corporate jets, private rail cars and pleasure yachts."[35] On one occasion FTC Chairman Paul Rand Dixon told a business audience: "I've come here with the high hope that I can persuade you that the Federal Trade Commission is not the socialistic, bureaucratic, dam-yankee tool of the devil that may have been pictured to you. I'd like to convince you that you've got a real friend in the FTC—a real friend. . . ."[36]

Industry spends considerable money lobbying and attempting to influence regulators and key legislators. In 1963 former FPC Commissioner Howard Morgan wrote President Kennedy that he did not wish to be reappointed to the commission, adding:

> Ordinary men cannot administer [the regulatory] laws today in the face of pressures generated by huge, huge industries. . . . The big problem in the regulatory field is not influence peddling and corruption as that word is commonly understood. . . . But abandonment of the public interest can be caused by many things, of which timidity and a desire for personal security are the most insidious. This Commission, for example, must make hundreds and even thousands of decisions each year, and many of which award scores and hundreds of millions of dollars in a single case. A Commissioner can find it very easy to consider whether his vote might arouse an industry campaign against his reconfirmation by the Senate.[37]

Not surprisingly, the regulatory agencies often lack resources and frequently do not press for more or effectively utilize those at their disposal. So poorly funded are the inspection programs authorized by the Walsh-Healy Act that inspectors cannot hope to examine more than 2 to 3 percent of the workers covered. The U.S. Geological Survey, which is supposed to police the oil-drilling industry, has seventeen inspectors to watch over 4,500 oil wells. The Federal Renegotiation Board (FRB), which is responsible for some $60 billion in government contracts, has a staff of 200 people. Admiral Hyman Rickover, after documenting the FRB's failures, termed it about as effective as putting a Band-Aid on cancer.[38]

The Federal Power Commission has a staff of 1,000 and a budget of $20 million to supervise corporations whose assets run into the billions and who employ tens of thousands of people. CAB has a staff of 665 and a budget of $13 million to police thirty-seven scheduled airlines doing an annual business exceeding $10 billion. The FCC has a budget of $32 million and a staff of 1,662 to police the $4 billion telecommunications industry, including the giant AT&T. And Chairman Paul Rand Dixon, a self-confessed "friend" of business, made a habit of returning funds to Congress, although, with a budget of $17 million and a staff of 1,300, the FTC lacked the resources to police hundreds of thousands of businesses on behalf of consumers. The Nader report charged that during the last decade the FTC did little to give its enforcement functions the necessary muscle but made only a minimal effort to press for adequate funds or statutory authority.[39]

In view of the strength and resources available to industry and the lack of talent and resources available to the regulatory agencies, it is not surprising that government has not been remarkably successful in protecting the public welfare. One important reason for this failure is the influence of able and expensive law firms retained by the private entrepreneur. **The Regulatory Agencies as Failures**

In 1964, while researching *Unsafe at Any Speed*, Ralph Nader learned of a 1955 agreement among automobile manufacturers that restrained the development and installation of antipollution devices. Nader's complaint to the antitrust division of the Justice Department resulted in the convening of a grand jury, at which Nader corroborated his charges in minute detail. Justice Department attorneys concluded that the agreement accomplished noncompetitive and delaying activities; the signatories agreed that they would not competitively publicize solutions to the pollution problem, that they would adopt a uniform date for the discovery and announcement of antipollution devices, and that they would install devices only on a mutually agreeable date.

The big four auto manufacturers engaged Lloyd and Pickering to fight the charges of collusion and conspiracy. The auto manufacturers arranged a series of meetings with Donald Turner of the Justice Department's anti-trust division at which they convinced Turner that the auto industry did not wish to violate the law. Turner decided not to press charges and wrote Nader:

> . . . The joint research venture among the auto companies, though in my opinion is unlawful . . . was not in the category of "per se" offenses and . . . most of the alleged restrictions were agreeably ancillary to the joint undertaking. I will not pretend that a reasonable man, particularly if he had a more evangelical approach to anti-trust than I have, could not have decided differently. . . .[40]

The Department did not ask the grand jury for an indictment, and the jury did not hand one down.

In 1968 the Justice Department drafted a complaint charging auto manufacturers with restraint of trade in the years 1961, 1962, and 1964. The industry urged that it be let off with a consent decree and pressed negotiations with the Justice Department. Nader complained that such negotiations undermined public confidence in antitrust enforcement because they are made without citizen access or publicity on which to base an informed opinion.

The manufacturers were again successful. The department ruling required, among other things, that they withdraw from the 1955 agreement and that a joint statement be submitted by the industry to government agencies concerned with pollution control. The effect of this action was to tell the auto companies that they had not done a nice thing and not to do it again. One government study estimates that pollution costs $13 billion annually, half that expense traceable to automobiles. An incensed Nader wondered after five years of litigation whether it would not have been better to hold a public trial exploring the nature and depth of the corporate crime.[41]

Another interesting case involved the giant Upjohn Company and its product Panalba, its legal defenders Covington and Burling, and the Federal Drug Administration. Under 1962 legislation, the FDA was authorized to use the National Academy of Science to test and pass on the safety of drugs. The academy recommended that production of Panalba be discontinued because of adverse reactions attributed to some of the drug's ingredients. Accordingly, the FDA ordered its production to cease as of 31 May 1968.

Covington and Burling appealed the decision and enlisted the aid of Michigan Representative Gerry Brown, whose constituency included Upjohn. Brown obtained a congressional hearing, and succeeded in getting a resolution passed to withhold publicity warning doctors of possible hazards, and urged resumed certification. Despite FDA protests, the Department of Health, Education and Welfare ordered that Panalba remain on the market. Covington and Burling obtained an injunction from federal court barring further FDA action against Panalba. Finally, in March 1970, the FDA won its case against Upjohn in the Supreme Court.

During the seventeen months that Upjohn had been contesting the case, it reaped $2.5 million, 12 percent of its domestic sales, while fighting a losing battle. Dr. Lester Breslow, president of the American Public Health Association, said of the Panalba case in November 1969: "The administrative and judicial action to assure continuing sales was clearly designed to protect the interests of the drug manufacturers, not to avoid hazards to patients taking the drug."[42]

In 1972 Ralph Nader charged that the Civil Aeronautics Board approved anticompetitive practices, permitted discriminatory personnel practices and overpriced tickets, and tended to overestimate airline financial difficulties. Nader charged that under Secor Browne the CAB had become the "most valuable minion" of the airline industries rather than a protector of the public interest and that Browne should resign.[43] The CAB's discouragement of competition has stifled aviation innovation. The nonscheduled airlines, which offer great savings to the American public, were suppressed and ultimately forced out of business by CAB actions.[44]

America's airlines have been the beneficiaries of more than $4 billion for improving safety, $1 billion in subsidies, and billions more in military research and development programs with consequential benefits to civilian aircraft. The Federal Aviation Administration and the CAB regulate the most favored industry. In one case, however, the CAB planned badly in granting a license to Northeast Airlines to fly from New York to Florida. The company went from a surplus of $831,000 in 1956 to a deficit of $44 million in 1962, and the CAB had to ask for additional subsidies. In the early 1960s, James M. Landis criticized the "hodgepodge of routes," and President Kennedy criticized the CAB for a lack of thoughtful planning.[45]

Citing failures to prosecute Firestone zealously for exaggerated claims of tire safety and Geritol for its promises of rejuvenation, Nader's report chided the FTC:

> Rather than vigorously using its enforcement tools, the agency has declined to act with energy and speed. It has refused to recommend criminal action and sought to give the violators of the law not just one free bite, provided by the cease and desist order procedure, but many more. The additional bites are provided by the FTC's refusal to bring action against those violators who ignore and even flout established cease and desist orders and by the invention of the complex system of "voluntary" enforcement procedures. Rather than bite down hard on the volunteers, the agency prefers a toothless attempt to gum to death.[46]

The idea that America can avoid both the excesses of capitalism and the nationalization of industry by government regulation has been with us since 1887. But critics such as Theodore Lowi and Ralph Nader have cast much doubt on this view. Frequently shrouded in secrecy, the regulatory process is hampered by partisan politics. Agencies are too often captured by the industries they are supposed to regulate. Corporate influence in the legislatures, courts, and the regulatory agencies themselves often neutralizes the few good works that they attempt. These failures have not gone unnoticed, and a number of individuals and groups have addressed themselves to attempts to salvage the regulatory process.

In 1971 the Advisory Council on Executive Organization (Ash Committee) recommended that the regulatory agencies be administered by a single administration and that key agency decisions be reviewed by a special court. John Moore, a student of the regulatory process, has recommended the following reforms: decentralized offices to provide greater access by the public; independent advisory boards to help offset the problem of cooptation; and a public council to provide competent representation for noncorporate elements of our society. Moore feels that the president should have a greater stake in the agencies carrying out basic objectives and that deregulation should be considered in certain areas of the economy.[47]

The revitalization of the FTC under Caspar Weinberger and his successors has demonstrated that the regulatory agencies can be made to work. In 1973, heightened consumer interest resulted in the creation of a new regulatory agency, the Consumer Product Safety Agency. Pondering the future of this as well as of older agencies, one cannot help but reflect on what an ICC staff member told a *Time* reporter on publication of the Nader study of that organization: "Don't panic. It just dies down. . . . Forget it."[48] Too often the American public does allow it to die down and pays accordingly.

ABUSES OF BUREAUCRATIC POWER

Above the entrance to Los Angeles City Hall is a quotation from Cicero: "He who violates his oath profanes the divinity of faith itself." The most cursory examination of American history reveals that the public bureaucracy has frequently been guilty of great abuses of power—the treatment of American Indians by the Bureau of Indian Affairs and the War Department during the nineteenth and twentieth centuries is an outstanding example.[49] But bureaucratic power has increased alarmingly during the past twenty years, and the abuse of power unearthed in recent decades is shocking to those who had believed in the essential integrity of America's public service. Abuses of power have been documented at every level of government, from local police to the White House. The following section will examine some of these abuses as well as the character of those who commit them.

The police. Street crime and violence, the need for adequate police protection, the attitude of courts toward criminals, and the need to protect our civil rights were among the campaign issues that were dramatically juxtaposed when the Democratic party, the world's oldest major political party, met in Chicago in August 1968 to nominate a candidate for the presidency. The party was riven by the Vietnam War issue and by loyalty to different candidates, including Vice President Hubert Humphrey, Minnesota Senator Eugene McCarthy, and the tragically slain Senator Robert F. Kennedy.

From the Station House to the White House

Chicago was expecting thousands of demonstrators, from peaceful supporters of the major candidates to Yippies and the militant wing of the Students for a Democratic Society (SDS), the Weathermen. To meet them, the city's 11,900-man police force was placed on twelve-hour shifts and supported by 5,000 Illinois National Guardsmen and 6,500 U.S. Army troops. The city resembled an armed camp; one protestor held up a sign reading "Welcome to Prague"—an ironic reference to the recent Soviet invasion of that martyred Czech city. Ignoring the lessons of the peaceful 1963 March on Washington, Chicago's Mayor Richard Daley refused to permit demonstrators the use of Lincoln Park, which would have made the task of police control much easier.

During the course of the convention, law enforcement officers were the targets of provocation ranging from obscenities to thrown rocks. Some provocations were planned; others were reactions to police brutality. For example, as one young man and his girlfriend were leaving Lincoln Park on orders of the police, the police threw him down and dragged his companion along the ground, beating her on the legs, arms, and back with their batons. The young man attempted to help her but was thrown back several times by the police and clubbed on the hands five or six times before he succeeded in pulling her away. Near Old Town, according to an eyewitness report, police were indiscriminately beating anyone who was not a law enforcement officer.

On Tuesday, a federal legal official was permitted to accompany a group of approximately fifteen police who cursed young people, daring them to come near and be beaten. A protestor walking in the opposite direction was kneed in the groin. An incoherent drunk was sprayed with mace in the eyes. On Wednesday a high-ranking Chicago police official admitted that police had gained control of the area near the Conrad Hilton Hotel. On the same day, a federal official observed that the police were striking people with evident malice.

In addition to physical brutality and deprivation of civil rights, police abuse at the Chicago convention also took the form of an assault on the mass media. Some 60 of the 300 newsmen present suffered injuries to themselves or to their equipment or were arrested. Many were physically attacked by police, and in thirteen instances photo or recording equipment was deliberately damaged.[50] Police were also excoriated for their antiriot activities in Newark, Washington, D.C., Los Angeles (Watts), and Detroit as well as for police action against the Black Panthers in the late 1960s.

An equally grave problem has been presented by police infiltration of civilian gangs. In order to combat lawlessness in society, police have recently resorted to the infiltration of suspect groups. In a famous example, a young man known as "Tommy the Traveler," claiming to be an SDS organizer but in reality an undercover agent for the government, sojourned the campuses of upstate New York, furthering his credibility by punching a dean of students and teaching students how to prepare Molotov cocktails. Tommy left a trail of violence behind him, causing many to wonder whether it was the proper task of government to preach violence to students, to infiltrate their classes, or to spy on their conduct.

In May 1970 police infiltrated the home of Professor David Lykken of the University of Minnesota who had merely convened a meeting of citizens opposed to the deployment of missile bases in North Dakota. The Minnesota Supreme Court dismissed the case; but the question remains: what will happen if fear of the police outweighs the right of dissent?[51]

The mails. Laws protecting the privacy of first-class mail have been on American statute books since 1789. The U.S. Supreme Court has ruled that this right is as inviolate as the right to privacy in one's own home. First-class mail can be opened only if it is undeliverable and if there is no return address; to seize and search it requires the authorization of a court and a warrant. As the following examples show, however, there has been widespread evasion of these laws by the government.

The U.S. Postal Service admits that since 1942 post offices throughout the country have been turning over to the IRS first-class mail addressed to businesses that have been seized for tax arrears by the Internal Revenue Service. In 1962 this practice was extended to private business mail. In one instance, officials from the IRS opened, read, and even answered a letter. Controversial senators have also had their mail intercepted and examined by the Post Office. A Senate investigating committee revealed that from 28 October to 16 November 1952 the Washington, D.C. Post Office had been asked to furnish the names, addresses, and postmarks of mail going to the home of Wisconsin Senator Joseph R. McCarthy. Although this was done at the request of a Senate investigating committee, the Post Office neverthe-less violated the law by cooperating.

In 1964 a Senate subcommittee investigating invasion of privacy asked Postmaster General John A. Gronouski for a list estimated to contain the names of 24,000 persons whose mail had been opened illegally. Gronouski refused, saying that to do so would violate the civil liberties of innocent people, jeopardize national security, and cripple criminal investigations. The subcommittee observed in its reply that Gronouski seemed unaware that the civil liberties of those 24,000 persons might already have been violated by the placing of a mail watch without permission or statutory authority.[52]

The Post Office is not the only agency guilty of violating the privacy of the mails.[53] In 1973 the chairman of the Federal Power Commission ad-mitted that his office routinely intercepted and opened mail addressed to members of the FPC staff from representatives in Congress. Chairman John N. Nassikas feebly justified this practice by stating that, in the past, congres-sional mail to his agency had been lost or delayed in processing.[54]

The credibility gap. The phrase "credibility gap" originated in the 1960s and still retains considerable political currency. Only in the last two decades have Americans come to believe that their government routinely lies to them. Much bureaucratic deception has been related to national defense. Although the burdens of defense make certain claims to secrecy legitimate, the government has also lied and withheld information from the public, not because the nation's defensive posture so dictated but to make an ad-ministration look good or to protect the image of certain incumbents.

The *Pentagon Papers* revealed how the government withholds and covers up information, as well as the capricious way in which government can and does classify, declassify, and leak information. On 30 August 1963, for ex-ample, Roger Hilsman, undersecretary of state for the Far East during the Kennedy administration, wrote a memo urging that the U.S. encourage a coup against South Vietnamese President Diem and suggesting that Diem be treated in any manner suggested by his generals. At that time the docu-ment was classified as top secret, but it was later declassified by President Johnson, presumably to tarnish the Kennedy-Camelot image and to injure the presidential aspirations of Robert Kennedy. Although reporters refused to print the story, it was finally revealed in a paper presented to the Ameri-can Historical Society in 1971. In short, what is secret and what is not is often a matter of capricious personal interpretation.[55]

In addition, the government has used information leaks for its own advantage and sought to suppress information that might injure it. An in-teresting example from the Nixon administration illustrates this. In August 1970 a story appeared in *Life* charging that Senator Joseph D. Tydings of Maryland, a leading Democratic foe of Nixon's policies, had used his influence to promote a Florida-based company of which he was a major stockholder. Specifically, it charged that Tydings was trying to obtain an Agency for International Development loan guarantee for a $7 million housing project in Nicaragua. The story was written by William Lambert, a Pulitzer Prize winner who had obtained his information from Charles W. Colson, special counsel to President Nixon (and later imprisoned for his role in the Watergate scandals). The story was a major blow to Tydings's reelection bid and undoubtedly contributed to his defeat by his Republican challenger, Glenn Beall, Jr. Thus, through a carefully calculated information leak, the Nixon administration was able to further its own ends.

One of the first major cases of governmental deception occurred during the administration of President Eisenhower. This was the U-2 incident involving a spy plane piloted by Francis Gary Powers who was paid by the CIA to spy on the Soviet Union. Aware of the flights, Eisenhower allowed them to continue despite his pending summit conference with Soviet Premier Nikita Khrushchev, assured that the plane contained adequate detonation devices to self-destruct in the event of capture.

On 5 May 1960 Khrushchev announced that an American plane had been shot down while violating Soviet air space. The first American reaction was a NASA announcement that a weather plane had been missing on a flight from Turkey since 1 May; on 6 May a State Department spokesman expressed certainty that there had been no deliberate attempt to violate Soviet air space. But the Soviets had captured the plane and its pilot. The State Department then admitted the nature of the flight but stated that it had not been authorized in Washington—a lie, as Eisenhower had approved it. In this tragic way the American public learned of a clandestine operation that had been going on for years.[56]

The case of Tibetan guerrillas being militarily trained in Colorado by the CIA provides still another example of governmental deception.[57] In 1951, troops of the Peoples' Republic of China occupied Tibet, though allowing the country's spiritual leader, the Dalai Lama, to remain enthroned. By mid-1950 Tibetan guerrillas had initiated military operations against the Chinese. The U.S. government, although in sympathy with the Tibetans, remained officially helpless to interfere until Allen Dulles, then director of the CIA, conceived a plan to screen Tibetan refugees coming through the Himalaya Mountains, offering the most promising candidates military training in the United States. The American-trained Tibetan would then be returned to his country to continue his fight against the Chinese.

Camp Hale, Colorado, offered an isolated setting similar to the terrain of Tibet, and by 1958 Tibetans were receiving CIA training there. But in July 1959 the CIA became concerned about the adequacy of its measures to hide the Camp Hale operation because the *Denver Post* had reported that the

Defense Atomic Support Agency was carrying out top-secret testing there. Although Camp Hale was administratively attached to nearby Fort Carson, top officials at the fort were not informed about its activities. On 7 December 1961 an Air Force C-124 aircraft loaded with Tibetans made an unexpected stop at Petersen Field, Colorado, near Kersaid, a private air school. The event attracted attention but reports were silenced by the army, and the *New York Times* honored the government's request not to pursue the events at Petersen Field.

The Tibetan training operation was abandoned in April 1962. But because the American public did not learn about it until 1973, such issues as the use of the monies to support clandestine operations, the CIA's violation of its own 1947 mandate by engaging in domestic operations, and the failure of Congress to supervise the CIA were not debated.[58]

It cannot be denied that some aspects of military operations require secrecy, but democracy demands that such events as foreign intervention and bombing should require the consent of the governed. Over a period of fourteen months in 1969–70, the United States secretly dropped 104,000 tons of bombs in 3,630 sorties over Cambodia, during the course of which the military falsified records and the Nixon administration consistently lied to Congress and the people, saying that Cambodian neutrality was being respected. On 3 March 1970 President Nixon told the American people: ". . . North Viet Nam has occupied sanctuaries all along the Cambodian frontier with South Viet Nam. For five years neither the U.S. nor South Viet Nam has moved against those enemy sanctuaries because we did not wish to violate the territory of a neutral nation."[59] The Cambodian cover-up may well have been the greatest systematic deception in American history.

The White House. Among the most shocking revelations of the Watergate hearings in the summer of 1973 were those involving the use of a new intelligence agency to curb dissent and the establishment of a White House "enemies list." Presidential counsellor John W. Dean, III, revealed that in July 1970 President Nixon had approved a domestic intelligence plan that included burglary, blackmail, the opening of mail, using foreign embassies for illicit purposes, and monitoring the telephone and telegraph communications of dissident domestic groups.

The plan required an unprecedented cooperative effort by the CIA, FBI, NSA, and Defense Intelligence Agency. One approach for domestic operations called for a new cadre of CIA superagents whose identity could not be traced and who could be concealed from all but a few high-ranking authorities.[60] This was supposed to be done for national security reasons, although one official admitted that "in many ways it seemed like just an excuse for domestic spying."[61]

Although such activities had been in use from 1941 to 1965, many Americans found it difficult to equate protesting college youth and antiwar matrons with Nazis and Communists. Much of the dissent arose from the poor, from minorities, students, and opponents of the war whose protests were grounded in social reality. Indeed, many of the changes they demanded would eventually be accepted by many Americans. Although the Nixon administration faced serious domestic turmoil from student protests, Black Panthers, and Weathermen, it was difficult to disagree with Senator Sam Ervin's characterization of the plan as the product of a Gestapo mentality.[62] The plan apparently arose from an obsession with radicalism, but the administration's reaction was at best unrealistic.[63] There were enough federal, state, and local agencies to deal with these problems without the creation of a secret White House Gestapo.

Tom Wicker, a newspaper columnist, noted that all staff aides accepted the plan. Men like Watergate intruder James McCord felt that there was only one legitimate value and that was that the United States is the most powerful and benign nation on earth. All other values were inoperative.[64] FBI Director J. Edgar Hoover and President Nixon found the plan indefensible, according to Wicker, but Nixon finally acknowledged its existence, claiming that it was dictated by the needs of national security. The distinguished historian Page Smith feels that Watergate represented a culmination of values that had preceded the Nixon administration and was linked to a set of attitudes that had permitted the CIA to pursue dubious operations in Guatemala, the Bay of Pigs, Tibet, and Southeast Asia.

Another of John Dean's shockers was the disclosure of a file entitled "Opponents List and Political Enemies Project." Although it was never established as an active concept, the disclosure of the existence of such a list in America was sensational. Dean said that the objective was to "screw" the administration's opponents in any way possible, including using the Internal Revenue Service and withholding federal contracts.

The list included all twelve black congressmen then in office, such distinguished journalists as Tom Wicker and James Reston, such prominent scholars as Arthur Schlesinger, Jr. and Noam Chomsky, businessman Stuart Mott, television correspondent Daniel Schorr, former Defense Secretary Clark Clifford, United Auto Workers President Leonard Woodcock, Mayor John Lindsay, and actors Paul Newman and Gregory Peck. Among the organizations on the list were Common Cause, the Committee for an Effective Congress, the Brookings Institution, and the Congress of Racial Equality (CORE). The only crime these individuals and organizations had committed was to oppose some or all of the policies of the Nixon administration. If government bureaucracy compiles enemy lists of those who merely disagree with its policies, it is superfluous to add that our liberties rest on quicksand.

BUREAUCRATS: WHAT MANNER OF MEN?

During the 1960s and 1970s our bureaucracy was too often staffed and led by arrogant men—"team players" whose blind loyalty to the president diminished their own individuality and usurped respect for democratic ideals at the same time that it was expected to advance their own careers. That "loyalty had always been rewarded in the [Nixon] administration" was abundantly confirmed by the Watergate hearings.[65] Herbert L. Porter, a young aide in the Committee to Re-elect the President, admitted that he had twice committed perjury to fulfill his role as a team player, stating proudly, "I have been guilty of a deep sense of loyalty to the President of the United States."[66] The make-up of the man is illustrated by the following dialogue between Porter and Senator Howard Baker of Tennessee.

> *Baker:* Did you ever think of saying, "I do not think this is quite right. This is not the way it ought to be?"
>
> *Porter:* Yes, I did.
>
> *Baker:* What did you do about it?
>
> *Porter:* I did not do anything.
>
> *Baker:* Why didn't you?
>
> *Porter:* In all honesty, because of the fear of group pressure that would ensue, of not being a team player.[67]

Maurice Stans, former secretary of commerce and finance director for the Committee to Re-elect the President, was asked by aide Hugh Sloan whether Jeb Magruder, deputy director of the committee, could have $83,000 to pay Watergate burglar G. Gordon Liddy. Stans quashed all questions about the purpose of this expenditure by replying, "I do not want to know, and you do not want to know."[68] Watergate intruder James McCord admitted being a long-time CIA team player who never questioned high-level officials.[69] McCord told of pressures from the White House to assure his silence and of promises of financial support for his family while he was in prison. This message was conveyed to John J. Caulfield, a high-ranking official in the Treasury Department, who regarded political espionage as congruent with his own service to the president.[70]

William Sloan Coffin, Jr., a former teacher and chaplain of Jeb Magruder at Williams College, attributed Magruder's downfall to a narrow, elitist education, to the times in which he lived, and to his conformity to the success ethic of his day—a combination of popularity, power, and money. Admitting that he and his fellow teachers at Williams might have done better by Magruder and his contemporaries, Coffin nevertheless observed that you don't have to be evil to do evil, that it was possible to be, like Magruder, "a nice guy but not yet a good man." "You have a lot of charm but little inner strength," he had once told Magruder. "And if you don't stand for something, you're apt to fall for anything."[71]

Magruder testified in his own defense that he had participated in administration law breaking in reaction to the law breaking he saw around him. But, Coffin argued, Martin Luther King, Jr. and the antiwar protesters had agitated against what they believed to be illegal, against laws whose constitutionality could only be tested by disobedience; they had campaigned openly and gone to jail for their activities. Magruder and his colleagues, on the other hand, had violated the law and usurped civil liberties in secret. There is a difference, Coffin asserted, between being true to the Constitution and being true to the man who hires you.[72]

David Halberstam felt that Nixon's bureaucrats were a new breed of men with great ambition and an amazing capacity to subjugate all for the good of the president, and that this was good, of course, for their own careers. They were fascinating in their manipulation of processes and techniques.[73]

> They may not know or care whether the elevators work in the summer in Harlem or whether the very richest members of the the society pay any income tax. . . . But they are expert at going into a foreign city and stringing the electronics necessary to get the Man on television, to get the right camera angles, laying down the television dollies just so. They seem more linked to the men like them in other countries than to their own society. One thinks of them and senses the new breed coming into power in Eastern Europe, the *apparatchik,* as manager; function and career over belief, what can the State do for us; they are all interchangeable parts with those in other governments.
>
> And they can, upon returning home, issue decrees saying that crime in the streets has been defeated, the cities have been saved, inflation curbed. They will not, after all, make the mistake of having Him televised visiting a ghetto and saying that crime in the streets has been curbed or visiting a meat market and talking about how they ended inflation. They are modern men, truly Orwellian; reality is not real life, reality is saying it on television.
>
> Morality is what you can get away with.[74]

That people who dissent from the consensus and refuse to be team players are consistently barred from government is one of the persistent failures of bureaucracy. Chris Argyris, chairman of Yale's Department of Administration Science, did a study of the Foreign Service and characterized the behavior of most of its officers as "withdrawal from interpersonal openness; mistrust of others' aggressiveness. . . ."[75] Foreign Service training emphasized the maxim "Find out who Big Brother is, and knuckle under."[76]

Before the opening of a Foreign Service recruitment drive on the campuses in 1965, a young officer asked what to do about students who felt misgivings about the war and was told to say that there was no place in the Foreign Service for nonsupporters of the war.[77]

The Nixon and Johnson administrations were particularly harsh on individualists. Of Nixon's cabinet, David Halberstam wrote: "They are not prized for their individualism. Individualism is dangerous; there is only one individual; only one voice; only one ego. Were there moments of individualism in Hickel, Romney, Peterson, et. al.? Did they make the mistake of believing that a cabinet official was his own man? Out!"[78] Lyndon Johnson forced out all who would not agree with his Vietnam policy—Undersecretary of State George Ball, Undersecretary of State for the Far East Roger Hilsman, Deputy Director of the Peace Corps Bill Moyers, and eventually Secretary of Defense Robert McNamara. Indeed, Johnson would compel a dissenter publicly to defend presidential policy, hoping that this would tie him to the policy and make him less likely to resign in protest; thus, George Ball was dispatched to Paris in December 1964 to defend America's policy in Southeast Asia.[79]

The U.S. Army, too, frequently crushed dissent. In early 1963 four American officers and senior advisers serving in the Mekong Delta saw that our South Vietnamese allies did not want to fight and that the enemy was winning the war. Colonel Fred Ladd, Lieutenant Colonel John Paul Vann, Colonel Wilber Wilson, and Colonel Dan Porter were all experienced career officers who had been specially trained for their positions.

But Colonel Ladd was criticized for his pessimistic reports. Lieutenant Colonel Vann, chastised by General Paul D. Harkins for calling the action in his area a defeat and for having discussed the situation with American reporters, became a "nonperson" whose future reports were ignored. After consulting with his sympathetic fellow officers, Colonel Porter enraged General Harkins by filing the most pessimistic report of the war to date. Although senior officer reports were normally circulated to other top advisers, the general intended to see to it that this report was "sanitized" and only then, if it still contained anything of value, circulated. With that, Colonel Porter resigned. Described as one of the Army's most dedicated officers, Lieutenant Colonel Vann soon followed his example.[80]

President Nixon's pre-Watergate staff was full of arrogant men indifferent to other points of view and to the bureaucratic process as well. H. R. Haldeman once stated brusquely that all presidents need an SOB and that he was Nixon's.[81] When it was suggested that the president send personal good wishes to a Republican senator who was fatally ill, Haldeman intercepted the message and penciled the notation, "Wait until he dies."[82]

The president's staff was especially insensitive to the importance in a free society of the legislature and the press. Senators with two and three decades of experience were treated disdainfully and regarded as mere legislative cannon fodder. Even the GOP National Chairman, Senator Robert Dole, complained of an absence of legislative understanding with the White House staff. Another staunch Nixon supporter, Senator Peter Dominick of Colorado, was miffed when Nixon bypassed him and a bill in his area of seniority was defeated.[83]

Deeply antagonistic toward the press, the Nixon White House staff never made public statements, never appeared in public or submitted to news conferences. After reading a mildly critical piece by John Osborne in *New Republic*, Haldeman sent him word to the effect that it was the worst piece of journalism he had ever seen.[84] To the men who had engineered the "selling of the president," the nation's press was merely something to be manipulated so that the Man could have four more years.

The Kennedy and Johnson administrations were no less arrogant. As David Halberstam summed up JFK's glittering staff:

> . . . They carried with them an exciting sense of American
> elitism, a sense that the best men had been summoned forth from
> the country to harness the American dream to a new American
> nationalism, bringing a new, strong, dynamic spirit to our historic
> role in world affairs; not necessarily to bring the American dream
> to reality here at home, but to bring it to reality elsewhere in the
> world. It was heady stuff, defining the American dream and
> giving it a new sense of purpose, taking American life which had
> grown too materialistic and complacent and giving it a new and
> grander mission.
>
> That special hubris about the American-age remained with
> some Kennedy people long after it had gone sour and indeed came
> apart. In 1968, when the horror of war and Gene McCarthy's
> success in New Hampshire had finally driven Robert Kennedy
> from his role of Hamlet, Theodore Sorensen was to write for his
> announcement speech—"At stake is not simply the leadership of
> one party, and even our own country; it is our right to the moral
> leadership of this planet."[85]

The two men who perhaps best symbolized the arrogance of the Kennedy and Johnson years were McGeorge Bundy, special assistant to President Kennedy for national security affairs, and Walt Whitman Rostow, chairman of the Policy Planning Council under Secretary of State Dean Rusk. Bundy's appointment was not happenstance; he had literally and figuratively been born and bred to it. Rostow was an inventive scholar but also a dogmatic man who lacked skepticism; not surprisingly, he was one of the last believers in the Vietnam War.[86]

The best and brightest were bound together by the belief that intelligence and reasoning could solve all problems.[87] This self-confidence helped to explain their fundamentalist feelings about the so-called domino theory, Ho Chi Minh, and Diem. They were fascinated by guerrilla war. They were ". . . aggressive, self-confident men, ready to play their role, believing in themselves, in their careers, in their right to make decisions here and overseas, and supremely confident in what they represented in terms of excellence."[88] The French failure in Vietnam was dismissed because, as Dean Rusk put it, "we were a can-do nation, and a great nation could do anything if it put its shoulder to the wheel."[89] McNamara, Bundy, and Rusk were all bright men, but their arrogance produced the greatest foreign policy blunder in recent American history.

Finally, our bureaucracies have too often been staffed by people more concerned with their own advancement and the interests of their own organization than with the interests of the nation and its citizens. Several instances from the army, FBI, and CIA corroborate this.

While covering the Vietnam War in 1963, David Halberstam filed a report with the *New York Times* documenting the growing strength of the enemy and the decline of our allies. The article suggested that the situation in the Mekong Delta was tenuous and that American optimism was as groundless as that of the French had previously been. When President Kennedy asked the army for its reaction to the story, the task of preparing the reply was not given to army intelligence but to General Richard Stillwell. The Stillwell report, compiled without consulting advisers in the Delta region, found Halberstam's report unfounded. Although the *Pentagon Papers* would later vindicate Halberstam, outright misreporting did not impede Stillwell's career. Halberstam noted: "Loyalty was not to the President of the United States, to truth or integrity, or even to subordinate officers risking their lives; loyalty was to the last to superiors and career."[90]

The Watergate entanglements also revealed how, in order to protect their own careers, high-ranking individuals permitted their organizations to be manipulated by political staffers. John Mitchell admitted holding discussions in his office about the use of bugging, kidnaping, and prostitution to cripple the Democratic party at the time that he was Attorney General of the United States and his office was the Department of Justice. Former Acting Director of the FBI, L. Patrick Gray, admitted giving John Dean free access to FBI Watergate files even after admitting his suspicion that Dean and others were trying to manipulate the FBI and CIA in an attempted cover-up. Gray accepted the files from convicted burglar E. Howard Hunt and later destroyed them. He also permitted presidential assistant John Ehrlichman to conceal a meeting with CIA Director Helms at which they compared notes on the cover-up. The CIA provided Hunt and Liddy with wigs, false papers, and cameras used in the break-in of the office of Dr. Daniel Ellsberg's psychiatrist. During the 1972 election, Helms stood silently by, allowing the public to be deceived in order to protect his career and the CIA's good name.[91]

Thus America's bureaucracy has failed the nation by having committed physical abuses, lied, deceived, spied, and denied people their rights. It has too frequently been staffed by men who are arrogant and contemptuous of democratic processes, who have overemphasized the importance of being team players, and who have placed their own careers and the interests of their organizations above the well-being of the nation. What can be done to ameliorate these conditions and make our bureaucracies both responsible and responsive to the nation's citizenry is the subject of the chapter that follows.

CASE STUDY 1

Mau-Mauing the Flak Catchers

TOM WOLFE

Michael Harrington's *The Other America* (1962) shocked this nation into acknowledging that poverty is not only one of our greatest problems but a national scandal as well. During the Kennedy, Johnson, and Nixon administrations, the responsibility of dealing with this problem was met in a variety of ways. Returning from a vacation in Bimini, presidential aspirant John Kennedy expressed shock at the conditions in West Virginia's Appalachia region and vowed during the 1960 presidential primary to do something to ameliorate them. As president, Kennedy did win some legislation to this end, including a manpower retraining act to help unemployed miners learn new skills.

Following his landslide victory in 1964, Lyndon Johnson, with great fanfare, launched a War on Poverty as the gem of his Great Society and, in the course of his tenure in office, obtained passage of the Equal Opportunity Act, creating the Office of Economic Opportunity (OEO), which administered a number of programs (VISTA, Head Start, Job Corps, Legal Services) aimed at eradicating poverty in America. But America surrendered before the War on Poverty had gained significant momentum, and the program gradually succumbed—a victim of its own inefficiency, the Vietnam War, the absence of an articulate clientele group, and the Puritan ethic that was repelled at the thought of a "dole" for the poor.

In 1973 President Nixon appointed Howard Phillips, a conservative ideologue, to preside over the death of the OEO. Some of the more successful programs were transferred to other departments; others were terminated. The Tom Wolfe selection that follows, which deals with poverty-level job seekers in San Francisco in 1967, illustrates problems of bureaucratic responsibility and insensitivity, of credibility gap, and of bureaucracy's inability to achieve at times what it was created to achieve. As you read this selection, consider these questions:

1. *What did the job seekers want, and were their demands reasonable?*
2. *How would you evaluate the technique they used to obtain their goals?*
3. *Why was the bureaucracy incapable of meeting their demands?*
4. *Based on this episode, what changes would you make in the poverty program to make it more effective?*

Anyway, the word got around among the groups in the Mission that the poverty program was going to cut down on summer jobs, and the Mission was going to be on the short end. So a bunch of the groups in the Mission got together and decided to go downtown to the poverty office and do some mau-mauing in behalf of the Mission before the bureaucrats made up their minds. There were blacks, Chicanos, Filipinos, and about ten Samoans.

The poverty office was on the first floor and had a big anteroom; only it's almost bare, nothing in it but a lot of wooden chairs. It looks like a union hall minus the spittoons, or one of those lobbies where they swear in new citizens. It's like they want to impress the poor that they don't have leather-top desks. . . . All our money goes to you. . . .

So the young aces from the Mission come trooping in, and they want to see the head man. The word comes out that the No. 1 man is out of town, but the No. 2 man is coming out to talk to the people.

This man comes out, and he has that sloppy Irish look like Ed McMahon on TV, only with a longer nose. In case you'd like the local viewpoint, whites really have the noses . . . enormous, you might say . . . a whole bag full . . . long and pointed like carrots, goobered up like green peppers, hooked like a squash, hanging off the face like cucumbers. . . . This man has a nose that is just on the verge of hooking over, but it doesn't quite make it.

"Have a seat, gentlemen," he says, and he motions toward the wooden chairs.

But he doesn't have to open his mouth. All you have to do is look at him and you get the picture. The man's a lifer. He's stone civil service. He has it all down from the wheatcolor Hush Puppies to the wash'n'dry semi-tab-collar shortsleeves white shirt. Those wheatcolor Hush Puppies must be like some kind of fraternal garb among the civil-service employees, because they all wear them. They cost about $4.99, and the second time you move your toes, the seams split and the tops come away from the soles. But they all wear them. The man's shirt looks like he bought it at the August end-of-summer sale at the White Front. It is one of those shirts with pockets on both sides. Sticking out of the pockets and running across his chest he has a lineup of ball-point pens, felt nibs, lead pencils, wax markers, such as you wouldn't believe, Paper-mates, Pentels, Scriptos, Eberhard Faber Mongol 482's, Dri-Marks, Bic PM-29's, everything. They are lined up across his chest like campaign ribbons.

He pulls up one of the wooden chairs and sits down on it. Only he sits down on it backwards, straddling the seat and hooking his arms and his chin over the back of the chair, like the head foreman in the bunkhouse. It's like saying, "We don't stand on ceremony around here. This is a shirtsleeve operation."

"I'm sorry that Mr. Johnson isn't here today," he says, "but he's not in the city. He's back in Washington meeting some important project deadlines. He's very concerned, and he would want to meet with you people if he were here, but right now I know you'll understand that the most important thing he can do for you is to push these projects through in Washington."

The man keeps his arms and his head hung over the back of the chair, but he swings his hands up in the air from time to time to emphasize a point, first one hand and then the other. It looks like he's giving wig-wag signals to the typing pool. The way he hangs himself over the back of the chair—that keeps up the funky shirtsleeve-operation number. And throwing his hands around—that's dynamic. . . . It says, "We're hacking our way through the red tape just as fast as we can."

"Now, I'm here to try to answer any questions I can," he says, "but you have to understand that I'm only speaking as an individual, and so naturally none of my comments are binding, but I'll answer any questions I can, and if I can't answer them, I'll do what I can to get the answers for you."

And then it dawns on you, and you wonder why it took so long for you to realize it. This man is the flak catcher. His job is to catch the flak for the No. 1 man. He's like the professional mourners you can hire in Chinatown. They have certified wailers, professional mourners, in Chinatown, and when your loved one dies, you can hire the professional mourners to wail at the funeral and show what a great loss to the community the departed is. In the same way this lifer is ready to catch whatever flak you're sending up. It doesn't matter what bureau they put him in. It's all the same. Poverty, Japanese imports, valley fever, tomato-crop parity, partial disability, home loans, second-probate accounting, the Interstate 90 detour change order, lockouts, secondary boycotts, G.I. alimony, the Pakistani quota, cinch mites, Tularemic Loa loa, veterans' dental benefits, workmen's compensation, suspended excise rebates—whatever you're angry about, it doesn't matter, he's there to catch the flak. He's a lifer.

Everybody knows the scene is a shuck, but you can't just walk out and leave. You can't get it on and bring thirty-five people walking all the way from the Mission to 100 McAllister and then just turn around and go back. So . . . might as well get into the number. . . .

One of the Chicanos starts it off by asking the straight question, which is about how many summer jobs the Mission groups are going to get. This is the opening phase, the straight-face phase, in the art of mau-mauing.

"Well," says the Flak Catcher—and he gives it a twist of the head and a fling of the hand and the ingratiating smile—"It's hard for me to answer that the way I'd like to answer it, and the way I know you'd like for me to answer it, because that's precisely what we're working on back in Washington. But I can tell you this. At this point I see no reason why our project allocation should be any less, if all we're looking at is the urban-factor numbers for this area, because that should remain the same. Of course, if there's been any substantial pre-funding, in Washington, for the fixed-asset part of our program, like Head Start or the community health centers, that could alter the picture. But we're very hopeful, and as soon as we have the figures, I can tell you that you people will be the first to know."

It goes on like this for a while. He keeps saying things like, "I don't know the answer to that right now, but I'll do everything I can to find out." The way he says it, you can tell he thinks you're going to be impressed with how honest he is about what he doesn't know. Or he says, "I wish we could give *everybody* jobs. Believe me, I would like nothing better, both personally and as a representative of this Office."

So one of the bloods says, "Man, why do you sit there shining us with this bureaucratic rhetoric, when you said yourself that ain't nothing you say that means a goddam thing?"

Ba-ram-ba-ram-ba-ram-ba-ram—a bunch of the aces start banging on the floor in unison. It sounds like they have sledge hammers.

"Ha-unnnnh," says the Flak Catcher. It is one of those laughs that starts out as laugh but ends up like he got hit in the stomach halfway through. It's the first assault on his dignity. So he breaks into his shit-eating grin, which is always phase two. Why do so many bureaucrats, deans, preachers, college presidents, try to smile when the mau-mauing starts? It's fatal, this smiling. When some bad dude is challenging your manhood, your smile just proves that he is right and you are chickenshit—unless you are a bad man yourself with so much heart that you can make that smile say,

"Just keep on talking, sucker, because I'm gonna count to ten and then *squash* you."

"Well," says the Flak Catcher, "I can't promise you jobs if the jobs aren't available yet"—and then he looks up as if for the first time he is really focusing on the thirty-five ghetto hot dogs he is now facing, by way of sizing up the threat, now that the shit has started. The blacks and the Chicanos he has no doubt seen before, or people just like them, but then he takes in the Filipinos. There are about eight of them, and they are all wearing the Day-Glo yellow and hot-green sweaters and lemon-colored pants and Italian-style socks. But it's the headgear that does the trick. They've all got on Rap Brown shades and Russian Cossack hats made of frosted-gray Dynel. They look *bad.* Then the man takes in the Samoans, and they look worse. There's about ten of them, but they fill up half the room. They've got on Island shirts with designs in streaks and blooms of red, only it's a really raw shade of red, like that red they paint the floor with in the tool and dye works. They're glaring at him out of those big dark wide brown faces. The monsters have tight curly hair, but it grows in long strands, and they comb it back flat, in long curly strands, with a Duke pomade job. They've got huge feet, and they're wearing sandals. The straps on the sandals look like they were made from the reins on the Budweiser draft horses. But what really gets the Flak Catcher, besides the sheer size of the brutes, is their Tiki canes. These are like Polynesian scepters. They're the size of sawed-off pool cues, only they're carved all over in Polynesian Tiki Village designs. When they wrap their fists around these sticks, every knuckle on their hands pops out the size of a walnut. Anything they hear that they like, like the part about the "bureaucratic rhetoric," they bang on the floor in unison with the ends of the Tiki sticks—*ba-ram-ba-ram-ba-ram-ba-ram*— although some of them press one end of the stick onto the sole of their sandal between their first two toes and raise their foot up and down with the stick to cushion the blow on the floor. They don't want to scuff up the Tiki cane.

The Flak Catcher is still staring at them, and his shit-eating grin is getting worse. It's like he *knows* the worst is yet to come . . . Goddamn . . . that one in front there . . . that Pineapple Brute . . .

"Hey, Brudda," the main man says. He has a really heavy accent. "Hey, Brudda, how much you make?"

"Me?" says the Flak Catcher. "How much do I make?"

"Yeah, Brudda, you. How much money you make?"

Now the man is trying to think in eight directions at once. He tries out a new smile. He tries it out on the bloods, the Chicanos, and the Filipinos, as if to say, "As one intelligent creature to another, what do you do with dumb people like this?" But all he gets is the glares, and his mouth shimmies back into the terrible sickening grin, and then you can see that there are a whole lot of little muscles all around the human mouth, and his are beginning to squirm and tremble. . . . He's fighting for control of himself. . . . It's a lost cause. . . .

"How much, Brudda?"

Ba-ram-ba-ram-ba-ram-ba-ram—they keep beating on the floor.

"Well," says the Flak Catcher, "I make $1,100 a month."

"How come you make so much?"

"Wellllll"—the grin, the last bid for clemency . . . and now the poor man's eyes are freezing into little round iceballs, and his mouth is getting dry—

Ba-ram-ba-ram-ba-ram-ba-ram

"How come you make so much? My fadda and mudda both work and they only make six hundred and fifty."

Oh shit, the cat kind of blew it there. That's way over the poverty line, about double, in fact. It's even above the guideline for a family of twelve. You can see that fact register with the Flak Catcher, and he's trying to work up the nerve to make the devastating comeback. But he's not about to talk back to these giants.

"Listen, Brudda. Why don't you give up your paycheck for summer jobs? You ain't doing shit."

"Wellll"—the Flak Catcher grins, he sweats, he hangs over the back of the chair—

Ba-ram-ba-ram-ba-ram-ba-ram—"Yeah, Brudda! Give us your paycheck!"

There it is . . . the ultimate horror. . . . He can see it now, he can hear it. . . . Fifteen tons of it. . . . It's horrible . . . it's possible. . . . It's so obscene, it just might happen. . . . Huge Polynesian monsters marching down to his office every payday. . . . Hand it over, Brudda . . . ripping it out of his very fingers . . . eternally. . . . He wrings his hands . . . the little muscles around his mouth are going haywire. He tries to recapture his grin, but those little amok muscles pull his lips up into an O, like they were drawstrings.

"I'd gladly give up my salary," says the Flak Catcher. "I'd *glad*ly do it, if it would do any good. But can't you see, gentlemen, it would be just a drop in the bucket . . . just a *drop in the bucket!*" This phrase *a drop in the bucket* seems to give him heart . . . it's something to hang onto . . . an answer . . . a reprieve. . . . "Just consider what we have to do in this city alone, gentlemen! All of us! It's just a *drop in the bucket!*"

The Samoans can't come up with any answer to this, so the Flak Catcher keeps going.

"Look, gentlemen," he says, "you tell me what to do and I'll do it. Of *course* you want more summer jobs, and we want you to have them. That's what we're here for. I wish I could give everybody a job. You tell me how to get more jobs, and we'll get them. We're doing all we can. If we can do more, you tell me how, and I'll gladly do it.''

One of the bloods says, ''Man, if you don't *know how,* then we don't *need* you.''

''Dat's right, Brudda! Whadda we need you for!'' You can tell the Samoans wish they had thought of that shoot-down line themselves— *Ba-ram-ba-ram-ba-ram-ba-ram*—they clobber the hell out of the floor.

''Man,'' says the blood, ''you just taking up space and killing time and drawing pay!''

''Dat's right, Brudda! You just drawing pay!'' *Ba-ram-ba-ram-ba-ram-ba-ram*

''Man,'' says the blood, ''if you don't know nothing and you can't do nothing and you can't say nothing, why don't you tell your boss what we want!''

''Dat's right, Brudda! Tell the man!'' *Ba-ram-ba-ram-ba-ram-ba-ram*

''As I've already told you, he's in Washington trying to meet the deadlines for *your* projects!''

''You talk to the man, don't you? He'll let you talk to him, won't he?''

''Yes . . .''

''Send him a telegram, man!''

''Well, all right—''

''Shit, pick up the telephone, man!''

''Dat's right, Brudda! Pick up the telephone!'' *Ba-ram-ba-ram-ba-ram-ba-ram*

''Please, gentlemen! That's pointless! It's already after six o'clock in Washington. The office is closed!''

''Then call him in the morning, man,'' says the blood. ''We coming back here in the morning and we gonna *watch* you call the man! We gonna stand right on *top* of you so you won't forget to make that call!''

''Dat's right, Brudda! On *top* of you!'' *Ba-ram-ba-ram-ba-ram-ba-ram*

''All right, gentlemen . . . all right,'' says the Flak Catcher. He slaps his hands against his thighs and gets up off the chair. ''I'll tell you what. . . .'' The way he says it, you can tell the man is trying to get back a little corner of his manhood. He tries to take a tone that says, ''You haven't really been in here for the past fifteen minutes intimidating me and burying my nuts in the sand and humiliating me. . . . We've really been having a discussion about the proper procedures, and I am willing to grant that you have a point.''

''If that's what you want,'' he says, ''I'm certainly willing to put in a telephone call.''

''If we *want!* If you *willing!* Ain't no want or willing *about* it, man! You *gonna* make that call! We gonna be here and *see* you make it!''

''Dat's right, Brudda! We be seeing you''—*Ba-ram-ba-ram-ba-ram*—''We coming *back!*''

And the Flak Catcher is standing there with his mouth playing bad tricks on him again, and the Samoans hoist their Tiki sticks, and the aces all leave, and they're thinking. . . . We've done it again. We've mau-maued the goddamn white man, scared him until he's singing a duet with his sphincter, and the people sure do have power. Did you see the look on his face? Did you see the sucker trembling? Did you see the sucker trying to lick his lips? He was *scared,* man! That's the last time that sucker is gonna try to *urban-factor* and *pre-fund* and *fix-asset* with us! He's gonna go home to his house in Diamond Heights and he's gonna say, "Honey, fix me a drink! Those mother-fuckers were ready to kill me!" That sucker was some kind of *petrified* . . . He could see eight kinds of Tiki sticks up side his head. . . .

Of course, the next day nobody shows up at the poverty office to make sure the sucker makes the telephone call. Somehow it always seems to happen that way. Nobody ever follows it up. You can get everything together once, for the demonstration, for the confrontation, to go downtown and mau-mau, for the fun, for the big show, for the beano, for the main event, to see the people bury some gray cat's nuts and make him crawl and whine and sink in his own terrible grin. But nobody ever follows it up. You just sleep it off until somebody tells you there's going to be another big show.

And then later on you think about it and you say, "What really happened that day? Well, another flak catcher lost his manhood, that's what happened." Hmmmmmm . . . like maybe the bureaucracy isn't so dumb after all. . . . All they did was sacrifice one flak catcher, and they've got hundreds, thousands. . . . They've got replaceable parts. They threw this sacrifice to you, and you went away pleased with yourself. And even the Flak Catcher himself wasn't losing much. He wasn't losing his manhood. He gave that up a long time ago, the day he became a lifer. . . . Just who is fucking over who. . . . You did your number and he did his number, and they didn't even have to stop the music. . . . The band played on. . . . *Still*—did you see the *look* on his face? That sucker—

CASE STUDY 2

Managing the News in Vietnam
JOHN MECKLIN

During the course of the Vietnam War, more than 40,000 young people were cut down in their prime; more than 300,000 were wounded; and the psychological cost to hundreds of thousands of American servicemen may never be ultimately assessed. The financial cost to the United States of this war exceeded $150 billion. But the Vietnam War cost America more than money and lives. From its earliest days it evoked such a degree of spying, lying, and manipulative deception on the part of public bureaucrats as to shake the faith of the American people in the essential integrity of their government.

Spying on civilian antiwar protesters by army plainclothesmen; lies to Congress, the press, and the public by persons at the highest levels of government; large-scale cover-ups by the air force—all were widespread and commonplace. But political deception is not new in American history, and, as the following selection indicates, the Nixon administration did not hold a monopoly on it. The author, John Mecklin, was a public affairs officer at the U.S. Mission in Saigon during the early 1960s. As you read this selection, ask yourself:

1. *What was wrong with the way in which the U.S. Mission obtained its information?*

2. *In what ways did the U.S. Mission deceive the press and the American public, and why did it do so?*

3. *What would you have done in Mecklin's place?*

4. *How could the press have better covered the war?*

. . . We were stuck hopelessly with what amounted to an all-or-nothing policy, which might not work. Yet it *had* to work, like a Catholic marriage or a parachute. The state of mind in both Washington and Saigon tended to close out reason. The policy of support for Diem became an article of faith, and dissent became reprehensible.

In its dealings with newsmen, the U.S. Mission thus was often wrong about the facts, in a situation of utmost importance to the U.S. national interest, in support of a controversial policy that was costing the lives of American servicemen. Even if conditions had otherwise been normal, this was incompatible with the inquisitive, skeptical nature of American journalism, and trouble would have been inevitable. Unhappily conditions were not otherwise normal.

The breakdown of communication between the U.S. Mission and American newsmen, and thus the American public, was further exacerbated by the special political considerations that enveloped our operations in Vietnam like a terminal-care oxygen tent.

For one thing the U.S. decision in 1961 to intervene massively in Vietnam amounted to outright abrogation of the Geneva Agreement of 1954. (The U.S. was not a signatory but it pledged itself unilaterally to honor the agreement.) The agreement provided that there be no increase in foreign forces in Vietnam above the level at that time. In the case of the U.S., this was some 685 men. There was also a provision limiting introduction of armaments which was similarly dumped in the trash can of history.

It was characteristic of the schoolbook morality that so often inhibits U.S. foreign policy that the Kennedy Administration was extremely uneasy about this, despite the fact that the Communists flagrantly violated the agreement years before we did.

Secondly Washington was worried about the propaganda and diplomatic ammunition that the U.S. intervention in Vietnam would provide the Communists, not only in Southeast Asia but globally. This no doubt resulted in part from the fact we had been so badly burned so recently in the Bay of Pigs, but it was an unrealistic concern. Any increased American effort in Vietnam was certain to stir a storm of Communist talk about American "imperialism," and so on, and there was nothing we could hope to do about it—except to make it work, which would more than cancel out the damage of any amount of Communist propaganda.

Thirdly the Kennedy Administration knew that U.S. support for Vietnam had never been popular among American voters, and it feared that increased "involvement" might lead to damaging domestic political repercussions. President Kennedy was one of the most politically sensitive men who ever occupied the White House, making this consideration particularly important.

The problem was further compounded by the attitude of the Vietnamese Government toward the press. Columnist Joseph Alsop described it as "idiotic." The Diem regime reacted to newsmen as though they were a foreign substance in the bloodstream, in uncontrollable convulsions.

Ambassador [Frederick E.] Nolting called the problem a "clash of cultures," as indeed it was. It was also a clash of centuries: the twentieth versus, let's say, the sixteenth. To the Ngo Dinh family with its Mandarin background, and its feudalistic form of government, the average freewheeling American newsman seemed both incomprehensible and dangerous. The family could not understand why the American press would publish anything that was derogatory to an ally locked in battle against an enemy who was also an American enemy. It demanded the same blank-check support from the press that it was receiving from the U.S. Government.

After a good many years of trying, the Americans persuaded Diem early in 1961 to hire a professional public relations consultant. The contract went to a New York agency, at a reported fee of $100,000. An American expert turned up in Saigon, but the experiment fizzled. One reason was a morass of financial complications. Another was the suspicion among some newsmen in Saigon that one of the expert's functions was to keep track of their activities for the palace. . . .

The [Diem] regime was not malicious, not particularly self-seeking about this. The palace seldom lied intentionally to the press. It often tried to persuade reporters to accept absurdities, but it usually believed them itself—and regularly tried to sell the same absurdities to the U.S. Mission, often, unhappily, with greater success.

Almost nothing was done to provide essential working facilities for newsmen. Vietnam was a nation at war, yet the only official spokesman for the Vietnamese armed forces was an obscure Lieutenant Bang, who could seldom be found. Military developments were reported in a daily communique, but it was regularly three or four days behind the news, and always played down setbacks. It was largely ignored. There were three or four relatively competent civilian information officers, but they too were difficult to find, especially when the news was bad.

The newsmen, of course, found other sources for the news, and increasingly treated the regime's communiques with the contempt they invited. This, in turn, outraged Diem and the Nhus, who tended to blame the U.S. Mission. Like politicians all over the underdeveloped world, they believed that the U.S. Government controlled the American press, just as they controlled the Vietnamese press. No amount of patient explanation could persuade them of the reality that the American newsmen not only were wholly independent of government control but in fact regularly transmitting dispatches that the U.S. Mission considered to be damaging to the U.S. interests.

This created a dangerous vicious circle. The Diem regime, recognizing that it could not persuade the newsmen, sought to control them. It tried to limit their movements around the country, to block their sources, and to keep them under surveillance. It lifted their dispatches out of the cable office—in violation of international communications codes—and had them translated for private circulation inside the government. And it protested vigorously to the U.S. Mission about everything it disliked in the newsmen's reports, sometimes calling us on the carpet for dispatches that had not yet been published in the newspapers to which they were addressed. The protests would often interfere with negotiations between the Mission and the regime on more important issues.

This still further poisoned the Mission's attitude toward the newsmen. We rationalized our attitude like this:

1. Success of the struggle against the Viet Cong depended importantly on persuading the Diem regime to heed U.S. advice.

2. The regime believed, however wrongly, that the U.S. press reflected the views of the U.S. Government and therefore blamed the U.S. Government for press reports that it disliked.

3. Such reports angered the regime and made it reluctant to accept American advice on matters of importance to the war effort.

4. Newsmen who wrote such dispatches were therefore damaging the U.S. national interest. To put it another way, it became unpatriotic for a newsman to use an adjective that displeased Mme. Nhu.

Completing the vicious circle, this kind of thinking led the Mission to react with sympathy to the regime's complaints, in the understandable human hope that by doing so we could get on with other business. Occasionally it worked that way. More often our sympathy simply tended to encourage the regime to more complaints. This also tended to identify the Mission with the regime's hysterical attitude toward the press, including eventually even its physical reprisals against newsmen.

Together all these special considerations led to an official U.S. policy on press relations that attempted on one hand to discourage publicity of any sort about our operations in Vietnam, and on the other to pamper the Diem regime.

At the outset, in 1961 and early 1962, the American buildup was treated like a clandestine operation, producing some memorable absurdities. When the aircraft carrier *Core* tied up at a dock in the Saigon River, for example, newsmen at the rooftop bar of the Majestic Hotel across the street could almost flick a cigarette down among the helicopters cluttering her flight deck. Yet if one of them asked if that was an aircraft carrier across the street, the official reply was supposed to be "no comment." The Mission was forbidden to discuss arrivals of military personnel or materiel of any sort.

This kind of foolishness quickly stirred the wrath of newsmen working in Vietnam, especially when the Viet Cong began killing Americans who were clearly engaged in combat missions. Excessive American secrecy became a news story in itself and was widely reported, with the implication that the U.S. Government was cheating on its own people, trying to fuzz up a policy that was costing the lives of American servicemen. The main result of the secrecy was considerably more publicity than the U.S. buildup would otherwise have generated. It also provoked indignant editorials and, more importantly, queries from congressmen.

By early 1962 difficulties with the press had reached a point where Washington ordered a reexamination of information policy. The result was a new directive, State Department cable No. 1006 of February 21, 1962—two months before my arrival—which was supposed to "liberalize" the policy. It was "liberal" in the sense that it recognized the right of American newsmen to cover the war in Vietnam, but it was otherwise little more than codification of the errors the Mission was already committing.

The text of the cable, which was classified, was not released, but it was shown to members of the House Subcommittee on Foreign Operations and Government Information headed by Rep. John E. Moss, Democrat, of California. The Subcommittee's report on October 1, 1963, paraphrased the cable as saying:

> News stories criticizing the Diem government "increase the difficulties of the U.S. job."
>
> Newsmen "should be advised that trifling or thoughtless criticism of the Diem government would make it difficult to maintain cooperation" with Diem.
>
> Newsmen "should not be transported on military activities of the type that are likely to result in undesirable stories."

The Subcommittee's report commented: "The restrictive U.S. press policy in Vietnam . . . unquestionably contributed to the lack of information about conditions in Vietnam which created an international crisis. Instead of hiding the facts from the American public, the State Department should have done everything possible to expose the true situation to full view." . . .

Feuds between newsmen and government officials had long been commonplace. During a World War II press conference, for example, President Roosevelt contemptuously presented a Nazi Iron Cross to an unfriendly reporter, implying that his reporting had been helpful to Hitler. Conflict was built in under the American system of checks and balances—the clash of the people's fundamental right to know versus the government's duty to guard secrets that would help the nation's enemies.

In Vietnam the feud reached a degree of bitterness such as I had never before encountered in some twenty years of foreign duty.

I was treated to a disconcerting glimpse of the official attitude toward newsmen on my first morning in Saigon. My advice was invited on a press conference to be given later that day by two American sergeants who had just been released after several weeks in the jungle as prisoners of the Viet Cong. The Communists had given them a fistful of propaganda leaflets to distribute among their comrades—the standard claptrap appealing to peace-loving Americans to cease participating in this dirty imperialist war against the peace-loving Vietnamese people and go home.

To my surprise an American military officer suggested that the sergeants be ordered not to tell the press about the leaflets. "Why should we help the V.C. circulate their propaganda?" he asked. He seemed to be saying that he thought American newspaper readers might be swayed by it. I objected and argued that, as a matter of principle, the sergeants should be instructed to withhold only sensitive military information of possible help to the V.C. In any case, I said, Americans don't take that kind of propaganda seriously, just as we all had laughed at Tokyo Rose and Axis Sally during World War II.

Came the press conference. After the sergeants had recounted their adventures, Peter Kalischer of the Columbia Broadcasting System asked: "Did the V.C. give you anything to bring out?" One of the sergeants looked Kalischer in the eye and replied: "No, sir."

It was an evident falsehood, obviously on orders, in equally obvious disregard of my recommendation. As is usually the case, the lie didn't work. Kalischer had visited the spot where the sergeants had come out of the jungle, talked to the American authorities there and heard about the leaflets. He even had a copy of one of them in his pocket when he asked the question. The lie was duly reported by newspapers, TV and radio all over the United States the next morning.

From some officials of the U.S. Mission, misleading a newsman was almost instinctive, if only as a way to get rid of him. It was a curious phenomenon, not necessarily malicious. These officials were men of high personal integrity, who would never dream of deceiving their wives or a colleague, or a friend. They seemed to regard a journalist as a natural adversary who was deliberately trying to sabotage the national interest, or as a child who would not understand and should not be asking about grown-up affairs in any case. Once in a press statement, for example, a senior American officer—I think inadvertently—used a figure on Viet Cong casualties that was absurdly inflated. I asked one of his aides to consider issuing a correction. "That would only draw attention to it," he replied, closing the matter.

To the best of my knowledge, no responsible U.S. official in Saigon ever told a newsman a really big falsehood. Instead there were endless little ones. They were morally marginal and thus difficult to dispute.

One day in 1962 a delegation of angry newsmen came to see me to complain that the U.S. Mission had been lying to them. I asked for examples. They could think of only two. One was our report that an American soldier was drowned when he fell from a boat on an "outing," when in fact the boat had been fired on by Viet Cong. The second was an official announcement that Vietnamese forces had rescued the American crew of a downed aircraft, when in fact they had been rescued by an American search party. I explained that in both cases our initial reports had been based on erroneous information from our own people, and I said I thought these were poor examples to support an accusation of lying.

What I did not say, could not say in my position, was that I understood their point exactly, that there had been so many little deceptions that they no longer believed anything we said on any subject.

A man from Mars admitted to official inner circles in both Vietnam and Washington could have been excused if he got the impression that the newsmen, as well as the Viet Cong, were the enemy. . . .

There was a patronizing, holier-than-thou tone in the official attitude toward the press. We repeatedly received cables from Washington using expressions like "tell the correspondents" to do so and so, or "explain how they were wrong" to write such and such. This was like trying to tell a New York taxi driver how to shift gears. Newsmen the world over are extraordinarily jealous of their prerogatives, often suffer from an inferiority complex, and react violently to any kind of pressure on their reporting.

Still worse was the frequent official suggestion that a "negative" reporter was somehow un-American. Visiting Saigon on one occasion, Admiral [Harry D.] Felt was asked a difficult question at a press conference. "Why don't you get on the team?" he snapped at the offending reporter. The local press corps was outraged. Similarly Ambassador Nolting once asked a newsman to "give President Diem the benefit of the doubt," implying that the press had been slanting its dispatches against Diem. The point was not entirely unjustified, but Nolting was never forgiven the remark.

This was characteristic of the whole sorry mess. Neither Felt nor Nolting was deliberately trying to needle the newsmen, nor even aware that what he said would be so strongly resented. With one or two exceptions the same insensitivity was true of the other senior officers in Saigon. There was a self-righteous witlessness about the official attitude toward newsmen that was hard to explain in men of such long and varied careers in the public service.

The Mission persisted in the practice of excessive classification, under the secret fraternity doctrine of State Department Cable No. 1006, to a degree that denied newsmen access to whole segments of U.S. operations in Vietnam. During the time I was there, whether or not napalm (jellied gasoline) was being used against the Viet Cong was technically classified, despite the fact that *Life* Magazine in early 1962 published a cover photograph in color of a napalm attack in Vietnam. The classification presumably was removed after Secretary [Robert] McNamara, in a press conference on April 24, 1964, admitted that napalm was being used, though he insisted this was only "very rarely."

Newsmen were forbidden (until mid-1964) even to visit the airfield at Bien Hoa, outside Saigon, where an important part of the U.S. Air Force effort in Vietnam was based. (This was the same base so disastrously hit by Viet Cong mortars in November 1964.) This was part of a near total ban on publicity about the Air Force. Inevitably it backfired.

Much of what the Air Force was doing was "blown" by Captain Edwin Gerald ("Jerry") Shank, T-28 fighter-bomber pilot who was killed in Vietnam, in letters to his wife that were widely published in the spring of 1964. There was eloquent comment on the U.S. Mission's policy toward the press, and how it affected many of the Americans out there, in this passage (*U.S. News & World Report,* May 4, 1964) of a letter dated January 20, 1964:

> "What gets me most is that they won't tell you people what we do over here. I'll bet you that anyone you talk to does not know that American pilots fight this war. We—me and my buddies—do everything. The Vietnamese 'students' we have on board are airmen basics (raw recruits). The only reason they are on board is in case we crash there is one American 'advisor' and one Vietnamese 'student.' They're stupid, ignorant sacrificial lambs, and I have no use for them. In fact, I have been tempted to whip them within an inch of their life a few times. They're a menace to have on board. . . ."

Surely it would have made more sense to invite the press to report the life and activities of Captain Shank and the other American fliers in Vietnam, and thus to give them some of the credit they so richly earned, than to have the story appear in this bitter, sensationalized form, coupled with an accusation from a dead hero that the U.S. Government had misled the American public about his work. Shank's letters were dramatic proof of a basic reality, that secrets don't keep in a situation as confused and controversial as Vietnam.

Excessive classification infected newsmen with distrust of everything we did and said on the understandable assumption that we probably were not telling the whole truth.

One of the spectaculars of the American performance in Vietnam was the compulsive official optimism about the state of the war. This was partly explained by the common ailment of "career involvement," a man's natural inclination to make his work look good. It was partly caused by the fact that Diem liked to be praised, and was inclined to regard as an enemy anyone who failed to praise him. Praise became part of the "advisory" technique. Mainly, however, the unrealistic optimism about Vietnam in both Washington and Saigon was defensive, a silly effort to counter hostile press reporting—in some ways like the losing candidate on election night who keeps pleading for everyone to wait for the upstate returns.

There were some memorable extravagances. Lyndon Johnson, who visited Vietnam in 1961 as Vice-President, compared Diem publicly with Winston Churchill. Secretary McNamara called him "one of the great leaders of our time." After a visit in 1962 General Taylor claimed to have found "a great national movement" that was crushing the Viet Cong. Ruefully I must confess helping to draft a speech by Ambassador Nolting in 1962 forecasting that "the Republic of Vietnam will take its place in history as the country where the tide of Asian Communism was reversed and the myth of Communist invincibility forever shattered." McNamara, Felt and Harkins repeatedly predicted publicly that the war would be in hand by 1964 or 1965, often coupling their remarks with disdainful references to "slanted" or "irresponsible" press reporting from Saigon.*

In early 1963 Senator Mike Mansfield visited Saigon and departed *without* commenting on the war at all. Things had reached such comic opera proportions that the newsmen regarded this as news and reported it widely.

Way-out official optimism and public abuse of the press often led the newsmen to look for more bad news to justify their previous reporting, further outraging the VIP optimists. Official restrictions on fresh, unedited news, under Cable No. 1006, similarly led the newsmen to look for private sources of their own. They were plentiful, and many of them were malcontents: resentful aircraft crews who were taking most of the American casualties, incompetent officials seeking recognition that had been denied in the public service, neurotics whose vanity was massaged by the attention of reporters from big-time organizations, or sincerely indignant officers who believed the Kennedy Administration was leading the U.S. to disaster in Vietnam and were willing to risk a jail term (by compromising secrets) to appeal their case to the U.S. public.

To protect such sources as these the newsmen used terms like "informed Americans" or "American observers" or "knowledgeable American sources" in their dispatches. Just as regularly each such story would provoke a protest from the Vietnamese Government, or Washington, or both, and the Mission would receive instructions to prevent any further stories attributed to "American sources." This was roughly like trying to prevent a reporter visiting a city of twenty thousand population from talking to anyone, yet some very important people in Washington apparently believed it could be done. The usual result was, first, a massive security investigation which always failed to uncover the source of the story; second, a directive reiterating previous instructions on how to talk to newsmen without saying anything; and third, a rash of indignant stories accusing the Mission of trying to "intimidate" news sources.

There was a particularly spectacular leak in late February 1963. It concerned a change in the rules of engagement for helicopter gunners. The principle was that they could open fire only in self-defense. Previously this had been interpreted to mean they could only fire when fired upon from the ground. The new order said that gunners now could fire if they observed the

---

*A ditty, sung to the tune of "Twinkle, Twinkle, Little Star," circulated through American field messes in Vietnam. I can recall only the first two verses:

We are winning:	If you doubt me,
This I know.	Who are you?
General Harkins told me so.	McNamara says so too.

V.C. preparing to shoot, i.e., the Americans could shoot first in self-defense. It was a sensible but also sensitive order, first because the change would be of great interest to the V.C. and, second, because it suggested further U.S. "involvement" and thus invited political repercussions.

It leaked so rapidly that stories appeared in the press before the new rules had even taken effect. This was hardly surprising. The order had to be circulated among something like a thousand persons, most of them young, embittered helicopter crewmen who had lost buddies to V.C. fire, and many of whom were close personal friends of newsmen. It should have been obvious from the outset that it could not be suppressed and that the only hope for avoiding page-one headlines was to call in the newsmen, tell them about it and appeal for it to be played down. Most of them would have cooperated. Instead the attempt to keep it from them led to sensationalized publicity all over the world.

Altogether the Mission's press policy tended to encourage soreheads while it outraged the newsmen. Its gumshoe investigations of leaks poisoned the American community with doubt and suspicion of colleagues, further depressing morale in an extraordinarily difficult situation. And it was unworkable anyway.

NOTES

1. William E. Connolly, "The Challenge of Pluralist Theory," in *Bias of Pluralism*, ed. William E. Connolly, pp. 3–4.

2. Ibid.

3. Theodore Lowi, *The End of Liberalism*, pp. ix–xiv.

4. Ibid., pp. 107–87.

5. Ibid., pp. 101–15.

6. Robert H. Buckhorn, *Nader*, p. 269.

7. Cited in Lucia Mouat, "The Quiet Men Who Patrol U.S. Skies," *Christian Science Monitor*, 25 October 1972, p. 7.

8. Louis M. Kohlmeier, *The Regulators*, p. 31.

9. Robert C. Fellmeth, *Interstate Commerce Ommission*, pp. 34–36.

10. Edward F. Cox et al., *The Nader Report on the Federal Trade Commission*, p. 110.

11. Ibid., pp. 106–10.

12. Ibid., pp. 108–10.

13. Ibid., pp. 111–15.

14. Bernard Schwartz, *The Professor and the Commissions*, pp. 210–13.

15. Kohlmeier, *The Regulators*, pp. 219–27.

16. David Wise, *The Politics of Lying*, p. 254.

17. John Heber, "Nixon Imprint Is Deep at Regulatory Agencies," *New York Times*, 6 May 1973, p. 1.

18. Ibid.

19. Lucia Mouat, "The Regulators," *Christian Science Monitor*, 24 October 1972, p. 9.

20. Lucia Mouat, "How High Should Gas and Electric Rates Be?" *Christian Science Monitor*, 28 October 1972, p. 7.

21. Fellmeth, *Interstate Commerce Ommission*, pp. 1–11.

22. Ibid., pp. 140–54.

23. Ibid.

24. Joseph C. Goulden, *The Superlawyers*, p. 196.

25. Cox, *Nader Report*, pp. 120–22.

26. Robert Engler, *The Politics of Oil*, p. 318.

27. Goulden, *Superlawyers*, p. 182.

28. Engler, *Politics of Oil*, especially p. 70.

29. Ibid., p. 321.

30. Ibid., p. 319; John M. Pfiffner and Robert V. Presthus, *Public Administration*, 5th ed. (New York: Ronald Press Co., 1967), pp. 452–53.

31. Cited in Engler, *Politics of Oil*, p. 325.

32. Ibid.

33. Ibid.

34. Fellmeth, *Interstate Commerce Ommission*, p. 19.

35. Ibid.

36. Cox, *Nader Report*, p. 38.

37. Ibid., p. 82.

38. Jethro K. Lieberman, *How the Government Breaks the Law*, p. 246.

39. Cox, *Nader Report*, pp. 89–90.

40. Goulden, *Superlawyers*, p. 344.

41. Ibid., pp. 340–52.

42. Ibid., p. 214; the remainder, ibid., pp. 209–14.

43. Mouat, "Men Who Patrol Skies," p. 7.

44. Kohlmeier, *The Regulators*, p. 115.

45. Ibid., p. 166.

46. Cox, *Nader Report*, p. 64.

47. John E. Moore, "Recycling the Regulatory Agencies," *Public Administration Review* 32 (July–August 1972): 291–98.

48. Fellmeth, *Interstate Commerce Ommission*, pp. 316–25.

49. Dee Brown, *Bury My Heart at Wounded Knee.*

50. Walker Commission, *Rights in Conflict*, pp. 1–11.

51. Lieberman, *How the Government Breaks the Law*, pp. 79–81.

52. Omar Garrison, *Spy Government*, pp. 109–19.

53. Ibid.

54. "The Open Mail from Congress," *San Francisco Chronicle*, 5 July 1973.

55. Wise, *Politics of Lying*, pp. 117–33.

56. Thomas B. Ross and David Wise, *The U-2 Incident;* and ibid., pp. 33–36.

57. Wise, *Politics of Lying*, pp. 162–78.

58. Ibid.

59. Cited in "The Cambodia Coverup," *San Francisco Chronicle*, 29 July 1972.

60. *Newsweek*, 14 June 1973, p. 28.

61. Ibid.

62. Ibid.

63. Ibid., p. 27.

64. Page Smith, "And Then Came Watergate," *Los Angeles Times*, 11 June 1973.

65. Cited in *Newsweek*, 4 June 1973, p. 18.

66. Walter Ragaber, "Taking Stock and Taking Aim," *New York Times*, 3 June 1973, sec. 4, p. 1.

67. *Newsweek*, 25 June 1973, p. 23.

68. Ibid.

69. Robert J. Donovan, "The Watergate Scandal," *Los Angeles Times*, 12 June 1973.

70. Cited in *Newsweek*, 4 June 1973, p. 18.

71. William Sloan Coffin, Jr., "Not Yet a Good Man," *New York Times*, 19 June 1973, p. 27.

72. Ibid.

73. David Halberstam, "The Worst and the Grayest," *Playboy*, July 1973, p. 151.

74. Ibid.

75. Cited in William A. Bell, "The Cost of Cowardice," in *Inside the System*, ed. Charles Peters and John Rothchild, pp. 169–80.

76. Ibid., p. 170.

77. Ibid., p. 168.

78. Halberstam, "The Worst and the Grayest," p. 151.

79. David Halberstam, *The Best and the Brightest*, p. 505.

80. Ibid., pp. 202–3.

81. R. W. Apple, Jr., "Haldeman the Fierce, Haldeman the Faithful, Haldeman the Fallen," *New York Times Magazine*, 6 May 1973, p. 104.

82. Ibid.

83. Spencer Rich, "Few Tears in the Senate at Downfall of Nixon's Police Guard," *Los Angeles Times*, 29 April 1973.

84. R. W. Apple, Jr., "The Truth Is Forcing Its Way Out," *New York Times*, 10 June 1973, sec. 4, p. 1.

85. Halberstam, *The Best and the Brightest*, p. 41.

86. Ibid., pp. 43–44.

87. Ibid., p. 44.

88. Ibid., pp. 122–23.

89. Ibid., p. 328.

90. Ibid., p. 210.

91. Herbert Scoville, "Are the Plumbers Worse than the Leak?" *New York Times*, 7 June 1973, p. 3.

SELECTED BIBLIOGRAPHY

Apple, R. W., Jr. "Haldeman the Fierce, Haldeman the Faithful, Haldeman the Fallen." *New York Times Magazine,* 6 May 1973, pp. 38–39.

———. "The Truth Is Forcing Its Way Out." *New York Times,* 10 June 1973, sec. 4, p. 1.

Bell, William A. "The Cost of Cowardice," In *Inside the System,* edited by Charles Peters and John Rothchild, pp. 169–80. New York: Praeger Publishers, 1973.

Brown, Dee. *Bury My Heart at Wounded Knee.* New York: Holt, Rinehart & Winston, 1971.

Buckhorn, Robert H. *Nader: The Peoples' Lawyer.* Englewood Cliffs, N.J.: Prentice-Hall, 1972.

Connolly, William E. "The Challenge of Pluralist Theory." In *Bias of Pluralism,* edited by William E. Connolly, pp. 3–4. New York: Atherton Press, 1969.

Cox, Edward F.; Fellmeth, Robert C.; and Schulz, John E. *The Nader Report on the Federal Trade Commission.* New York: Richard W. Baron Publishing Co., 1969.

Engler, Robert. *The Politics of Oil.* Chicago: Phoenix Books, 1961.

Fellmeth, Robert C. *Interstate Commerce Ommission: The Report on the Interstate Commerce Commission and Transportation.* New York: Grossman Publishers, 1970.

Garrison, Omar. *Spy Government.* New York: Lyle Stuart, 1967.

Gellhorn, Walter. *When Americans Complain.* Cambridge, Mass.: Harvard University Press, 1968.

Goulden, Joseph C. *The Superlawyers.* New York: Dell Publishing Co., 1972.

Halberstam, David. *The Best and the Brightest.* New York: Random House, 1972.

———. "The Worst and the Grayest." *Playboy,* July 1973, p. 151.

Kohlmeier, Louis M. *The Regulators.* New York: Harper & Row, 1969.

Lieberman, Jethro K. *How the Government Breaks the Law.* New York: Stein & Day, 1972.

Lowi, Theodore. *The End of Liberalism.* New York: W. W. Norton & Co., 1969.

Moore, John E. "Recycling the Regulatory Agencies." *Public Administration Review* 32 (1972): 291–98.

Mouat, Lucia. "How High Should Gas and Electric Rates Be?" *Christian Science Monitor,* 28 October 1972, p. 7.

———. "The Quiet Men Who Patrol U.S. Skies." *Christian Science Monitor,* 25 October 1972, p. 7.

———. "The Regulators: Their Impact on U.S. Life." *Christian Science Monitor,* 24 October 1972, p. 9.

Rieselbach, Leroy N. *Congressional Politics.* New York: McGraw-Hill, 1973.

Ross, Thomas B., and Wise, David. *The U-2 Incident.* New York: Random House, 1952.

Schwartz, Bernard. *The Professor and the Commissions.* New York: Alfred A. Knopf, 1959.

Walker Commission. *Rights in Conflict.* New York: Bantam Books, 1968.

Wise, David. *The Politics of Lying.* New York: Random House, 1973.

9

CONTROLS OVER THE BUREAUCRACY

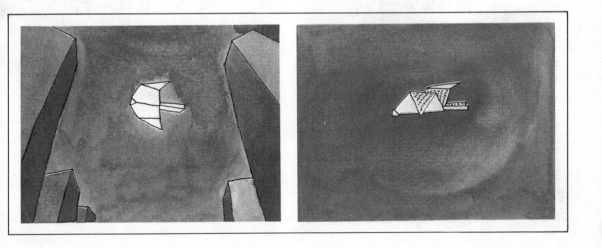

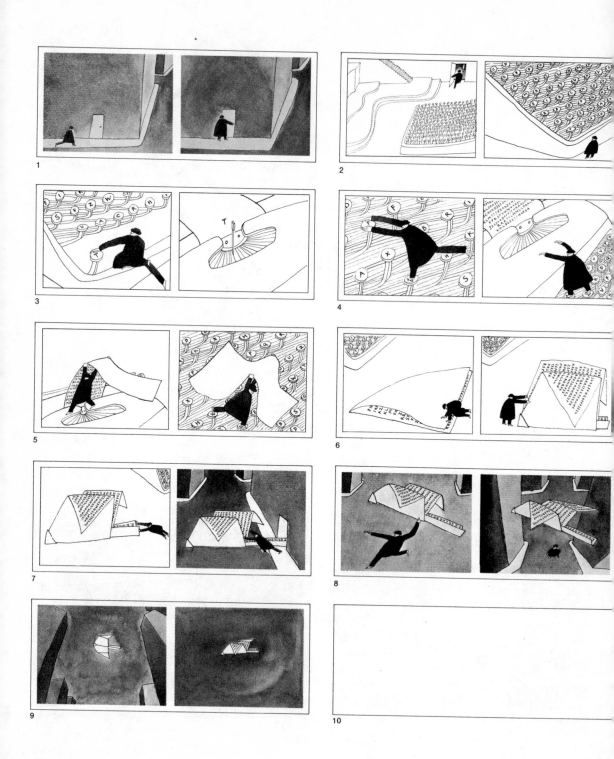

*Feuds between newsmen and government officials had
long been commonplace. . . . Conflict was built in under
the American system of checks and balances—the clash
of the people's fundamental right to know versus the
government's duty to guard secrets that would help the
nation's enemies. In Vietnam the feud reached a degree
of bitterness such as I had never before encountered in
some twenty years of foreign duty. . . . A man from Mars
admitted to official inner circles in both Vietnam and
Washington could have been excused if he got the
impression that the newsmen, as well as the Viet Cong,
were the enemy. . . .*

Managing the News in Vietnam
JOHN MECKLIN

9 It should be emphasized that the majority of American bureaucrats are probably honest, hard-working, unappreciated public servants whose decency is assumed and whose good deeds are quickly forgotten. But as Robert Kennedy once observed in discussing the relationship between civil servants and public individuals exposed to injuries for which there are no legal remedies: "I am not talking . . . about persons who injure others out of selfish or evil motives. I am talking about the injuries which result simply from administrative convenience, injuries which may be done inadvertently by those endeavoring to help—teachers and social workers and urban planners."[1] Britain's great constitutional lawyer, A. C. Dicey, warned that "wherever there is discretion, there is room for arbitrariness."[2] In short, all human institutions contain persons whose motives are less than lofty. The question is how the citizen can be protected against bureaucratic injury, whether it is intended or not.

All bureaucratic societies have sought to provide checks on bureaucratic usurpations. The Soviet Union has its procurators who are supposed to see to it that citizens and administrators alike adhere to the law. In Great Britain, the "question hour" permits members of Parliament an opportunity to seek redress for their constituents in cases involving bureaucratic impropriety. France's Conseil d'État is a highly acclaimed administrative court

341

that has exercised its responsibilities with objectivity, independence, and competence. The Scandinavian countries have had considerable success with the ombudsman. In the United States, the legislature was intended to be the chief check on bureaucratic irresponsibility. This section will discuss the major traditional checks on bureaucracy as well as some of the newer concepts, including the ombudsman, Nader's Raiders, Common Cause, and NOGO-POGO alternatives.

TRADITIONAL CONTROLS

Legislative Control   Arthur MacMahon has noted that "legislative oversight of administration is a familiar and well-grounded assumption of responsible government."[3] In the United States, legislative control is exercised primarily through the power of the purse, control over personnel, investigations, the legislative veto, and organizational control.

Power of the purse. Because few policies or bureaucracies can be maintained without money, the power of the purse—or the ability of the legislature to influence the flow of financial resources to the bureaucracy—is Congress's most important and fundamental instrument of control over the bureaucracy; at the state level it also constitutes the chief control over the executive.[4]

Financial control is exercised through legislative committees and also through the General Accounting Office (GAO). Legislative committees, especially the Appropriations Committee of the House of Representatives, are important to the control process because they are likely to limit or curtail funds for organizations and programs with which they are not in sympathy— hence the powerful inducement for administrators to heed the words and desires of the legislature. Richard Fenno observed in 443 separate case studies that the full House of Representatives accepted 87.4 percent of the Appropriations Committee's recommendations.[5] The GAO was created in 1921 to audit the books of federal agencies and to report its findings to Congress. Its function, as Joseph P. Harris has observed, is to assess the soundness of an agency's accounting and financial system and to appraise its overall efficiency.[6]

Control over personnel. State and national legislatures can influence bureaucracy by their methods of controlling personnel policies. These methods include Senate confirmation of nominations, the congressional power of impeachment, the passage of laws affecting classified services, and the use of indirect pressures.[7]

Unless it perceives a conflict of interest, a lack of qualification, fundamental disagreement over policy, communist sympathies, or personal vendettas, the Senate normally confirms executive nominations. Of 700,000 nominations submitted to Congress by presidents Truman, Eisenhower, and Kennedy, only 12 were withdrawn because of possible Senate opposition. President Johnson had no senate rejections, though he did withdraw some nominations.[8]

More recently, however, the Senate has failed to confirm a number of nominations. The nomination of John Knowles as assistant secretary of Health, Education and Welfare was blocked because the American Medical Association regarded him as too liberal on the issue of public medicine. President Nixon's 1973 appointment of Robert H. Morris, formerly a lawyer for Standard Oil of California, to the Federal Power Commission was not approved. In July 1973 the Senate Foreign Relations Committee refused to confirm Nixon's appointment of G. McMurtrie Godley, former ambassador to Laos, as assistant secretary of state for the Far East because of the appointee's previous connections with Vietnam policy.

Congress also has the power to impeach the executive branch, although this has been attempted only twice in American history and in both cases the necessary two-thirds majority vote was lacking. All states except Oregon can impeach a governor, but this, too, has happened only four times in a century.[9]

Congress exercises a direct influence over various classified services by means of laws affecting internal personnel policy, the outside activities of bureaucrats, and bureaucratic growth, as well as by means of several committees that watch over the classified services. Internal personnel policy is affected by the passage of laws dealing with bargaining rights, fringe benefits, special allowances, leaves of absence, and so forth. Congressional attempts to control the outside activities of bureaucrats include the Hatch Act (1939), which seeks to limit partisan political involvement, and House Un-American Activities Committee investigations to ferret out subversives in government.

The Jensen Amendment of the early 1950s sought to limit bureaucratic growth, and the Whitten Amendment of 1950 to limit the number of full-time federal employees, although the net effect of both was only to increase the number of temporary employees in government.[10] In addition, several committees, notably those dealing with the civil services, maintain a close watch over the classified services.

Legislatures can also influence bureaucratic personnel policies indirectly. As a result of negative congressional reports and of "passing the word" to key decision makers, thousands of bureaucrats have been removed, reclassified, hired, and fired. The motives behind these actions are normally both positive and benign.[11]

Investigations. The objective of legislative investigations is to gather information on the basis of which to pass or bar future legislation. Either by a standing committee or by special committees, Congress and state legislatures are empowered to investigate any part of government at will—a powerful check with which bureaucrats must contend as they pursue their activities.

The first major congressional investigation centered on the failure of Major General Arthur St. Clair's expedition against the northwestern Indians in 1792. More famous investigations in American history include the Joint Committee on the Conduct of the Civil War (1861); Senator Harry Truman's inquiry into defense mobilization and efficiency during World War II; Senator Estes Kefauver's committee studying the drug industry during the 1950s; the House Un-American Activities Committee (HUAC) investigations in the 1940s and 1950s; Senator Joseph McCarthy's probe of Communists in government in the early 1950s; and most recently Senator Sam Ervin's investigation of presidential campaign practices.

Senator Truman's committee was fair and judicious and saved the public billions of dollars. The efforts of HUAC and McCarthy were criticized by many as witch hunts and personal vendettas that often violated the civil liberties of witnesses. Senator Kefauver's efforts resulted in useful new legislation, although they arose out of his campaign for national office. There can be no question that the Ervin committee's revelations were of monumental significance.

Legislative veto. The legislative veto permits Congress and its committees to block executive actions and requires that an executive agency submit to a committee or subcommittee within a specific period—usually thirty, forty-five, or sixty days—before acting on certain matters. These vetoes have appeared on the statute books since 1920. By the time of the Eighty-ninth Congress (1965–66), 19 percent of the statutes enacted into law contained legislative vetoes dealing with such matters as control of real property, the transfer of public buildings, and stockpiling. Many presidents, particularly Lyndon Johnson, have vigorously opposed legislative vetoes on the grounds that they impede the prerogatives of the chief executive.[12]

Organizational control. Legislators have the power, with or without executive consent, to create or abolish departments and agencies, to specify their internal structures, and to insist on or to refuse administrative changes. Since 1945, Congress has refused one-third of all presidential reorganization requests, including President Kennedy's attempt to create a Department of Urban Affairs,[13] while the establishment of an Assistant Secretary for the U.S. Fish and Wildlife Service was done against executive opposition.

Congress has frequently refused presidential requests for administrative reform, though it will sometimes insist on administrative changes to facilitate congressional control, as in 1952 when the passport and visa offices of the State Department were transferred to the Bureau of Security and

Consular Affairs. Some executive-legislative organizational goals are written into law, such as the supposed independence of the regulatory agencies from the executive branch. Occasionally agencies are required to exchange data with one another; others are required to consult with advisers and committees established by law. All these regulations are designed to enhance legislative control over bureaucracy.[14]

How effective are these tools in controlling bureaucracy? "If I were grading the legislature," said a former Pennsylvania state legislator and assistant to Governor Milton J. Shapp, "I would give them a B-minus on constituent homework; a C-plus on the quality of legislation, and a D on legislative oversight."[15] According to Stephen K. Bailey, a generation of political scientists has virtually agreed that Congress has performed the task of legislative oversight badly.[16] This failure can be attributed to a lack of commitment, technical expertise, necessary information, and time on the part of individual legislators, to "whirlpools of influence," and to the fragmentary character of the legislative process.

Effectiveness of Legislative Control

A 1970 study of the relationship of twenty-three congressmen to the federal regulatory agencies revealed a general lack of commitment to the task of legislative oversight and a sense of greater rewards to be found in constituent responsibilities.[17] As one congressman put it, "There is always an election around the corner, and what we do between times has to have something in it that we can sell back home."[18] Among others, Senator John J. Sparkman of Alabama was troubled by the question of how legislators can be motivated to do tedious, nonglamorous work.[19]

Congressmen see agencies as impenetrable mazes and the inexpert efforts of lay legislators as exercises in futility. Most congressmen are trained in the law and lack specialized technical expertise in other fields. As one remarked: "The regulatory agencies are pretty technical. Most of us don't know enough about it to even begin to ask intelligent questions."[20] In addition, and not only because facts pertaining to defense are frequently withheld from it by the executive branch, Congress often lacks the information to do its job properly. Historian Henry S. Commager has asked why Ralph Nader seems to know more than Congress about the problems facing the United States.[21]

Other factors inhibit effective legislative oversight as well. Legislators often develop rewarding relationships which they prefer not to endanger by the exercise of energetic oversight. Congressmen from oil-producing states, for example, will not press for a zealous Federal Power Commission. A legislator who finds it more rewarding in terms of patronage and projects for his own district to side with the president or governor will not want to do anything to embarrass the executive's administration or to offend strong economic interests that might hurt him politically. These relationships are what Ernest S. Griffith has referred to as "whirlpools of influence.[22]

John Bibby's study of the Senate Committee on Banking and Currency stressed that the political orientation of the committee chairman strongly influences the committee's activity. If the chairman is policy oriented, he and the committee will tend to avoid legislative oversight. If he is service oriented, he will permit legislative oversight if his colleagues are interested.[23] Congressmen may see legislative oversight as politically advantageous, of course. Service on the Ervin committee, for example, has undoubtedly enhanced the careers of several of its members.

Even when legislative attention is given to administrative oversight, the efforts are (in Emmette Redford's words) often "spotty, spasmodic, and sometimes cursory."[24] Examining three thousand pages of a congressional committee analysis of the 1950 defense budget, Warner Schilling found the emphasis centered on financial trivia with little information concerning policy alternatives not already covered by the press.[25] In his study of the Department of Health, Education and Welfare, Ira Sharkansky suggests that congressional oversight stresses that which is believed to be in the public eye. The House Armed Services Committee, for another example, tends to emphasize real estate transactions instead of focusing on the effectiveness of military policy decisions.[26]

In addition, Congress tends to accept the findings of its committees without serious review or criticism. For more than twenty years it has treated the federal budget in a piecemeal fashion, failing to examine revenue and expenditures in a broad perspective—a disjointed procedure (characteristic of most aspects of congressional legislation) that has made it impossible to fix responsibility for budget failures.[27] Senator William Brock of Tennessee sums up the problem by asking: "Why don't we treat these problems in the context of the whole . . . ? We simply can't have a housing policy without considering transportation in the urban community. Why not deal with the problem of the urban community? Why not deal with the problem of the human being?"[28]

In addition to legislative oversight, the courts, party influence, the press, public opinion, and professional ethics have all exercised traditional, if imperfect, control over the bureaucracy. Theoretically, the courts can review any decision made by the bureaucracy or the chief executive. The due process clauses of the Fifth and Fourteenth amendments have been cited to nullify many administrative acts. In 1952 the Supreme Court declared that President Truman had seized the steel mills illegally and ordered that they be returned to private management. In 1970 the Supreme Court refused to permit the attorney general to prevent publication of the *Pentagon*

Papers. Thus the courts have been effective instruments in checking administrative abuses, but court battles are often long, expensive procedures. It cost Daniel Ellsberg more than $1 million, for example, to contest the *Pentagon Papers* case.

The influence of political parties, the press, and public opinion has been powerful but sporadic. The 1952 Republican presidential campaign emphasized the corruption in President Truman's administration and was undoubtedly responsible in part for the subsequent election of President Eisenhower. The persistent efforts of the *Washington Post* to expose the Watergate affair showed the press at its best, but such penetrating investigative reporting is rare. Although Senator George McGovern tried to arouse public opinion in reaction to Watergate and the ill-conceived Soviet grain deal of 1971, the public overwhelmingly ignored him.

The hope that professional ethics will serve as an internal check, encouraging honesty and efficiency among public servants and professionals, is naive. Law is the major profession of many of the leading public administrators of this country, but Watergate has caused many to wonder about the nature and efficacy of the American Bar Association's code of ethics. Ralph Nader has observed: "The best lawyers should be spending their time on the great problems—on water and air pollution, on racial justice, on poverty and juvenile delinquency . . . but they are not. They are spending their time defending Geritol, Rice Krispies and oil import quotas."[29] Most professional organizations tend to support the status quo. Thus the AMA strenuously opposed Medicare even though its final passage would benefit millions of Americans.

SOME NEW ALTERNATIVES

The ombudsman. In most cases, an ombudsman is a legal officer appointed by, and responsible to, the national parliament for the purpose of supervising the public service and its employees. His primary concern is with the observance of national laws, but his central preoccupation is the protection of citizens' liberties and rights.

Originating in Sweden in 1809, the office of ombudsman was established in Finland in 1919, in Denmark in 1955, and for the armed services in West Germany the same year; subsequently, Norway, New Zealand, Israel, Canada, and Tanzania borrowed the concept in varying forms. Hawaii was the first state in the U.S. to adopt the office in 1967, followed in the same year by New York's Nassau County and the city of Buffalo. The ombudsman has been institutionalized on several of the nation's university campuses, as well as within the attorney general's office in the state of Wisconsin.

The utility of the ombudsman can perhaps best be illustrated by three cases from the experience of Alfred Bexlius, Sweden's ombudsman for civil matters.[30] In one case, an unfaithful wife complained to the police of mistreatment by her husband, a habitual drunkard. On orders of the police physician, the man was sent to a mental hospital where he was held for eight months. On receipt of his complaint, the ombudsman took the case to Sweden's highest medical board for advice, and the board decided that there were insufficient medical grounds for the man to have been detained in a mental hospital against his will. Instead, he should have been sent to a hospital for alcoholics, where he would have been detained no longer than three or four months. Although the ombudsman did not find enough evidence to prosecute the police physician, he did request that the government grant compensation to the aggrieved man.

In a 1961 case, the ombudsman learned that the president of a private Swedish airline had arranged a good will trip from Sweden to Paris and that among his guests were the director of the Civil Aviation Inspectorate and his wife. Although the director, who had been invited because of his official position, had requested and received permission from his superior, the Director General of the National Board of Civil Aviation, the ombudsman ruled that he should not have accepted because his participation in the trip impaired public confidence in his official role. Both men were prosecuted and fined, and the action was upheld by the Swedish Supreme Court.

For a final example, a Swedish court wrongly ordered a man who was under arrest to pay the cost of his return flight from the United States to Sweden. In reviewing this man's complaint about another aspect of the case, the ombudsman inadvertently discovered the error. The judge could not be faulted as the law was obscure on this point. Nevertheless, the ombudsman requested that the man be reimbursed for the cost of the involuntary trip. These cases are not earthshaking, but to the aggrieved parties they were very real and important. In each case, the redress awarded helped to uphold justice as well as the sense that bureaucracy can be bent to human needs.

The need for some type of ombudsman in this country has long been recognized; indeed, several versions already exist. In almost every major city, newspapers or radio and television stations offer "activist" programs that air citizens' complaints. The *Buffalo Evening News,* for example, ran a feature entitled "Newspower" that received 313 complaints in six months—a demonstration of public concern that gave impetus to the creation of an ombudsman in that city.[31] Former Mayor John Lindsay of New York City created "little city halls" in the boroughs to act as ombudsmen. For decades the U.S. Army has had its inspector general, which, although an imperfect instrument, permits soldiers to bypass their superiors in complaining of abuses.

Nevertheless, adopting the ombudsman concept in its more formal manifestations would pose many problems in this country, which is neither as small nor as homogeneous as those nations in which the office has so far proved effective. In other nations the ombudsman is a totally independent agent who has access to all relevant documents and deliberations; but his ability to remedy grievances depends not only on his own investigatory power but also on the power of public opinion to compel an erring official to alter his course.

In the United States, the president can still order the bureaucracy to withhold important, or even potentially important, information under the doctrine of executive privilege. The 1967 Freedom of Information Act was supposed to facilitate access to bureaucratic activities, but, as the Nader studies show, it has not been overwhelmingly successful in this regard. In addition, American ombudsmen might be hindered by the American concept of separation of powers. New York City's attempt to create this office foundered on the jealousy between a Republican mayor and a Democratic city council, a conflict typical in American politics.

Another major roadblock to the adoption of this office is that many American legislators believe that acting as ombudsmen is a major part of their own job and a key factor in their electoral success. Former Senator Joseph Clark of Pennsylvania, who estimated that he received between one thousand and ten thousand letters per week, felt that answering his mail and other routine duties is what impressed constituents, not speeches on the great issues of the day.[32] A recent study revealed that 75 percent of all congressmen felt that interceding with the bureaucracy on behalf of their constituents was the most time-consuming aspect of their work.[33]

The office of ombudsman offers a number of important advantages over our traditional means of controlling bureaucracy. Unlike the courts, the ombudsman offers free service to citizens who wish to use him. Unlike legislators, he would be politically neutral. Relieving the burden on legislators, he would bring greater expertise to individual problems and complaints. Ideally, bureaucrats would be protected against unjust accusations; public servants would be more responsive to client wishes, knowing that the ombudsman was waiting in the wings; and public confidence in the public service would improve with the knowledge that redress of grievances is possible.

The office of ombudsman need not proliferate a swollen and costly bureaucracy of its own. The New Zealand ombudsman has only one assistant and costs the nation only $30,000 per year. The Government Accounting Office has already been cited as a constitutional precedent for the creation of an ombudsman.[34] Donald Rowat has estimated that the United States could establish an operational ombudsman with a staff of one hundred persons in regional offices around the country.[35]

The NOGO-POGO alternative. After an extensive study of bureaucratic abuses, Theodore Becker rejected the ombudsman on the grounds that his powers are too limited to initiate investigations of high government officials. Becker is suspicious of a pseudodemocratic office staffed by nonelected people and regards the ombudsman as an aristocrat in democratic clothing who will seduce the American people into thinking that they are in the hands of a compassionate surrogate government.

Becker urges two paths of action. First, we must replace the obsolete, inadequate laws now on the books and enact strict new laws to prevent governmental lawlessness. Second, he believes that we need a comprehensive antigovernment or countergovernment resembling the loyal opposition, or shadow government, in Britain. Becker's proposed "Negative Ortho-Government" (NOGO) would monitor the positive policy-making government (POGO), or the incumbents. NOGO would be elected by the people. A counterjudiciary would also be elected but would serve for life. Elections would present candidates for both governments and would emphasize both the positive and negative actions of incumbents. Although these proposals sound somewhat impractical, Becker reminds us that it takes a diamond to cut a diamon.[36]

Ralph Nader and company. Ralph Nader, one of the most controversial and enigmatic forces to emerge in American public life in several decades, is the first-generation offspring of Lebanese parents who felt a deep obligation to better American society. Not surprisingly, he was an early champion of many causes. While still an undergraduate at Princeton and years before the publication of Rachel Carson's *Silent Spring,* he tried to publicize the dangers of DDT. During his years at Harvard Law School in the early 1960s, he championed the cause of the American Indian, an issue that did not gain national attention until the Wounded Knee episode of 1973.

Nader first achieved public attention with the publication of *Unsafe at Any Speed,* a critical scrutiny of General Motors's compact automobile, Corvair. For the first time, someone said plainly that automobiles were dangerous and that auto manufacturers had a responsibility to protect the people who buy them by providing safer designs and equipment. The book resulted in a Senate investigation of auto manufacturing chaired by Senator Abraham Ribicoff of Connecticut. Nader's appearance before the committee and the fact that his book substantiated a number of fatal accidents involving GM cars caused the company to hire a private detective to investigate his life and social activities with the object of destroying his credibility. This bit of spying cost General Motors $425,000, which Nader later collected in a violation of privacy suit.

What does Nader hope to achieve? In opening his appeal to Public Citizen, an organization to support his activities, he argued:

> It is abundantly clear that our institutions, public and private, are not performing their proper functions and are wasting resources, concentrating power, and serving special interests at the expense of voiceless citizens and consumers. . . . A way must be found for the individual citizen to provide an impact on government agencies and corporate board rooms. Government agencies often serve as protectors of the industries they are supposed to regulate. Bureaucrats cannot easily overcome the pressure brought by the hundreds of special interests in Washington and state capitols. A primary goal of our work is to build countervailing forces on behalf of citizens who do not become jaded, bureaucratized or co-opted.[37]

Nader has developed a number of citizen organizations that aim at providing counterweights to bureaucratic irresponsibility. One of the most famous is Nader's Raiders, whose first team was assembled during the summer of 1968 and was heavily staffed by Ivy League bluebloods, including William Howard Taft IV from the Yale-Harvard law schools and Nixon's future son-in-law, Edward Cox, from the Princeton-Harvard law schools. The Raiders' first target was the FTC. The students earned between $200 and $1,000 for a ten-week period and worked from twelve to sixteen hours a day. One student described his work as the equivalent of attempting to do a Ph.D. dissertation in ten weeks.[38]

In 1969 Nader launched his Center for the Study of Responsive Law, whose employees received between $10,000 and $15,000 per year. During 1969–71 the center produced nineteen major reports covering such topics as the ICC and FCC, mining in West Virginia, and the corporate activities of E. I. duPont de Nemours in Delaware. In 1972 the center assembled 500 students to evaluate the voting records of members of Congress and also published *Who Runs Congress?* At various stages of completion in 1972 were studies of the relationship to the government of the National Academy of Sciences, the pulp and paper industry in Maine, and the use of think tanks by the federal government. Nader places great emphasis on students, and, under his aegis student fees financed citizen action groups organized by students at the universities of Minnesota and Oregon. By 1972 there were ten Nader-run organizations, including the Center for Auto Safety and the Clearinghouse for Professional Responsibility.

Nader's impact has been considerable. He is personally, or largely, responsible for the passage through Congress of a number of major bills, including the Natural Gas Pipeline Safety Act, the National Wholesome Poultry Products Act, the Wholesome Meat Act, the Mine Health and Safety Act, and the Federal Highway Safety Act, and his influence has had a far-reaching effect on the regulatory agencies as well. Following the Nader report on the Federal Trade Commission, the "old gray lady" was transformed into a relatively dynamic organization. Millions of automobiles have been recalled as a result of Nader's influence and activity on behalf of automotive safety. In 1973, as previously noted, Robert H. Morris's appointment to the Federal Power Commission was refused Senate confirmation because it was doubted that a former lawyer for Standard Oil of California could be a sincere, impartial consumer advocate. In 1973, too, the Consumer Product Safety Commission was created to ensure the safety of millions of products.

Common Cause. In 1970, John W. Gardner, former secretary of the Department of Health, Education and Welfare, launched an organization called Common Cause, citing three basic reasons why institutions and societies lose their adaptability.

> First, the dominant groups weave an impenetrable web of procedure, law and social structure to preserve their power and in doing so, cut themselves off from their sources of rejuvenation, uncomfortable challenges, and dissent. Second, the forces of inertia, habit and custom elevate existing procedures to inviolable traditions. . . . Meeting current challenges becomes less important than preserving familiar arrangements. Third, a society loses motivation, conviction, confidence, and morale that characterized it in its days of vitality. It no longer believes in anything, least of all itself. The vision fades. The ideal fails.[39]

Common Cause emphasizes access, responsiveness, and accountability —factors sorely needed if our bureaucracies are to be made responsible to those whom they serve. Gardner emphasizes the need for accountability because, after elections, lobbyists (the representatives of special interests) don't pack up and go home. Gardner wants Common Cause to monitor the activities of legislatures and bureaucracies and to lobby for laws that will open up the system.[40] He is concerned that legislatures, regulatory agencies, and governmental agencies often make decisions in secret. Common Cause hopes to break this wall of secrecy.[41]

Gardner is firmly committed to America's political system but admits that interest-group liberalism has failed. The clash of interest groups over problems of urban blight and air and water pollution has not served the public interest. By balloting its members, Common Cause would determine the issues most vital to the public interest and would then lobby for them. Common Cause would not hold a monopoly on these activities, but could nevertheless make a significant contribution. By 1972 the organization, claiming almost a quarter-million members, had helped to defeat the Supersonic Transport and had successfully lobbied for opening up the congressional seniority system and for a more effective campaign spending law.[42]

The Common Cause suit against the Committee to Re-elect the President, which was in violation of that law, was an important contribution to the Watergate revelations.

Public interest law. Nader's activities have generated a new public interest (*pro bono*) law greatly influencing both the American legal profession and the nation's bureaucracy. Many young lawyers are no longer interested in "whoring for the corporations" but devote all or part of their energies to public interest law. Several leading Washington law firms permit their attorneys to devote part of their time to *pro bono* law. Examples: Richard Copaker, a young associate of Covington and Burling, fought to stop the U.S. Navy from using the Puerto Rican island of Culebra as a naval gunnery range; public interest lawyer Benny Kass sued American Airlines for deceptive advertising; Bruce Montgomery of Arnold and Porter led the fight against the Alaska pipeline; Charles Halpern of the Center for Law and Social Policy fought the Alaska pipeline and the use of DDT and insecticides; and Joseph Rush, a private labor attorney, pressed the Labor Department and Congress to investigate the murders of United Mine Workers leader Joseph Yablonski and his wife and daughter.[43] The *pro bono* work of Wilmer, Cutler, and Pickering included contesting high utility rate charges to the poor in Appalachia, assisting complaints of military abuses, and combating the erection of freeways that threatened scenic sections of Memphis and New Orleans.[44]

After graduating from the Columbia University Law School in 1965, John Benzhaf led the fight for equal time against cigarette smoking, his efforts resulting in $175 million in free time to counteract cigarette commercials. As a professor at the George Washington University School of Law, he has encouraged his students to get the Federal Trade Commission to prevent Campbell from selling mislabeled soup, to prosecute Firestone for deceptive tire advertising, to force oil companies to post octane ratings and to disclose the truth about saturates.

Public interest law is not confined to Washington, D.C. One of the few genuine successes of the aborted War on Poverty was its legal service program, parts of which have survived in various regions of the country in the form of privately organized store-front law firms funded by VISTA. One such store-front located in San Francisco's poverty-ridden Mission District was run by two young law school graduates whose cases typically involved drugs, welfare hassles, evictions, and utility cutoffs. Both planned to remain in public interest law after their tour with VISTA was completed.[45]

Although public interest law has achieved significant gains and offers a genuine hope for controlling American bureaucracy, certain caveats must be made. Ralph Nader and company are muckrakers in the best American tradition, but muckrakers come and go in our history (the Progressive muckrakers died with World War I and the Roaring Twenties). Some of Nader's reports, such as those dealing with old age convalescent homes and with land use in California, have been criticized as superficial and inaccurate. In addition, Nader relies heavily on the young who are willing to work long hours for little pay. But youthful zeal tends to flag in time, and tomorrow's young people may be less idealistic than those of today. Finally, in contrast to corporations, which have large, full-time, well-paid staffs, most of Nader's efforts are not well financed. Thus, public interest is still a perhaps; not so the legal apparatus of America's corporations and public bureaucracies.

In summary, socialism and nationalization are anathema to most Americans. Alone among the modern industrialized nations, we have sought to regulate rather than to nationalize public utilities by establishing supposedly expert, independent regulatory agencies to protect consumer interests in such areas as railroads, airlines, and telecommunications. In too many cases, however, the regulatory agencies have succumbed to the industries they are supposed to regulate. Their expertise has been compromised by partisan politics and by presidential and congressional meddling. Many of their procedures are clandestine, and their few good efforts are often neutralized by the vast legal and financial resources at the disposal of the regulated industries.

Bureaucratic abuses have arisen from the fact that our bureaucracies have been manned by many individuals more interested in advancing their own causes and careers, or those of their superiors or agencies, than in observing democratic precepts. Clearly, America needs techniques to control its bureaucracies. Traditionally we have relied on legislative oversight, political parties, the courts, public opinion, the press, and professional ethics to prevent abuses; but these means are limited and obviously have not prevented abuses from occurring, and their failure has caused students of public administration to examine some of the alternatives discussed in this chapter. The chapter that follows will describe some of the contemporary trends in public administration, including comparative and developmental administration, the New Public Administration, and semi- and nonbureaucratic organizations. The book ends with a review of some of the major themes discussed throughout the preceding chapters.

NOTES

1. Cited in Walter Gellhorn, *When Americans Complain,* p. 209.

2. Cited in D. C. Rowat, "Ombudsman for North America?" *Public Administration Review* 24 (December 1964): 231.

3. Arthur MacMahon, "Congressional Oversight of Administration," *Political Science Quarterly* 63 (March 1973): 161–90.

4. Bell Zeller, ed., *American State Legislatures*, p. 174.

5. Richard Fenno, "The House Appropriations Committee," *American Political Science Review* 56 (June 1962): 323.

6. Joseph P. Harris, *Congressional Control of Administration*, p. 155.

7. Stephen K. Bailey, *Congress in the Seventies*, p. 89.

8. Ibid., p. 90.

9. Coleman B. Ransone, Jr., *The Office of the Governor in the United States* (Tuscaloosa: University of Alabama Press, 1965), p. 370.

10. Leroy N. Rieselbach, *Congressional Politics*, pp. 309–10.

11. Bailey, *Congress in the Seventies*, p. 42.

12. John S. Saloma, III, *Congress and the New Politics*, p. 139.

13. Bailey, *Congress in the Seventies*, p. 92.

14. Rieselbach, *Congressional Politics*, pp. 300–310.

15. Cited in William J. Keefe and Morris S. Ogul, *The American Legislative Process*, p. 475.

16. Bailey, *Congress in the Seventies*, p. 87.

17. Seymour Scher, "Conditions for Legislative Control," in *The Congressional System*, ed. Leroy N. Rieselbach, pp. 389–411.

18. Ibid., p. 395.

19. Saloma, *Congress and the New Politics*, p. 153.

20. Scher, "Conditions for Legislative Control," p. 396.

21. Taylor Branch, "Profiles in Caution," *Harper's*, July 1973, p. 68.

22. Rieselbach, *Congressional Politics*, p. 298.

23. John F. Bibby, "Committee Characteristics and Legislative Oversight," *Midwest Journal of Political Science* 5 (1966): 305–24.

24. Emette S. Redford, "A Case Analysis of Congressional Activity," *Journal of Politics* 122 (1960): 258.

25. Warner Schilling, Paul Y. Hammond, and Glenn H. Snyder, *Strategy, Politics and Defense Budgets*, p. 62.

26. Ira Sharkansky, "An Appropriations Committee and Its Client Agencies," *American Political Science Review* 59 (September 1965): 622–28.

27. Lewis A. Dexter, "Congress and the Making of Military Policy," in *New Perspectives on the House of Representatives*, ed. Robert L. Peabody and Nelson W. Polsby, pp. 305–324.

28. Branch, "Profiles in Caution," p. 69.

29. Robert H. Buckhorn, *Nader*, p. 302.

30. These cases are taken from Albert H. Rosenthal, "The Ombudsman," *Public Administration Review* 24 (December 1964): 227.

31. William H. Argas and Milton Kaplan, "The Ombudsman and Local Government," in *Ombudsman for American Government*, ed. Stanley V. Anderson, pp. 101–35.

32. Gellhorn, *When Americans Complain*, p. 75.

33. Ibid., p. 157.

34. William B. Gwyn, "Transferring the Ombudsman," in Anderson, *Ombudsman for American Government*, pp. 42–92.

35. Rowat, "Ombudsman for North America?" p. 232.

36. Theodore Becker, *Government Anarchy and the POGO-NOGO Alternative*, pp. 231–44.

37. Buckhorn, *Nader*, pp. 154–55.

38. Ibid., pp. 88–89.

39. John W. Gardner, *In Common Cause*, p. 99.

40. Ibid., pp. 19–20.

41. Ibid., p. 81.

42. *Common Cause Report from Washington* 3, no. 2 (December 1972): 9.

43. Goulden, *The Superlawyers*, pp. 353–55.

44. Ibid., p. 362.

45. Mildred Hamilton, "Legal Team Goes to Bat for the Poor," *San Francisco Chronicle*, 15 July 1973.

SELECTED BIBLIOGRAPHY

Anderson, Stanley V., ed. *Ombudsman for American Government*. Englewood Cliffs, N.J.: Prentice-Hall, 1969.

Argas, William H., and Kaplan, Milton. "Ombudsman and Local Government." In *Ombudsman for American Government*, edited by Stanley V. Anderson, pp. 101–35. Englewood Cliffs, N.J.: Prentice-Hall, 1969.

Bailey, Stephen K. *Congress in the Seventies*. New York: St. Martin's Press, 1970.

Becker, Theodore. *Government Anarchy and the POGO-NOGO Alternative*. New York: Stein & Day, 1972.

Bibby, John F. "Committee Characteristics and Legislative Oversight." *Midwest Journal of Political Science* 5 (1966): 305–24.

Branch, Taylor. "Profiles in Caution." *Harper's*, July 1973, p. 69.

Buckhorn, Robert H. *Nader: The Peoples' Lawyer*. Englewood Cliffs, N.J.: Prentice-Hall, 1972.

Dexter, Lewis A. "Congress and the Making of Military Policy." In *New Perspectives on the House of Representatives*, edited by Robert L. Peabody and Nelson W. Polsby, pp. 305–24. Chicago: Rand McNally & Co., 1963.

Fenno, Richard. "The House Appropriations Committee." *American Political Science Review* 56 (1962): 323.

Gardner, John W. *In Common Cause*. New York: W. W. Norton & Co., 1972.

Gellhorn, Walter. *When Americans Complain*. Cambridge, Mass.: Harvard University Press, 1968.

Goulden, Joseph C. *The Superlawyers*. New York: Dell Publishing Co., 1972.

Harris, Joseph P. *Congressional Control of Administration*. New York: Doubleday & Co., 1964.

Keefe, William J., and Ogul, Morris S. *The American Legislative Process*, 3d ed. Englewood Cliffs, N.J.: Prentice-Hall, 1973.

MacMahon, Arthur. "Congressional Oversight of Administration: The Power of the Purse." *Political Science Quarterly* 63 (1973): 161–90.

Redford, Emette S. "A Case Analysis of Congressional Activity: Civil Aviation." *Journal of Politics* 122 (1960): 258.

Rieselbach, Leroy N. *Congressional Politics*. New York: McGraw-Hill, 1973.

Rosenthal, Albert H. "The Ombudsman: Swedish Grievance Man." *Public Administration Review* 24 (1964): 226–33.

Rowat, D. C. "Ombudsman for North America?" *Public Administration Review* 24 (1964): 226–33.

Saloma, John S., III. *Congress and the New Politics.* Boston: Little, Brown & Co., 1969.

Scher, Seymour. "Conditions for Legislative Control." In *The Congressional System,* edited by Leroy N. Rieselbach, pp. 389–411. Belmont, Calif.: Wadsworth Publishing Co., 1970.

Schilling, Warner; Hammond, Paul Y.; Snyder, Glenn H. *Strategy, Politics and Defense Budgets.* New York: Columbia University Press, 1962.

Schwartz, Benjamin A. "Congressional Ombudsman Is Feasible." *American Bar Association Journal* 56 (1970): 57–59.

Sharkansky, Ira. "An Appropriations Committee and its Client Agencies." *American Political Science Review* 59 (1965): 622–28.

Sweig, Franklin M. "The Social Worker as Legislative Ombudsman." *Social Work,* 14 January 1969, pp. 25–33.

Zeller, Bell, ed. *American State Legislatures.* New York: Thomas Y. Crowell Co., 1954.

CON-
TEMPORARY
TRENDS

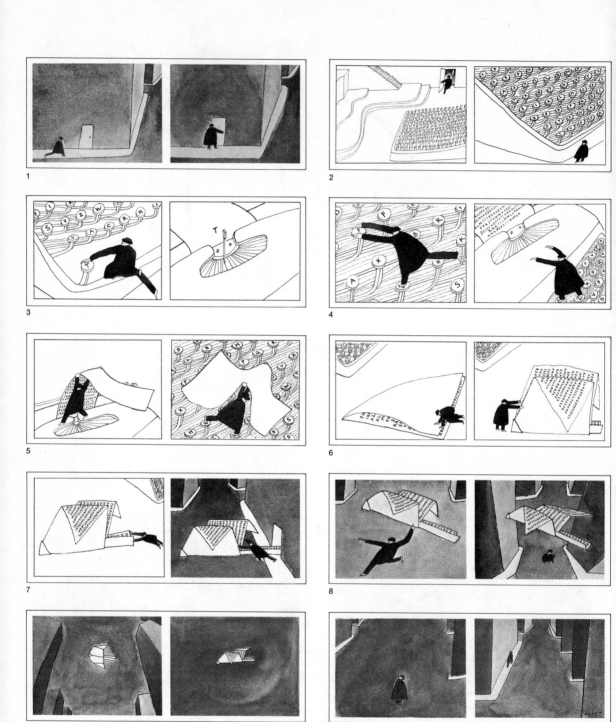

1

2

3

4

5

6

7

8

9

10

10 Both the theory and practice of public administration are undergoing close scrutiny and substantial change at the present time. In the hope of reforming American administrative practices, much serious thought, pragmatic as well as speculative, is being given to identifying the various roles and types of bureaucracies in the United States and elsewhere in the world. The pursuit of social equity, especially, is a major concern of, and a point of departure for, those who are exploring the meaning and implications of the New Public Administration,[1] whose preoccupations range from questions of moral and ethical probity to matters of personnel administration, collective bargaining, employee participation in the making and carrying out of policy, and the goals of the budgetary process.

This chapter begins with an examination of a number of administrative subfields that have influenced the theory and practice of American public administration. The second section explores the meaning and significance of social equity and the New Public Administration. The chapter, and the book, concludes with a discussion of alternatives to traditional bureaucratic organization and a speculation about possible future trends.

PUBLIC ADMINISTRATION AND THE WORLD

Comparative Public Administration

American public administration has long suffered from culture boundedness; the occasional examination of other systems has usually been confined to those of a few nations in Western Europe. But the radical alteration of America's role in world politics during the post–World War II period caused a number of scholars, led by Robert Dahl, to deplore the absence of a universal administrative science and to complain that the discipline as then constituted was parochial, formal, and legalistic.[2]

After World War II, scores of nations with weak and primitive economies would soon be free of American, Belgian, British, French, Italian, and Portuguese colonial rule. Whether they would embrace liberal democracy or some form of dictatorial rule would depend in part on how well their public bureaucracies enabled them to cope with the challenges of modernization and technological development. It was hoped that a science of comparative public administration would provide insights into such problems and yield some useful hypotheses about administrative behavior in general.[3]

Comparative public administration is a method that ". . . indicates differences in form and process within varying contexts; identifies the range across which administrative phenomena vary; and demonstrates the patterns whereby certain features of administrative systems tend to occur together." Two important thinkers in this field are Ferrel Heady and Fred Riggs.

In attempting to develop a classification scheme or typology for comparative public administration, Ferrel Heady addressed himself to three central questions.[4] First, what major characteristics distinguish the composition, hierarchical patterns, and behavioral patterns of bureaucracies? Second, to what extent are bureaucracies multipurpose organizations—i.e., making as well as administering policy? Third, what, and how effective, are the major methods of those organizations, such as legislatures, that attempt to control bureaucracies? Heady concluded that all bureaucracies fall into the following categories: traditional autocratic, bureaucratic elite, polyarchical competitive, dominant party semicompetitive, mobilization, and communist totalitarian.[5]

In traditional autocratic systems, the ruling elite is drawn from families having monarchic or autocratic status. The civil and military bureaucracy is the instrument of the elite, who rely on it to make changes they want and to prevent those they do not. There is little economic progress because the political elite has little interest in it, and the system tends therefore to change slowly if at all. Ethiopia, under Haile Selassie, and Iran are good examples of traditional autocratic systems, but many nations in the Near East and North Africa also fit the pattern.

Bureaucratic elite systems are those in which traditional elites have been displaced by civil or military career officials. Modernizing goals are articulated by this elite though not necessarily shared by the general population. Political parties and participation are not highly developed. Countries that fall into this category include Thailand, Nicaragua, South Korea, Iraq, Indonesia, Syria, Guatemala, and Paraguay.

In polyarchical competitive systems, the prefix *poly* denotes a distribution of power among several elites, including merchants, landlords, labor leaders, and intellectuals. Like the United States and many Western European nations, these systems permit popular participation, free elections, an open political party system, and the vesting of policy-making authority in representative institutions. Because these governments need popular support, they tend to have short-range goals and somewhat limited ability to extract services and to regulate. Military interventions may occur but are regarded as temporary. Israel, Lebanon, Argentina, Greece, Brazil, Ceylon, Nigeria, Turkey, Jamaica, Costa Rica, Malaysia, and the Philippines number among this group.

Dominant party semicompetitive systems exhibit an appearance of permitted opposition; but the majority party is closely associated with the battle for colonial freedom or nationalism, and opposition parties, though tolerated, are normally treated as treasonous. In Mexico, for example, the Partido Institucional Revolucionario (PRI) is associated with the 1917 Revolution, and in India the Congress party is equated with freedom from British rule.

Mobilization systems often have a charismatic leader and aggressive young elites interested in development and nationalism. The bureaucracy is controlled, loyal, and neutral, commanding high status and attracting many of the nation's best-trained people; party or military bureaucrats are often placed in the national civilian bureaucracy for the purpose of controlling it. In recent years, Nasser's Egypt, Nkrumah's Ghana, Tunisia, Mali, and Guinea have been examples of mobilization systems.

Communist totalitarian systems are one-party states committed to a Marxist-Leninist philosophy. Since the state mobilizes and directs all economic and social activities in society, communist bureaucracies are extremely complex. The Party serves as the control mechanism, and its bureaucracy parallels the civilian one. Life is difficult for Communist bureaucrats because they must prove their loyalty to the Party and its ideological tenets as well as their competence as bureaucrats, and the two are not always compatible. The Soviet Union and its Eastern European allies, including Hungary, East Germany, Poland, and Czechoslovakia, exemplify this type of system.

In summary, Heady's typology reveals the variety of political and administrative relationships possible. Perhaps not all nations (for example,

Yugoslavia) fit neatly into his schematization of administrative life, but it is a starting point for an analysis of diverse administrative systems.[6]

Borrowing from the vocabulary of optics, Fred Riggs uses Weber's concept of ideal types to describe the administrative process in developing areas.[7] In less developed, "fused" societies, administrative structures (bureaucracies, legislatures, etc.) have several functions, so that a tribal chief, for example, may also be judge and jury or even a god. In more developed societies, which Riggs terms "diffracted," administrative structures are more specialized, and the division of labor is more pronounced.

Midway between these two types lie "prismatic" societies in which fused and diffracted traits are combined. That is, some structures are specialized and others are multifunctional, and old and new forms may overlap. Nepotism may persist, for example, despite the existence of a highly developed civil service system and competitive civil service testing for personnel. The economic system may combine barter with the market system in a bazaar-canteen model whose administrative counterpart is to be found in Riggs's concept of *sala* (the Spanish word for "government office" in Latin America). Sala officials use both administrative rationality and nonadministrative criteria in performing their duties—e.g., an agricultural official may hire a witch doctor to bless a tractor.

Riggs believes that his prismatic-sala model enables us to understand the problems of emerging societies that elude established social science concepts. It may make sense, for example, to speak of public administration as a separate institution and discipline in the United States, but it would not be a sensible characterization of administration in Iran, Indonesia, or Malagasy. Although attempts to apply Riggs's model have had only limited success to date, the model is valuable because it is grounded in empirical evidence in Southeast Asia and provides a unique conceptualization of the role of bureaucracy in transitional societies.[8]

As already noted, not all nations fit neatly into schematizations of administrative life; but that does not diminish the value of attempting to gain insights into administrative behavior in general by examining how specific nations and cultures cope with their unique administrative problems. Harry Eckstein has suggested, for example, that a nation's political institutions must, if they are to survive, be congruent with that nation's political culture.[9] The public bureaucracy of Italy provides a good illustration of the administrative challenges confronting a fascinating and troubled nation with a fragmented political culture. Prince Metternich is alleged to have once observed that the word Italy was merely a geographical expression.

The Italian bureaucracy. For centuries Italy was comprised largely of warring city-states, and the cleavage between the northern and southern portions of the country remains intact to the present day. Geographically, the nation is divided by mountains and islands, producing areas with different cultures and dialects—Sardinia and Sicily are examples. Economically and socially, the north has developed more extensively than the south, owing to its proximity to, and good communications with, the rest of Europe. The movements of which Italians are proudest—the Renaissance, the unification of 1861, the World War II resistance to German occupation during which 100,000 Italians died, and the post–1945 Economic Miracle—have for the most part been northern accomplishments.

The south has developed a culture that is more Mediterranean in character. Despite massive efforts to improve the quality of life in the south, hundreds of thousands of southerners migrate annually from the squalor of Calabria and Sicily to the bright lights and freeways of Milan and Turin, causing serious social tensions in those cities.[10] Unlike the north, traditional structures mean more than formal legal structures in the south, where intense family loyalties preclude corporate efforts with outsiders—a condition Banfield has termed "amoral familism."[11]

Other factors divide the Italian nation as well. Religion, especially the authority and status of the Roman Catholic church, has been a burning issue since the Vatican refused to grant diplomatic recognition to the newly unified country in 1861; clerics and anticlerics have feuded relentlessly throughout the postunification period. Voter alienation, too, has been a pronounced feature of post-1945 Italian political life, with two-thirds of the industrial workers voting for Marxist-socialist parties. The vast divisions in nineteenth-century Italian society caused Massimo d'Azeglio to remark, "We have made Italy, now we must make Italians"—in many ways an apt comment today.[12]

The Italian bureaucracy reflects these problems of division and alienation. Like most of their national institutions, the civil service does not have the confidence and respect of the Italian people. It is accused of being overpaid and underpaid, overstaffed and understaffed, overcautious and overzealous, ineffective and corrupt—and it is all of these things. Despite efforts to improve emoluments, the civil service has been unable to attract the best minds of the country. Overcentralization often prevents the rational use of personnel. Some offices are overstaffed and others suffer acute personnel shortage. Since 1945 the Foreign Office has had too many ushers, doorkeepers, and custodial workers at a time when it lacked the consular and diplomatic staff necessary to meet the nation's international commitments.[13] Many civil service jobs are nonrational, created primarily to alleviate the severe unemployment problem in the south; and many of these low-skilled jobs are not abolished even when technological improvements have made their existence superfluous. In addition, the laws under which the administration operates are often antiquated, illogical, uncoordinated, and self-defeating. Overzealous civil servants fear being reported for violating the law. (Two civil servants whose enterprise had made possible significant discoveries of antipolio vaccine were charged with misappropriation of funds, which they had, in fact, misappropriated in order to accomplish their work.)

Italian civil service employees are drawn predominantly from the south, with 36.8 percent of the population supplying 62.2 percent of the administrative class, 75 percent of the prefects, and 77 percent of the judges, notwithstanding that southerners reflect their region's conservative orientation and distrust of government. Southerners are partial to the church and to big business, the traditional forces operating in and controlling the south.[14] Not surprisingly, La Palambara's study revealed Italian labor to be pro–big business and the church, believing the bureaucracy to be antilabor.[15]

The Italian bureaucracy has not lacked achievements, however. In spite of chronic political instability, it has been a relatively important unifying force within the political system. There can be no question that it deserves some of the credit for the post–1945 Economic Miracle. In addition, the state-owned and operated ENI (*Ente National Idrocarburi*, or National Hydrocarbon Corporation), which has provided energy-poor Italy with both energy and balance of payment surpluses, has been among the most successful enterprises of the postwar period.

In sum, the Italian bureaucracy reflects both the traditional and modern elements, as well as the cleavages and alienation, that characterize Italy as a nation.[16] Concern about problems such as these has helped give rise to two distinct areas of public administration: international administration and developmental administration. The Italian nation has sought the help of international administrative agencies, especially the Common Market and the United Nations, to solve some of its problems, while southern Italy, specifically, provides an excellent illustration of the need for a viable theory of developmental administration.

International Administration

Although they did not become really important until the end of World War II, international administrative systems are not new. The International Postal Union and the Pan American Union (now the Organization of American States) were both established during the nineteenth century. The League of Nations was created after World War I in an attempt to prevent another worldwide conflagration. Among them, organizations like the United Nations, the Common Market, NATO, and the Organization for African Unity, all created since 1945, employ tens of thousands of people. Ideologically, they emphasize humanitarian choices, such as peace, human unity, and equality. In addition, they are trying to protect man's environment and to reduce the violence, disease, pain, and genocide that often lead to war.

Often criticized for not living up to their ideals, international organizations can progress only as far as the sovereign states of the world permit. They have limited formal powers, no independent source of money, and no military forces of their own. Before this century, no group of bureaucrats had attempted to work novel and uncharted areas, control population growth, improve health and educational standards in less-developed areas, police international crime, disarm the world, or maintain peace among hostile nations. The achievement of these goals has been sought with few formal sanctions, scant resources, and little cooperation. International organizations have had to chart their own courses—to experiment, improvise, and rely on appeals to idealism.

Among other problems, many have questioned whether international civil servants can subordinate their national loyalties to the international organization. Former Soviet Premier Nikita Khrushchev, for example, questioned the loyalties of UN Secretary Dag Hammarskjöld and demanded a three-man secretariat to supervise the organization. Member nations argue about the number and placement of their citizens in the various organizations. The organization's official language, too, is often a bone of contention. Uncertainty surrounds the existence of these organizations, and their dependence on international member nations for resources precludes effective planning.

Nevertheless, international organizations have enjoyed many important successes. NATO has been a major factor in assuring the stability of postwar Europe. The UN has been an umbrella for a number of organizations doing useful work for the world, including the International Monetary Fund, UNICEF, and the World Health Organization. The humanitarian efforts of the UN saved the lives of hundreds of thousands of refugees in postwar Europe, and its peacekeeping efforts in the Congo, Cyprus, and the Middle East have been significantly instrumental in containing international violence during more recent times. As people become more aware that the world's fate depends on interdependent efforts such as these, the importance of international administrative systems will grow accordingly.[17]

Developmental Administration

Developmental administration was nurtured in the post–World War II period with the desire of wealthier nations to aid those that were less so. Special attention was given to nations attempting to transform themselves from colonial dependencies to sovereign states. It was hoped that a transference of resources and know-how would facilitate their transformation from technologically backward nations into more productive, self-sufficient countries. Bureaucrats of the donor and recipient nations would play a central role in this process. But the task has proved difficult, and the results, especially of U.S. bilateral aid, have been mixed.

Developmental administration raises perplexing questions. Which countries need help most? Which organizations—public or private, national or multinational—should be enlisted to help? Could the recipient governments better accomplish the task without foreign aid experts? Where would aid produce the best possible results? For whom? What would the price be?

Pakistan provides an example of developmental administration gone wrong. Ayub Khan's widely hailed Decade of Development (1958–68) meant "development" of the rich and continued squalor for Pakistan's masses. The program relied on private enterprise as the engine of growth. Growth rates averaged from 6 to 7 percent per year; but in 1968, 66 percent of the nation's industrial wealth was concentrated in the hands of twenty families who controlled 80 percent of the nation's banking and 97 percent of its insurance industry. Pakistan also had a colonial-style bureaucracy, an archaic accounting system, and severe organizational and management limitations. Yet its Decade of Development was hailed by American aid officials as an excellent example of planned economic development.[18]

For another example: Project Camelot, which was enthusiastically suggested by social scientists interested in testing hypotheses about nation building, change, and development in a cross-cultural setting, was a Pentagon project administered by American University in Washington, D.C. Its purpose was to examine prerevolutionary countries and to devise ways of coping with potentially revolutionary situations. A pilot program was begun in Chile in 1965; but local newspapers carried stories of American spying, the U.S. ambassador claimed he knew nothing about the project, and the uproar caused President Johnson to cancel the Chilean project as well as similar ones in Columbia and Brazil. In the view of a leading critic, Project Camelot had wrongly assumed that change was bad, and social scientists had assumed a Pentagon point of view much as industrial sociologists adopt a managerial perspective.[19] The ability to accept change and the role of social scientists in foreign public policy remain problems for developmental administration.

Nevertheless, developmental administration can play a vital role both domestically and abroad. As Gerald Caiden notes:

> The goal of development is not westernization or modernization into industria, but the employment of modern techniques, both technical and social, in the pursuit of societal objectives. It is the attainment of results, not rationality, form or ritual. To achieve this end, ideology of development is essential, something Weidner has described as a "state of mind" which fosters a belief in equitable

progress. Esman sees it as (a) doctrine incorporating a reliance on ideology for decision-making criteria, (b) priority to fundamental social reform, (c) political and social mobilization, (d) latitude for competitive political action and interest articulation, (e) ethnic, religious and regional integration, (f) governmental guidance of economic and social policy, and (g) commitment to the future.[20]

In a sense, all nations are undergoing political development. In the United States, for example, Appalachia and the Ozarks might be fruitful areas for testing some the concepts of developmental administration.

TOWARD A NEW PUBLIC ADMINISTRATION

Public administration is today striving to achieve greater efficiency, economy, and administrative effectiveness by finding ways to offer improved and expanded services with the resources available or by providing the same or improved services at less cost. To these goals the New Public Administration adds the pursuit of social equity—finding ways to eradicate discriminatory practices in the making and execution of public policy.[21]

What is meant by *equity?* In its general definition:

Equity denotes the spirit and the habit of fairness, justness, and right dealing which would regulate the intercourse of men with men—the rule of doing to all others as we desire them to do to us. . . . It is therefore the synonym of natural right or justice. But in this sense its obligation is ethical rather than jural, and its discussion belongs to the sphere of morals. It is grounded in the precepts of the conscience, not in any sanction of positive law.[22]

But one of the foremost exponents of social equity, H. George Frederickson, argues:

The phrase "social equity" is used here to summarize the following set of value premises. Pluralistic government systematically discriminates in favor of established stable bureaucracies and their specialized minority clientele (the Department of Agriculture and large farmers as an example) and against those minorities (farm laborers, both migrant and permanent, as an example) who lack political and economic resources. The continuation of widespread unemployment, poverty, disease, ignorance, and hopelessness in an era of unprecedented economic growth is the result. This condition is morally reprehensible and if left unchanged constitutes a fundamental, if long-range, threat to the viability of this or any political system. Continued deprivation amid plenty breeds widespread militancy, and so forth. A Public Administration which fails to work for changes which try to redress the deprivation of minorities will likely be eventually used to repress those minorities.[23]

In Frederickson's view, administrators must comprehend the ethical framework on which society and government are based if they are to make equitable decisions on behalf of the disadvantaged. Unfortunately, administrators are neither impartial, preoccupied with moral considerations, nor necessarily concerned with the effects of their decisions on the disadvantaged. Social equity—improving the political position and economic well-being of minorities in society—is therefore not only a laudable goal, but the pursuit of it is an end in itself.

Proponents of the New Public Administration argue that a commitmitment to the policies and organizational structures that promote social equity constitutes a healthy desire for change, which in turn would enhance the goals of efficiency, economy, and administrative effectiveness. This does not mean change for the sake of change or major constitutional changes in the structure of government. The New Public Administration is more concerned with advocating, or experimenting with, modified-bureaucratic or nonbureaucratic decentralized organizational forms for the purpose of inducing administrative change in the traditional entrenched bureaucracy. Insofar as the public service employee all too often follows accepted procedures automatically, without considering ultimate goals and outcomes, the adoption of counterbureaucratic administrative methods may have a positive effect on organizational personnel.

The decision of the U.S. Supreme Court in the case of *Griggs* v. *Duke Power Company* (8 March 1971) and the potential for organizational change offered by program budgeting systems illustrate both the advantages and the administrative pursuit of social equity.

From the institution of merit criteria and a civil service system to the establishment of affirmative actions programs, many significant steps have been taken to provide equal opportunity in employment. Today the courts have moved to obligate the government to guarantee individual equality of access to civil service positions as well as individual due process in the competition for jobs. In the case of *Griggs* v. *Duke Power Company*—a classic example of social inequity under Title 7 of the Civil Rights Act of 1964—common laborers who wished to enter low-skill positions in departments other than the company's "labor division" were required to present a high-school diploma and to perform satisfactorily on two aptitude tests.

On the grounds that a man does not need a high-school diploma in order to be a good janitor, the court deemed these tests non–job related and discriminatory, especially against blacks, who were the most frequent aplicants for positions in the categories in question. Although the court did not specify what constituted proper selection and promotion procedures, *Griggs* was nevertheless a landmark in the legal definition of social equity and an important step toward assuring the applicability of tests to jobs and equal employment opportunities.

Eliminating such tests may bring higher social benefits but may also result in lowered efficiency owing to the lowering of value qualities. That is, social equity may be at odds with efficient economic administration, and some administrators may object strongly to achieving social equity, racial or otherwise, at the expense of the organization. Because some elected officials may represent substantial opposition to the New Public Administration and because the courts are less vulnerable than administration in this regard, greater judicial control over administrative agencies may result in order to enforce matters pertaining to social equity.

Examining alternative programs is a central aspect of the New Public Administration and a basic technique of programming-planning-budgeting systems as well. Because cost-benefit analysis or PPBS can compel legislatures and bureaucracies, military and nonmilitary alike, publicly to justify and defend their decisions regarding the expenditure of public funds, they can also be used as devices for organizational change in the interests of social equity.

In order to save considerable money for other programs, possibly including domestic programs, for example, former Secretary of Defense Robert McNamara wanted both the navy and air force to use the TFX fighter plane. But some military officials were more concerned that their own department should obtain new resources and weapon systems than they were with economic concerns or considerations of equity. Thus, in his efforts to gain greater control over the Defense Department from the military, McNamara did not advocate outright change but used PPBS as an agent of change in the name of improved economy. Using PPBS in this way, however, assumes that an informed public will respond to the disclosure of inequities with sufficient vigor to demand a change. H. George Frederickson notes that, in general:

> New public administration is concerned less with the Defense Department than with defense, less with civil service commissions than with the manpower needs of administrative agencies on the one hand and the employment needs of the society on the other, less with building institutions and more with designing alternative means of solving public programs. These alternatives will no doubt have some recognizable organizational characteristics and they will need to be built and maintained, but will seek to avoid becoming entrenched, non-responsive bureaucracies that become greater public problems than the social situations they were originally designed to improve.[24]

New Public Administration faces difficult problems, not the least of which involves upper and lower management relations. Specialists who are qualified to build new organizational structures may not be available in sufficient numbers to advocate such changes as informal decentralization. In addition, upper-level management may oppose the ideas of specialists and lower-level administrators who advocate the New Public Administration. Because it seeks methods by which lower levels of organization and less-influential minorities can receive equal or favored treatment, the New Public Administration and its ideas are not likely to improve this relationship.

Administrative reforms, undoubtedly involving a political process and possibly societal reform as well, are necessary to accomplish the goals of the New Public Administration, and it is axiomatic in administrative reform that changes must be made through an existing organizational system that is in turn itself transformed in some way. Administrative reform can arise from three sources: from those who wish to change an organization that fails to satisfy the clientele it serves; from those who favor reform whenever an administration fails to achieve a defined level of performance; and from those who wish continually to reform an organization until their own vision of administrative perfection is realized. However reform is accomplished, private and public organizations alike must develop a more profound awareness of social responsibility. As one study has concluded, public administrators will have to shift their emphasis away from purely political considerations and more toward social and ethical problems. They must, in short, broaden their concern.[25]

Finally, proponents of the New Public Administration regard hierarchies as counterproductive and advocate modified hierarchic systems as part of their program for reform and change.[26] Organizational changes for modifying hierarchies include such alternatives as decentralization and group decision making. Other alternative types, including semibureaucratic and collective organizations, will be examined in the concluding section of this chapter.

BUREAUCRATIC, SEMIBUREAUCRATIC, AND NONBUREAUCRATIC ORGANIZATIONS*

The bureaucratic organization, with management personnel at the top who set policy and workers at the bottom who carry it out, is the model for the contemporary organization of factories, universities, schools, hospitals, and

*This section was written by Professor Frank Lundenfeld of Cheyney State College, Cheyney, Pennsylvania.

government bureaus in capitalist and socialist countries alike. Because it is so pervasive, it is difficult to imagine alternatives to bureaucracy. In addition, because bureaucracy enables small elites to exercise enormous power through their control of governments and corporations, the widespread adoption of nonbureaucratic alternatives in capitalist countries would imply a change in power relations, or an end to the traditional power of the capitalist class. Capitalism requires some form of bureaucratic organization, which, ". . . with its reliance on multiple levels of authority and supervision and its emphasis on discipline and predictability, is probably the only way of ensuring efficient production using alienated labor."[27] Nevertheless, viable alternatives do exist and are to be found among the interstices of American society, in, for example, free schools, health collectives, food co-ops, legal collectives, producers' collectives, newspaper and magazine collectives, and some political collectives.

Bureaucracies and collectives occupy the extreme ends of an administrative continuum and differ pointedly in respect to position stratification, role differentiation, and type of member commitment. Bureaucratic organizations are distinguished by a hierarchy of positions, specialized roles, and employees who are instrumentally committed—i.e., who work chiefly for pay. Collectives, or nonbureaucratic organizations, feature equality instead of hierarchy, generalized roles, and members whose commitment arises chiefly from their mutual friendship and moral allegiance to the goals of the organization. Members participate in collectives because they want to, not because they have to.[28] Semibureaucratic organizations generally fall between these two extremes, though they resemble bureaucracies more than they resemble collectives.

Collectives imply some form of socialism and could exist on a large scale if people no longer needed to hold jobs to make a living—that is, if people were guaranteed a minimum level of basic economic security. Those who cannot entirely accept bureaucracy in its present condition may find a semibureaucratic or collective model more appropriate to today's needs. But the implementation of collectives will be part of a revolutionary change and will not precede such change on any large scale. As long as power relations remain unaltered in this country, any discussion of alternatives to bureaucracy will be largely theoretical.

Participants in semibureaucratic organizations are still in it for the money, but money plays a less important part in their motivation than it does in bureaucracies. Also, in a society in which organizations are constantly forming, disintegrating, and re-forming with new members and new purposes, participants must be able to detach from one another emotionally and re-

**Semi-
bureaucratic
Organizations**

Table 8 THREE TYPES OF ORGANIZATION

	Bureaucracies	Semi-bureaucratic Organizations	Collectives
Examples	Division of General Motors; welfare agency	University research group; factory comanaged by workers	Health collectives; free school
Dimensions			
Differentiation	Specialized roles	Roles sometimes specialized, sometimes not	Generalized roles
Stratification	Hierarchy of positions (line organization); authority at the top	Some hierarchy; staff rather than line predominates; authority in experts *and* at the top	Equality; authority in collectivity
Members' Commitment	Instrumental (salaries primary)	Instrumental/moral	Moral/effective

attach to others in a brief period of time. Thus in the typical semibureaucratic organization there may be a high moral commitment to organizational goals but only a moderate degree of friendship among members.

Contrary to popular stereotype, not all contemporary corporations are run like rigid military bureaucracies. While such forms of organization may have been efficient for nineteenth-century industrial empires, modern businesses have begun to discover the advantages of freer, more democratic forms of organization. Indeed, as Bennis and Slater have observed, democracy may be the best way to operate a business under the conditions of a changing environment. With uncertain markets and competition from new technologies, semibureaucratic organizations have the greater flexibility needed to adapt to altered circumstances.

In a way, semibureaucratic systems are the answer to management's dream. They provide higher quality, faster service and greater output, with fewer employees, lower costs, and higher morale, all without relinquishing the prerogative of management to set overall policy. Among the worthwhile values that predominate in the new forms of business enterprise, Bennis and Slater include:

1. Full and free communication, *regardless of rank and power.*
2. A reliance on consensus, rather than the more customary forms of coercion or compromise to manage conflict.
3. The idea that influence is based on technical competence and knowledge rather than on the vagaries of personal whims or *prerogatives of power. . . .*[29]

Bennis and Slater do not suggest that rank and power should disappear from business organizations, nor does such a suggestion appear in the human relations literature on the subject. The central problem is how to humanize capitalist organizations so that they benefit employer and employee alike, without, however, challenging the basic prerogatives of management.

Businesses are gradually adopting more democratic methods, including the participation of workers in management, because such methods work. In most organizations, job specialization continues; indeed, in research groups it may form the basis around which a team of experts in different fields joins together to solve a problem. In others, however, such as the new Procter and Gamble plant in Lima, Ohio, specialized jobs have disappeared except for that of the boss responsible to management, who is still at the head of the plant.[30]

The more democratic the organization, the greater is the workers' influence on decisions. Thus, for management, the basic problem arising from worker participation is one of control. When democracy goes too far, the very function of managers may be called into question, which is what happened when the Polaroid Corporation instituted job enlargement for a group of 120 machinists on a "crash" production project. In place of the usual eight-hour-a-day routine, the machinists each had one hour's training plus two hours in coordinating activities and five hours at the machines. The program was too successful, and worried management reverted to the old system when it found that workers had little need for managers under the new one.

Limited forms of worker participation in management have spread in some advanced capitalist countries in Europe—in France and Germany notably but in socialist Yugoslavia as well. These systems give employees some voice in setting policies, but for the most part they serve the same integrative functions as trade unions in maintaining the stability of their respective systems. That is, they allow worker participation but without relinquishing management's prerogative to maintain overall control and high productivity. In Western Europe, according to Clegg, "the ideological foundations of capitalism's acceptance of workers' participation in management lie in a defined policy to contain and avoid social conflict by limited concessions."[31]

Collectives   Collectives are groups of persons gathered together to work toward some goal of mutual group interest. They are held together by friendship, commitment to others in the organization, or loyalty to an ideal—for example, a shared desire to provide a socially useful product or service—rather than by expectations of pay or other compensation. Members are often unpaid; and even when they are paid, they may continue to work during months when the organization is too poor to afford their salaries.

An outgrowth of the political opposition movement and the counterculture of the 1960s, some collectives include radical change in the larger society among their long-range goals, while others have no explicit political purpose. Thus the members of many food co-ops believe their only goal is to obtain organically grown low-cost foods; likewise, many free school participants say that they are more interested in building a healthy learning environment than in changing the world.

In the capitalist countries, most contemporary collectives function, at least to some extent, outside the existing political-economic system, offering an alternative to that system and its power-centered values. In collectives, equality prevails over hierarchy, roles are generalized rather than specialized, and authority resides in the collectivity.[32] All members are regarded as equal, with equal rights of decision; indeed, in many collectives the process of democratic decision making is as important as the product or task goals to which the group is devoted.[33]

This is not to suggest that collectives are either disorganized or necessarily inefficient. Most collectives delegate responsibility in some way—either in the form of subcommittees assigned to specific functions or of officers selected for particular jobs. But officers, if any, remain in office only at the pleasure of the members; and where there is a division of labor there is usually job rotation as well, so that differentiation is temporary and does not give rise to a hierarchy of officers or participants of "important" committees versus ordinary members.

That collectives must spend their time arguing endlessly about trivia is a misconception—some do but many do not. Committee members or officers are presumed to know what they are doing. The chairperson decides how to facilitate business meetings; the bookkeeper, how to keep records; and any members who hold these jobs may innovate. The consensus process used in seeking unanimous agreement is more time-consuming than the majority vote system, but debate is usually reserved for important issues. Members have the right to suggest new policies or to question the decisions of committees or delegated officers. A member who feels strongly enough about an issue can make the whole collective think about the dissenting viewpoint instead of being arbitrarily overridden by the majority. A frequent answer to criticism is to ask the critic to assume the responsibility in question.

Collectives vs. communes. Communes differ from collectives in terms of exclusivity, goals, and degree of emotional identification with the group. Communes are usually more exclusive and harder to join than collectives, are typically oriented around "just living," and mostly lack clear-cut goals. Those that are goal oriented (to spread the word of God, for example) or that produce as well as consume are also collectives. Although good interpersonal relationships are important in a collective, perhaps more as a means of facilitating goals than as an end in themselves, the task orientation of collectives generally means less emotional involvement with the group than is characteristic of communes.

The Israeli kibbutzim and certain American utopian communities are both communes and collectives. In some groups the communal aspect is separated from the collective: members of the political collectives that make up the Philadelphia "Movement for a New Society" also live in communal households, but the households often contain persons from different collectives or even members of no political collective at all. Twin Oaks, a utopian community in Virginia modeled after Skinner's Walden Two, also functions as a collective whose sixty members are encouraged to work in community agriculture and industries, although each may do several different jobs during the same day or week.[34]

Collectives vs. bureaucracies. Joyce Whitt has observed that collectives can be contrasted with bureaucracies in some twenty different aspects.[35] The distinctions in stratification, role differentiation, and member commitment remain primary, however, with other differences flowing from these.

Collectives are more democratic than bureaucracies, partly because authority resides in the whole organization rather than in any given member at the top. Although executives are sometimes elected, their function is more often to implement than to make decisions, while such decisions as are made are subject to review and change by the membership. Collectives, too, are typically small in size (usually numbering fewer than fifty members) because direct democracy, with or without specialized coordinators, works best when members are few.

Knowledge sharing is one of the most vital and significant modes to arise from the deemphasis of collectives on rigid stratification and professional role differentiation. Although some collectives have formalized written procedures, for example, their function differs greatly from that in bureaucracies, and they are used far less often in collectives than in bureaucracies. Secret documents and files are a mark of bureaucracy. Collectives, on the other hand, may use written documents for the purpose of helping new members to become more readily assimilated to the organization or to facilitate job rotation by sharing vital knowledge among all members. Indeed, shared knowledge forms the basis for socialization into temporary specialized roles in some collectives. Thus the Questa Food Co-op in San Luis Obispo, California, prepared a job description booklet for its fifty members so that everyone would be familiar with all the jobs that had to be done and with the working of the collective as a whole.

The writing of doctors' prescriptions in Latin, using brand names instead of generic names for medication, is another example of a common bureaucratic mode whose effect is only to mystify patients, making them dependent on the specialized knowledge of the physician. Health collectives, however, try to share their medical knowledge as widely as possible with their clients in order to make them less dependent on so-called expert advice. The absence of role differentiation also means that collectives place less emphasis on professional credentialing—i.e., hiring on the basis of degrees, examinations, and so forth. Public-school teachers must have certificates, degrees, and diplomas, but free-school teachers are hired on the basis of ability, rapport, and interest. Many have official credentials, but competent persons are seldom rejected by free schools for lack of them.

Finally, as a consequence of their smaller size and of the commitment of members to friendship and identification with the goals of the organization, interpersonal relations tend to be warmer, more personal, and usually more friendly in collectives than in bureaucracies. But, because of the secondary importance of material rewards, collectives are more fragile than bureaucracies and may dissolve when members feel they have accomplished their goals. Bureaucratic organizations have a high persistence over time. In fact, the continuity of the bureaucratic organization often becomes an end in itself, so that as soon as one goal is fulfilled, new goals are found to justify its continuing existence.[36]

The preceding chapters demonstrate that scholars have been closely studying the nature of bureaucratic phenomena from the time of Max Weber to the present day. Chapters 2 and 3 examined formal and informal organizational structure through the eyes of these scholars; chapter 4 explored the strengths and weaknesses of decision making in relation to good organizational communication; chapters 5 and 6 focused largely on management and policy aspects of organizations, such as personnel and budgetary matters.

Chapter 7 indicated that the growth of a large and powerful American bureaucracy reflects public demands for increased governmental services and social programs. That a large and powerful public bureaucracy struggles with many chronic and serious problems was suggested in chapters 8 and 9, which also asserted that administrative responsibility, legal and social equity, and bureaucratic responsiveness are the crucial elements in public administration today. The concluding chapter has looked at some of the more recent subfields of organizational administration, including comparative, developmental, and international administration and the New Public Administration, and has also examined semibureaucratic and collective alternatives to formal bureaucracy.

The major question raised by these chapters is whether bureaucracy serves itself or the needs of the people. Although growing professionalism in public administration and the emergence of ombudsmen reflect trends aimed at ensuring bureaucratic neutrality and fairness, it must be said in the final analysis that bureaucracy can be only as efficient and effective as the people who staff it, only as sensitive and responsive as those in and out of government want it to be, and only as legitimate as individual administrators and a watchful educated public demands. Ultimately, therefore, a watchful and educated public should and must demand the highest standards of professional performance on the part of its public administrators, because in one way or another, administration touches all of us.

The job market generally requires us to work within an organization, either corporate or public, and to go through the personnel process of being recruited, socialized, promoted, or, in some cases, fired. Our economic viability and promotional potential depends to a great extent on how well we function within the organization. Our overall satisfaction often depends on how well we adapt to the bureaucratic environment. Even outside the organization, the services we seek, receive, or are denied, whether from public or private organizations, will influence the quality of our national, international, and individual lives.

NOTES

1. H. George Frederickson, "Toward a New Public Administration," in *Toward a New Public Administration: The Minnowbrook Perspective*, ed. Frank Marini (Scranton, Pa.: Chandler Publishing Co., 1971); Dwight Waldo, ed., *Public Administration in a Time of Turbulence* (Scranton, Pa.: Chandler Publishing Co., 1971); and Louis C. Gawthrop, *Administrative Politics and Social Change* (New York: St. Martin's Press, 1971).

2. Ira Sharkansky, *Public Administration* (Chicago: Markham Publishing Co., 1970), p. 15.

3. Robert Dahl, "The Science of Public Administration: Three Problems," *Public Administration Review* 34 (winter 1974): 1–11.

4. See Joseph La Palombara, "Development: Notes, Queries and Dilemmas," in *Bureaucracy and Political Development*, ed. Joseph La Palombara (Princeton: Princeton University Press, 1967), pp. 34–60.

5. Ferrel Heady and Sybil L. Stokes, ed., *Papers in Comparative Public Administration* (Ann Arbor, Mich.: Institute of Public Administration, 1962), pp. 10–11.

6. Ibid., chap. 6; and John Rehfuss, *Public Administration as Political Process* (New York: Charles Scribner's Sons, 1973), p. 182.

7. Fred W. Riggs, *Administration in Developing Areas* (Boston: Houghton Mifflin Co., 1964), pp. 206–312.

8. See James Brady, "Japanese Administrative Behavior and a Sala Model," in *Readings in Comparative Public Administration,* ed. Nimrod Raphaeli (Boston: Allyn & Bacon, 1967), pp. 433–56.

9. Harry Eckstein, *Division and Cohesion in Democracy: A Study of Norway* (Princeton: Princeton University Press, 1966).

10. Joseph La Palombara, *Interest Groups in Italian Politics* (Princeton: Princeton University Press, 1964), p. 61.

11. See Edward Banfield, *The Moral Basis of the Backward Society* (New York: Free Press, 1959).

12. Cited in Dante Germino and Stafo Passigli, *The Government and Politics of Contemporary Italy* (New York: Harper & Row, 1968), p. 1.

13. John C. Adams and Paolo Barile, *The Government of Republican Italy,* 3d ed. (Boston: Houghton Mifflin Co., 1963), pp. 114–15.

14. Norman Kogan, *The Government of Italy* (New York: Thomas Y. Crowell Co., 1962), p. 102.

15. See La Palombara, *Interest Groups in Italian Politics,* chaps. 8 and 11.

16. See Gabriel Almond and Sydney Verba, *The Civic Culture* (Boston: Little, Brown & Co., 1965), pp. 308–12.

17. Most of this information is from Gerald E. Caiden, *The Dynamics of Public Administration: Guidelines to Current Transformations in Theory and Practice* (New York: Holt, Rinehart & Winston, 1971), pp. 264–72.

18. See Garth Jones, "Failure of Technological Assistance," *Journal of Comparative Administration* 2 (May 1970): 10–11, 30.

19. Irving Louis Horowitz, *The Rise and Fall of Project Camelot* (Cambridge, Mass.: M.I.T. Press, 1967), pp. 3–41.

20. Caiden, *Dynamics of Public Administration,* p. 296.

21. Frederickson, "Toward a New Public Administration," p. 311.

22. Henry Campbell Black, *Black's Law Dictionary,* 4th ed. (St. Paul, Minn.: West Publishing Co., 1957), p. 634.

23. Frederickson, "Toward a New Public Administration," p. 311.

24. Ibid., p. 312.

25. Gawthrop, *Administrative Politics and Social Change,* pp. 106–7.

26. Frederickson, "Toward a New Public Administration," p. 312.

27. See Richard C. Edwards, in Richard C. Edwards, Michael Reich, and Thomas E. Weisskopf, *The Capitalist System* (Englewood Cliffs, N.J.: Prentice-Hall, 1972), p. 118.

28. For this reason Theobald has suggested the term *conservative* for this type of organization (see Robert Theobald, "All Necessities Freely Available," in *Radical Perspectives on Social Problems,* 2d ed., ed. Frank Lindenfeld [New York: Macmillan Co., 1973], pp. 219–28).

29. Warren G. Bennis and Philip E. Slater, *The Temporary Society* (New York: Harper & Row, 1968), p. 4. Emphasis added.

30. See David Jenkins, *Job Power* (New York: Doubleday & Co., 1973), chap. 12.

31. Ian Clegg, *Workers' Self-Management in Algeria* (New York: Monthly Review Press, 1971), p. 19. In principle, workers' participation in management means that authority is shared and that policy decisions are not made only at the top. In practice, even in the best representative

councils, the elected representatives become more involved in policy matters, but the rank and file remains apathetic.

32. Jenkins, *Job Power,* chap. 15.

33. Rosabeth Moss Kanter and Louis A. Zurcher, Jr., "Concluding Statement: Evaluating Alternatives and Alternative Valuing," *Journal of Applied Behavioral Science* 9, nos. 2–3 (1973): 388–90.

34. See Kathleen Kinkade, *A Walden Two Experiment* (New York: William Morrow & Co., 1973).

35. Joyce Rothschild Whitt, "Resistance to Authority and Bureaucracy: Toward an Alternative Model of Organization and Legitimacy" (Unpublished paper, xeroxed, University of California, Santa Barbara, 1973).

36. See David Sills, *The Volunteers* (Glencoe, Ill.: Free Press, 1957), p. 62.

INDEX

383